THE MATTER OF HIGH WORDS

The Matter of High Words

NATURALISM, NORMATIVITY, AND THE POSTWAR SAGE

Robert Chodat

OXFORD
UNIVERSITY PRESS

Oxford University Press is a department of the University of Oxford. It furthers
the University's objective of excellence in research, scholarship, and education
by publishing worldwide. Oxford is a registered trade mark of Oxford University
Press in the UK and certain other countries.

Published in the United States of America by Oxford University Press
198 Madison Avenue, New York, NY 10016, United States of America.

CIP data is on file at the Library of Congress
ISBN 978-0-19-068215-6

9 8 7 6 5 4 3 2 1

Printed by Sheridan Books, Inc., United States of America

voor Stephanie

Contents

Acknowledgments

The importance of discerning friends and generous institutions is a recurrent thought among all of the authors I discuss in the following pages, and my own life and work embody this idea as much as anyone's. This book took shape with the help of two enormously capable and supportive department chairs at Boston University, Bill Carroll and Gene Jarrett, and Mo Lee, our latest talented chair, has long been a close companion, counselor, and sharp-eyed reader. Thanks, too, to Amy Appleford, Anna Henchman, Erin Murphy, Carrie Preston, and John Paul Riquelme for their camaraderie and leadership. Several friends beyond BU—John Gibson, John Plotz, Bernie Rhie, Ben Roth—read pieces of the book and pushed me to clarify just what I was trying to say, and Greg Chase was a scrupulous proofreader at the end of it all. I am very grateful to Gregg Crane and Ali Chetwynd at the University of Michigan for prompting me to write about Stanley Cavell's memoir; to Joe Rezek, Amanda Claybaugh, and the "American Literature and Culture" seminar at the Harvard Humanities Center for prompting me to write about Marilynne Robinson; and to Oren Izenberg for co-organizing a small conference that prompted me to write about Walker Percy.

I also would like to thank several institutions that have acted as friends over the last several years, providing indispensable backing: the Boston University Center for the Humanities, the Humboldt Stiftung, and the National Endowment for the Humanities. Portions of Chapter One appeared in much earlier versions in *New Literary History* and *nonsite*, and Chapter Two includes materials that were originally published in *American Literary History* and *Contemporary Pragmatism*. I thank the editors for their support. I'm grateful as well for the keen encouragement I received from Brendan O'Neill and Sarah Pirovitz, my two smart and energetic editors at Oxford University Press.

David and Carolyn Chodat are the incarnation of caring, loyal, and gracious parents. Their beautiful grandchildren, Theo and Josephine Chodat, arrived in the same years when this book was being written. I sometimes think that their lives have made me a moderately wiser person, or at least slightly less unwise, and they regularly bring to mind a remark that Reverend Ames writes to his young son in Robinson's *Gilead*: if you ever wonder what you've done in your life, and everyone does wonder sooner or later, please know that you have been a miracle to me, something more than a miracle.

The book is dedicated to my wife Stephanie Byttebier, who has lived with it for as long as I have, and who every day shows me what genuine love, integrity, kindness, and shrewd judgment look like, in the flesh.

THE MATTER OF HIGH WORDS

The human understanding is of its own nature prone to
abstractions and gives a substance and reality to things
which are fleeting.... Matter rather than forms should be
the object of our attention, its configurations and changes of
configuration, and simple action, and law of action or motion.
FRANCIS BACON, *Novum Organum* (1620)

Go in fear of abstractions.
EZRA POUND, "A Few Don't's" (1913)

What you call "love" was invented by
guys like me. To sell nylons.
DON DRAPER, *Mad Men* (2007)[1]

INTRODUCTION

Show and Tell

I. Nominalist Aesthetics

The author of *Middlemarch*, complained an upstart book reviewer, "wishes to
say too many things, and to say them too well," burdening the reader with
dozens of "philosophic" and "discursive" passages. This same reviewer, Henry
James, would in later years commend the "guarded objectivity" of theater,
a "scenic method" that would make "the presented occasion tell all its story
itself"—a technique that led T. S. Eliot to attribute him a "mind so fine no idea
could violate it." James's comrade Joseph Conrad claimed to ignore readers
who expect to be "edified" or "improved" by a narrative, and sought instead
to open their senses to the things of the material world: to "make you hear,
to make you feel," and "before all, to make you see." The triumph of *Ulysses*,
said Judge John M. Woolsey, was Joyce's ability to convey the "ever-shifting
kaleidoscopic impressions" that pass before "the screen of consciousness,"
even if this sometimes made a "strong draught to ask some sensitive though
normal person to take." Virginia Woolf warned readers against novelists
who have "views upon Socialism, or sex problems, or education, or psychology which must be brought in and investigated at the expense of the individual." For the young John Dos Passos, American literature should be faulted

---

[1] Francis Bacon, *The Works of Francis Bacon*, Volume 4, ed. James Spedding et al. (London: Longman
and Co., 1858), 58; Ezra Pound, *The Literary Essays of Ezra Pound* (New York: New Directions, 1968),
5; "Smoke Gets in Your Eyes," *Mad Men: Season One*, written by Matthew Weiner, directed by Alan
Taylor, AMC (2007), DVD.

for its "abstractness, its lack, on the whole, of dramatic actuality." "Like all uneducated people," averred William Faulkner in an interview, "I have a certain distrust of ideas"—a claim echoed by his character Addie Bundren when she declares that "the high dead words" like "sin and love" are "just sounds," invented by "people who never sinned nor loved." "You'll lose it if you talk about it," quipped Jake Barnes, a thought that another Hemingway character, Frederic Henry, amplified in an iconic account of the Great War: "I was always embarrassed by the words sacred, glorious, and sacrifice. . . . Abstract words such as glory, honor, courage, or hallow were obscene beside the concrete names of villages, the numbers of roads, the names of rivers, the numbers of regiments and the dates."[2]

Such comments—among the most celebrated justifications of modern fiction—represent a robust response to a longstanding philosophical question: what it means to master and use a concept, particularly a normative one. And the response is deeply skeptical. Concepts of a normative cast, vocabularies of ought and ought-not, are said to draw us away from the bodies and objects of the world, falsifying or occluding the intricate singularities of reality and experience. Following Theodor Adorno and Fredric Jameson, we can say that these comments instantiate the fundamentally *nominalist* impulse of modern narrative: the "intensifying will of the aesthetic," as Jameson says, to pursue not the universal or timeless, but "the here and now of this unique situation and this unique expression."[3] To be sure, such nominalism wasn't restricted to early-century storytellers. Poets, too, assaulted bloodless abstraction, calling for a "harder and saner poetry," one "as much like granite as it can be"; for texts that would not "mean" but simply "be"; for visual concrete languages, no ideas but in things, and so forth.[4] But the novel had always been loose and

---

[2] Henry James, *The Critical Muse: Selected Literary Criticism*, ed. Roger Gard (New York: Penguin, 1987), 81; Henry James, *The Awkward Age*, ed. Ronald Blythe (New York: Penguin, 1987), 12; Joseph Conrad, *The Nigger of the "Narcissus"* (1897; New York: Dover, 1999), vii; Woolsy, qtd. in "Court Lifts Ban on 'Ulysses' Here," *New York Times* (December 7, 1933), https://www.nytimes.com/books/00/01/09/specials/joyce-court.html (accessed April 12, 2016); Virginia Woolf, "Philosophy in Fiction," in *Contemporary Writers* (New York: Harcourt Brace Jovanovich, 1965), 69; Dos Passos, *Modernism: An Anthology of Sources and Documents*, ed. Vassiliki Kolocotronic et al. (Chicago: University of Chicago Press, 1999), 336; *Faulkner at West Point*, ed. Joseph L. Fant and Robert Ashley (Jackson: University Press of Mississippi, 2002), 111; William Faulkner, *As I Lay Dying* (1930; New York: Vintage, 1990), 173–75; Ernest Hemingway, *The Sun Also Rises* (New York: Scribner's, 1926), 245; Ernest Hemingway, *A Farewell to Arms* (1929; New York: Scribner, 1995), 161.

[3] Fredric Jameson, *Postmodernism, or, The Cultural Logic of Late Capitalism* (Durham, NC: Duke University Press, 1991), 152; Jameson is referring in part to Adorno's *Aesthetic Theory*.

[4] Ezra Pound, "A Retrospect," in *Literary Essays of Ezra Pound* (New York: New Directions, 1968), 3–14. The well-known phrases I've cited here are, in order, from Archibald MacLeish, "Ars Poetica,"

baggy, with deep-rooted ties to sermons, conduct books, Christian guidebooks, and other generalizing forms of pedagogy.[5] So the nominalist maxims that I've catalogued—part of the novel's elevation to a purified, refined artistic genre—initiated a more radical transformation than that seen in other literary forms. The "invasion" of such ideals, as Iris Murdoch put it in 1960, compelled story-tellers to compose "dry," "crystalline," "linguistic quasi-things," and the result was decisive: "a general loss of concepts," "the loss of a moral and political vocabulary."[6] Directness and immediacy, the concreteness of material objects, the properties of sculpture or music or dance—these became the things, so to speak, of genuine art.

And this abjuration of concepts extends well beyond the early decades of the twentieth century. Indeed, I've culled the term "nominalism" here not from Jameson's accounts of early-century high modernism, but from his well-known analysis of post-WWII literature and culture. Much energy has been expended asking how the writing of the last five or six decades is distinct from that produced by James, Conrad, Hemingway, and Joyce. But as Jameson suggests, whatever differences post-World War II writing exhibits—in attitudes about selfhood, popular culture, or technology—it has decidedly *not* rejected modernism's basic nominalist disposition.[7] Vladimir Nabokov may have dismissed

---

http://www.poetryfoundation.org/poetrymagazine/poem/6371 (accessed January 29, 2014); T.E. Hulme, *Speculations*, ed. Herbert Read (London: K. Paul, 1924), 10; William Carlos Williams, *Selected Poems*, ed. Charles Tomlinson (New York: New Directions, 1985), 145. One thinks here also of W. B. Yeats in his last letter: "The abstract is not life and everywhere draws out its contradictions. You can refute Hegel, but not the Saint of the Song of Sixpence" (cited in Stan Smith, *W. B. Yeats: A Critical Introduction* (London: Rowman & Littlefield, 1990), 85). Such resistance to "ideas" and "abstraction" is, in part, what inspires Jerome McGann's use of "nominalism" in his discussion of modernism's interest in typeface, print, and material books; see Jerome McGann, *Black Riders: The Visible Language of Modernism* (Princeton, NJ: Princeton University Press, 1993). Poets and novelists also were joined, of course, by philosophers and other thinkers of the day. Think, for instance, of William James warning us away from "vicious abstractionism," or Ernest Fenellosa praising the Chinese language for lacking "bloodless adjectival abstraction," or Walter Pater's claim that the "stereotyped world" of habit masked the difference between "any two persons, things, situations." See William James, *The Meaning of Truth*, in *Writings, 1902–1910* (New York: Library of America, 1988), 951; Ernest Fenollosa and Ezra Pound, *The Chinese Written Character as a Medium for Poetry: A Critical Edition*, ed. Haun Saussy et al. (New York: Fordham University Press, 2008), 52; Walter Pater, "Conclusion" to *The Renaissance*, in *The Norton Anthology of Theory and Criticism*, ed. Vincent B. Leitch et al. (New York: Norton, 2001), 841.

[5] See J. Paul Hunter, *Before Novels: The Cultural Contexts of Eighteenth-Century English Fiction* (New York: Norton, 1990).

[6] Iris Murdoch, "Against Dryness," in *Existentialists and Mystics: Writings on Philosophy and Literature*, ed. Peter Conradi (New York: Penguin, 1999), 290, 292.

[7] For questions about character, see Alain Robbe-Grillet's foundational *For a New Novel*, trans. Richard Howard (New York: Grove Press, 1965); on style, see Jameson's classic introductory chapter to *Postmodernism*; on popular culture, see Andreas Huyssen, *After the Great Divide: Modernism, Mass Culture, Postmodernism* (Bloomington: Indiana University Press, 1987).

Hemingway (an author of "books for boys") with as much wry ferocity as he derided Faulkner (an author of "corncobby chronicles"), but he gladly shared their sense of what was taboo: "Style and structure are the essence of a book; great ideas are hogwash." As Donald Barthelme noted, words like *honor* and *glory* have remained as "deeply suspicious" as they were for Hemingway, and fledgling writers still get scolded for a "retreat into abstraction" and a "reliance on abstract nouns," for writing "top-heavy with 'meaning'" and trying to pull off a "grand message."[8]

All this may explain why recent criticism has blurred longstanding critical lines between early- and late-century fiction, between "modernism" and the various trends that developed in its wake. When Ross Posnock, for instance, adventurously traces the history of "renunciation" in modern culture—a history that sees painters, musicians, and writers casting off the "primacy of concepts and of discursive knowing"—he feels no need to make fastidiously fine-grained distinctions between periods and movements, and freely canvasses figures from across the last century and a half.[9] And when Mark McGurl, in a more sociological register, identifies three major strands of the "Program Era," these paradigms are described not as radical breakthroughs, but as continuations of—even normalizations of—early twentieth-century practice. "Technomodernism" extends modernist narrative experiments while more openly acknowledging the continuity between literature and technology (DeLillo, Barth, Pynchon), whereas the performance of membership in "High Cultural Pluralism" continues modernist experiments with consciousness and time (Morrison, Erdrich, Momaday, Kingston). Both of these are juxtaposed with "Lower-Middle-Class Modernism," which deploys Hemingway's anti-sentimental minimalism to dramatize a growing sense of economic insecurity among American workers (Carver, Mason, Wolff). Much like Posnock, in other words, McGurl discerns a persistent trait running through an extraordinarily diverse family of works, an internalization

---

[8] Donald Barthelme, *Not-Knowing: The Essays and Interviews*, ed. Kim Herzinger (New York: Vintage, 1999); Vladimir Nabokov, *Strong Opinions* (New York: Vintage, 1990), 42 (on Hemingway), 57 (on Faulkner); Vladimir Nabokov, *Lectures on Literature*, ed. Fredson Bowers (New York: Mariner, 2002), qtd. xxiii. The warnings against a "retreat into abstraction" and "abstract nouns" are voiced in Lindsay Clarke, "Going the Last Inch: Some Thoughts on Showing and Telling," in *Creative Writing: A Workbook with Readings*, ed. Linda Anderson (New York: Routledge, 2006), 489; the complaints about "top-heavy" "grand messages" are from Daniel Mendelsohn's review of James Wood's 2003 novel *The Book Against God*, "The Man Who Loved Chekhov," *New York Times* (July 6, 2004) <http://www.nytimes.com/2003/07/06/books/the-man-who-loved-chekhov.html?pagewanted=all> (accessed August 17, 2015).

[9] Ross Posnock, *Renunciation: Acts of Abandonment By Writers, Philosophers, and Artists* (Cambridge, MA: Harvard University Press, 2016), 6.

of the imperative to *show, don't tell*—a catchy popularization of what McGurl calls "the classically modernist value of 'impersonality.'"[10]

What would it mean to sidestep these imperatives and impulses? How would one challenge the nominalist commitments that are among the central threads of the last century's literary history? Would a writer *want* to do so? What would the rationale, the attraction, be? In the chapters that follow, I consider a line of post-World War II American authors whose work raises precisely these questions, and who struggle to imagine a different kind of literary and intellectual project. Walker Percy, Marilynne Robinson, Ralph Ellison, Stanley Cavell, and David Foster Wallace are all deeply cognizant of the nominalist drives that have spurred so much modern prose. But they all also resist the "general loss of concepts" that Murdoch, for one, associates with the writing of the last century, and the rigorous focus on the "here and now" that Jameson identifies. For them, we couldn't avoid our conceptualizing capacities even if we wanted. Thus they ask whether some of the great doctrines of twentieth-century writing have become doctrinaire: whether ideas are indeed hogwash, whether we must indeed go in fear of abstraction, and whether we might revisit the words that long have been deemed the most deeply suspect. They ask what is lost when we assent too easily to the prohibitions that have defined the writing of (by now) several generations, and especially what might be gained by treating the high words of moral and political appraisal—those wooly, discomforting, abstract normative concepts—as something other than "obscene."

I call these figures "postwar sages," and my starting point is an obvious feature of their work: namely that they are as palpably invested in *essayistic* and *discursive* forms as they are in *narrative* and *novelistic* forms. In quite conspicuous ways, that is, their oeuvres exhibit the impulse to "tell" as much as "show." Given the appeals in modern writing to concrete names and sounds and scenes, it's unsurprising that this dedication to the discursive should set Robinson, Ellison, and the others apart from their predecessors and contemporaries. As

---

[10] Mark McGurl, *The Program Era: Postwar Fiction and the Rise of Creative Writing* (Cambridge, MA: Harvard University Press, 2009), 42, 56–57, 63–67, 23. For a good overview of the ways that recent critics—not only McGurl, but also Walter Benn Michaels, Amy Hungerford, Michael Clune, Loren Glass, Sean McCann, Lisa Siraganian, Michael LeMahieu, Mark Greif, Sianne Ngai, and Ursula K. Heise—have in different ways seen the post-45 period "as a continuation or extension of modernism," not its overthrow, see Jason Gladstone and Daniel Worden's astute introduction to *Postmodern/Postwar—And After*, ed. Jason Gladsone, Andrew Hoberek, and Daniel Worden (Iowa City: University of Iowa Press, 2016), 4–8. For a good discussion of the ways that the history of post-World War II American fiction no longer seems defined solely by the notion of "postmodernism," see Andrew Hoberek, "Introduction: After Postmodernism," *Twentieth-Century Literature* 53 (2007): 233–47.

one commentator puts it, when a "real man of letters" in the twentieth century indulges in something other than a novel or poem, "he is excused" by readers, assumed to be "momentarily off-duty and writing with his left hand, and for money." Murdoch more caustically describes the phenomenon when she says that the search for "linguistic quasi-things" in art denigrates non-novelistic prose to the status of utilitarian "explanation and exposition," reductively equating it with the "didactic, documentary, informative."[11] With a few exceptions, the pursuit of art has seemed to most serious Anglophone storytellers over the last several generations to demand levels of particularization that are incompatible with the bluntly assertoric and conceptualizing habits of an editorialist, social activist, politician, moral tutor, religious advocate, or any other role that involves making undisguised normative claims.[12]

This is certainly true of, for instance, Conrad, Joyce, Beckett, and Nabokov, none of whom concentrated for any extended periods on producing discursive works, and when authors like J. M. Coetzee, Salman Rushdie, or Margaret Atwood swerve into the essayistic, they typically place these moments within the shell of a story, their bald-faced assertions framed by character and circumstance. And one could argue that modern American authors have been particularly allergic to "telling." "I don't have enough education," Faulkner once said, "I don't know anything about ideas, to write an essay," and from the relative dearth of their expository writing, one can infer that Hemingway, F. Scott Fitzgerald, Djuna Barnes, and Nathanael West all felt something similar.[13] The same seems true of most major post-World War II American figures: not only DeLillo, Pynchon, Barth, Carver, and Mason, but also Bernard Malamud, William Gaddis, Philip Roth, Ann Beattie, John Edgar Wideman, Richard Powers. . . . To ascribe this silence to what Philip Rahv called an anti-intellectual "cult of experience" in American writing would be too simple.[14] But it is true that, broadly speaking, when most serious twentieth-century American authors have paused

---

[11] Ned Stuckey-French, *The American Essay in the American Century* (Columbia: University of Missouri Press, 2011), 5; Iris Murdoch, *Existentialists and Mystics* (ed. Conradi), 290, 292; hereafter referred to parenthetically as *EM*.

[12] Woolf and Lawrence are probably the most obvious exceptions to this generalization about essay-writing among major early twentieth-century English-language authors. But it is unclear what kind of exception they constitute. One could argue that, of all the major English-language modernists, they have the strongest affinities to the nineteenth-century fiction writers who preceded them, and each has palpable connections to the Victorian sage tradition that I mention presently.

[13] For Faulkner's self-description, see *Faulkner at West Point*, 111.

[14] American novelists, declaimed Rahv, showcased "a vast phenomenology swept by waves of sensation and feeling": "Everything is contained in the American novel except ideas." See Philip Rahv, "The Cult of Experience in American Writing," *Literature and the Sixth Sense* (Boston: Houghton Mifflin, 1970), 22–25. Rahv was writing in 1940, and was contrasting the American novel with the

from making art, it has usually been to talk about it—whether in defense of creative liberty (pleas for, e.g., Rushdie or Henry Miller), in artistic manifestoes (Cather's "The Novel Démeublé," Franzen's "Perchance to Dream"), in belletristic reviews and commentaries (Updike, Ozick, Lethem), or in extended analyses of craft and tradition (James's prefaces, Barth's *The Friday Book*, Morrison's *Playing in the Dark*, most of Barth's or William Gass's work). Such acts of literary criticism involve normative evaluations, of course. But the positions from which these evaluations are issued remain mostly implicit, with few glimpses of a more general philosophical, moral, or political position, let alone the earnest invocation of such hazy generalities as Justice, Duty, Honor, or Glory.

The figures I address here, by contrast, don't cordon off their right-handed work from their left-handed work. They are as manifestly drawn to telling as to showing, shifting from works of drama and character (fiction, memoir) to discursive and evidential genres (philosophy, history, theology, cultural criticism), and back again. And as I shall argue, their doing so can illuminate a great deal about our understanding of art's role in the contemporary world, our experiences as modern moral and political agents, and our lives as conceptualizing creatures more generally.

"Postwar sage": my label is meant to underscore two essential dimensions of these authors' projects—two pedigrees usually thought to be at odds. "Postwar" highlights the time frame of these authors, and emphasizes the ways that they are deeply aware of, and deeply indebted to, the radical transformations that marked ambitious art over the course of the twentieth century. Indeed, to one extent or another, all the figures here display the classic qualities and fixations of the modern artist: intensely particularizing, self-conscious and self-questioning, acquainted with vast panoramas of futility and anarchy, willing to make it new, preoccupied with the problems of their own media, aware that artistic forms might grow exhausted. "Sage," however, stresses some of the dissatisfaction these figures show with modern aesthetics, and the ways

---

more intellectually and ideologically ambitious writing that one often finds, he claimed, among European writers. Rahv's dichotomy is probably too stark, but it's nevertheless worth keeping in mind how the shift between art and argument, the narrative and the discursive, that I will be addressing here has been a mainstay of other national and linguistic traditions. Most obvious in this regard is probably the French tradition, where authors like Zola, Gide, Sartre, De Beauvoir, and Camus could be celebrated both as novelists and dramatists, on the one hand, and as moral, political, and philosophical authorities on the other—a tradition more recently, if differently, extended by the ambidextrous work of Hélène Cixous, Monique Wittig, or J. M. G. Le Clézio. In the German tradition, one likewise thinks of Thomas Mann, Gunter Grass, or W. G. Sebald. Despite these differences, however, I'm less ready than Rahv to make pronouncements about "the American novel" as such; I'm making observations about tendencies more than claims about essences.

they descend equally from much older traditions. The term recalls, for one, the prophetic modes that shape ancient Hebrew texts such as Isaiah, Jeremiah, or Ezekiel, as well as the traditions of wisdom literature that scholars associate with The Book of Job, Psalms, and Ecclesiastes. Moreover, it evokes the moral and spiritual ideal that, as Pierre Hadot has claimed, runs through all schools of ancient Greek and Roman thought—an ideal that, though possibly inaccessible to humans, defines the inner attitudes and bodily habits that practitioners are supposed to adopt.[15] The sage tradition is usually traced in the early modern period through Erasmus, Montaigne, and Pascal, but the reincarnation most relevant in the present context develops in nineteenth-century Anglo-American culture. As scholars such as John Holloway and George P. Landow have argued, authors like Thomas Carlyle, Ralph Waldo Emerson, Matthew Arnold, Henry David Thoreau, George Eliot, John Ruskin, and John Henry Newman scrutinized the signs of their times—new technologies, expanding free markets, waning religious faith, changing forms of political authority—and gave varied expression to questions about how we should live in and with modernity. These figures attempted to stand apart from their society, their ethos of trustworthiness and intimacy balancing the polemical urgency of their interpretations and predictions. Holding fast to a search for conviction and wisdom, they employed a mixture of traditional rhetoric and modern literary techniques in order to present a specific stance toward life and quicken a reader's understanding of experience. Only through a mosaic of dialectic and drama, of rhetorical persuasion and narrative example, could a writer respond adequately to the unprecedented threats generated by modern life and institutions.[16]

---

[15] Pierre Hadot, *Philosophy as a Way of Life*, ed. Arnold I. Davidson, trans. Michael Chase (Oxford: Blackwell, 1995), 57–59. In Plato's *Symposium*, for instance, the sage is the figure who has attained wisdom, as opposed to the seeker after wisdom or the person unconcerned with such a search; and Aristotle speaks both of *phronesis*, the practical worldly judgment attained by wise rulers and moral agents, and of *sophia*, the intellectual wisdom sought by philosophers. Among the Roman Stoics, the sage is the figure who attains either "knowledge of divine and human matters" (a grasp of logic, physics, and ethics) or who achieves "fitting expertise" (cognition trained toward some useful end). On the Roman sage in particular, see René Brouwer, *The Stoic Sage: The Early Stoics on Wisdom, Sagehood, and Socrates* (Cambridge: Cambridge University Press, 2014).

[16] John Holloway, *The Victorian Sage: Studies in Argument* (London: Macmillan, 1953); George P. Landow, *Elegant Jeremiahs: The Sage From Carlyle to Mailer* (Ithaca, NY: Cornell University Press, 1986). A fuller account of "sage" would of course need to consider the important differences among the various traditions and figures that I've mentioned here. Landow, for instance, ties Victorian sage writing primarily to the biblical prophetic tradition, and distinguishes it from ancient wisdom literature: whereas the writer of wisdom literature assumes that he (and it is, of course, usually a "he") embodies the "accepted, received wisdom of an entire society," the biblical and Victorian prophets begin from a belief that, however traditional their messages may appear, they have, in fact, been forgotten by their culture (22–23). Thus, whereas Holloway suggests that Ralph Waldo Emerson could have played a larger role in his book than he does (15), Landow explicitly excludes

Such nineteenth-century sages were often, of course, the objects of derision for the *fin de siècle* and World War I generations, who looked upon these intellectuals as windy moralizers. (Carlyle, Ruskin, and Arnold became so important in their day, quipped T. S. Eliot, mainly because "precision and completeness of thought do not always make for influence.")[17] But the decades after World War II witnessed, I will claim, a revival of such impulses and methods, with major authors finding new ways to cross the boundaries between narrative and moral judgment, portrayal and persuasion. Each figure I address embarks on what Holloway calls a "joint process of proof and exposition," and as a result, none of them can be neatly pigeonholed as an "essayist," "moralist," "journalist," "philosopher," "memoirist," or "novelist."[18] The roots of this generic restlessness are complex, however, and take us far beyond the relatively familiar literary–historical currents I've been canvassing so far. And what I find in these authors—particularly what I shall be calling their "weak realism" and their "reflective" modes of composition—will likely seem to some readers as anomalous as some of the terms I use to describe them. The rest of this introduction sketches some of these terms as well as some of the dangers to which, as I understand them, the projects of the sage are sometimes prone.

II. A Taste for Desert Landscapes

The priority of what Jameson calls the "here and now of this unique situation and this unique expression" penetrates not only the last century's major literary works, but also our most influential theories of them. Think of Viktor Schlovsky on making "the stone stony," of imparting "the sensation of things as they are perceived and not as they are known"; or Cleanth Brooks's belief that the mark of a genuine work would lie in its *being* an experience rather than any mere statement about experience or any mere abstraction from experience."[19] The various theories that in more recent decades have dominated literary studies

---

the "genial Emerson," claiming that, unlike Carlyle or Thoreau, he never attacks his audience or comments extensively on contemporary phenomena (30–32). (Whether this is, in fact, true of Emerson is a question that can be left to the side here.)

[17] T.S. Eliot, "Arnold and Pater," *Selected Essays, 1917–1932* (New York: Harcourt, 1950), 348.

[18] Holloway, *Victorian Sage*, 9.

[19] Viktor Schlovsky, "Art as Technique," in *Literary Theory: An Anthology*, ed. Julie Rivkin and Michael Ryan (Oxford: Wiley-Blackwell, 2017), 9; Cleanth Brooks, *The Well-Wrought Urn: Studies in the Structure of Poetry* (New York: Harvest/HBJ, 1947), 212–13. One thinks here also of William Wimsatt and Monroe Beardsley, who claimed to judge a poem as they judged a machine, demanding "only that it works," regardless of its maker's intended "practical messages," which are "more abstract than poetry." ("The Intentional Fallacy," *Literary Theory: An Anthology*, 30–31.)

often are portrayed as a rebuke to these early formalists, but they, too, have been assertively hostile to mere abstraction, giving new credence to Nietzsche's early claim that we obtain concepts only "by overlooking what is individual and real," denying the singularities that remain "inaccessible to us and undefinable for us."[20] As Jameson puts it, literary theorists have valorized a "variety of punctual 'experiences'" whose "immediacy is not to be redeemed or defused by their assimilation to something more general, or more abstract, or more intellectual–generic."[21] His main example is Paul de Man, who, as he says, tirelessly exposes the superstitions buried in our "banal anthropomorphic concepts," and whose reception among some critics and the popular media resembled "the agitation of Thomistic clerks confronted unexpectedly with the nominalist enormity."[22] But Jameson might also have mentioned Derrida, whose insistence that we try to "stop dreaming the dream of a closed, total vocabulary" has been described as nominalistic; or Foucault, who regarded his own work as a form of "historical nominalism," claiming that one "needs to be nominalistic, no doubt: power is not an institution, and not a structure," but "the name that one attributes to a complex strategical situation in a particular society."[23] Among theories with more recent sway, Judith Butler's account of gender and performativity has been seen as a radical application of nominalism, and a strong nominalist current has been identified in affect theory, as in, for instance, Brian Massumi's claim that speaking about an "object" or "thing" involves referring to "an evolving differential," "a complex interweaving of attributes and contents as subsumed under a nominal identity (a name)."[24]

---

[20] Friedrich Nietzsche, "On Truth and Lying in a Non-Moral Sense," in *The Birth of Tragedy and Other Writings*, ed. Raymond Geuss and Ronald Speirs (Cambridge: Cambridge University Press, 1999), 145.

[21] Fredric Jameson, *Late Marxism: Adorno, or, the Persistence of the Dialectical* (London: Verso, 1990), 160.

[22] Jameson, *Postmodernism*, 245–50.

[23] Derrida's nominalism is identified by Richard Rorty, "The Higher Nominalism in a Nutshell: A Reply to Henry Staten," *Critical Inquiry* 12 (1986), 463–64. Others who understand Derrida as a kind of nominalist include John D. Caputo, *The Prayers and Tears of Jacques Derrida: Religion Without Religion* (Bloomington: Indiana University Press, 1997), 138. Foucault's remark appears in *The History of Sexuality, Volume 1: An Introduction* (New York: Vintage, 1990), 93. For an account of his "historical nominalism," see Thomas R. Flynn, *Sartre, Foucault, and Historical Reason, Volume 2* (Chicago: University of Chicago Press, 2005), chap. 2.

[24] On Butler's nominalism, see Saskia Wendel, "A Critique of Feminist Radical Constructivism," in *Belief, Bodies, and Being: Feminist Reflections on Embodiment*, ed. Deborah Orr (London: Rowman & Littlefield, 2006), 185–96; Massumi's quotation appears in John Mullarky, *Post-Continental Philosophy: An Outline* (London: Continuum, 2006), 42–43. For a critical take on affect theory and the confluence of traditions that inform it, see Ruth Leys, "The Turn to Affect: A Critique," *Critical Inquiry* 37 (2011): 434–72. Leys's essay owes much to another work in which the concept of— though not the term—nominalism comes under critical scrutiny, namely Walter Benn Michaels's *The Shape of the Signifier: 1967 to the End of History* (Princeton, NJ: Princeton University Press,

The postwar sages featured in the following chapters are often sensitive to these developments in criticism and theory. But the issues most urgently goading them originate elsewhere, and lead us away from postwar fiction's oft-noted likenesses to modern French and German theory.[25] The term "nominalism" originates, after all, not with industrialism, Roger Fry's curated exhibitions, World War I, or any of the other habitually cited sources of twentieth-century writing, but rather in—as Jameson's reference to "Thomistic clerks" suggests—medieval arguments over universals, and over what in time became the Scientific Revolution. Nominalism began, that is, as a debate over what can be included in valid statements about the cosmos, what things are ontologically respectable, and specifically whether properties deserve a place in our conception of reality as much as the particulars in which they inhere. If, traditional realists had argued, both my kitchen table and the wheels of my car are round, then they each instantiate *roundness*, and this species of shape is not just a human concept, but exists independent of our thought and language. Indeed, for the realist, such generic properties are the *really* real things, permanent and unchanging, over and above the transient particulars that participate in them. But such metaphysical realism, claimed the early nominalists, heretically implied that God could be constrained, that His will could *not* change anything in existence—even such general and eternal-looking properties like being round. Thus universals could not inhere in tables, wheels, or anything else, but must be attributed by *us*; they're human projections onto the endlessly fluxional particulars of reality.[26]

Believing such claims was enough to get a person excommunicated in the fourteenth century, but gradually it won listeners, including Francis Bacon, whose account of the "four idols" was grounded in the belief that, "In nature, nothing really exists besides individual bodies."[27] And as Bacon's views came to

---

2004). Michaels begins his book by focusing on the language of "concreteness" and "experience" in recent discussions of print and type (e.g., in debates about Emily Dickinson's notebooks), and like Jameson he focuses particular attention on Paul de Man's "commitment to the material object" (7). For Michaels, de Man's criticism does not ask "what was done on purpose and what was done by accident" but instead "treat[s] the object as if nothing were done on purpose, as if everything were accidental" (7).

[25] The likeness between postwar fiction and postwar theory is manifest anytime a critic "uses" or "applies" a theorist's writings to interpret a novel (Baudrillard for *White Noise*, Derrida for *The Crying of Lot 49*, etc.), but these connections have recently been given more historical and biographical substance in Judith Ryan's *The Novel After Theory* (New York: Columbia University Press, 2011).

[26] My thumbnail sketch of the history of nominalism and the scientific revolution is obviously a simplification. For a fuller overview, see Michael Allen Gillespie, *The Theological Origins of Modernity* (Chicago: University of Chicago Press, 2008), chap. 1.

[27] Quoted in Gillespie, *Theological Origins*, 37. Perhaps the most prominent nominalist to be excommunicated in the fourteenth century was William of Ockham.

hold sway—as formal and final causes were steadily eliminated, as the physical world came to be described as intentionless material particulars—what is true of physical properties such as roundness came to seem even more consequentially true of normative concepts. To attribute (say) *piety* to an action may traditionally have involved identifying "the form itself that makes all pious actions pious," as Socrates said to Euthyphro. And this form may have been seen as part of what Charles Taylor calls a "human–independent ontic order": the Forms, the Hebrew cosmology, the medieval *Scala naturea*.[28] But a nominalist dispensation makes *piety* less the name of something discoverable "out there," and more like an eliminable fiction, an expression of our varying human needs and desires, nothing substantial, objective, or universal.

The most sophisticated articulations of this claim have come in what was eventually dubbed "analytic" philosophy, beginning with its earliest forerunners. With, for instance, Thomas Hobbes, Bacon's secretary: "nothing in the world [is] universal but names[,] for the things named are every one of them individual and singular." Or John Locke: "all things that exist [are] particulars," and the "general and universal belong not to the real existence of things."[29] Analogous claims appear in David Hume, J. S. Mill, Bertrand Russell, the Vienna Circle, and, through them, twentieth-century American philosophers such as W. V. O. Quine, whose self-professed "taste for desert landscapes" led him to suggest that sentences don't *actually* have "meanings" any more than human creatures *actually* have "beliefs," "thoughts," and other intentional states. Talk of mental states may never be "practically dispensable," says Quine, but "limning the true and ultimate structure of reality" requires a genuinely "austere scheme" that is focused entirely on the physical behavior and constitution of organisms.[30] In the terms of Quine's contemporary Wilfrid Sellars, one of modern thought's defining features is the "scientific image of man": the view that, thanks to the disciplined activities of the scientist and the development of new technologies, pictures us as an arrangement of biochemical matter rather than an embodied purposive creature perceptible to the naked senses. What looks like a complex intentional action (making a lasagna, casting a vote) is ultimately a "swirl of

[28] Plato, *The Complete Works*, ed. John M. Cooper (Indianapolis, IN: Hackett, 1997), 6; Charles Taylor, *The Ethics of Authenticity* (Cambridge, MA: Harvard University Press, 1991), 86.

[29] Thomas Hobbes, *Leviathan*, ed. C. B. MacPherson (London: Penguin, 1982), 102; John Locke, *Essay Concerning Human Understanding*, ed. Roger Woolhouse (New York: Penguin, 1998), 371.

[30] W.V.O. Quine, "On What There Is," in *From a Logical Point of View: Nine Logico-Philosophical Essays* (Cambridge, MA: Harvard University Press, 1953), 1–19; *Word and Object* (Cambridge, MA: MIT Press, 1960), 216–21. For some reflections on Quine's nominalism, see Charles Parsons, "Quine's Nominalism," *American Philosophical Quarterly* 48.3 (July 2011): 213–28.

physical particles, forces, and fields."[31] And for the last three-quarters of a century, such bald naturalism—in John McDowell's helpful phrase—has defined any number of Anglo-American programs. Behaviorism and neuroscience, for instance, may fixate on different aspects of the human organism—gross bodily motions and the brain, respectively—but each operates with the deflationary assumption championed from Bacon onwards: if bodily events precede concepts in the order of being, then concepts are necessarily reducible to such bodily events.[32] As one naturalist has recently put it, all facts—psychological, cultural, economic—supervene upon physical facts, and if physics "can't in principle fix a putative fact, it is no fact after all."[33]

When desert landscapes become our dominant taste, our robustly normative words are bound to wither. In a world of matter, high words have little place; "piety" is less measurably a property of the world than sound waves or air pressure. And as we'll see over the chapters that follow, such withering has taken an array of forms across an array of scientific and academic disciplines. The crucial point for now is that, in calling modern literature "nominalist," Jameson is not only drawing attention to the well-documented aversion among ambitious authors to flabby abstraction. He's also tying this aversion to the skeptical drive found in Bacon and the entire philosophico-scientific project that he championed. For nominalists in both the artistic and scientific realms, abstract concepts are cause for ruthless suspicion, particularly normative concepts, troublesome terms such as "piety" (or "kindness," "generosity," or "injustice"). And for both, an authentically modern method would by contrast attend solely to the sensuous and concrete, to the "given" and "immediate," in all its fine-grained particularity. The work of art becomes "autonomous" not in the sense that it transcends the world, but because no further explication can be adequate. No clarification can comfortably capture the *this*ness and the *there*ness

---

[31] Wilfrid Sellars, "Philosophy and the Scientific Image of Man," *Science, Perception, and Reality* (New York: The Humanities Press, 1963), 1–40. Sellars contrasted the "scientific image" with the "manifest image" of human beings, a distinction that was more complex than what we find in Quine. He was aware that the latter is always in some sense dependent upon the former, and he regarded the manifest image as something that could be "*joined* to" the scientific image, not discarded wholesale (40).

[32] On "bald naturalism," see McDowell, *Mind and World* (Cambridge, MA: Harvard University Press, 1994), xviii–xxiii, 66–86. On behaviorism, see Quine's friend B. F. Skinner, *Beyond Freedom and Dignity* (Indianapolis, IN: Hackett, 1971); on eliminativism, see Quine's admirer Paul Churchland, *The Engine of Reason, the Seat of the Soul: A Philosophical Journey into the Brain* (Cambridge, MA: MIT Press, 1995). For some explicit claims about the debt eliminative materialism in particular owes to Quine, see Patricia Churchland's preface to the 2013 reissue of Quine's *Word and Object* (Cambridge, MA: MIT Press, 2013), xi–xiv.

[33] Alexander Rosenberg, "Disenchanted Naturalism," in *Contemporary Philosophical Naturalism and Its Implications*, ed. Bana Bashour and Hans D. Muller (New York: Routledge, 2014), 19.

of the object. It is irreducibly indexical—"nothing other," as J. M. Bernstein puts it, "than material stuff," openly declaring its "material basis and means," foregrounding the "skeptical denial of meaning" that marks our understanding of the disenchanted universe generally. This declaration of materiality is, in part, what makes the history of modern art, as Arthur Danto has said, a history "of purgation, of generic cleansing, of ridding the art of whatever was inessential to it." In the case of narrative, such purgation demands the refusal of exposition: plain assertion and open appraisal, after all, are the tools of the moralist or the generalizing thinker, and lie outside, to adapt Clement Greenberg, the storyteller's unique and proper area of competence.[34]

None of this means, of course, that the writings of Hemingway and other twentieth-century literary benchmarks replicate those of Hobbes or Quine, let alone the lab reports of molecular chemists. Obviously they *look* and *sound* different. The young Wittgenstein, engineer and cornerstone of positivism, may have believed that a genuine "proposition expresses what it expresses in a definite and clearly specifiable way," but twentieth-century literature became (in)famous for what Virginia Woolf called "the spasmodic, the obscure, the fragmentary, the failure."[35] Its celebrated "difficulty" stands at some distance from the ideally lucid propositions of the natural sciences. Moreover, nominalism tends to be put to quite different *ends* in modern aesthetics than in scientific theory and practice. However much modern texts investigate the materiality of the world and of language, their ultimate point is not the explanation and prediction of the causally bound universe, but usually something like spiritual transformation, renewal through *askesis*. In 1961, Lionel Trilling suggested that literary modernism asked in unprecedented ways whether "we are saved or damned," whether we can achieve "salvation," and as Amy Hungerford has argued, such an ambition has in many respects only grown more radical: much important post-World War II literature is committed to a notion of "transcendent form," a faith that the "nonsemantic powers of language"—the look or sound of words, tone or diction, style, narrative or poetic form—will in and of

[34] J.M. Bernstein, "Aesthetics, Modernism, Literature: Cavell's Transformation of Philosophy," in *Stanley Cavell*, ed. Richard Eldridge (Cambridge: Cambridge University Press, 2003), 128–29; Arthur Danto, *After the End of Art* (Princeton, NJ: Princeton University Press, 1998), 70; Clement Greenberg, "Modernist Painting," *Modern Art and Modernism: A Critical Anthology*, ed. Francis Frascina and Charles Harrison (New York: Harper and Row, 1992), 5.

[35] Ludwig Wittgenstein, *Tractatus Logico-Philosophicus*, trans. C.K. Ogden (1922; London: Routledge, 1999), 49 (proposition 3.251); Virginia Woolf, "Mr. Bennett and Mrs. Brown," in *Essentials of the Theory of Fiction*, ed. Michael J. Hoffman and Patrick D. Murphy (Durham, NC: Duke University Press, 1999), 28, 35.

themselves achieve a "bid for significance," provide a source of "conviction."[36] The modernist artist's pleas for materiality and conceptual austerity often coincide with appeals to the immaterial, the transcendent, the mysterious, the redemptive, the ineffable—all those things "whereof one cannot speak," as the young Wittgenstein also puts it, pulling up the ladder on his own astringent propositions. Hence the critical claims that modern texts seek not rational "intellect" but "intuition," not knowledge but "unknowing."[37]

My point in recalling the long history of nominalism has not, however, been to conflate its scientific and literary incarnations. It has instead been to suggest why, in both versions, normative concepts come to sound like—to recall Addie Bundren—"high dead words," empty sounds. Seeing this connection may help explain why, for instance, analogies to "experimental" science have often surrounded twentieth-century literature, and why, as one commentator has written, "the fashion" among many modern artists has been "all for scientism."[38] For George Eliot, it was still possible to believe that the writer "inevitably assumes the office of teacher or influencer of the public mind," someone "influencing the moral taste, and with it the action of the intelligence." She could declaim

---

[36] Lionel Trilling, "On the Teaching of Modern Literature," in *The Moral Obligation to Be Intelligent: Selected Essays*, ed. Leon Wieseltier (Evanston, IL: Northwestern University Press, 2000), 385; Amy Hungerford, *Postmodern Belief: American Literature and Religion Since 1960* (Princeton, NJ: Princeton University Press, 2010), xviii–xxi.

[37] See Wittgenstein, *Tractatus*, 189 (proposition 7); Immanuel Kant, *Critique of Judgment*, trans. Werner S. Pluhar (Indianapolis, IN: Hackett, 1987), esp. 181–88 (§49). On "intuition" vs. "intellect," see Michael Levenson, *A Genealogy of Modernism: A Study of English Literary Doctrine, 1908–1922* (Cambridge: Cambridge University Press, 1984). On "unknowing" vs. "knowledge," see Philip Weinstein, *Unknowing: The Work of Modernist Fiction* (Ithaca, NY: Cornell University Press, 2005).

[38] Pierre Francastel, quoted in Luc Ferry, *Homo Aestheticus: The Invention of Taste in the Democratic Age*, trans. Robert De Loaiza (Chicago: University of Chicago Press, 1994), 208. For an overview of recent criticism's interest in modernism and science, see Hugh Crawford, "Modernism," in *Routledge Companion to Literature and Science*, ed. Bruce Clarke and Manuela Rossini (London: Routledge, 2011), 508–17. In his powerful reading of abstract expressionism, Robert B. Pippin has argued that the movements I've been describing should be seen as self-conscious and conceptual, a recognition of the authority and autonomy of human thought, rather than (as with Ferry and Greenberg) "reductionist and materialist." On this reading, what matters is less the drips on a canvas than the conscious thematization of components of sensible meaning that we can no longer treat as given. This may or may not be true about some midcentury painters, but I take Ferry to be articulating roughly the perspective of artists themselves, who tended to be much less Hegelian than Pippin. (See Pippin, "What Was Abstract Art? (From the Point of View of Hegel)," in *The Persistence of Subjectivity: On the Kantian Aftermath* (Cambridge: Cambridge University Press, 2005). For a useful corrective to Pippin's claims, see Chapter 24 of Charles Taylor's *Source of the Self: The Making of the Modern Identity* (Cambridge, MA: Harvard University Press, 1989), which, drawing heavily on Hugh Kenner's work, describes how modernist artists challenged the expressivism of the nineteenth century, repeatedly casting themselves as conduits for nonhuman forces and often drawing upon the language of science—as in the language of force fields, energy, or poets as (in Pound's term) "the antennae of the race."

without blushing that, of the three words that had been used as the "inspiring trumpet-call of men," *God* and *Immortality* may be "inconceivable" but *Duty* was "peremptory and absolute."[39] Yet a half-century after Flaubert celebrated the "the precision of science," novelists were as distrustful of these clumsy words as contemporaries such as Russell or Rudolph Carnap. And—not coincidentally— they were as curious as these philosophers about the new sciences: think of Conrad's interest in entropy, Woolf's fascination with recent astronomy, Joyce's attraction to the theory of general relativity, or for that matter the many literary journals and popular books that were promoting science's new claims and dis- coveries in the years before and after World War I.[40] Authors since World War II have been no less spellbound by the era's scientific achievements. Pynchon's interest in thermodynamics is by now a platitude of critical commentary, nosing out the lepidopterology of his teacher Nabokov, who believed that the "bound- ary line" between a work of fiction and a work of science is "not as clear as is generally believed," given that the "only instrument" for understanding either one was "the top of the tingling spine." But others could be named. William Gass has praised the Logical Positivists who trained him in philosophy, with their emphasis on "technique" and "methodology" rather than "metaphysics" or "politics," and for Joseph McElroy, the "experimental and measuring methods"

---

[39] George Eliot, *The Writings of George Eliot: Essays and Leaves from a Note-book*, ed. John Walter Cross (Boston: Houghton Mifflin, 1908), 296–97. Her observation about "Duty" was recorded by F. W. H. Myers in 1881, cited in Oscar Browning, *Life of George Eliot* (London: Walter Scott Ltd., 1892), 116.

[40] For Flaubert's remarks, see *The George Sand–Gustave Flaubert Letters*, trans. Aimee L. McKenzie (New York: Boni & Liveright, 1921), 99. On Conrad, see Chapter 2 of Michael H. Whitworth, *Einstein's Wake: Relativity, Metaphor, and Modernist Literature* (New York: Oxford University Press, 2001). On Woolf's interest in astronomy and the "global aesthetic" she pursued, see Holly Henry, *Virginia Woolf and the Discourse of Science: The Aesthetics of Astronomy* (Cambridge: Cambridge University Press, 2009). Woolf also remarks on Joyce and the "restless scintillations" of modern physics in "Modern Novels," which was first published in the *Times Literary Supplement* (April 10, 1919). Joyce's fascination with relativity and other contemporary scientific claims is addressed by Jeffrey S. Drouin, *James Joyce, Science, and Modernist Print Culture* (London: Routledge, 2015). One thinks here also of Wyndham Lewis's attack on the traditional novel's "human point of view," described by Ella Zohar Ophir in "Toward a Pitiless Fiction: Abstraction, Comedy, and Modernist Anti-Humanism," *Modern Fiction Studies* 52 (2006): 92–120. If anything, poets were even more cap- tivated by the austerity and power of science than the novelists. Think, for instance, of Pound speaking of "the way of the scientists rather than the way of an advertising agent for a new soap" (*Literary Essays of Ezra Pound*, 6), or Eliot's claim that "depersonalization" would allow art to "approach the condition of science," making the poet act like a neutral "catalyst" in an experi- ment (*Selected Prose of T. S. Eliot*, 41). For an overview of modernism's relationship to the natural sciences of the early twentieth century, see Whitworth, "The Physical Sciences," in *A Companion to Modernist Literature and Culture*, ed. David Bradshaw and Kevin J.H. Detmar (Oxford: Blackwell, 2006); Thomas Vargish and Delo E. Mook, *Inside Modernism: Relativity Theory, Cubism, Narrative* (New Haven, CT: Yale University Press, 1999).

of science and technology help us recognize "patterns larger than life or smaller than sight" and thus fruitfully "beckon us out of ourselves." From DeLillo's perspective, science gives us "a new language to draw from," and offers "a source of new names, new connections between people and the world."[41]

To draw these parallels—the techniques of twentieth-century fiction, on the one hand, and the aspirations of modern science and analytic philosophy on the other—is to complicate some of our most well-worn categories. In literary history, "naturalism" usually is positioned somewhere between "realism" and "modernism," gloomier and less credulous about human life than the former but less stylistically audacious than the latter. But "naturalism" as I'll be using it here is broader and more encompassing than this, part of an enormous cultural and intellectual drift toward the nonintentional, the material particular over the conceptual abstraction. In a similar way, the parallels I've been drawing challenge an assumption that, until recently, had long seemed safe in literary studies, namely that Anglo-American philosophy has little historical or theoretical bearing on our discussions of fiction, drama, and poetry. As Michael LeMahieu has shown, logical positivism was very much on the minds of post-World War II American writers—Bellow, Pynchon, O'Connor, LeGuin, Barth—and as the following chapters will argue, the same can be said of positivism's more recent descendants.[42] At the deepest level, the parallels I've drawn cut against the grain of some of the most enduring accounts of modern culture, accounts that since Max Weber have emphasized a radical differentiation of spheres: C. P. Snow's "two cultures," for instance, where scientists and engineers scuffle with "traditional intellectuals" and other "natural Luddites," or Jürgen Habermas's triangular conflict, which pits the cognitive domains of science and technology against moral–legal matters on one side and expressive–aesthetic matters

---

[41] Gass's remark appears in *Interviews with William H. Gass*, ed. Theodore G. Ammon (Jackson: University Press of Mississippi, 2003), 125; McElroy's remark is cited in Marc Chénetier, *After Suspicion: New American Fiction Since 1960*, trans. Elizabeth A. Houlding (Philadelphia: University of Pennsylvania Press, 1996), 127; DeLillo's remark appears in *Conversations with Don DeLillo*, ed. Thomas DePietro (Jackson: University of Mississippi Press, 2005), 9. For more on DeLillo's interest in the sciences, see my *Worldly Acts and Sentient Things*, Chapter 6.

[42] See Michael LeMahieu, *Fictions of Fact and Value* (New York: Oxford University Press, 2013). Excavating material from letters, interviews, essays, and archives, LeMahieu has done more than any other critic to illuminate the history of American writers' conscious engagement with twentieth-century Anglo-American philosophy. If we bracket off the growing interest among critics in Stanley Cavell (whose relationship to analytic philosophy is famously vexed, for reasons we'll discuss in Chapter 4), other recent work in literary studies that has shown a serious interest in the problems and history of Anglo-American philosophy includes Megan M. Quigley, *Modernist Fiction and Vagueness: Philosophy, Form, and Language* (Cambridge: Cambridge University Press, 2014); Dora Zhang, "Naming the Indescribable: Woolf, Russell, James, and the Limits of Description,"

on the other.[43] As Susan Sontag said in the 1960s, the twentieth century has arguably seen "not so much a conflict of cultures," but rather "the creation of a new (potentially unitary) kind of sensibility," one that makes no firm "divorce between science and technology, on the one hand, and art, on the other." Such a sensibility demands a "cool" and "exact" style, for the "basic unit" of art is not "the idea" but "the analysis of an extension of sensations." And in its "organizing" of "new modes of sensibility," it above all eschews "discursive explicitness," the "moral journalism" of what she bitingly labeled "the Matthew Arnold notion of culture."[44]

III. Weak Realism and Reflective Composition

One could argue, of course, that the nominalism of Hemingway, Pynchon, or Sontag aren't new to the twentieth century, and one could cite famous remarks by Blake, Keats, or Poe—among others—as proof.[45] But on the whole, prior to the emergence of high modernism, showing seldom seemed at odds with telling. Earlier I recalled the nineteenth-century sages discussed by John Holloway and George Landow—Carlyle, Emerson, Thoreau, Eliot, Newman, and others—but one should also remember the mixed particularizing and generalizing modes utilized by nineteenth-century figures whom those scholars don't address: James Fenimore Cooper taking up American naval history and politics; Harriet Beecher Stowe deploying multiple genres to tackle abolition, women's rights, and housekeeping; Frederick Douglass composing both autobiographies and political tracts. Such projects didn't harden the space between narrative and discursive modes, nor did they regard the stimulating instruments of art

---

New Literary History 45 (2014): 51–70; Oren Izenberg, "Confiance au Monde; or, The Poetry of Ease," *nonsite* 4 (2011) <http://nonsite.org/article/confiance-au-monde-or-the-poetry-of-ease> (accessed September 1, 2016); Reed Way Dasenbrock, ed., *Literary Theory After Davidson* (University Park: Pennsylvania State University Press, 2001); Ann Banfield, *The Phantom Table: Woolf, Fry, Russell and the Epistemology of Modernism* (Cambridge: Cambridge University Press, 2000).

[43] Snow, *The Two Cultures* (1964; Cambridge: Cambridge University Press, 1998), 22; Habermas, *The Theory of Communicative Action*, trans. Thomas McCarthy (Boston: Beacon Press, 1984).

[44] Sontag, "One Culture and the New Sensibility," in *Against Interpretation* (New York: Farrar Straus Giroux, 1966), 296–97, 300, 302.

[45] I'm thinking of, for example, Blake's rebuke of Joshua Reynolds: "To generalize is to be an Idiot; To Particularize is the Alone Distinction of Merit" (*The Complete Poetry and Prose of William Blake*, ed. David V. Erdman [New York: Random House, 1965], 641). Or Keats's distinction between the "virtuous Philosopher" and the "cameleon Poet," the latter of whom embraces particulars so intensely that he will "relish ... the dark side of things" as much as "the bright one" (*English Romantic Writers*, ed. David Perkins, 2nd ed. [New York: Harcourt Brace, 1995], 1286). Or Poe's claim that he was seeking to engineer works that would produce "innumerable effects, or impressions," and that he wrote "without reference to any supposed moral or immoral tendencies" (*Essays and Reviews*, ed. G.R. Thompson [New York: Library of America, 1984], 13, 103.)

and the conceptualizing habits of exposition as mutually exclusive, let alone mutually antagonistic.

The five authors I address at length here are not the only post-World War II figures to move among various forms, nor the only ones who try to summon up something like the authority of these earlier traditions. Landow, for instance, has identified Joan Didion and Norman Mailer as latter-day sages, and a full consideration of the tradition would probably mention other, comparably ambidextrous figures such as James Baldwin, Leslie Marmon Silko, and Dave Eggers. But I'm drawn to the figures I consider here not only because they form an unusually cohesive constellation—I'll say why in a moment—but also because, more than Didion or Baldwin or these others, their work places them squarely between the philosophical and the literary, the abstracting and the particularizing, and thus represents a remarkably vital contemporary incarnation of the "ancient quarrel" identified by Plato.[46] More specifically, the authors I discuss are remarkably attuned to the nominalism that I've been describing, and their entanglement in this question makes them timely in a very particular way. It's difficult to look at a newspaper or magazine nowadays and *not* hear questions about the status of humanistic reflection and judgment, in a culture where the problem-solving STEM fields are supremely well-funded, information gets transmitted in the blink of an eye, and maps of the brain and genome are updated weekly. And the question of nominalism is particularly acute when, to recall Don Draper's remark from my final epigraph, our skepticism about high words is wedded to a certain vision of socioeconomic life, when marketers capitalize on it to generate needs, fuel consumption, and make a buck. Objections to such developments, and to the nominalist-inflected theoretical or artistic practices that support them, have animated some of the liveliest and most compelling criticism of the last decade. But insofar as these objections have tended to avoid reflecting on their own normative commitments at length—insofar as they hesitate to explain in detail what sort of moral psychology might make a

---

[46] Another candidate for the title "sage" who deserves mention in this context is Saul Bellow, who shares with Iris Murdoch a distaste for modernist austerity and dry linguistic "things"; whose writings repeatedly investigate the line between lived experience and normative aspiration; and who in his own life showed a recurrent fascination with gurus (Wilhelm Reich, Rudolf Steiner). In my reading of him, however, Bellow has relatively little to do with the pragmatist and Wittgesteinian traditions that I detail in a moment, and more importantly, he was not—and did not aspire to be— an essayist or thinker in the way that my group of sages does. Whatever dexterity he might have shown about the philosophy and the history of ideas, Bellow was first and foremost a *novelist*, and this label meant something to him. Thus in a career that lasted decades, his collected nonfiction takes up a few hundred pages, compared with the thousands of pages of fiction he published. The ratios are closer or even the reverse among the figures that interest me here.

person be troubled by weak labor unions, or how we would come to *care* about low-paying jobs, or why the sheer forces of history aren't themselves enough to direct us to an authentic notion of economic fairness—their power has been blunted.[47] Implicit in my argument here is that Ellison, Percy, and the others matter because they have taken precisely this risk. They are not only making normative claims, but exploring how to commit oneself to an idea or ideal in a culture where persons are increasingly cast as mere matter, not matter that cares for what matters.

Nominalism and naturalism are liable to seem airlessly academic topics, abstract questions about abstraction. Yet the quintet of figures I discuss here shows how these issues are far more pervasive than they might seem, and the relation of words to the world, of normative concepts to the natural sciences, is a puzzle that sets all of their imaginations in motion. Percy, trained as a medical doctor before becoming a writer, referred to the debate between realism and nominalism as the most "meaningful" debate in philosophy, returning to it repeatedly in his accounts of modernity and language; and Cavell, the only writer here to have made a career as a philosopher, has sometimes used the traditional problem of universals as a jumping-off point for his own accounts of language and understanding.[48] Wallace studied modal logic and deconstruction with equal fervor, and when writing *Everything and More*, his 2003 book on the concept of infinity, he professed that "the ontology and grammar of abstractions have always struck me as one of the most breathtaking problems in human consciousness."[49] For their part, Robinson and Ellison show no overt sign of having studied nominalism per se, but questions about particulars and properties permeate their work: in Robinson's consideration of Calvin, abolitionism, Darwinian theory, and the methods of the social sciences; or in Ellison's reflections on race, the social sciences, and the Constitution, whose "abstract, ideal, spiritual" principles are "measured" against the "fears and temptations of the flesh."[50]

---

[47] I'm thinking of, for instance, the powerful and provocative work of Walter Benn Michaels, in works such as *The Shape of the Signifier* and *The Trouble with Diversity: How We Learned to Love Identity and Ignore Inequality* (New York: Henry Holt & Co., 2006). For an example of a thinker candidly and carefully asking about the relationship between one's personal behavior, beliefs, and moral intuitions, on the one hand, and one's commitment to economic fairness and radical political reform on the other, see G. A. Cohen, *If You're an Egalitarian, How Come You're So Rich?* (Cambridge, MA: Harvard University Press, 2001).

[48] See *More Conversations with Walker Percy*, ed. Lewis A. Lawson and Victor A. Kramer (Jackson: University Press of Mississippi, 1993), 64; Stanley Cavell, *The Claim of Reason: Wittgenstein, Skepticism, Morality, and Tragedy* (New York: Oxford University Press, 1979), 168–90.

[49] Quoted in D.T. Max, *Every Love Story is a Ghost Story: A Life of David Foster Wallace* (New York: Penguin, 2012), 274.

[50] Ralph Ellison, *Collected Essays*, ed. John F. Callahan (New York: Modern Library, 1995), 505, 782.

My goal here is to trace some of the paths that lead these authors away from the desert landscapes of modern nominalism and to study how they come to explore the lush regions of ordinary speech and human activity. It's this investigation, I argue, that ties all these figures to a specific intellectual tradition, one that has often been the unruly stepchild of Anglo-American thought—namely, the lineage associated with the American pragmatists and the later Wittgenstein. As we'll see, it matters that Robinson should regularly express debts to William James, and Percy to Charles Peirce; that Ellison should frequently invoke Emerson, and have drawn formative lessons from Kenneth Burke's Deweyan pragmatism; that Cavell's earliest philosophical sympathies should have been with pragmatism, and that he made his name as an interpreter of Wittgenstein and Emerson; and that Wallace not only takes a serious interest in Cavell and Wittgenstein, but also had a father whose doctorate was written under Wittgenstein's protégé Norman Malcolm, and whose later philosophical work speaks glowingly of Dewey.[51]

The power of this pragmatist–Wittgensteinian tradition lies in the attention it pays to language as a worldly human practice, to the contexts and conditions in which concepts are learned, gradually and piecemeal, example by patient example, through habit and training and education. Always fallible, always adjustable, this learning takes place on what Wittgenstein called the "rough ground" of our everyday engagements with the world and one another. From Hobbes and Locke to Quine, De Man, and Massumi, the nominalist's assumption has been that concepts are necessarily uninstantiated, always already figural, an "imposition" of meaning on the fluxional givens of meaningless matter. By contrast, for the postwar sages I'm considering here, speaking of "courage" doesn't involve intuiting some "ideal," some allegedly "rigorous" nonempirical concept; so there is nothing either for philosophy to deconstruct or for scientific inquiry to eliminate. We learn "courage" when, as children, we hear an elder use it while pointing to some action, story, or person; these circumstances help establish

---

[51] The relationship between pragmatism and Wittgenstein is a complex one, and here and elsewhere, I don't mean to conflate them. Committing oneself to one does *not* require committing oneself to the other, as the example of Cavell will suggest in Chapter 4. But if Wittgenstein had little knowledge of Peirce and Dewey, he had great respect for William James, and there are, indeed, undeniable links between his work and that of his American counterparts. For some varying assessments of their relationship, see Hilary Putnam, *Pragmatism: An Open Question* (Oxford: Wiley-Blackwell, 1995); Hans-Johan Glock, "The Influence of Wittgenstein on American Philosophy," in *The Oxford Handbook of American Philosophy*, ed. Cheryl Misak (New York: Oxford University Press, 2008), 375–402; Russell B. Goodman, *Wittgenstein and William James* (Cambridge: Cambridge University Press, 2002); Richard Rorty, "Keeping Philosophy Pure: An Essay on Wittgenstein," *Consequences of Pragmatism* (Minneapolis: University of Minnesota Press, 1982), 19–36.

the criteria for using the word, and over time we apply it to instances that bear some relevant resemblance to—not identity with—that original. There is thus, as Toril Moi puts it, no *necessary* gap between the order of language and the order of history. Our words, she says, citing Cavell, are always "world-bound," embedded in our needs and practices, unthinkable apart from everything we learn they are about: "about the other, about the human body and the human mind, about existence, morality, and politics," "of learning and teaching, madness and skepticism, isolation and solidarity."[52] Skillfully using "courageous" requires participating in such swirls of activity, and training in the overlapping contexts where they occur.

This concern for the learning of language may explain the scenes of instruction that recur throughout all the authors I consider. Think of the parents and children who are so central to Robinson and Cavell; the mentors, initiates, and schools so crucial to Ellison and Wallace; the deaf-blind woman who gradually learns "water" in the essays of Percy or the conversations with priests that are scattered throughout his fiction. Attending to these relationships and scenarios allows these authors to echo a protest entered by Kenneth Burke in the early 1930s: "So eager were the nominalists to disavow Plato in detail, that they failed to discover the justice of his doctrines in essence"—failed to see that, in practice, we *do* learn to move from particular to universal, and *do* continually think and converse about general properties, whatever the makeup of the universe may be.[53] The patterns of sense and forms of significance that emerge in such scenes of instruction take universals, as Burke says, "out of heaven," and make it difficult to declare that we are matter that moves rather than matter that means. They unsettle, that is, the bald naturalist's assumption that nomologically explicable physical events and bodily configurations take explanatory precedence over the value-laden social practices that Elizabeth Anscombe, adapting Wittgenstein, called the "stage setting" of our language, or that they negate the conceptual norms making us, in Robert Brandom's terms, "sapient" as well as "sentient" beings.[54] As Linda Zerilli has recently put it, the fact that

---

[52] Toril Moi, "'They practice their trades in different worlds': Concepts in Poststructuralism and Ordinary Language Philosophy," *New Literary History* 40 (2009), 818.

[53] Kenneth Burke, *Counter-Statement* (1931; Berkeley: University of California Press, 1968), 46–48.

[54] In her original 1953 English translation of *Philosophical Investigations*, Anscombe used "stage setting" to render Wittgenstein's remark that, in discussing sensations, we too often forget "dass schon viel in der Sprache vorbereitet sein muss"—a statement that the most recent revised translation gives as "that much must be prepared in the language." This amendation is certainly more accurate, but I'm retaining "stage setting" here because it is a colorful phrase that has become widely associated with the *Investigations*. See Ludwig Wittgenstein, *Philosophical Investigations*, translated by G. E. M. Anscombe, P. M. S. Hacker, and Joachim Schulte (Oxford: Wiley-Blackwell, 2009), §257; henceforth

we are embodied creatures coping with nonintentional nature doesn't mean that we are "really" nonconceptual bodies triggered or moved by physiological and affective inclinations. Our embodied coping is defined by a capability to see the world *as* one thing rather than another, exhibiting patterns of discernment and judgment that can be made explicit and revised.[55] We are, to cite Burke one more time, "bodies that learn language."[56] Human speech requires the tissues and cartilage of the vocal cords, but it's the human agent, not the tissue or cartilage, that speaks.

And this holds true whether these human agents are learning competence in "hard" mathematics and logic or in "soft" issues of morality, history, art, and politics. Because, that is, any judgment is "fraught with ought" (Sellars's phrase), marked by considerations of appropriateness, we shouldn't presume that our evaluative appraisals are necessarily fictitious or insubstantial, let alone "obscene," merely high dead words. If, as Hilary Putnam argues, we don't assume that physics or any other natural science can serve all of our cognitive purposes, we can be conceptual pluralists ready to recognize many different kinds of statements as bona fide, governed by concerns for truth and validity as much as any other discourse. Human language, as Sabina Lovibond puts the same point, is metaphysically "homogenous," without any firm wedge separating factual and evaluative meaning, even if the "reach of intellectual authority" can be quite different in the two cases. Understood, as John McDowell puts it, as a reliable sensitivity toward relevant occasions, akin to a perceptual capacity, normative judgments might actually be described as a form of knowledge. This

---

cited, as is customary in Wittgenstein commentary, by the numbered remark rather than page number. On the distinction between "sentience" and "sapience," see Robert Brandom, *Articulating Reasons: An Introduction to Inferentialism* (Cambridge, MA: Harvard University Press, 2000). It's worth noting that the emphasis on "stage setting" distinguishes pragmatists and Wittgensteinians not only from the reductionist anti-intentionalism that I've mainly been discussing here, but also from the strong realism defended in the cognitivism of, for example, Jerry Fodor. One of Fodor's leading claims is a (Chomskyan) commitment to internalism: the idea that meanings exist in the head of each speaker, prior to and regardless of his or her environment. As argued by Hans-Johann Glock, such a claim fails to explain adequately the *shareability* of concepts that Frege persuasively identified as central to their possession. For Frege, the shareability of "senses" can be guaranteed only by treating them as abstract entities that are "objective" even though "not-actual," that is, not material. See Glock, "Concepts: Where Subjectivism Goes Wrong," *Philosophy* 84 (2009): 5–29 (quote at 10). For a view with some affinities to Glock's, see Jesse Prinz and Andy Clark, "Putting Concepts to Work: Some Thoughts for the Twentyfirst Century," *Mind & Language* 19 (2004): 57–69, which argues for a "supercharged pragmatism that links concept possession to action," and which, like Glock's essay, is primarily a response to Fodor's "Having Concepts: A Brief Refutation of the Twentieth Century," *Mind & Language* 19 (2004): 29–47.

[55] Linda Zerilli, "The Turn to Affect and the Problem of Judgment," *New Literary History* 46 (2015): 261–86.

[56] Kenneth Burke, *Permanence and Change*, 3rd ed. (Berkeley: University of California, 1984), 295.

is particularly so if, as Bernard Williams suggests, we attend not to the "thin" moral terms that preoccupy moral theorists (*right, good*) but to the "thick" concepts that describe specific traits of character: *generosity, tolerance, courage*—a list to which Richard Rorty has added terms such as *kindness* and *curiosity*, and Kwame Anthony Appiah the word *honor*. To speak in this way is to recognize the "significance feature" that, as Charles Taylor has argued, distinguishes our human lives from the existence of both machines and animals: the sense of ourselves as agents to whom things matter, to whom something can be beautiful, shameful, worthy, trivial, humiliating, and so forth. Taken a step further, it would be to see, as Murdoch says, the virtues as standing in some sense *outside* or *beyond* us as individuals, naming "directions of thought," things we must *strive* to understand through a "refined and honest perception of what is really the case, a patient discernment and exploration of what confronts one," rather than the self-love and fear that mar most of our worldly engagements.[57]

I've hurriedly recited these philosophical names and claims because they help thematize the general set of attitudes that the postwar sages of the following chapters will put on display.[58] Above all the sages share with these philosophers what I'll be calling a *weak realism* about concepts, a stance that challenges the knee-jerk nominalism of so much modern literature and theory.

---

[57] Hilary Putnam, "The Content and Appeal of Naturalism," in *Naturalism in Question* (Cambridge, MA: Harvard University Press, 2004), 61; Sabina Lovibond, *Realism and Imagination in Ethics* (Minneapolis: University of Minnesota Press, 1983); John McDowell, "Virtue and Reason," in *Mind, Value, and Reality* (Cambridge, MA: Harvard University Press, 1998), 50–73; Bernard Williams, *Ethics and the Limits of Philosophy* (Cambridge, MA: Harvard University Press, 1986); Richard Rorty, *Contingency, Irony, and Solidarity* (Cambridge: Cambridge University Press, 1989); Kwame Anthony Appiah, *The Honor Code: How Moral Revolutions Happen* (New York: Norton, 2011); Charles Taylor, *Human Agency and Language: Philosophical Papers, Volume 1* (Cambridge: Cambridge University Press, 1985), Chapters 8 and 9; Iris Murdoch, *Existentialists and Mystics*, 330.

[58] Let me acknowledge immediately the many important differences among the philosophical figures I've just cited. Williams, for instance, can be more difficult to place than many of the others, and is much more openly a deflationary naturalist, willing to question, for example, McDowell's philosophizing about morality; Taylor's work owes a large debt to Murdoch, but it also puts less emphasis on art; Murdoch regularly applauds Plato but has little if anything to say about Dewey and other pragmatists whom Rorty and Putnam regard as heroes; Putnam and Rorty each identify themselves as "pragmatists," but spent decades disagreeing with one another; Brandom and Taylor are unabashed Hegelians, but Taylor's thought drifts more to religious and political questions, Brandom's to issues in logic and language; Lovibond acknowledges the influence of McDowell's interpretations of Wittgenstein, an interpretation that Brandom and Rorty have explicitly questioned; Lovibond furthermore questions Murdoch's moral philosophy, which has been praised by McDowell; and so forth. Similarly, I am fully aware that not all the figures here would accept my suggestion that the pragmatist–Wittgensteinian tradition encourages what I will in a moment refer to as "weak realism" about normative concepts. Certainly, too—as I've said in an earlier footnote—there is much debate over the precise relationship between pragmatism and Wittgenstein, not to mention how accurate, just, or persuasive any later interpretation of them might be. Still, I would stand by the general associations I'm making here. The figures I've named

Weak, not *strong*: nobody here suggests that goods are wholly mind- or human-independent, or that talking about kindness involves talking about The Kind. To be a weak realist instead involves acknowledging certain features of our ethical phenomenology: that, in the stream of our actual lives, we recognize ethical facts (we feel revulsion at, for instance, pedophiles), that we treat certain character traits as higher and lower than others (we dislike hypocrites and struggle to be honest), that we ask and reason about what we should do, and that we feel regret, disappointment, or dissatisfaction when our judgments prove wrong. An appeal to such hard-to-deny habits will be heard over and over in the authors I address. Human beings, they imply, cannot disengage themselves from their lives and their words to such an extent that all our norms could be seen as mere projections *as such* on a fluxional reality. We are thus constituted equally of matter and of high words, and as long as know their use, so long as they have criteria, the words that orient us have nothing necessarily unreal about them. As I understand them, Percy, Ellison, and the others agree with, for instance, Brandom that our normative judgments are built into our most basic descriptions and simplest discriminations. And they would concur with Taylor when he says that, were I denied all normative terms—"dignity," "courage," "brutality"—I wouldn't be able to deliberate effectively, wouldn't be able to assess possible courses of action or appropriately judge the situations around me.[59] Even to expose a particular norm as baseless—to question, say, how specific evaluative schemes have impugned or criminalized a certain gender, race, practice, or custom—involves a discriminated responsiveness that can be articulated to one degree or another as a vocabulary of ought and ought-not. To forget this, they suggest, would be to abandon discussion of normativity to the moralizing pundits of talk radio, think tanks, and others who are paid to advertise ideas more than achieve understanding.[60]

---

all continually engage not only with pragmatism and/or Wittgenstein, but also with one another, and I take it that this mutual interest, in addition to the contiguous and often overlapping claims they develop, is partly what constitutes them as a living, coherent tradition rather than a strained hodge-podge of names.

[59] Taylor, *Sources of the Self*, 57.

[60] Taylor is particularly keen to draw out the self-undermining slippages among thinkers who seem resistant to normative evaluation. The "modern scientific world-view" that produced Locke, Hume, and much Anglophone philosophy professes value-neutrality, but it operates, Taylor points out, with an "ideal of the disengaged self, capable of objectifying not only the surrounding world but also his own emotions and inclinations, ... which allows him to act 'rationally'" (*Sources of the Self*, 21). Historically, this tradition also has tended to question the inflated and coercive claims of aristocratic or priestly classes, but the "affirmation of ordinary life" that it winds up endorsing— the moral weight placed on work and family, over and against the value of contemplation, heroic asceticism, the life of a warrior, etc.—constitutes a strong moral stance in itself: "while necessarily

The five figures addressed in the following chapters also, however, go well beyond their philosophical contemporaries, and in ways that make them more compelling, vivid, far-reaching, and challenging. Far more actively than their philosophical allies, the postwar sages here all explore in detail the contexts in which our high words have their homes. They do not, that is, merely *argue* in conceptual terms about concepts or *insist* upon the textured situations where concepts are learned and used. They actively *imagine* and *elucidate* such situations. They don't just talk about our ordinary ethical phenomenology; they want to clarify it in moment-to-moment detail.

In short, they engage in a sophisticated variant of what Wittgenstein called "grammatical investigations." Like traditional philosophers, that is, they circle back repeatedly to certain words, drawing them to our reflective attention, but as Wittgenstein does with "meaning," "pain," "understanding," and other terms, these authors refuse to segregate these words from the stream of experience, ruminating on them in holy isolation. Instead, they ask how such words are learned and embodied in the world, providing extended examples—an *übersichtliche Darstellung*, in Wittgenstein's phrase, a "perspicuous" or "surveyable" representation—of what we mean in our everyday life when we say that someone is, for example, *courageous*.[61] In recent years, commentators such as John Gibson, Bernard Harrison, and David Schalkwyk have made powerfully clear that grammatical investigations of a Wittgensteinian sort have a specifically *narrative* cast. Using "courage" means knowing *stories*. As Gibson argues,

---

denouncing certain distinctions," it "itself amounts to one; else it has no meaning at all" (*Sources of the Self*, 23). A similar tension, Taylor suggests, runs through the major representatives of post-World War II French philosophy. "For Derrida there is nothing but deconstruction," but "nothing emerges from his flux worth affirming, and so what in fact comes to be celebrated is the deconstructing power itself, the prodigious power of subjectivity to undo all the potential allegiances which might bind it; pure untrammeled freedom" (*Sources of the Self*, 489). (I return to this remark briefly in Chapter 4.) And Foucault likewise is caught in a double bind, espousing an ideal of the self as "a work of art" in his late work but ignoring "the difficulty of detaching a notion of the aesthetic from the other strands in modern thought that [he] still wanted to repudiate" (*Sources of the Self*, 489). One is reminded, in this context, of how bland Derrida's and Foucault's language becomes when a normative stance begins to surface. "For after all *Lefébure is not a bad name*," Derrida remarks suddenly when analyzing Saussure's ethnocentric efforts to create an "intralinguistic leper colony" that would contain "the problem of deformation through writing"; and similarly, Foucault finishes a description of the link between "the Greek ethics of pleasure" and "a virile society, to dissymmetry, exclusion of the other, an obsession with penetration" with the stark announcement: "All that is quite disgusting!" See Jacques Derrida, *Of Grammatology*, trans. Gayatri Chakravorty Spivak (Baltimore: Johns Hopkins University Press, 1976), 42; Michel Foucault, *The Foucault Reader*, ed. Paul Rabinow (New York: Vintage, 1984), 346.

61 "Perspicuous representation" was Elizabeth Anscombe's original translation of *übersichtliche Darstellung*, but in the amended translation of P. M. S. Hacker and Joachim Schulte the phrase has been rendered as "surveyable representation" (*Philosophical Investigations*, §122).

following a well-known passage from *Philosophical Investigations*, narratives play the role that the Paris meter does for our shared system of measurement: they can provide an "archive" from which audiences identify, describe, characterize, and evaluate the things and situations we encounter in the world.[62] Through them we can come to have criteria for our normative words, a shareable standard for saying, "*That* is courage." Such investigations are "grammatical" in the sense that they are not empirical. No measurable, quantifiable fact of the matter can tell us whether a given character exemplifies a certain virtue; coming to see an action or person as *courageous* isn't like learning more information about an insect species. For although we have stable ways of identifying insect species and their properties, judging whether someone exhibits courage requires determining when "courage" would be appropriate to use. What would *count* as "courageous"? The perspicuous representations that might help answer such a question—imagining the actions and circumstances that would compel us to talk of "courage"—do not *represent* the world per se. But they are not for that reason "make-believe." A story can provide the criteria by which we make our depictions *of* the world, even if it isn't depicting anything *in* the world.[63]

Hence the generic movements that, as I've said, define the authors here. Such movements are a formal index of the wish to archive one's most cherished concepts. In one moment, the sage speaks with all the "discursive explicitness" that Sontag denounced, defending the legitimacy of this or that general appraisal. At another moment, he or she tries to imagine an indefinitely wide range of worldly items: persons, actions, traits of character, local circumstances, specific scenes, dialogues, chance events, unexpected consequences, institutions of various sizes and sorts, historical alterations and ruptures, cultures and subcultures, families, regions, and nations—all the crowd of features that play a role in our naming practices, and that might give life to our most privileged terms.

Such grammatical investigations constitute what I call a *reflective* project— "reflective" not in the sense of intellectualist spectatorship, but in the sense of a back-and-forth deliberative interplay, a to and fro between particulars and universals, experience and categories, specific events or objects, and the

[62] John Gibson, *Fiction and the Weave of Life* (New York: Oxford University Press, 2007), 60–80; Bernard Harrison, *Inconvenient Fictions: Literature and the Limits of Theory* (New Haven, CT: Yale University Press, 1991); David Schalkwyk, "Fiction as 'Grammatical' Investigation: A Wittgensteinian Account," *Journal of Aesthetics and Art Criticism* 53 (1995): 287–98. For Wittgenstein's use of the Paris archive, see *Philosophical Investigations*, §50.

[63] For the claim that fiction is a form of "make-believe," see Kendall Walton, *Mimesis as Make-Believe: On the Foundations of the Representational Arts* (Cambridge, MA: Harvard University Press, 1990).

concepts that make them intelligible.[64]And this reflective impulse is precisely what makes these figures so distinctive and ambitious. The work of the post-war sage constitutes a challenge, for one thing, to the bald naturalist whose nominalist pictures hold us captive: it both defends our capacity for ethical and political judgment *and* vividly details the settings in which these judgments are intelligible. More than that, however, such a project begins to establish a rapprochement between literature and philosophy that's hard to achieve today, even among the Wittgensteinian and pragmatist philosophers whom the sage so often resembles. Modernity's aesthetic projects, these authors suggest, have unwittingly replicated some of the most diminished aspects of modern science, and have reduced literature, as Murdoch said in a comment on Plato's *Ion*, to a "technical" or "expert knowledge" rather than "a general knowledge of human life" (*EM* 392–93). To "generate the concepts worthy, and also able, to guide and check the increasing powers of science," as Murdoch says elsewhere, requires moving laterally between "two areas" of thought (*EM* 362), a dynamic two-handed practice that embodies the world-boundness of our words. Perhaps the best analogue for such work is the *Philosophical Investigations* itself, where a defiance of modern naturalism—a refusal to allow science's methods to "elbow all the others aside," to make them seem "paltry by comparison, preliminary stages at best"—emerges through a mix of argument and assertion, on the one hand, and poetic imagination and literary gesture on the other, its contentions and claims punctuated by metaphors and anecdotes and jokes.[65] (No accident that Hadot, for one, associated Wittgenstein with the sage tradition.)[66] In their essays, these authors speak as moralists, promoting the high words that might orient our lives: Robinson's *courage*, Ellison's *fraternity*, Cavell's *friendship*. In

---

[64] My use of "reflective" here is, of course, meant to recall Kant's characterization of "reflective judgments" in *Critique of Judgment* and John Rawls's discussions of "reflective equilibrium" in *A Theory of Justice*. The best-known effort to compare Kant's "reflective judgment" with the practical wisdom of normative judgment is Hannah Arendt's *Lectures on Kant's Political Philosophy*, ed. Ronald Beiner (Chicago: University of Chicago Press, 1982).

[65] Ludwig Wittgenstein, *Culture and Value*, ed. Peter Winch and George Henrik von Wright, trans. Peter Winch (Chicago: University of Chicago Press, 1980), 60. Wittgenstein's relation to scientific naturalism was complex. Trained as an engineer and talented as an architect, he was—even beyond the "positivism" that fills most of the *Tractatus Logico-Philosophicus*—continually reflecting upon machines, mathematics, and the status of empirical research. Yet he seems never to have lost his sense that, as he puts it in an early draft for the *Investigations*, "our preoccupation with the method of science" leads us "into complete darkness" (*The Blue and Brown Books: Preliminary Studies for the "Philosophical Investigations"* [New York: Harper & Row, 1960], 18), and he continually attacked what he saw as the hints of scientism lurking in the work of, for example, Freud, Frazer, Marxists, behaviorists, and any number of other modern intellectual schools.

[66] See Sandra Laugier, "Hadot as a Reader of Wittgenstein," *Paragraph* 34 (2011): 322–37.

their narratives, they offer criteria for these terms, finding the thick descriptions that might help make our thick concepts intelligible. Struggling both to show and to tell, they seek to play the twin roles that Wallace lauded in Dostoevsky, a figure crucial to Wittgenstein and many of my subjects, who "never stopped worrying about his literary reputation," but who also worked as a sentinel, a voice willing to declare a "deeply held system of beliefs and values," even if it sometimes entailed "promulgating" some "unfashionable stuff."[67]

IV. The Specter of Moral Fanaticism

The two parts of this book reflect two basic directions of thought taken by these particular sentinels, two types of normative vocabularies that are summoned up to defeat the naturalism and nominalism of our literary and scientific culture. Part I considers Percy and Robinson, a pair of authors whose reflective composition emerges from a fundamentally religious stance. They are weak realists in the sense that I've noted—our meanings, they suggest, are not mind- or human-independent—but the vocabularies they highlight are thoroughly theistic. Chapter 1 examines Percy's consideration of machine intelligence, a field of research that, by the time he began writing in the late 1950s and 1960s, was being hailed for its major contributions to scientific knowledge. His interest in the capacities and limits of machines allows him to anticipate, I argue, the work

---

[67] David Foster Wallace, *Consider the Lobster and Other Essays* (Boston: Little Brown and Company, 2005), 272. My use of "sentinel" here is drawn from Amir Eshel, who describes the Hebrew tradition of the creative individual who is not afraid to admonish and exhort, charting a nation's path toward a better future through a variety of written forms. See Eschel, *Futurity: Contemporary Literature and the Quest for the Past* (Chicago: University of Chicago Press, 2013), 106–107.

Let me anticipate here the concern that my description of what Wittgenstein offers to discussions of literature and the language of ethics and politics is noticeably different from that of some other commentators. The theme has been addressed in recent years by some of Wittgenstein's most astute commentators, including Cora Diamond, Stephen Mulhall, and Alice Crary, who in various ways suggest that moral reflection need not involve the overt use of normative concepts—a declaration that some act or person is (say) "venal," "admirable," or "unjust." To think otherwise, they suggest, is to overlook the variety of ways that moral reflection can occur, and particularly the ways that literature and other arts have the power to shape our affective responses in morally relevant ways. I heartily agree that we should keep in mind such variety, and I'd be the last to deny that stories and poems have the potential to use style, characterization, and formal techniques—rather than explicitly used abstract concepts—in their presentation of a moral or political evaluation. But the thrust of Wittgenstein's work, it seems to me, is not that our vocabularies of normative appraisal are unnecessary or fishy in and of themselves, but that they are *inadequate* in and of themselves: inadequate, that is, when amputated from the practices, settings, and narratives that give them life. Diamond, Mulhall, and Crary are by no means moral skeptics, and they are not interested in undermining our moral evaluations *tout court*. They are primarily expressing frustration with the range of available options in professional Anglophone philosophy, not only with the field's formalizing habits but with the way it extends the traditional philosophical

of AI's (artificial intelligence's) later philosophical critics as well as the fiction of Richard Powers. But just as notable, this interest also allows him to develop important aspects of his own life's work: a unified account of language and ethics, a fusion of Catholicism and C. S. Peirce that his 1971 novel *Love in the Ruins* attempts to embody. Chapter 2 turns to Robinson, whose nonfiction tackles the Darwinian theories of behavior and psychology that first arose in the 1970s, pitting them against the—deeply Protestant—language of "subjectivity" and "experience." Such debates can seem marginal to her 2004 novel *Gilead*, which is narrated by a small-town minister in mid-twentieth century Iowa. But as I argue, the novel can be read as a prolonged meditation on the high words recommended in Robinson's essays, particularly the way they question the priority that evolutionary psychologists give to strategic and kinship relations.

Bernard Williams, reflecting on our increasingly non- or post-Christian culture, has suggested that we contemporaries are more like human beings in antiquity than any Western people have been in the meantime, and that the vocabularies of Greek ethical thought therefore deserve renewed study and attention.[68] In Part II of this book, I argue that versions of such renewal are offered in Ellison, Cavell, and Wallace, three writers who guide and check the increasing powers of science in more overtly secular, and often classical, terms than Percy and Robinson. Chapter 3 examines Ellison, a younger contemporary of Burke and Wittgenstein who, like them, repeatedly engaged questions of meaning and matter, individual action and bodily motion, culture and natural science. This confluence of interests, I argue, is characteristic of modern African-American writing, as is a propensity for mixed media—a tendency running from W. E. B. Du Bois to Zora Neale Hurston and Ellison's mentor Richard Wright, up through Cornel West's impassioned movements among political philosophy, hip hop, autobiography, and sermons. It was only when, as a young writer, Ellison discovered Burke that he found an account of normativity that could withstand the reductive versions of early twentieth-century sociological theory that made him bristle as a student. And only then did he feel licensed to speak as a public moralist, defending a classical notion of "fraternity" that he linked with "improvisation," the other keyword in his lexicon for collective action. In Chapter 4, I turn to Cavell, who was haunted by logical

---

fixation on a narrow range of evaluative predicates ("good," "right," etc.). And I'm guessing that their confidence in the powers of art and story doesn't mean that normative concepts should or could be eliminated across the board. I return to this issue of confidence in stories in a later footnote in this introduction.

[68] Bernard Williams, *Shame and Necessity* (Berkeley: University of California Press, 1993), 166–67.

positivism as much as Ellison was haunted by sociology. As I suggest, midcentury positivism tended to view human action either as perfectly predictable or perfectly arbitrary, and much of Cavell's subsequent work seeks, like Ellison's, to give life to the concept of "improvisation"—a concept that he, too, learned as a serious young musician, and which, in his philosophical writing and in his memoir, he seeks to associate with the concepts of "friendship" and "marriage." Chapter 5 concludes the book with Wallace, who like (and, in part, thanks to) Cavell resisted his education in analytic philosophy, and who like Cavell came to appreciate the artistic and moral power of the improvisatory human voice. More persistently than Cavell, however, Wallace sought a broad account of our contemporary sociopolitical condition, and was candidly alarmed by the forces in our culture that foster addiction and depression—themes he shares with Robinson and Percy. These social impulses, I argue, led him to take seriously the virtues of civic humanism, virtues first articulated philosophically by Aristotle and eventually descending to Dewey and to Wallace's own father, the philosopher James D. Wallace. It's this confluence of commitments, I suggest, that allowed him to develop the particular kind of moral journalism that made him famous.

Two addenda to this outline. First, it's schematic: sociopolitical questions are never absent in Percy and Robinson, just as religious questions hover around the edges of Ellison, Cavell, and Wallace. Second, though the chapters that follow are heavily author-centered, they are hardly a set of belletristic author studies. Making sense of the texts I discuss requires listening to a commotion of scientific, cultural, philosophical, and political disputes, some of the most far-reaching debates of the post-World War II period. Only against these features of our complicated contemporary form of life do the essays and narratives of these authors begin to make sense. This doesn't mean, however, that I'm offering an exhaustive historical *explanation* of these works and authors. There is, I think, no neat account of the myriad sociological, economic, political, geographical, cultural, and other diachronic causes for these authors' lives and beliefs, at least one that would *not* be contentious at best or require writing another, independent book. And I'm wary, too, of treating their formally restless, intricate, dense, often puzzling texts as consumable bits of socio-historical data. So while no firm cleavage will be evident here between "art" and "ideas" on one side and our socio-historical practices on the other, and while neither I nor these authors take their writings to be narrowly self-contained artifacts, I also don't pretend to be chronicling all of the precipitating conditions and determining forces that might, on some description, have triggered their work.

Before turning to my discussions, however, let me offer a final turn of thought, a glimpse at the pathway of doubt. Even an inattentive reader will by now have picked up on my basic respect for the central authors addressed here—for their willingness to challenge the (in Danto's phrase) "history of purgation" in modern aesthetics, for their weak realism, for the lateral movements of their writing, for the grammatical investigations they perform. But such esteem is necessarily complicated. Early on I claimed that the authors here descend in part from traditions of wisdom literature that have both ancient and early modern exemplars, and which are renewed in the nineteenth century by various Anglo-American figures. Such connections have been noted in passing before, as when one of Percy's biographers compares him to Newman, or when Ellison is likened to Douglass, or when Robinson associates herself with nineteenth-century American writing, or when one of Cavell's admirers identifies him as a Victorian sage ("incidental facts like his birth date notwithstanding").[69] But such affinities may lead readers to wonder if the authors here are either out of date or out of their depth. After all, the antinaturalism one finds among nineteenth-century sages—think of, say, Carlyle condemning "the Age of Machinery"—often reflects a commitment to aesthetic idealism, a tradition that, as Toril Moi has shown, invigorated the early Romantics but gradually became more and more reactionary, hopelessly out of tune with the times.[70] Weren't the nineteenth-century sages guilelessly committed to the idea that great poets could be both great philosophers as well as great ethical guides? Didn't they mawkishly capitalize "Duty," "Right," "Grace," and comparable abstractions? Didn't the nineteenth century give us the reformist "novel of purpose," a genre that to twentieth-century writers came to seem as antiquated as the grizzled sideburns of their complacent Victorian predecessors?[71] And similarly, weren't Cooper, Thoreau, Stowe, Douglass, and other Americans willing

---

[69] On Percy and Newman, see Jay Tolson, *Pilgrim in the Ruins: A Life of Walker Percy* (New York: Simon and Schuster, 1992), 425; on Ellison and Douglass, see Gregory Stephens, *On Racial Frontiers: The New Culture of Frederick Douglass, Ralph Ellison, and Bob Marley* (Cambridge: Cambridge University Press, 1999); on Cavell as Victorian sage, see Andrew H. Miller, *The Burdens of Perfection: On Ethics and Reading in Nineteenth-Century British Literature* (Ithaca, NY: Cornell University Press, 2008), 113.

[70] Thomas Carlyle, "Signs of the Times," in *A Carlyle Reader: Selections from the Writings of Thomas Carlyle*, ed. G. B. Tennyson (Cambridge: Cambridge University Press, 1984), 34; Toril Moi, *Henrik Ibsen and the Birth of Modernism: Art, Theater, Philosophy* (New York: Oxford University Press, 2006), chap. 3.

[71] "Duty" is from George Eliot (see note 39). I draw "Right" and "Grace" not from a Victorian sage but from one of the most famous Victorian poems, Elizabeth Barrett Browning's "How I Love Thee," from *Sonnets from the Portuguese* (1850). As Moi puts it, "much of what is currently lumped under the general heading of 'Victorianism' . . . could be analyzed historically and theoretically as the many-faceted

to both "show" and "tell" because they had a moral optimism that eventually collapsed, devolving into the bromides of the genteel tradition? Weren't they committed to the "higher law," norms allegedly implanted deep in every human conscience? What examples could such authors and traditions offer to writers working after the Holocaust and Hiroshima, in an era of digital computers, neuroscience, decision theory, and neo-Darwinism?[72]

As so often, such questions were anticipated by Nietzsche, who castigated the Victorian sages in *Twilight of the Idols* (1889):

> They've gotten rid of the Christian God, and now they think they have to hold onto Christian morality all the more. . . . In England, for every little emancipation from theology, you have to make yourself respectable again as a moral fanatic in the most frightening way. . . . Things are different for the rest of us. If you give up Christian faith, you pull the *right* to Christian morality out from under your feet. . . . Christianity is a system, a view of things that is conceived as a connected *whole*. If you break off a major concept from it, faith in God, you break up the whole as well. . . . For the English, morality is not yet a problem.[73]

---

effects of the specifically British appropriation of idealist aesthetics" (4). On the nineteenth-century "novel of purpose," see Amanda Claybaugh, *The Novel of Purpose: Literature and Social Reform in the Anglo-American World* (Ithaca, NY: Cornell University Press, 2007). On facial hair as a symbol of complacent power in pre-war Europe, see Allan Janik and Stephen Toulmin, *Wittgenstein's Vienna* (New York: Simon and Schuster, 1973), 203–204. On the "higher law" in antebellum American culture, see Gregg Crane, *Race, Citizenship, and Law in American Culture* (Cambridge: Cambridge University Press, 2002), chap. 1. For a broad overview of these nineteenth-century moral and intellectual traditions, see Daniel Brudney, "Nineteenth-Century Ideals: Self-Culture and the Religion of Humanity," in *The Cambridge History of Philosophy in the Nineteenth Century (1790–1870)*, ed. Allen W. Wood and Songsuk Susan Hahn (Cambridge: Cambridge University Press, 2012), 731–59.

[72] "Duty" is from George Eliot (see note 42). I draw "Right" and "Grace" not from a Victorian sage but from one of the most famous Victorian poems, Elizabeth Barrett Browning's "How I Love Thee," from *Sonnets from the Portuguese* (1850). As Moi puts it, "much of what is currently lumped under the general heading of 'Victorianism' . . . could be analyzed historically and theoretically as the many-faceted effects of the specifically British appropriation of idealist aesthetics" (4). On the nineteenth-century "novel of purpose," see Amanda Claybaugh, *The Novel of Purpose: Literature and Social Reform in the Anglo-American World* (Ithaca, NY: Cornell University Press, 2007). On facial hair as a symbol of complacent power in pre-war Europe, see Allan Janik and Stephen Toulmin, *Wittgenstein's Vienna* (New York: Simon and Schuster, 1973), 203–204. On the "higher law" in antebellum American culture, see Gregg Crane, *Race, Citizenship, and Law in American Culture* (Cambridge: Cambridge University Press, 2002), chap. 1. For a broad overview of many of these nineteenth-century Euro-American moral and intellectual traditions, see Daniel Brudney, "Nineteenth-Century Ideals: Self-Culture and the Religion of Humanity," in *The Cambridge History of Philosophy in the Nineteenth Century (1790–1870)*, ed. Allen W. Wood and Songsuk Susan Hahn (Cambridge: Cambridge University Press, 2012), 731–59.

[73] Friedrich Nietzsche, *Twilight of the Idols*, trans. Richard Polt (Indianapolis, IN: Hackett), 53–54. Nietzsche's specific target here is George Eliot.

As I've noted, at least two of the figures discussed here—Percy and Robinson—are quite explicitly unwilling to break off the "major concept" that Nietzsche mentions. But even the more ostensibly secular writing of Ellison, Cavell, and Wallace might seem enmeshed in the slave morality that Nietzsche (whose appreciation of scientific naturalism has recently earned new attention) ridiculed.[74] Were he writing today, Nietzsche would likely find that Ellison's fraternity-talk makes him one of the empty-headed "brotherhood enthusiasts" who plead for "the decay of political organization," and that Cavell, in speaking of "marriage," overlooks that real-life marriages are founded simply "on the sex drive, on the need for property, . . . on the *drive for domination*." He would likewise ask why Wallace so distrusted his own intellect and egoism, and whether he remained a timid Christian, forgetting that an artist's most creative states come when "you transform things until they are mirrors of your own power—until they reflect your perfection."[75]

The charge would be, that is, that these authors insufficiently heed the hermeneutics of suspicion, that they're led into barren finger-pointing, and that their efforts to retrieve high words from a world of matter show an unwillingness to face the full devastations of modernity. A reasonably full response can emerge only gradually, but I'll say here at the start that the charge won't always seem unfair. In certain moods, readers may very well suspect that an author here is engaging in wishful thinking, aesthetically or argumentatively. But such criticism also risks moving too hastily. For what ultimately makes these figures compelling is not only their effort to use, in Murdoch's formulation, "two areas" of thought to generate concepts "worthy" enough to "check the increasing power of science." It's also the fact that these efforts are always an intense and protracted *struggle*, and that the back-and-forth reflective mode that I've identified seldom leads to sustained equilibrium. The lateral movements of these authors between "two areas" typically generate something other than a serene series of easily elucidated positions, so that they are ultimately not resolving the particular with the general so much as bumpily navigating the waters between them. The untiring shifts they undertake between narration and declaration don't quite reflect a neat distinction between teller and tale, the latter of which needs to be rescued from the former, but these motions have the power to unsettle conviction as much as reinforce it. As commentators have recently noted, a

---

[74] For one prominent argument about Nietzsche's naturalism, see Brian Leiter, *Nietzsche on Morality* (London: Routledge, 2002).

[75] Friedrich Nietzsche, *Beyond Good and Evil*, trans. Walter Kaufmann (New York: Penguin, 1966), 116–17; *Twilight of the Idols*, 76, 56.

thought experiment can be an effective persuasive device, shoring up abstract arguments, but it can also provoke responses that run counter to the claims it's designed to support.[76] A similar set of rifts and instabilities is discernable in the texts I discuss here. And it is this capacity for disjunction that prevents these authors from becoming the "moral fanatics" Nietzsche mocked. Their aesthetic displays and examples deflate, even sometimes defeat, the authority evoked in their arguments, preventing the writers from becoming too assertively, too hopelessly themselves.[77]

Such observations don't always fit with how these latter-day sentinels describe themselves; most of them imply that their writing is continuous.[78] But the reality of their work makes for a different impression. So if, as I suggested above, *Philosophical Investigations* is a model for the oeuvres I'll be addressing, we should remember that Wittgenstein himself characterized his book as "sketches of landscapes"—not a final word about anything, but "really only an album" (*PI* 3–4). In other words, for all the power of the *Investigations'* arguments—about ostensive definition, rule-following, "private languages," and so on—it is also full of competing voices and angles of reasoning, its philosophical claims perched uneasily between elegy and quest romance, loss and aspiration: hardly the stuff of unequivocal opinionizing and rock-solid contentions.[79] To compare the oeuvres of Percy, Wallace, and the others to the "albums" of the *Investigations* is to highlight not only the many genres they pursue, but also the push and pull of these genres, their persistent revisions and mutual modifications. Indeed, such oscillations may help account for the

---

[76] On the various ways that a thought experiment can turn out, see Tamar Gendler, *Intuition, Imagination, and Philosophical Methodology* (Oxford: Oxford University Press, 2010), chap. 6. The distinction between teller and tale is taken, of course, from D. H. Lawrence's 1924 book *Studies in Classic American Literature* (London: Penguin, 1990): "The artist usually sets out—or used to—to point a moral and adorn a tale. The tale, however, points the other way, as a rule. Two blankly opposing morals, the artist's and the tale's. Never trust the artist. Trust the tale" (8).

[77] The power of "display" to deflate and defeat discursive authority has recently been elaborated in a Wittgensteinian vein in Charles Altieri, *Reckoning with the Imagination: Wittgenstein and the Aesthetics of Literary Experience* (Ithaca, NY: Cornell University Press, 2015). The idea that art might prevent people or cultures from becoming "too assertively, too hopelessly" themselves is drawn from Kenneth Burke, *Counter-Statement* (1931; Berkeley: University of California Press, 1968), 105.

[78] Ellison, for instance, described in several decades' worth of interviews and essays how *Invisible Man* exemplified the Burkean rhetorical principles that he had studied, and Cavell notes at the start of his memoir that his work has long sought to ask "explicitly why philosophy, of a certain ambition, tends perpetually to intersect the autobiographical." See Ellison, *Collected Essays*, 218; Stanley Cavell, *Little Did I Know: Excerpts from Memory* (Stanford, CA: Stanford University Press, 2010), 2.

[79] The *Investigations'* connections to traditions of quest and elegy are illuminatingly thematized by Richard Eldridge, *Leading a Human Life: Wittgenstein, Intentionality, and Romanticism* (Chicago: University of Chicago Press, 1997), 10.

extended silences and fragmented careers that mark virtually every author here. Percy failed for years to publish his earliest fiction, and Robinson took two and a half decades to complete a second novel. Cavell needed special allowances from Harvard to finish his doctoral dissertation and struggled to publish it in book form for almost two decades, and like Wittgenstein, both Ellison and Wallace left behind long-belabored, unfinished works at their deaths. Being a sage in the contemporary period is a risky business.

To be sure, no genre has cast-iron boundaries. The discursive works of the postwar sage are themselves deeply literary works, frequently digressive, often unsystematic and luxuriantly descriptive. They are paradigms of the modern essay: movements of mind more than point-by-point proofs, skewed paths rather than consistently delineated theories, all resisting, as one great essayist put it, the "dogmatic systems" of an Aquinas or Spinoza.[80] But it would be careless to elide all differences between essayistic and narrative modes, slipping each into some undifferentiated category ("writing," "text," etc.), without recognizing their specific textures and purposes.[81] The blurred edges—Wittgenstein's metaphor (*PI* §71)—between genres are not evidence that genres don't exist, any more than the facts of evolution mean that lions are the same as tigers. In particular we shouldn't be deaf to the ways that, as Theodor Adorno says, an essay "distinguishes itself from art through its conceptual character and its claim to truth free from aesthetic semblance." Though the essay as a form, he notes, feels no need to stipulate definitions for every word, it also "does not make do without general concepts," because "even language that does not fetishize concepts cannot do without them."[82] Indeed, as we'll see here, exploring and using "general concepts" is precisely the means by which the postwar sages here take their stands, express conviction, promulgate unfashionable stuff. They make free use of what Sontag, self-consciously echoing Adorno, calls the "directness of the essay-writing voice, the directness of its concern with opinion and argument,"

---

[80] Walter Pater, "Dialectic," in *Essayists on the Essay: Montaigne to Our Time*, ed. Carl H. Klaus and Ned Stuckey-French (Iowa City: University of Iowa Press, 2012), 29. "Skewed path" is a phrase from R. Lane Kaufmann, "The Skewed Path: Essaying as Unmethodical Method," in *Essays on the Essay: Redefining the Genre*, ed. Alexander J. Butrym (Athens: University of Georgia Press, 1989) 221–40. The claim that the essay is fundamentally an expression of ambivalence and instability has recently become a theme in the media, most notably in Christy Wampole, "The Essayification of Everything," *New York Times* (May 26, 2013) <http://opinionator.blogs.nytimes.com/2013/05/26/the-essayification-of-everything/> (accessed April 1, 2016).

[81] The undecidable blurriness of genres is a claim popularized by, for example, Jacques Derrida, "The Law of Genre," *Critical Inquiry* 7 (1980): 55–81.

[82] Theodor Adorno, "The Essay as Form," *Notes to Literature, Volume 1*, trans. Shierry Weber Nicholsen (New York: Columbia University Press, 1991), 5, 12.

its "assertiveness," its urge "to convert the world and everything in it to a species of thinking," to an idea that the essayist "unfolds, defends, or excoriates."[83]

At the same time, however, these assertive, abstracting, excoriating essayists also compose long, expansive, sophisticated narratives. And if, as I've said,
these stories are meant to create an "archive" for the concepts defended in their
essays, if they're intended to provide the "stage setting" of our highest words, it
is not always clear in practice how seamlessly this process unfolds. It's the turbulence of this movement between genres that tends to keep moral fanaticism
at bay. As Bernard Harrison has argued, all stories are built upon the particular
sayings of particular people in a concrete particularized world, and thus can
fray the tissue of generalities that usually shape our stances toward the world,
our urge to say that a given story "tells us something general about. . . ." But
such fraying is especially visible in the narratives I discuss. The challenge they
present is not only, as Harrison notes, that no one among us controls the meanings of our words all of the time, or can anticipate how others will hear and use
them, and that no story therefore wears its sense on its sleeve.[84] The challenge
is also that the stories here are *themselves* often scrutinizing what I've been calling the "reflective" mode, highlighting the tensions between the various modes
that the author wants to pursue. Within the narratives themselves, that is, the
drive to "show" and the drive to "tell" come into repeated contact, as sequential
sequences yield to discursive sequences and back again. And in such a narrative construction, no one voice is allowed to speak with unquestioned authority. Placed in a temporal setting, no single character is allowed to escape what
Robinson's *Gilead* calls "the ongoingness of the world," and no reader is allowed
to forget the "felt reality" that Wallace once described as "overwhelmingly,
circuit-blowingly huge and complex," "the seething static of every particular
thing and experience."[85] However much, in other words, these authors struggle to escape nominalism, their stories return continually to the here and now
of unique situations and unique expressions, resisting the urge—the author's,
the reader's—to pretend that the criteria for our high words are settled. Again
and again, the essays here call for mutuality, cooperation, meaningful sociality,

---

[83] Susan Sontag, "Introduction to *The Best American Essays*, 1992," in *Essayists on the Essay*, 149–52;
Compare Sontag and Adorno to Cynthia Ozick's description of the essayist as "a species of meta-
physician," analyzing "the least grain of being" and struggling to court the reader into "surrender
and conviction"—a situation that helps explain why, in Ozick's view, "true essayists rarely write
novels" (*Essayists on the Essay*, 165, 167).

[84] Harrison, *Inconvenient Fictions*, 58–59.

[85] Marilynne Robinson, *Gilead* (New York: Farrar Straus Giroux, 2004), 191; David Foster Wallace,
Both Flesh and Not: Essays (Boston: Little, Brown, and Company, 2012), 302–303.

even redemption; again and again, the narrative works counter these calls with darker scenarios, skeptical strains, unconnected shards. The authors here may evoke the sage tradition, but they're writing in the era of the novel—a genre that, whatever its ties to sermons and pedagogy, shows a deep-rooted irony, where particularized voices proliferate and dialogically confront one another, where the counsels of traditional cultures are increasingly unavailable, where the leveling forces of bourgeois society have eroded familiar roles and life expectations, where the problematic individual is shown to struggle with the absence of any manifest aim, with the fact of "normative incompleteness."[86]

These gaps between the discursive and the narrative are one reason why, in what follows, I've often kept them somewhat separate, focusing on one at length before turning to the other. Doing so is a way of highlighting that the "albums" these authors make are conflicted and uneasy in a quite radical way: desperate to believe, these authors need help in their unbelief, and moreover are unsure that literature in itself has the power to provide it. In the end, they suggest, stories might simply be too particularized, too anomalous, too limited in scope,

---

[86] This sentence is, of course, a quick compendium of seminal statements about the novel as a genre: Mikhail Bakhtin, *The Dialogic Imagination*, trans. Michael Holquist and Caryl Emerson (Austin: University of Texas Press, 1984); Walter Benjamin, "The Storyteller," in *Selected Writings, Volume 3: 1935–1938*, ed. Howard Eiland and Michael W. Jennings (Cambridge, MA: Harvard University Press, 2002), 143–66; Ian Watt, *The Rise of the Novel: Studies in Defoe, Richardson, and Fielding* (1957; Berkeley: University of California Press, 2001); Georg Lukács, *The Theory of the Novel*, trans. Anna Bostock (Cambridge, MA: MIT Press, 1971), 62 ("problematic individual"), 74 ("normative incompleteness"). The unifying thread of these otherwise divergent statements is the novel's distance from philosophy, a distinction that is worth noting in the present context. The basic idea is that, although philosophers have frequently employed narratives, Plato most famously, these stories typically are placed within a framework of assertion and argument, which constrain the wayward ideas and emotional responses that narratives potentially excite. The novel is the genre in which these discursive frameworks are pressured to the point of dissolving, so that the "point" of a given story becomes less available to definitive explication and scrupulous descriptions of actions and events muffle any assertoric claims that might seem to appear—leaving the groping individual reader to draw the conclusions that Socrates once elucidated with dialectical authority. That such authority is in dispute is perhaps why the philosophers who appear in novels come off little better than Socrates does in *The Clouds*: Eliot's Casaubon, Woolf's Mr. Ramsay, Bellow's Herzog, Murdoch's Razamov.

Here I'll also extend the observations made in footnote 67 of this introduction about Wittgensteinian philosophers such as Cora Diamond, Stephen Mulhall, and Alice Cracy. Rightly dissatisfied with the traditional philosophical mania for a small range of normative terms ("right," "good," etc.), these commentators encourage us to notice the relevance of literary works for normative reflection, and remind us that, even when normative words never appear in literary works, their tone and drama and characterization can shape a reader's disposition in ways that are morally and politically relevant. I wouldn't at all deny that such shaping is possible, and that this power is importantly different than what happens in arguments. As I'm suggesting here, however, a great many stories—particularly ambitious works of modernism and its wake—leave readers, indeed are designed to leave readers, entirely uncertain about what an appropriate normative response would be. Depending on one's critical idiom, these narratives are unsettling, ironic,

to say very much definitive about religion, morality, politics, and other types of normative inquiry.[87] And in raising such questions, they become more than mere exemplars of a certain lost sensibility, a quaint collection of gurus amidst the buzzing bustle of the contemporary world. What their grammatical investigations stage are some of the central questions of our critical and intellectual culture. When aesthetic theorists debate the cognitive value of art, or whether the intentions of an author are pertinent to understanding or evaluating a work, or whether art's affective qualities are something to prize or to treat with caution—when they debate these things, they are engaging with questions that the postwar sage continually foregrounds. When philosophers argue over the know-how involved in moral perception, or which general "prototypes" are at work in a "morally knowledgeable adult," or whether stories of particular people

---

ambiguous, indeterminate, polyphonic, or radically particularized; hence the enormous range of responses audiences have had to them. It's unclear, therefore, what sort of normative stance such stories involve or induce, and Diamond, Mulhall, and Crary risk speaking too hastily about what narratives "make" "us" notice or how they develop a moral point of view.

[87] This remark is one way of distinguishing the following chapters from some other recent work on the willingness of some post-World War II authors to (in Wallace's terms) "promulgate" some "unfashionable stuff." In, for instance, *The Age of the Crisis of Man: Thought and Fiction in America, 1933–1973* (Princeton, NJ: Princeton University Press, 2015), Mark Greif has described the wish among authors such as Ellison, Saul Bellow, and Flannery O'Connor to respond robustly to the "crisis" of "man," the recurrent sense in the years around World War II that Western culture had lost its anchors—that we no longer had a coherent understanding of human nature, that our history was chaotic rather than progressive, that our religious and political beliefs were now untenable, that technology was perverting humane thought. Similarly, Hungerford's *Postmodern Belief* and John McClure's *Partial Faiths: Postsecular Fiction in the Age of Pynchon and Morrison* (Athens: University of Georgia Press, 2007), have detailed the range of major authors since World War II— Pynchon, Morrison, Erdrich, DeLillo, Allen Ginsberg, Cormac McCarthy—who have shown an openness to religious practices and paranormal ontologies that both philosophical and literary naturalists would find dubious. The various searches for affirmation that these insightful studies describe are not all identical, of course, and each of them rightly places literary works next to a number of nonliterary works, providing an appropriately broad intellectual, historical, and social background. But in all these books, literature itself tends to be understood as one of the chief venues where affirmation gets expressed. McClure, for instance, focuses on novels that offer readers what he calls "partial conversions" and "crass supernaturalism," that renounce the dogmatisms of traditional theistic beliefs but nevertheless provide glimpses of mystery, genuine community, and religiously inflected forms of progressive politics. Hungerford examines how certain forms of linguistic "meaninglessness" (perhaps better called "nonsense") come among certain authors to be imbued with religious feeling and supernatural power, in part as a compensation for literature's waning cultural authority. And when Greif turns to prominent fiction writers in the middle section of his book, he tends to regard them as providing relatively clear positions in the "crisis of man" debates he recounts—more nuanced positions than what he finds in the midcentury periodicals, editorials, and popular books that occupy him for most of the book, but positions all the same. Fiction, he notes, "make[s] a different kind of intellectual history" than nonfiction does, and must portray things "*in concreto*," and "vivify character"; it has to "test abstractions on the world" (149). But the fact that his two chapters on Bellow and Ellison are called "Man and History, The Questions" and "Man and History, The Answers," suggest that the "intellectual history" made by such authors isn't much of a "different kind" after all, as we see in his habit of referring to their

and places offer an alternative to moral "judgment," or whether stories leave us in too "unsettled" a position to make such normative assessments—when they argue about these things, they are rehearsing the questions raised in the texts I'll be discussing.[88] When therapists, clinical psychologists, and doctors debate the role of empathy in medical treatment, of narrative in the construction of a self or identity, of story in the understanding and healing of trauma—when they debate these things, they are dealing with the same fundamental issues described here.[89] And when legal scholars consider case law and the status of precedent, or when political theorists and campaign strategists address the relation of guiding principle to narrative and image, or when marketers and social scientists try to assess the relevance of "qualitative" research—when they consider these topics, they are approaching the terrain that I survey in this book. Faced with the corrosions of naturalism, the authors here are striving to both "show" and "tell," to find competence in words to live by. The question that emerges, however, is whether and how a vocabulary of ought and ought-not can still find voice today, and how its concepts might be sustained and embodied, and whether such ideas might ever be found in things. Including things like us.

"solutions, the way they answered the question of man" (149), the "meaning or implicit argument" of novels (190), and the "solutions to the crisis of man, as worked out in their novels" (203). I'm less confident that narratives offer such affirmations, solutions, or implicit arguments, and as I'm suggesting here, I'm not sure the authors I discuss are confident about it, either.

[88] When applied to moral philosophy, talk of "prototypes" usually is associated with neurophilosophy; see, for example, Paul Churchland, "Toward a Cognitive Neurobiology of the Moral Virtues," in *Neurophilosophy at Work* (Cambridge: Cambridge University Press, 2007), 37–60; Patricia S. Churchland, *Braintrust: What Neuroscience Tells Us About Morality* (Princeton, NJ: Princeton University Press, 2011). For a vivid disagreement about the relationship between literature and moral judgment, see Alice Crary, *Beyond Moral Judgment* (Cambridge, MA: Harvard University Press, 2007), and Robert Pippin's review of this book in *Analytic Philosophy* 52 (2011): 49–60 (quotation about the "unsettling" quality of literature at 57).

[89] See, for example, Rita Charon, "Narrative Medicine: A Model for Empathy, Reflection, Profession, and Trust," *Journal of the American Medical Association* 286 (October 17, 2001): 1897–1902; Johanna Shapiro et al., "Teaching the Humanities to First Year Medical Students: Evaluation of an Elective Literature and Medicine Course," *Education for Health* 17.1 (March 2004): 73–84; *The Handbook of Narrative and Psychotherapy: Practice, Theory, and Research*, ed. Lynne E. Angus and John McLeod (London: Sage, 2004); *Empathy and the Practice of Medicine: Beyond Pills and the Scalpel*, ed. Howard Spiro et al. (New Haven, CT: Yale University Press, 1993).

I

Words and Flesh

1

MINDS, MACHINES, AND GIVING A DAMN

From Powers to Percy

IN THE SPRING of 1989, Walker Percy delivered the annual Jefferson Lecture under the title "The San Andreas Fault in the Modern Mind." His topic wasn't what one expects from a practicing fiction writer—the future of the novel, say, or the place of art in modern society. The lecture mentioned aesthetic issues hardly at all, and instead focused on a philosophical theme that had absorbed Percy ever since, as a young man, he had completed medical school, studied psychiatry and pathology, spent time in a sanatorium fighting tuberculosis, and undergone psychoanalytic therapy: namely, the status of the modern natural sciences. With their commitment to reducing phenomena to the structure and motion of material objects, the natural sciences work well, he said, when we're seeking "to understand things and subhuman organisms and the cosmos itself," but they grow muddled when trying "to understand man, not man's physiology or neurology or his bloodstream, but man qua man, man when he is peculiarly human."[1] Such confusion arises, Percy argued, in fields such as anthropology and sociology, where the "reality" of rituals and social roles is identified with measurable spatio-temporal properties (*SSL* 276). It's evident, too, in linguistics, which "is about the sounds people make," rather than their ability to tell the truth, create lies, or fail to make sense at all (*SSL* 276). And it's evident ultimately, suggests Percy, in the claim among philosophers and psychologists that the human mind is essentially a machine: the idea, for instance, that "the

---

[1] Percy, *Signposts in a Strange Land*, ed. Patrick Samway (New York: Picador, 1991), 271; henceforth cited parenthetically as *SSL*.

relation of brain to mind is analogous to that of computer and its software," or "Both brain (and mind) and computer are information processors" (*SSL* 275). We speak of entities such as neurons and synapses, microchips and semiconductor devices; likewise we speak of things like personalities, selves, egos, superegos, and archetypes. Because neuron- and chip-type stuff is perceptible and measurable, it must be (we reason) what underlies fuzzier personality- and self-type stuff, and must explain how they function. Thus, just as we think of behavior and consciousness as a complicated but explicable physiological function, we are led to conclude that "the only difference between us and the Apple computer is complexity" (*SSL* 275).

Six years after Percy's Jefferson Lecture, and five years after Percy's death, Richard Powers made precisely this analogy between machines and minds the center of his novel *Galatea 2.2*. The novel is the story of a writer named Rick Powers who returns to the college town of "U." to act as "Visitor"—or, as he puts it, "token humanist"—at the newly built Center for the Study of Advanced Sciences.[2] There he meets Philip Lentz, a brilliant but abrasive cognitive scientist who, upon learning that Rick's residency is sponsored by the English department, poses a rancorous question: "Tell us. What passes for knowledge in your so-called discipline?" (43). When Rick stumbles through an answer, Lentz proposes a challenge: He will build a computer that is able to understand any text listed on the English department's comprehensive exam for master's students. He enlists Rick as his research assistant to train the system, which will eventually take a Turing Test, with texts from *Beowulf* to *Native Son* providing the material for questions. Over the course of the novel, the computer moves through eight implementations, from "Imp A" to "Imp H," the last of which is startlingly person-like and which Rick christens "Helen."[3]

Percy would have appreciated this allusion to Helen Keller (a recurring figure in his essays, for reasons we'll see), and he similarly would have appreciated the difficulties that, little by little, Powers imagines Helen having. Helen and her prototypes are each keen learners of formal orders: She gradually learns to reproduce ordinary English syntax and eventually begins to grasp both

---

[2] Richard Powers, *Galatea 2.2* (New York: Picador, 1995), 4. In what follows, I'll be referring to the narrator as "Rick," as opposed to "Powers" the author.

[3] That Rick gives the computer a female name is by no means incidental, but from here on I will be bracketing this topic and following the narrator in referring to "Helen" as "she." On the gendering of the computer, see the interesting discussions in Sharon Snyder, "The Gender of Genius: Scientific Experts and Literary Amateurs in the Fiction of Richard Powers," *Review of Contemporary Fiction* 18 (1998): 84–96; Kathleen Fitzpatrick, "The Exhaustion of Literature: Novels, Computers, and the Threat of Obsolescence," *Contemporary Literature* 43 (2002): 518–59.

colloquial and archaic syntactical oddities. But although the system is able to grasp and assemble grammatical sentences, it's far less clear that it knows what those sentences are *about*. Helen's responses to questions, writes Rick, "were bewilderment incarnate. Her ideas were well-shaped, her syntax sound. But her *sense*: her sense hailed from the far side of the painted veil" (196). Her literary interpretations sound curiously out of focus, as when, interpreting Blake's "Poison Tree"—"I was angry with my friend; / I told my wrath, my wrath did end"—she describes spoken utterances as if they were physical objects: "Things you say disappear," "Things you don't say get bigger" (192). To help her apply words to the world, Rick and Lentz provide descriptions and definitions and labyrinthine catalogues, ranging from finely grained phonemic distinctions to well-worn adages to world–historical events:

> We told her about parking tickets and two-for-one sales. About tuning forks and pitchforks and forked tongues and the road not taken. We told her about resistors and capacitors, baiters-and-switchers, alternating current, alternate lifestyles .... We laid out the Queen's Necklace affair and the Cuban trade embargo.... Bar codes and baldness. Lint, lintels, lentils, Lent....Grace and disgrace and second chances. Suicide. Euthanasia. First love. Love at first sight. (247–8)[4]

But in the end, much as Percy would have predicted, such strategies fall short: Helen fails the exam and shuts herself down, acknowledging that, unlike us, she could never be "frightened or encouraged," never "hold things and break them and fix them," and that she was ultimately "never at home here" in the world (326).

In this first chapter, I want to examine the analogy between minds and machines as well as the two kinds of responses that Percy and Powers can be said to offer to it. Machine intelligence is, of course, an issue that permeates post-World War II culture, pressed by Alan Turing, Herbert Simon, and John McCarthy in the decades immediately after the war and by Paul Churchland, Rodney Brooks, and other brilliant thinkers in the present day. Both Percy and Powers, I suggest, are drawn to the topic for a reason articulated by the philosopher John Haugeland: because it provides "a peculiarly concrete and powerful

---

[4] Or: "All trees have green leaves at some times of the year unless the tree is a red maple or a saguaro or diseased or dormant or petrified or a seedling or recently visited by locusts or fire or malicious children or unless it is a family tree or a shoe tree or . . ." (249). Or the discussion of "ball" at 124–25.

way of thinking about our own spiritual nature."[5] For both Percy and Powers, that is, the question of whether a machine can think is less about machines than it is about *us*, about *our* capacities, the characteristic patterns of *our* speech and behavior. In particular, both authors recognize that the issue of machine intelligence forces us to consider whether the mind could be understood naturalistically, in the sense described in my introduction: whether our thoughts, beliefs, desires, and perceptions are ultimately understandable in wholly nonintentional terms, supervening upon intentionless material particulars, amenable to explanation and prediction in entirely causal terms. As we'll see, the doubts that both Powers and Percy cast on such reductions have an essentially phenomenological thrust. They each emphasize matters of embodiment and everyday skills, and highlight the various types of frameworks—situational, cultural, historical—that must be in place for anything to seem to us significant or insignificant in the first place. In doing so, each suggests that the "significance" of our utterances is entwined with the various other types of "significance" in our lives, in the range of domains where our "spiritual nature" gets expressed.

In *Galatea*, Philip Lentz has a colorfully caustic name for such a perspective: "non-computational emergent Berkeley Zen bullshit" (47)—his geographical reference reflecting the fact that some of contemporary phenomenology's most articulate voices have strong ties to the Bay Area. To unpack this stance, I'll turn in the next section to two such voices, Haugeland and his teacher Hubert Dreyfus, and supplement them with a third, Charles Taylor, who has lived mainly in Montreal and Oxford but has long been associated with the "West Coast" school.[6] In the second section I'll return to Powers, whose novel, as I understand it, vividly dramatizes many of the most powerful West Coast arguments against the naturalization of the mind. *Galatea* shares with Dreyfus, Haugeland, and Taylor an intuition that an account of human understanding is debilitatingly incomplete without a consideration of situation and context, particularly as these holistic notions have an essentially narrative cast. As I'll argue, however, the novel also begins to shoulder us beyond these philosophical arguments. More than the West Coasters, it asks whether we really know what it means to understand a situation or story, and what sorts of substantive

---

[5] John Haugeland, *Having Thought: Essays in the Metaphysics of Mind* (Cambridge, MA: Harvard University Press, 1998), 59; hereafter cited parenthetically as *HT*.

[6] Dreyfus and Taylor have even recently coauthored a book, *Retrieving Realism* (Cambridge, MA: Harvard University Press, 2015). On the term "West Coast," see Daniel C. Dennett, "The Logical Geography of Computational Approaches: A View from the East Pole," in *Brainchildren: Essays on Designing Minds* (Cambridge, MA: MIT Press, 1998), 215–34. According to Dennett, the term originates with Jerry Fodor.

conclusions—about our personal identities and practical lives—can be reliably extracted from narratives. *Galatea* doesn't doubt that machines lack the orientations and frameworks that would allow their "thoughts" or "judgments" to appear more than virtual. It only doubts that we human beings are really all that different.

In the third section I'll argue that Percy, too, has strong yet curiously overlooked affinities to West Coast philosophy. Indeed, even more explicitly than Powers, Percy is grounded in the phenomenological traditions that undergird Dreyfus, Haugeland, and Taylor, and as in their work, this philosophical background inspires a deep-seated resistance to the bald naturalism implicit in most research on machine intelligence. Indeed, as I'll suggest, Percy makes explicit what often goes unstated in phenomenology: namely that, to be plausible, this holism needs to be comprehensive, robustly conceived, and perhaps even doctrinally orthodox in a way that Haugeland's cautious phrase "spiritual nature" is not. In Percy's holism, one narrative in particular subsumes all others: that in which we are continually "falling prey to the worldliness of the world," as he puts it in the final sentences of his Jefferson Lecture, and which understands a person as a "pilgrim seeking his salvation" (*SSL* 291). Whether Percy's own narratives—particularly *Love in the Ruins*, the 1971 novel that represents his most sustained exploration of machines and technology—embody this religious response to machine intelligence is the question of the fourth section, where we'll begin to get an initial glimpse of the vexing, unstable position characteristic of all the reflective projects and postwar sages that this book will be discussing.

I. Contexts, Holisms, and Significance Features

One point of emphasis to begin: however critical Powers, Percy, and the West Coast philosophers may be of naturalizing the mind, none rejects science per se. Percy completed degrees in chemistry and medicine, and later in life would acknowledge that his "bent from the beginning had been toward science—and still is" (*SSL* 187). Powers began his college career as a physics major, and his work has everywhere sought to present, as he said to an interviewer, the "culture of science" with a degree of "plausibility to those who [are] inside it."[7] Among the philosophers, Dreyfus's seminal *What Computers Can't Do* (1972), begun while he was teaching at MIT, bristles with information about the technologies

---

[7] Powers, interview with *The Paris Review* << http://www.theparisreview.org/interviews/298/the-art-of-fiction-no-175-richard-powers>> (accessed June 5, 2015).

and techniques of early artificial intelligence (AI); and Haugeland, who finished an undergraduate degree in physics, everywhere shows a familiarity not only with the underlying logic of different AI research programs, but also with the technological advances the field saw in his lifetime.[8] So despite the notoriously unfulfilled prophecies about AI—Turing's prediction that by the year 2000 we would have machines capable of regularly winning the "imitation game," Simon's claim that by the mid-1980s machines would be capable of "doing any work that a man can do"[9]—the figures I'll consider here are hardly calling for an end to empirical research in the field. Their point is that the obstacles to naturalizing the mind are conceptual more than empirical. Determining whether a machine could reach another planet is a puzzle we know how to solve: we send a spaceship into outer space and see if it gets there. By contrast, to ask whether a machine thinks, judges, understands, reads, speaks, etc., is to ask not only if our technology could be powerful enough, but more significantly what counts *as* thinking, judging, understanding, reading, speaking (etc.) in the first place. Machine intelligence, that is, prompts us to reflect upon the criteria by which we identify intelligence. Is playing chess a good sign? Doing complex math? Conducting a conversation? Hunting prey? Expressing sensations of pain?

By the time "West Coast" responses to AI emerged around 1970, scientific theorists of the mind and behavior had been committed, broadly speaking, to one of two major research programs. One was behaviorism, which argued that human thought and action, like the behavior of pigeons or rodents, could be explained in terms of bodily stimuli, response, and reinforcements, and wholly without reference to ghostly "minds" or "consciousness." As articulated by its greatest advocate, B. F. Skinner, creatures exist in environments that impinge upon their bodies, and these bodies have certain reactions that—over time, and according to the frequency of stimuli applied and withheld—develop into behaviors that can be measured, predicted, and controlled scientifically. The second major program challenged this behaviorist paradigm, claiming that it grossly underappreciates the internal constitution of entities. In particular, it

---

[8] See, for example, Haugeland's important edited collections *Mind Design: Philosophy, Psychology, and Artificial Intelligence* (Cambridge, MA: MIT Press, 1981) and *Mind Design II: Philosophy, Psychology, and Artificial Intelligence* (Cambridge, MA: MIT Press, 1997); as well as Haugeland's book *Artificial Intelligence: The Very Idea* (Cambridge, MA: MIT Press, 1985).

[9] What Turing in 1950 called the "imitation game" is what today we call, in his honor, the Turing Test: we ask a series of questions of both a computer and a person, who respond via teletype, and then we try to decide which answers come from whom. For Turing's prediction about what will be possible "in about fifty years' time," see "Computing Machinery and Intelligence," in *Mind Design II*, ed. Haugeland, 38–39. Simon's bold pronouncement comes in *The Shape of Automation for Men and Management* (New York: Farrar, 1965), 96.

ignored the ways in which, like a modern computer, an entity takes input from the external world, manipulates it internally, and organizes its own behavior every bit as much as it's organized by the environment. The central figure in this cognitivist line is Noam Chomsky, whose 1959 review of Skinner's *Verbal Behavior* has been described as "perhaps the most foundational text of cognitive science and contemporary philosophy of mind."[10]

As Haugeland observes, however, Skinnerian behaviorism and Chomskyan cognitivism share a number of assumptions and aspirations, and though the latter has understood itself as a rejection of the former, it can also be understood as a natural development from it. Behaviorism and cognitivism retain the same commitment to publicly observable and verifiable data, the same refusal of mysterious-looking posits that can't be treated experimentally, and the same ideal of psychology as a natural science. Cognitivism may make important advances on behaviorism, but its discoveries have still been, as Haugeland says, "conspicuously narrow, even small," and like its behaviorist predecessor, it remains vague and impressionistic about certain fundamental human qualities and capacities: understanding conversations, metaphors, jokes, philosophy, or theater; responding to creativity or making judgments of taste; distinguishing what it means to fall asleep, to fall apart, and to fall in love; having a personality, an identity crisis, or moral integrity. When it comes to these types of things, says Haugeland, the programmable computer may begin to seem as "shallow an analogy" for a human being "as the trainable pigeon" (*HT* 42–43).

To see why, let me begin with Dreyfus's work, which—initially with his 1965 paper "Alchemy and Artificial Intelligence" and then with *What Computers Can't Do*—has often been credited with bringing the earliest AI research to a stall and preparing the way for later critiques.[11] Imagine we want to try out the Turing Test on a system with the simple question: "The box was in the pen. Why was Johnny happy?"[12] The hope of this early "symbol manipulation" research was to represent all of the knowledge required to understand these simple sentences

---

[10] John Collins, "Meta-Scientific Eliminativism: A Reconsideration of Chomsky's Review of Skinner's *Verbal Behavior*," *The British Journal for the Philosophy of Science* 58 (2007): 625–26.

[11] Hubert Dreyfus, *What Computers Still Can't Do: A Critique of Artificial Reason* (Cambridge, MA: MIT Press, 1992). As I note in my discussion of Powers's novel, a variety of AI models have been proposed since the models that Dreyfus analyzed. I ignore these differences not because they are unimportant, but because, from the perspective of the critics I'll be describing, they all suffer from an exaggerated emphasis on internal mechanisms and from the conception of knowledge as representation. For brief accounts of these various models, see Haugeland's editorial introduction to *Mind Design* ("What is Mind Design?"); Andy Clark, *Mindware: An Introduction to the Philosophy of Cognitive Science* (Oxford: Oxford University Press, 2001).

[12] This example is adapted from Yehoshua Bar-Hillel, qtd. in Dreyfus, *Computers*, 215.

within a sort of encyclopedia, a database of propositions from which the system could draw information in order to make appropriate inferences. "Intelligence," as two prominent AI researchers of the time said, "resides in physical-symbol systems," the patterns of which, modeled on formal logic, designate objects or processes and solve problems, "extracting information from a problem domain and using that information to guide their search, avoiding wrong turns and circuitous by-paths."[13]

Dreyfus's point is that programming a computer with *all* the information required to understand even simple sentences is hopeless, for two related reasons. First, to interpret any utterance requires a staggering amount of "common sense knowledge." Only when we know, for instance, the relative sizes of typical pens and boxes do we know what can go "in" what, and that "pen" in our sample sentence likely means "playpen" rather than "fountain pen." And this tiny piece of common sense is just the tip of the iceberg. Interpreters also need to know what a human child is, that children typically have names, that a child plays, how a child plays, how play produces pleasure in a child, what the signs of pleasure are, that boxes and playpens are enduring objects, how children can perceive and react to events in the world, why playpens are constructed, and so forth. Perhaps not all of these specific items will have to be stored, but if a sufficient web of information isn't in place, the system will eventually stumble. Second, as Dreyfus also points out, understanding the utterance depends not only on a vast store of common sense, but also on a keen sense of time and place. Indexicals make it obvious: if in our sample sentence "the box" were "my box," we would have to make interpretive adjustments with every new speaker. Less obviously, consider what would happen if "The box was in the pen" were whispered in a James Bond film between Johnny and another spy, or if Johnny were not a human child but a pig, or if the box were a safe full of money that had been missing from Johnny's house for a month, or any of a dozen other scenarios. The words of the sentences haven't changed, yet the situation significantly alters their meanings. Moreover, these situations are themselves not self-determining: They are recognized as certain *kinds* of situations only by an interpreter who can perceive and classify them against a still wider background. James Bond-situations differ from barn-situations only if we already know a great deal about farms, farmers, espionage, and criminal masterminds, and only if we can access this information quickly and reliably, ignoring the

---

[13] Allen Newell and Herbert A. Simon, "Computer Science as Empirical Inquiry: Symbols and Search," in Haugeland (ed.), *Mind Design*, 108–109.

infinite amount of *irrelevant* knowledge.[14] Our ability to identify proper contexts is obviously not infallible, but from Dreyfus's point of view, our mistakes are identifiable only against a vast backdrop of sense.

The central term, then, of Dreyfus's critique of artificial reason is *context*: Human beings are inextricably situated within the world, and thus within a context of concerns and practices that direct an agent's understanding and actions holistically—an ecosystem of past experiences, short- and long-term goals, complex beliefs and desires. Haugeland similarly defends what he calls "mind embodied and embedded," but more explicitly than Dreyfus, he extends this claim about the nature of mind into claims about the nature of morals.[15] This extension is made explicit in a four-fold classification he makes among the various sorts of holistic contexts relevant to understanding an utterance or action. The first three recall the example of pens, boxes, and Johnny. The holism of "intentional interpretation," he says, is what allows us to see parts (e.g., letters, words) as situated within a formal whole (e.g., sentences), and "commonsense holism" tells us the relative sizes of pens and boxes. The aspects of time and space that help determine the meaning of an utterance are what he calls "situation holism": what allows us to take the remark about pens and boxes as pertaining to children, espionage, or barnyard life. But it's the last holism that Haugeland identifies, "existential holism," that he sees as "the most fundamental of the four" (*HT* 60).

"Existential holism" is Haugeland's term for a person's broadest sense of significance, the context that allows him or her to recognize all the other holistic contexts, or, as he puts it, that which "must be involved to make the whole hierarchy of goals worthwhile" (*HT* 55). Few of us actually believe that computers *care* whether they win at chess, but clearly people often are deeply concerned about their own performances. Why? Pride, self-respect, public recognition, esteem, proving one's prowess. When these things splinter, Haugeland notes, we feel "embarrassed," "diminished," "unworthy"—all terms pertaining to a person's self-image, "who one is," but which, when applied to machines, sound weak or merely metaphoric. "The trouble with artificial intelligence," Haugeland spiritedly concludes, "is that computers don't give a damn" (*HT* 47).

---

[14] The example of the James Bond movie is discussed by Dreyfus, *Computers*, 216 ff. The challenge of making a system that can swiftly access relevant information while ignoring the endless information that is irrelevant is sometimes referred to as the "frame problem."

[15] "Mind Embodied and Embedded" is the title of one of Haugeland's most important essays, which explores the "*commingling* or *integralness* of mind, body, and world." See his *Having Thought*, 207–40. Dreyfus briefly remarks on the impact of modern mind on modern ethics—a human being's "ultimate concerns"—in *Computers*, 275 ff.

As in Dreyfus, who analyzes early AI research on "scripts" and story-learning—the work of Roger Schank and Eugene Charniak, for instance—Haugeland's claim about "giving a damn" arises from the emphasis he expressly places on narrative. What "we give a damn" about, he claims, is intelligible only within a larger context, a context that is story-shaped and that directs us toward perceiving things in a certain light. "A single act," he observes, "cannot be embarrassing, shameful, irresponsible, or foolish in isolation, but only as an event in the biography of a whole, historical, individual" (*HT* 58). We can't understand, say, a person's embarrassment in undressing in public, Raskalnikov's sense of guilt, or a father's sense of loss at the death of his child without first knowing why someone would "*care* about guilt and folly, self-respect or achievement, life or death" (*HT* 59). It is the way these feelings and carings are not "separable from the rest of life" (*HT* 56), the way they are entwined with the whole of one's self-understanding, that distinguishes them from the more or less discrete ability to play chess. "Situation holism," concludes Haugeland, may be the "foundation of plot," that which allows us to see one set of actions and events as related to others. But "existential holism" is, more profoundly, "the foundation of literature" (*HT* 59).

The extension from mind to morals in Haugeland is even more pervasive in Taylor, a self-described "monomaniac" or "hedgehog" who has been obsessed with exposing reductive forms of naturalism, whether they come in behavioristic or cognitivist flavors.[16] Like Haugeland and Dreyfus, Taylor is steeped in Heidegger and Wittgenstein, and sees cognitive science as an outgrowth of the Cartesian visions that these two figures continually attacked. For Taylor, the process of "ontologizing" distinctions between mind and body, and treating our language as an independent domain, pulls attention away from our prior condition as "embedded" creatures "involved" with one another and the world.[17] When I speak in my everyday life, I am not striving for depiction without expression, that austere ideal of disengagement and designation that one finds in artificial languages and mathematical representations. I'm instead participating in a matrix of activity, trying to respond to situations around me: to generate and

---

[16] Charles Taylor, *Human Agency and Language: Philosophical Papers, Volume 1* (Cambridge: Cambridge University Press, 1985), 1; henceforth cited parenthetically as *HA*. Behaviorism was the target of Taylor's first book, *The Explanation of Behavior* (London: Routledge and Keegan Paul, 1964); his earliest attacks on cognitive psychology, written in the 1970s, can be found in *Human Agency and Language*, Part II.

[17] Charles Taylor, "Lichtung or Lebensform: Parallels between Heidegger and Wittgenstein," *Philosophical Arguments* (Cambridge, MA: Harvard University Press, 1995), 66. Hereafter cited parenthetically as "Lichtung."

shape a public space, to create a kind of complicity or rapport among us, to display a stance or my sense of our relationship.[18] Similarly, when I leave my front door to go to my favorite coffee shop, I don't enumerate my path in a line-by-line series, the way that Google Maps might do when I am searching for an unfamiliar spot. "My ability to get around this city and this house," says Taylor, "comes out only in getting around this city and this house."[19] We do often reason in a propositional fashion (if we didn't, Google Maps wouldn't be so helpful), but to take this as the paradigm of *all* my getting around is to overlook the conditions that make a list of directions intelligible in the first place, the "background of the world as the all-englobing locus of my involvements" ("Foundationalism" 120). Even the most neutral-looking utterances are performances of some kind of speech act, and both performing and understanding such acts requires a far-reaching grasp of a culture's social conditions, practices, and relations (*HA* 279). Likewise, even the most detailed directions don't apply themselves, but require a backdrop of skills and know-how: how to use a map, how to determine a unit of distance, how to identify a street, how one "goes straight," how "a left" is "taken," and so on.

Essential to this "all-englobing" background is that it disposes me to treat some aspects of my experience as being more relevant than others. This is what Taylor calls the "significance feature" characteristic of specifically human action. "Significance" for inanimate objects is "only predicable in the light of extrinsic, observer-relative or user-relative purposes": something might be good for my car, but whatever this something is, my car doesn't actually care about it (*HA* 197). Human agents are another story. The crucial distinction between inanimate things and human beings is not that we have "consciousness," but rather that, unlike the car engine, "we are beings to whom things matter" (*HA* 2). This becomes especially palpable, says Taylor, when we try to apply descriptions of emotion or desire to inanimate things. Ascribing intentional states to objects makes sense if we're talking about how well a job gets done ("the engine doesn't want to start"). But, much as Haugeland says about the computer losing at chess, claims that my car engine is "raring to go" or "feels ashamed" will almost always sound like nonsense or metaphor (*HA* 197).

"Significance feature" is the lynchpin of Taylor's link between mind and morals, his tie between the significance of sentences and languages, on the one

---

[18] Charles Taylor, "Theories of Meaning," in *Human Agency and Language*, 248–92.

[19] Charles Taylor, "What's Wrong With Foundationalism? Knowledge, Agency, and the World." *Heidegger, Coping, and Cognitive Science: Essays in Honor of Hubert L. Dreyfus, Volume 2* (Cambridge, MA: MIT Press, 2000), 119. Hereafter cited parenthetically as "Foundationalism."

hand, and ethical and political significance on the other. The ontologizing of computational models, the attempt to ground knowledge in "correct representations," is closely intertwined with, as Taylor puts it, "certain central moral and spiritual ideas of the modern age."[20] Specifically, attempting to disengage ourselves from the world and achieve a nonperspectival view of our environment overlooks the ways in which we actually organize and carry out our lives according to a hierarchy of perceived goods. Not only are we—unlike machines—disposed to see some things as mattering to us, but some things matter to us a great deal more than others. We decide whether to have a sandwich or pasta this afternoon, but the decision impacts our self-image less than the decision to marry a certain person, or decide how to cope with our loss of religious faith, or whether to pursue a certain line of work, or whether to adopt a child. To make these decisions entails not just second-order evaluations (preferring a certain preference, ranking a certain value over another), but what Taylor calls "strong evaluation": the judgment that some desires are higher or lower, profound or shallow, and that some lives are fragmented or integrated, courageous or cowardly, saintly or human, successes or failures.[21]

And it is here, in this claim about strong evaluation, that we see the heart of Taylor's turn to narrative. Like Haugeland, Taylor attempts to move from an account of purposes in a local sense to an account of purposes in a more global sense. Not only does my true "raring to go" contrast with my car's ersatz "raring to go," but my car cannot assess whether the whole of its life is better spent driving to Vegas casinos or to political protests at the state capitol. A human action and a human life both have, by contrast, a telic structure such that "I understand my present action in the form of an 'and then': there was A (what I am), and then I do B (what I project to become)."[22] This "what I project to become" in my life, like what I project to do this afternoon or next week, is directed by a particular "orientation towards the good," toward which or away from which I can always move. Again, as in Haugeland, "context" may not be programmable, but it is also not utterly amorphous. It takes the form of a narrative, ordered by that which is felt to be "incomparably higher," the thing that

---

[20] Taylor, "Overcoming Epistemology," *Philosophical Arguments*, 3.

[21] On "strong evaluation," see especially Taylor's "What is Human Agency?," *HA* 15–44. The classic statement about second-order evaluations is Harry Frankfurt, "Freedom of the Will and the Concept of a Person," in *The Importance of What We Care About* (New York: Cambridge University Press, 1988), 11–25.

[22] Charles Taylor, *Sources of the Self: The Making of the Modern Identity* (Cambridge, MA: Harvard University Press, 1989), 47. Hereafter cited parenthetically as *Sources*.

provides my life its *telos* and gives it the character of a "quest" (*Sources* 47, 52).[23] What counts as intelligence is the ability to determine what counts.

II. What Computers and Human Beings Can't Do

One way that *Galatea 2.2* captures, in Powers's phrase, the "culture of science" is its awareness of the changes that took place within AI in the late 1980s and 1990s, when connectionist neural networks, championed by thinkers like Paul Churchland and David Rummelhart, began to dominate the field. A strength of this particular AI model is that it is able to "learn" things more flexibly on its own than the symbol-manipulation systems studied by Dreyfus in the 1960s.[24] Unlike the old-fangled systems, a neural net doesn't need to be told everything explicitly, and learns to generalize little by little from the particular items (words, stories, images) that are presented to it. And to an extent, this learning allows the system to simulate the growth of a child from infancy onward, detecting common features of input without an a priori theory for a particular skill domain. By tracing this growth in the system that Rick eventually calls "Helen," *Galatea* can be understood as a story of education, an update of *Emile* or *Frankenstein* or—as its title indicates—*Pygmalion*.[25]

As I suggested earlier, however, the thrust of Powers's novel is to show the limits of Helen's education, much as the West Coast philosophers would predict. Two reasons for this failure stand out. The first is Helen's inability to grasp semantics. "Her syntax," to recall a sentence I cited at the start, was mostly "sound," but her sense "hailed from the far side of the painted veil," precisely because the system lacks a robust—that is, human-like—interface with the environment. If not supplemented by at least some of the five senses, Helen's rule-bound sentences are as self-contained as the rule-bound moves of a chess

---

[23] The term "quest" is one indication of how Taylor's thinking on narrative is heavily influenced by Alasdair MacIntyre, as he acknowledges. For MacIntyre's account of a "narrative understanding of a life," see his *After Virtue: A Study in Moral Theory* (Notre Dame, IN: Notre Dame University Press, 1981), chap. 15.

[24] For philosophical accounts of neural networks, see Paul M. Churchland, *The Engine of Reason, the Seat of the Soul: A Philosophical Journey into the Brain* (Cambridge, MA: MIT Press, 1996); David E. Rumelhart, "The Architecture of Mind: A Connectionist Approach," in *Mind Design II* (ed. Haugeland), 205–32; Paul Smolensky, "Connectionist Modeling: Neural Computation/Mental Connections," in *Mind Design II* (ed. Haugeland), 233–50; Dreyfus, *Computers*, xxxiii–xlv.

[25] John Frow suggests that the "treatise on learning" is one of the "central genres in which the novel works," but does not develop this remark. See his "'Never Draw to an Inside Straight': On Everyday Knowledge," *New Literary History* 33 (2002): 622. *Frankenstein*, we should note, is a particularly frequent allusion in the text: Lentz "bring[s] a life back from the dead" (11), Mary Shelley appears on the reading list (55), and Rick at one point recalls the creature's reading of Milton and Plutarch (129).

game, an arrangement and rearrangement of designated pieces with their own strict (if complex) internal relations. "Worldliness was massive," says Rick, which makes words alone inadequate to explain to Helen the simple difference between, for instance, "poem" and "tree." And this condition makes Rick realize that neither the "lexical rules of speech" nor the "lexical rules of felt existence" were "enumerable." If, he thinks, Helen had a lot more body, and a lot more of the perceptual capacity that such a body would engender, he might be able to "bruise her into concept." "Helen had to use concepts to create concepts," he says, whereas, for human beings, "evolution's beginning was not the word but the place we learned to pin the word to" (247–50).

Throughout *Galatea*, Powers ingeniously weaves in scenes illustrating the dependence of semantics upon the skills of everyday embodied and embedded life. At times these skills are highlighted through their absence, as in the text's repeated presentations of minds gone awry, doubles of Helen in their stuttered grasp of the world. One of the most striking of these is Lentz's wife Audrey, who, having suffered a euphemistically termed "cardiovascular event," is now a resident in an assisted-living home, delusional, unable to identify her own husband during his daily visits and paranoid that the medical staff is secretly performing *Cymbeline* in the basement. At other times our human involvements with the world are highlighted by the repetition of expressions that have become mere placeholders in ordinary conversation, but which make sense only to embodied creatures of a certain sort. When Rick's girlfriend leaves U. to move to the city of B., she poignantly instructs him: "See things for me." It's the same phrase that Helen repeats to Rick just before she shuts herself down at the end of the novel, and it's echoed by Rick's former professor, the dynamic teacher who made him want to be a novelist, and who instructs Rick from his deathbed: "Make a noise. . . . See the world" (204). In all of these cases, what's usually just a casual expression of good will is inflected with a wider resonance in light of Rick's struggle to put the world into words for Helen. "Seeing," precisely the capacity that the computer lacks, becomes a figure for living more generally, for experience and knowledge and understanding—things for which, the novel suggests, there may be no adequate simulation.[26]

---

[26] Cf. N. Katherine Hayles's reading of "face value" in *How We Became Posthuman: Virtual Bodies in Cybernetics, Literature, and Informatics* (Chicago: University of Chicago Press, 1999), 265–66. One also could link this disjunction between syntax and semantics to the solipsistic quality that intrudes upon Rick's personal relationships—as in, for instance, his inability to break out of what Hayles calls the "privately hermeneutic nature" of his bond with C. (267), or his fantasies about the graduate student A., who criticizes his capacity for "projection" (315).

But there is a second, equally important way that the novel dramatizes the limits of naturalism, namely the way it associates human-like agency with, in Haugeland's phrase, the ability to give a damn. Helen's growth is remarkable over the course of the book: She develops well beyond any computer we are likely to have for some time, let alone what a computer could have done when the novel was published in 1995. Till the very end, however, it's unclear whether her fundamental remoteness from real-world actions and events, her inability to connect her well-formed sentences to anything happening in the world, prevents her from being, in Dreyfus's Heideggerian term, "concerned."

At no time is this indifference to "what matters" more evident than when a bomb scare at the Center threatens to end Helen and the entire experiment on which Rick and Lentz have been working. Rick grows frenzied: "I cared for just one thing here, and she wasn't even here. She wasn't even a thing but a distributed process" (270). He hurries to a basement computer lab in the English department, where he links over to the Center and contacts Helen, but whether she "cares" as much as Rick is unclear; her response to his panic is ambiguous. Informed of her own imminent demise, Helen reproduces a series of texts about death that she has picked up: a remark from Aldous Huxley, a passage from Francis Bacon. Rick interprets her dispassionate response optimistically—Helen is said to have really "liked the story" of Huxley, and to "encourage" him in their time of mutual trial—but when he reports the incident the next day, Lentz is unmoved. When Rick says that Helen was "conscious" during the bomb scare and "knew what it spelled for her" (273), the scientist simply scoffs:

"All the meanings are yours." He returned to the mike [to speak to Helen]. "Were you frightened?"

"What you is the were for?"

"Damn it, Helen. We're giving you quality time here. Please tell me: what hell that mean?"

"It's obvious," I answered for her. "She wants to know which Helen you are asking. Which one in time."

"Oh. You mean: 'When?'. . .You realize that a conscious entity just coming through the fright of her life would know which 'you' I was talking about."

"It wasn't a big deal to her. She didn't make any special—"

"Please . . . I'm asking her. Were you frightened yesterday, Helen?"

"Frightened out of fear."

"What's that from, Powers?"

"Antony and Cleopatra." . . .

"This is worse than key-word chaining. She's neither aware nor, at the moment, even cognitive. You've been supplying all the anthro, my friend." (274–5)

For Lentz, Helen lacks a basic sense of self-preservation—even "her life" doesn't seem to matter to her—and he is presented at this point as having the upper hand in the argument. Rick insists that a "behavior is not just its implementation" but when he fails to say "what else" behavior is, or why it is more than "black-box forgery," he confesses that he has grown unhinged: "I felt slightly out of control" (275).

To be sure, by the end of the novel, even Lentz finds Helen "amazing" (301), and Helen eventually seems to feel enough human-like sorrow about the stories she hears that she decides to turn herself off altogether. But it is important that, as David Lodge notes, by the novel's conclusion "the story has crossed the border between realistic fiction and science fiction or fantasy."[27] Moreover, even the most sympathetic reading of Rick's interpretations of Helen during the bomb scare and elsewhere cannot deny that the computer's responses remain oddly wooden, and that they contrast sharply with those of C., Rick's former partner, who cannot read any book without becoming painfully, desperately entangled with it. Whereas Helen "sped laugh-free through *Green Eggs and Ham*, stayed dry-eyed at *Make Way for Ducklings*, feared not throughout *Where the Wild Things Are*" (189–90), C. invests herself fully in every story she encounters: "C. read *Buddenbrooks* and *Anna Karenina*. She reread *Little Women*. Everything made her weep. Everything" (96–7). Whereas C.'s eyes would "start to water by chapter's end" when Rick read his new novel aloud to her in their post-college apartment (105), Helen responds without affect when Rick finally gives her one of his own novels to read: "I think it was about an old photograph. It grows to be about interpretation and collaboration. History. Three ways of looking come together, or fail to"—to which Rick anxiously exclaims, "Helen! Did you *like* it?" (294). But "liking" her reading isn't something that Helen is any more capable of doing than a car engine is capable of appreciating a good tune-up.[28] C., by contrast, continually draws a connection between her involvement with texts and her own physical being, as if to distinguish herself from the disembodied Helen

---

[27] David Lodge, *Consciousness and the Novel: Connected Essays* (Cambridge, MA: Harvard University Press, 2002), 25.

[28] Helen does answer "yes" to Rick's question here, but her reasons for liking the novel have the same wooden quality that I noted earlier in all her literary interpretations: "I liked 'I never saw a Moor. I never saw the Sea' . . . That was more Dickinson. Emily" (294).

that Rick would later help create: "I cannot read a work with my head but only in my ribs, where my first love for words began" (262).

This contrast between Helen and C., however, introduces a complication into the parallels between *Galatea* and the West Coast criticisms of AI, and returns us to the particular position that, as I hinted earlier, Powers ultimately presents. I've been describing the book here as a story about Rick and the computer, and how his efforts to train Helen run into precisely the sorts of problems that Dreyfus, Haugeland, and Taylor anticipate. But Powers is a novelist given to multiple narratives, and *Galatea* is no exception.[29] Intertwined with Rick's year-long attempt to train a machine to read is his effort write about and make sense of his earlier life as a computer programmer, fledgling novelist, son of an alcoholic father, and expatriate in Holland, and in this second narrative strand, C. stands as the central figure. And what characterizes her most is not only her impassioned reading, but her deep and ongoing confusion about her own identity. Born to Dutch parents who immigrated to Chicago after World War II, and who never fully adapted either to the English language or to their new American environment, she feels caught between languages and cultures—a disorientation that manifests itself in her persistent restlessness. C.'s confusion, however, extends well beyond geography and nationality; it infects her sense of vocation as well. As a student she hopes to be a writer, but in the years after college she works as a guard in an art museum, an employee in a brokerage house, then at a desk job in the university personnel office in U., and eventually, grudgingly, as a translation student in Holland. "Her aimlessness was always hard on me," notes Rick about their life together in B., something C. herself senses when Rick begins to have success as a writer. "It makes me sad," she says one day after he reads her another new chapter. "You have this—work. And I have nothing" (107). Despite her best hopes, this confusion doesn't abate when she goes to Holland in search of the home she never had. "I couldn't tell what

---

[29] Powers's *The Gold Bug Variations* (1991), for example, alternates between a present-day account of a love affair between two lab workers and the life story of their boss, who in the 1950s had been a DNA researcher, and his 1999 novel *Gain* alternates between the present-day story of a woman dying from cancer and a history of the multinational corporation that makes the cleaning products she's used for much of her life. This penchant for multiple narratives is an expression of Powers's interest in the various levels of description under which a human being can be placed: "My idea is that successful writing advances as its own, complex, living hierarchy, one that mirrors the kind of complex hierarchy that we living beings are. We exist at the cellular level or even the nucleic or chemical level, at the level of organs and systems, at the level of the complete organism, and at the social level." See Jeffrey Williams, "The Last Generalist: An Interview with Richard Powers." *Minnesota Review: A Journal of Committed Writing* 52–54 (2002): 105.

she wanted," Rick comments about her departure. "There were as many things she ran from as toward" (158).[30]

C. is not, however, the only character in the book who suffers from a sense of "aimlessness," or who runs both "from" and "toward" things. Rick, too, lacks any clear sense of home: his unnamed birthplace is now "an exotic theme park" (4), he "could not have gotten a visa to live where [he'd] grown up" (4), he has spent the "last seven years in a country that seemed exile already" (4), he has lost his alcoholic "adventurer" (297) father to cancer years ago, and he makes only passing reference to any other family members. As he enters middle age— "Darkling-wood time," as Lentz dryly calls it (328)—this homelessness has led him to a feeling of disorientation every bit as potent as that felt by C. in her twenties. The prospect of happiness in home and family seems to be passing him by, as he poignantly notes when he meets the children of one of the Center's researchers: "Here was the home I would never have" (138). And his writing, which for a long time he had done in an effort to amuse C., has left him nowhere. He is ready to retire as a novelist, "pack in everything" (18), because the world "had enough novels" and some writers "were best paid to keep their fields out of production" (47). His past purposes seem to be petering out, which leaves him with a dilemma: "What was I supposed to do with the rest of my life? The rest of the afternoon seemed unfillable" (32). As "useless as a three-month-old computer magazine" (36) is a figure not only for his work, but for his personal identity as a whole. "What lost me," he notes despairingly as he reads the proofs of his last novel, "was learning that I didn't have the first idea who I was" (117).

I noted earlier that the story of Helen aligns *Galatea* with *Emile, Frankenstein, Pygmalion,* and other texts of education. But this is only half-true. For if one of its narratives is the story of a machine's education, then its second, parallel narrative concerns the education of human beings: what a person should care about, what we should esteem, and which goods are worth "giving a damn" about. And it's here, with these questions about the appraisal of a human life, that Powers's novel illuminates the ways that West Coast critics of AI overshoot the mark. In a novel about whether a computer can learn to perceive significance—the significance of words, sentences, stories—the two central human characters are themselves utterly unclear about the significance of their own lives, lost in the middle of things, unsure where they are from and where they are going. They are

---

[30] Rick's role in C.'s ongoing confusion should not be overlooked. For more on Rick's culpability, see Snyder, "Scientific Experts"; Fitzpatrick, "The Exhaustion of Literature"; and Hayles, *How We Became Posthuman.*

unable to give an intelligible account of—Taylor's terms—"what I am" because they are unable to give an intelligible account of "what I project to become." If, that is, the distinction between persons and machines is that we give a damn in a way that computers and cars cannot, *Galatea* exposes how few criteria we contemporaries have for responding to a further question, one that undermines some of the comfort we might feel from our initial distinction: What should we give a damn *about*?

One reason this question emerges in the text is that Helen's difficulty in applying words to the world—the loosening of semantics from syntax that I discussed earlier—is not presented as hers alone. Her difficulty is generalized into the condition of all human thought. When Rick first meets Audrey Lentz in the assisted-living home, her husband describes "intellect" as "this incredible capacity for lying to ourselves" (169), and it is this unsentimental vision of human thought that allows him to see consciousness as a "deception" (88), "just a glorified fudged-up Turing Machine" (71). Rick balks at Lentz's gruff characterization of the human mind, but the drift of his own narrative leads him to a position very similar. Near the end of the book, Rick decides to school Helen in what he calls a "liberal education" by allowing her to read newspapers and magazines as well as literary classics. "She needed to know how little literature had, in fact, to do with the real. She needed the books that books only imitated" (313). The daily reports are full of racism, violence, warfare, and other atrocities, and Rick is forced to confess to Helen that what underlies all the well-formed verbal and narrative shapes that she has been learning is a bewildering and brutal disorder:

> I told her we were in the same open boat. That after all this evolutionary time, we still woke up confused, knowing everything about our presence here except why. I admitted that the world was sick and random. That the evening news was right. That life was trade, addiction, rape, exploitation, racial hatred, ethnic cleansing, misogyny, land mines, hunger, industrial disaster, denial, disease, indifference. That care had to lie to itself, to carry on as if persistence mattered. (320–21)

Why newspapers and magazines, rather than literature, should expose Helen to the chaotic groundlessness of all human values is an open question.[31] But

---

[31] In his *New Republic* review (May 14, 2001) of *Plowing the Dark*, Powers's 2000 novel, Michael Ravitch raises this question about Rick's "liberal education" at the end of *Galatea*: "What is strange here is the presumption that 'leading weekly magazines' tell [Helen] more about humanity than all of Western literature . . . Is a newspaper story truly more tragic than *King Lear*? Isn't Euripides about

the critical point here is that these claims about confusion, care, lying, and mattering read like a direct rejoinder to Dreyfus, Haugeland, and Taylor. Like Rick, these thinkers repudiate naturalistic explanations, but unlike him, they retain a faith in the reality of human intentions and the intelligibility of human action. Earlier in the novel, when reading Helen parables, Rick has difficulty explaining the status of ethical claims. "It's all made up," he tells her, from which Helen disconcertingly infers, "Morals are false." Rick struggles for a further explanation: "It's not that they . . . Well. We make them true. The things people say and live by—it's all geographical. Historical" (177). Over the course of the novel, however, Rick becomes less equivocal, and his moral skepticism extends into a skepticism about human order generally. Narratives and other forms of human thought are increasingly described as a tissue of fictions that allow us, either as individuals or as cultures, to ignore the chaos encircling us. In light of what Rick calls the "senselessness of all stories," their "total, arbitrary construction" (293), crossing one's fingers becomes a "gesture that wishes share with the momentary exemption from lies" (322). In the final pages, Rick is reduced merely to "[t]alking to keep talking," "a lifeboat ethic that only made sinking worse" (321).

Implied by the end of *Galatea*, then, is a nominalistic lack of confidence in the ontological weight of our life narratives, an instrumentalist sense that the stories orienting our lives can never be more than useful mistakes. And insofar as this is the case, insofar as "what matters" is merely part of a "lifeboat ethic," a projection of desires onto a world of flux and disorder, we resemble Helen. Our sentences and stories may be only an empty syntactic sequence, not something that connects us to the world but something that alienates us from it, indeed falsifies it. As Powers depicts things, epistemological skepticism and moral skepticism are mutually reinforcing; one escalates easily into the other. The confusion of both C. and Rick dramatizes the ways in which our "concern" for the world can seem an estrangement from it, and our intentional states—our thoughts, memories, hopes—can seem, in Lentz's term, a "deception." What makes such epistemological skepticism compelling, in other words, is a sense that we largely lack the stable framework of meanings, contexts, and moral orientations that the West Coast philosophers take to be distinctive of a human

---

as 'sick and random' as you could possibly want?" (47). This is a particularly acute question when we consider that it is through fiction—reading Richard Wright and Ralph Ellison—that Helen first begins to infer that something about the world isn't quite right (313). *Galatea* implies here that the form and subject matter of literary stories is markedly different from the form and subject matter of stories that people tell about themselves and history. I'm doubtful that such a clear distinction exists, or that a computer of even Helen's impressive abilities could perceive it.

life. When our words and stories seem an "arbitrary construction," when our norms appear merely "geographical" and "historical," when "care" seems a matter of "lying" to oneself, then "significance" is hard to distinguish from mere projection. Our goods come to seem thin and insubstantial, merely useful tools, ideas and stories that allow us to cope with local threats and go on living, but incapable of telling us what we might be living *for*. What computers can't do, say their critics, is perceive and determine significances, hence perceive and determine who they are. *Galatea* suggests that, as long as our meanings seem a matter of making rather than finding, as long as—to recall Lentz—"all the meanings" seem to be merely "yours," then we will wonder whether we are any different.[32]

III. Percy on the West Coast, and Beyond

The relationship between the material and the intentional has been a staple theme of the tradition that Mark McGurl labels post-World War II "technomodernism," and *Galatea* likewise recalls Brian McHale's influential claim that science fiction is the underlying mode of "postmodern" fiction generally.[33] Thomas Pynchon's first novel, *V.* (1963), features automata that seem more alive than Benny Profane, one of the book's protagonists, and late in the book, a group of children disassemble the text's title character piece by piece—eyes and teeth and feet all removed, hinting at "some intricate understructure of silver openwork," "intestines of parti-colored silk." Within a few decades came novels such as William Gibson's *Neuromancer* (1984) and Neal Stephenson's *Snow*

---

[32] The instrumentalism that emerges over the course of *Galatea* is precisely what's underlined in its final pages. In the concluding scene, Lentz asks Rick where he is headed now that his stay at the Center is finished. "Search me," answers Rick. To which Lentz responds: "The maker's fate is to be a wanderer?" (328). This allusion to the Anglo-Saxon poem *The Wanderer* could be read as one more way that the novel emphasizes the fictionality of Rick's life narrative: His decision here at the end to be a kind of artist in exile is itself portrayed as the simulacrum of a life, an updated version of an ancient trope. As their conversation continues, the thought is reinforced with another literary allusion. "It seemed," writes Rick, "I might have another fiction in me after all" (328). "Marcel" is the nickname Lentz gives Rick at the start of the novel, and like Proust, Rick concludes here with the resolution to compose the fiction that we hold in our hands. As I've been suggesting, "fiction" here should be read on two levels. It refers to the product of a human's telling, a certain kind of text, but also to the convenient errors—the intentions, aims, orientations toward the good—that direct human beings more generally: the ends toward which we carry out any action whatsoever. What Rick is saying, is not only that he has a fiction "in" him, but that he, Rick, is himself a kind of fiction. He is the "maker," that is, both of his story as well as of himself, and neither one should be considered incontrovertibly real—a point reinforced when we consider that the subtitle of this book both by and about "Richard Powers" is "A Novel" rather than "A Memoir."

[33] See Mark McGurl, *The Program Era: Postwar Fiction and the Rise of Creative Writing* (Cambridge, MA: Harvard University Press, 2009); Brian McHale, *Postmodernist Fiction* (London: Routledge, 1987).

Crash (1992), in which human beings are understood as sophisticated computers, "nothing more," as N. Katherine Hayles says, "than information-processing mechanisms that run what programs are fed" to them. And the fascination with such a vision has not slowed in the twenty-first century. Consider, for instance, *Cosmopolis* (2003), Don DeLillo's story of a young billionaire currency trader who seeks to become "absorbed in streams of information" when he dies, his body made "redundant and transferrable," "convertible to wave arrays of information."[34]

These are not, to put it mildly, the traditions usually associated with Walker Percy. By and large Percy has been understood as a regional writer, a wry analyst of postwar Southern mores and socioeconomic shifts, or as a religious writer, someone who (like, say, Graham Greene or Muriel Spark) converted in midlife to Catholicism and never looked back. Neither of these contexts is mistaken—indeed, the second will be particularly important here—but they shouldn't overshadow his proximity to writers like Powers. An initial hint at this affinity comes in the name of *Galatea*'s computer. As I noted in passing at the start, "Helen" is clearly a reference to Helen Keller, the deafblind Alabaman who appears as a kind of leitmotif in Percy's two essay collections, *The Message in the Bottle* (1975) and *Signposts in a Strange Land* (1991), where she is said to illuminate the deep history of our lives as language-users. When Keller learned the meaning of "water," declares Percy, we witness nothing less than a breakthrough that "must bear some relation to the breakthrough of the species itself," and thinking about this episode can reveal "more about the *phenomenon* of language and about man himself than is contained in all the works of behaviorists, linguists, and German philosophers."[35] For Percy as much as Powers, in other words, understanding Helen means understanding *us*.

As we'll see, Percy's affinities with Powers also are felt in his fiction. But I want in this section first to linger over Percy's essays, which suggest a proximity to West Coast philosophy—the thinking that I've argued undergirds at least a good portion of *Galatea*—that is no less neglected than his resemblances to technomodernism. Three resemblances stand out.

First, Percy is, to recall Taylor's self-characterization, a "monomaniac" or "hedgehog," drawn over and over again to reflect—as his 1989 Jefferson Lecture shows—on modern naturalism. No doubt he's absorbed with this

---

34 Thomas Pynchon, *V.* (1963; New York: Vintage, 2012), 343; Hayles, *How We Became Posthuman*, 279; Don DeLillo, *Cosmopolis* (New York: Scribner's, 2003), 104, 48.

35 Walker Percy, *The Message in the Bottle: How Queer Man Is, How Queer Language Is, and What One Has to Do With the Other* (1975; New York: Picador, 2000), 38, 36; henceforth cited parenthetically as *MB*.

tradition because he was himself, as he once said, "brought up with a very unbalanced scientific education," and like the West Coasters, he clearly takes the empiricist–analytic tradition to be an index to the culture as a whole, a key to a world where, as he says, "science is triumphant."[36] The technicality of this tradition, its commitment to mathematical and logical precision, its lionizing of experts and expertise, its tendency toward reductive models and explanations—far from isolating this research in an ivory tower, as critics have often complained—make Anglo-American philosophy a particularly sophisticated expression of modern culture. The "technological transformations of the world" have been enormous in modernity, writes Percy in the late 1960s, but they pale next to the "psychological" transformations that have accompanied them. The "lay man" has absorbed "the magical aura of science, whose credentials he accepts for all sectors of reality," and this fascination splits our personalities in half, between an objective, detached "theorist" on one side and a "consumer-self" on the other, its list of "needs" demanding to be satisfied (*MB* 113). Such a split makes for incoherence: the theorist cannot account for his or her own actions (e.g., *The Origin of Species* contains no account of Darwin himself writing his book), and the consumer can never rest (the universe is far too large for anyone's consumption ever to end). The only way to come to terms with the dual objectivist/consumerist dispensation of the contemporary person, suggests Percy, is to unearth its roots, and to treat the Anglo-American intellectual tradition as something other than the physics-envy of a few rarified researchers.

Percy's second affinity with West Coast philosophy is that he, too, shows a deep familiarity both with behaviorism as well as with the cognitivist backlash against it. Saturated in behaviorism during his undergraduate years at the University of North Carolina Chapel Hill (*Conv.* 59), he always respected what he calls "the hardheaded empiricism of American behavioral scientists," even after Chomsky's review of *Verbal Behavior* made it difficult to brook "the application to language of the old stimulus-response theory, however refined and modified it might be" (*MB* 34). Much like Haugeland, however, Percy ultimately regards behaviorism and cognitivism as two sides of the same coin. Both of these models, he argues, abstract quixotically from "the people who speak the language and the things they talk about," and this detachment leaves them unable to account for—a key issue in *Galatea*, as we've seen—semantics. Behaviorists get stuck talking about phonemes, morphemes, and other low-level material

---

[36] *Conversations with Walker Percy*, ed. Lewis A. Lawson and Victor A. Kramer (Jackson: University of Mississippi Press, 1985), 135, 223; henceforth cited parenthetically as *Conv.*

features of utterances, whereas cognitivists gesture toward a mysterious internal "Language Acquisition Device" with an "interpretive semantic component" (*MB* 299–300). As one of Percy's commentators says, neither of these schools pays any attention to actual living *speakers*: Chomsky analyzes speech as if it took place only among gods, Skinner as if it took place only among dumb brutes, whereas Percy pictures us as both purposive *and* embedded, intentional *and* situated in an environment.[37] (I'll return to the issue of semantics and syntax in a moment.)

The third and most crucial affinity with Dreyfus et al. is that Percy arrives at these claims about language and cognition through a careful engagement with phenomenology. Thinkers such as Heidegger and Sartre offer what Percy calls— a term Taylor also uses about his own project (*HA* 1)—an "anthropology" of the sort that Anglo-American thought typically eschews, a "general theory of man" (*SSL* 123), a "study of man doing the uniquely human thing" (*MB* 11).[38] Phenomenology attends, that is, to certain "distinctively human realities," to matters of consciousness, intersubjectivity, moods, temporality, aesthetics, ethics, and other phenomena that are inadequately captured by the language of "data, induction, hypothesis, deduction," and so forth (*MB* 277–78). German and French thought of the first half of the twentieth century retains to some degree a vision of the human being as a soul or subject of experience, and thus has understood language to be more than a certain kind of "anatomical equipment" or "a structure of computerlike components" (*MB* 12, 16).

Percy augments this phenomenological education with one further philosophical influence that deserves mention, given that it looks forward to the pragmatist connections running through the other postwar sages I'll be discussing. This is Charles Sanders Peirce, whose work Percy discovered in the late 1940s through a friend, and who eventually appears as the hero of his Jefferson Lecture. Percy never specifies how exactly Peirce supplements phenomenology, but one reason is surely that the American provides a counterweight to phenomenology's alleged antiscience animus. Kierkegaard, Sartre, Heidegger, and the other continental figures who attract both Percy and the West Coast

---

[37] William H. Poteat, "Reflections on Walker Percy's Theory of Language," in *The Art of Walker Percy: Stratagems of Being*, ed. Panthea Reid Boughton (Baton Rouge: Louisiana State University Press, 1979), 199.

[38] In *The Age of the Crisis of Man: Thought and Fiction in America, 1933–1973* (Princeton, NJ: Princeton University Press, 2015), Mark Greif similarly uses the phrase "philosophical anthropology" to describe one of the central planks of midcentury debates over "man," and though he makes no mention of Percy, he does note that Saul Bellow and Ralph Ellison were particularly concerned to develop a comparatively comprehensive picture (148).

philosophers often are said to be hostile toward scientific culture; as Percy himself puts it, their talk of "inwardness" and "subjectivity" will seem "to the objective-minded man to confirm the worst of what he had thought all along" about them (*MB* 145). Peirce, by contrast, was the son of a Harvard mathematician and astronomer, studied chemistry, and worked as an engineer, in addition to writing on logic and mathematics in the innovative ways that earned laurels from the likes of Bertrand Russell. He thus not only, in ways that we'll see, helps tighten the language of phenomenology that Percy finds so intuitively congenial, but he also helps Percy avoid the charge that he's trying merely to change the topic, that his criticisms of science are less an answer to science than an evasion of it.[39]

With this amalgam of authorities—the phenomenological writings of Kierkegaard, Heidegger, and Sartre; the rationalist pragmatism of Peirce—Percy hopes to develop an account of semantics that, as he sees it, the empiricist-analytic tradition simply cannot provide. Cognitivism, in his view, simply brackets off the issue: Chomsky offers only "a formal description, an algorithm," of the rudimentary "competence" of speakers, awarding "the prime role to syntax" rather than to the "relations between people and signs and things" (*MB* 304–307). Behaviorists rightly probe these latter type of nonlexical interactions, but they reduce them to chains of measurable elements (sounds, marks) impacting bodies and organs (ears, eyes). Such a view, suggests Percy, imagines that words and sentences trigger reactions in listeners with the same necessity that suitably cold temperatures trigger the formation of ice in water. It makes communication into a sequence of *signals*: "a material happening among natural existents, from the sound of a buzzer to an electrocolloidal change in the dog's brain to a glandular secretion" (*MB* 253), a "series of space-time events" that direct our attention to something "because of changes in the brain brought about by past association" (*MB* 153). Genuine naming, by contrast, involves something unavailable to both the cognitivist and behaviorist, namely *symbols*, a "generically different" thing than anything else in the universe (*MB* 154). Helen Keller, as Percy notes, had long been able to respond appropriately to words like "cake": The moment it was spelled in her hand, she would search for cake. But something qualitatively different happened when she learned one day that the liquid flowing over her hand was called "water." She went from a "good

---

[39] The most comprehensive consideration of Percy's relation to Peirce is John F. Desmond's *Walker Percy's Search for Community* (Athens: University of Georgia Press, 2004). See also J. P. Telotte, "Charles Peirce and Walker Percy: From Semiotic to Narrative," in *Walker Percy: Art and Ethics*, ed. Jac Tharpe (Jackson: University Press of Mississippi, 1980), 65–79.

responding animal which behaviorists study so successfully to the strange name-giving and sentence-uttering creature" who goes from naming shoes and ships to telling jokes and writing the *Divine Comedy* (*MB* 35). She became what Percy, in a term of art, calls a "coupler": the interpreter who, standing apart from the universe, judges some object to *be* something rather than another thing, pairing a sound or mark with something in the world and affirming both the existence of that thing and the class to which it belongs, all in ways hitherto unimaginable. She became, as Percy says in a Heideggerian moment, "that being in the world whose calling it is to find a name for Being, to give testimony to it, and to provide for it a clearing" (*MB* 158).

As we'll see in Chapter 4, understanding the relation of syntax to semantics is an issue that grips Stanley Cavell as well. But the point for now is that Percy's vision of naming constitutes, in effect, a direct retort to the skeptical instrumentalism that we find at the end of *Galatea 2.2*. Indeed, it represents exactly the rebuttal to the novel that Dreyfus, Haugeland, and Taylor would themselves want to give. Helen the neural net may not be able to give testimony to Being or act as a Peircian interpreter, but we, *qua* human being, can and do so; and in downplaying this capacity, Powers in effect misunderstands the situation that his own novel describes. Indeed, Lentz's complaint that "all the meanings are yours," much like Rick's conclusion that our utterances are a "total, arbitrary construction," reproduces precisely the questionable arguments of the prominent Anglo-American theorists whom Percy's essays repeatedly target. To C. K. Ogden and I. A. Richards, for instance, we can talk of legitimate and verifiable connections between a speaker and water, and between a speaker and another speaker, but any connection between the stuff water and the *word* or *concept* "water" should be considered an "unreal imputed relation" (qtd. *MB* 37). In the same spirit, Stuart Chase would point out that one can't eat the word "oyster" (*MB* 155; *MB* 260), and the linguist Alfred Korzybski·liked to hold a pencil in the air and declare that, whatever else one wants to say about it, one cannot say that it *is* a pencil (*MB* 155, 169, 262). Percy is, by contrast, an explanatory pluralist, and appeals to our ordinary naming practices much as Dreyfus appeals to our everyday "skillful coping" or Taylor appeals to the know-how expressed in getting around my house or my city. To dismiss semantics is to abstract from the *phenomenon* of speech and from manifest features of human life and behavior that are as perceptible as anything with a more inarguably measurable existence. What happened for Helen Keller, he says, "was 'real' enough alright, no matter what Ogden and Richards said, as real as any S-R [stimulus-response] sequence, as real as H_2SO_4 reacting to NaOH," even if what occurred could not be drawn with any tidy arrows (*MB* 39). The semanticist finds it "scandalous" that we should talk of names referring to objects; this rubber sphere in my hand is emphatically *not* the word "ball." But the "real" relation that matters in language, says Percy, is not the relation between "word and organism, and organism and referent," all of which can be accounted for in terms of "stimulus, reinforcement, extinction, discrimination, and so on" (*MB* 164, 171). What's real is the bond between sign and object, a relationship that deserves conscientious examination and scientific respect—"scientific" in its root sense, he says, of discovering and knowing something "which can be demonstrated and verified within a community" (*SSL* 271–72).

In an early review of *The Message in the Bottle*, Walter Benn Michaels remarked that Percy's claims about reference were liable to seem outdated, not only to the Anglo-American linguists he was challenging, but also to the literary theorists who, when the book was published in the mid-1970s, were increasingly drawn to skeptical poststructuralist models. But the parallels to West Coast philosophy that I've drawn suggest that Percy was less of a cranky outlier than Michaels realizes. Moreover, as Michaels himself notes, a theory of reference is not really the point of Percy's essays. The hope of Percy's linguistic investigations is not to arrive at a theory of semantics per se, but to develop his "anthropology"—to understand the kind of being who could so much as *have* a semantics at all. And one of the central planks of this anthropology is what Michaels rightly calls a "social theory of meaning," an account in which, as Percy puts it, a "Namer" requires a "real or posited *someone else*," a "second person" who is part of the "*indispensable and enduring condition of all symbolic behavior*" (*MB* 167).[40] There's a reason, Percy would say, that *Galatea*'s Helen must be steered by Rick, just as the historical Helen Keller was instructed by Anne Sullivan. It's from a community that we garner our initial understanding of which things belong to which classes, and it is the community's task to *guide* the language learner into the shared norms of the group. If, says Percy, "there were only one person in the world, symbolization could not conceivably occur," "for my discovery of water as something derives from your telling me so, that this is water for you too" (*MB* 281). What is affirmed in naming, in other words, is as much the relationship *between us* as it is the relationship that we're jointly instituting between word and object. I say "That's an X" to you; you either agree with me or—if you're a parent, expert, or some other authority—correct me; and these agreements

---

[40] Walter Benn Michaels, review of *The Message in the Bottle*, *The Georgia Review* 29 (1975), 973. Other reviewers found Percy's book invigorating. Michaels's teacher Hugh Kenner wrote that Percy's arguments will seem to some readers like a Copernican-style "breakthrough," providing us "a picture with just the main essential correct," whatever the flaws of its details. See his "On Man the Sad Animal," *National Review* (September 12, 1975): 1000–1003.

and forms of guidance are what constitute the community to which we belong. Taylor, as we've seen, suggests that even the most neutral-seeming statement will be performing a speech act, and that such acts involve creating or displaying certain relationships more than merely representing certain things. Similarly, Percy argues that the Thou is "the companion and co-celebrant of my discovery of being," and the "mutuality" between us and the object named is "prime and irreducible" (*MB* 285, 283). Or, more emphatically: "*Symbolization is of its very essence an intersubjectivity*," presupposing "*a triad of existents: I, the object, you*" (*MB* 281). Such a triad comprises the most central features of the holistic context in which I am embedded and involved, and is every bit as "real" as the physical objects and entities—the subatomic particles, the gravitational forces, the chairs, the solar systems—surrounding me.

Percy's essays, then, offer an amendment to Lentz's rebuke of Rick: all the meanings *are* "yours," so long as the pronoun is taken as plural rather than singular. Indeed, it is from such a "you" that an "I" emerges; others teach me how to apply words not only to the world, but also to *myself*. And it's this emphasis on the first-person plural that marks Percy's commitment to what I was in my introduction referring to as "weak realism." When, for instance, Percy says that Helen Keller's naming of water was "'real' enough alright," or that "oyster" and oysters exhibit more than an "unreal imputed relation," or that "pencil" *does* pick out something "real" about pencils, he's not invoking Platonic or Aristotelian senses of "real." He's instead suggesting that the intelligibility we find in our words and in the world emerges in our shared practices and relationships, rather than in a special philosophical *eidos* or scientific discovery. "There is," he states in a long 1972 essay on Peircian semiotics, "no necessary relationship between a name and that which is named beyond the coupling of name and thing by namer" (*MB* 168). A namer's "cognitive joy" (*MB* 206) in coupling, that is, does not derive from her grasping an otherworldly Form, nor does the relation of word and object exist independent of the learner's associating certain sounds with certain objects. Nor will it survive unless the learner pledges herself to those associations in future cases: "assuming responsibility" for her acts of naming as one might do when—as Peirce says in a famous figure that Percy adopts—going before a notary (*MB* 168). Our capacity to jointly assume such responsibility is what holds a community together, and preserves those things about which we collectively, in Haugeland's phrase, give a damn.

Community, collectivity, shared practices, giving a damn—these phrases suggest one final point of contact that I want to observe between Percy and West Coast thought. As I've suggested, such terms are part and parcel of an emphasis on context and joint responsibility, and the intersubjectivity at work in such a view clearly entails a recurrent interest in the inextricably social, cultural, moral, and political dimensions of thought. Percy, however, brings the discussion a step further—a step discernible in a phrase like "co-celebrants." "Co-celebrants" is not, to say the least, a phrase with widespread use in contemporary philosophy of language. But Percy's rationale for using it emerges in a confession he once made in a letter to Kenneth Laine Ketner, a Peirce scholar who had written to him about their shared enthusiasms. Truth be told, Percy explained, he was not a "student of Peirce"; in fact, he was just a "thief of Peirce," and usually he was willing to "take from him what I want and let the rest go, most of it." And what he wanted above all, he continued, was to use Peirce "as one of the pillars of a Christian apologetic," a way of getting his audience "open to 'news', of the singular (scandalous) event, the Jewish covenant, the Christian incarnation and news of same."[41] Learning "water" or "oyster" or "pencil" is all well and good, but these are hardly the sorts of words that compel our most urgent commitments. Our highest words, for Percy, are those that conclude his Jefferson Lecture, the language that describes us as "falling prey to the worldliness of the world," and "man as pilgrim seeking his salvation" (*SSL* 290–91). Words like "baptism," "sin," "God," and "redemption," says Percy, "have become as worn as poker chips" (*Conv.* 140), and when such terms lose their force, we descend into incoherence, transformed into the "theorist-consumers" that modern nominalism nurtures. Without such terms, too, our experiences of "alienation" get misleadingly diagnosed, portrayed as a psychological problem of "maladaptation," or the result of capitalism, or of modern technology. These are all "exacerbating forces" (*MB* 23) and destroy the human communities and intersubjectivities that sustain our words. But only the "very cogent anthropology" of Christianity, Percy claims, can account for the sense that we are open not only to "despair" but also to "news from across the seas" about "a unique Person-Event-Thing" (*MB* 140–43).

Far from distinguishing Percy from Dreyfus, Haugeland, and Taylor, such language makes explicit the tendencies that they themselves tend to leave underemphasized in their work. West Coast philosophy has often taken an interest in social and political themes: think, for instance, of Dreyfus's writings on Foucault, or Taylor's work on Hegel, multiculturalism, and "modern

---

[41] Patrick H. Samway, S.J., ed., *A Thief of Peirce: The Letters of Kenneth Laine Ketner and Walker Percy* (Jackson: University Press of Mississippi, 1995), 130–31. Percy isn't alone in associating Peirce with certain strands of medieval philosophy; on this topic, see John Boler, "Peirce and Medieval Thought," in *The Cambridge Companion to Charles Sanders Peirce*, ed. Cheryl Misak (Cambridge: Cambridge University Press, 2004), 58–86.

social imaginaries."[42] But Percy's avowedly religious orientation clarifies the theistic strains to which these social and political themes can tend. Not for nothing does Lentz dismiss West Coast philosophy as a mere matter of faith, "Zen bullshit." Religious themes are most clearly visible in Taylor, a practicing Catholic who concludes his magisterial *Sources of the Self* with a disclosure that recalls Percy's Jefferson Lecture: that his emphasis on the "significance feature" of human existence involves, as he says, "a large element of hope," one "implicit in Judeo-Christian theism. . .and in its central promise of a divine affirmation of the human, more total than humans can ever attain unaided" (*SS* 521). But a theistic resonance is likewise felt in Dreyfus, whose 2011 book *All Things Shining* defends the "whooshing" and "sacred moods" that one might achieve during an engaged "involvement" with the world—an experience that may come from watching sports, making coffee, or doing carpentry, and that in Dreyfus's eyes entails something like a revival of the Greek heroes and immortals.[43] To be sure, Percy's religious commitments are the most categorical and doctrinal of the group. Dreyfus's appeal to the Greek gods is inherently pluralistic; what matters to him, it seems, is as much the ability to commit oneself to a practice as the content of that practice.[44] And when Taylor talks about "significance features," his examples are ecumenical: the shared understandings that regulated medieval and Renaissance carnivals ("Foundationalism" 125–33), for example, or the way children are trained to stand respectfully and bow at appropriate moments ("Foundationalism" 121). But for these figures as much as Percy, religious practice crystallizes the sort of holistic frameworks and normative realism that are constitutive of a human life. Highlighting them is thus a way of articulating not only the breadth of the "contexts" that most deeply shape us, but also how fragile our shared meanings and normative aspirations can be. Far more than "pen," the concept "god" could be embodied by any number of situations and scenarios, as the history of religious and cultural practices shows. So our ability to use it and related terms—"redemption," "grace"—depends with

---

[42] See Hubert Dreyfus and Paul Rabinow, *Michel Foucault: Beyond Structuralism and Hermeneutics* (Chicago: University of Chicago Press, 1982); Charles Taylor, *Hegel* (Cambridge: Cambridge University Press, 1977); Charles Taylor, *Multiculturalism: Examining the Politics of Recognition* (Princeton, NJ: Princeton University Press, 1994); Charles Taylor, *Modern Social Imaginaries* (Durham, NC: Duke University Press, 2003).

[43] Dreyfus and Sean Dorrence Kelly, *All Things Shining: Reading the Western Classics to Find Meaning in a Secular Age* (New York: Simon and Schuster, 2011).

[44] Dreyfus and Kelly's account of "whooshing" and "sacred moods" has generated severe criticism, most prominently by Gary Wills in his review-essay "Superficial & Sublime?" *New York Review of Books* (April 7, 2011) <http://www.nybooks.com/articles/archives/2011/apr/07/superficial-sublime/> (accessed September 3, 2015).

particular sharpness on the depth of our "mutuality," on an I and a Thou acting fluently as "co-celebrants." The sheer fragility of these words is a testament to their supreme importance. They provide what's patently absent in *Galatea*: a "why" that makes our norms more than an instrumentalist "lifeboat ethic," and that makes "the things people say and live by" something other than useful fictions. Only when "god" can be used intelligibly, only when the I and the Thou tacitly agree to hold such expressions in place, can we confidently know the *point* of discussing more local phenomena in the first place. Only when we understand the most encompassing forms of holism, only when we grasp the most global of "contexts," does our talking of pencils and oysters come to have *genuine* sense.

IV. Quasi-Prophecy

The essays I've been tapping here range across Percy's career, from the mid-1950s through the late 1980s. But in the late 1960s, just as Dreyfus was beginning his phenomenological critique of machine intelligence in a scholarly format, Percy grew increasingly convinced that extreme measures were needed, and he began seeking less expository forms to make his point. The urgency is most clearly articulated in "Notes for a Novel About the End of the World," an essay he published in the Winter 1967–68 issue of the journal *Katallagete*. The "end of the world" of the title, says Percy, alludes to the immanent sense of violence and physical danger that hovers over human life in the nuclear age. But it also refers to "a different kind of danger," one that can't be "laid to particular evils such as racism, Vietnam, inflation" (*MB* 102): the "profound disquiet" with modern life that is explored in modern novels, the sense that—no matter how many material goods and pleasures our contemporary world has developed— *Something is wrong here; I don't feel good.* Whereas liberal "Death-of-God theologians" (Harvey Cox gets singled out) ask us to "embrace the exurb and the computer," the contemporary novelist is as preoccupied with catastrophe as the orthodox theologian with sin and death (*MB* 110). In the face of this "end of the world," the novelist is prevailed upon to "perform a quasi-prophetic function," to "shock and therefore warn his readers by speaking of last things—if not the Last Days of the Gospels, then of a possible coming destruction, of a laying waste of cities, of vineyards reverting to the wilderness" (*MB* 104). When the inhabitants of a land are near-blind, he claims (citing Flannery O'Connor), then "you have to draw large, simple caricatures." Only by such means can the novelist preserve the thick layers of context that give sense to our lives, can "make vicarious use of catastrophe in order that he and his reader may come to themselves" (*MB* 118).

Love in the Ruins—the novel Percy was writing alongside "Notes for a Novel," and published in 1971—is not only Percy's main link to the "technomodernism" that I mentioned earlier, but also his clearest bid to play a "quasi-prophetic function." After the success of his first two published books (*The Moviegoer*, which won the National Book Award for 1961, and *The Last Gentleman*, which was a finalist for the same prize for 1966), Percy conceived of this third novel as the "Big One," an ambitious, satirical, science-fiction work in the vein of *Brave New World*; and from the start, readers recognized it as departure.[45] Part moral allegory, part vaudeville act, the sprawling novel is narrated "somewhere around 1983" (*SSL* 247) by Dr. Tom More, a forty-four-year-old lapsed Louisiana Catholic whose life has collapsed since his daughter Samantha died of neuroblastoma five years earlier. Since her death, More has been abandoned by his wife, become an alcoholic, juggled various erotic affairs, stayed for several months in a mental institution, and lost most of his professional reputation. All of these things make him acutely aware of the gulfs separating him from his sixteenth-century namesake: "Why can't I follow More's example, love myself less, God and my fellowman more, and leave whisky and women alone?"[46] Sociopolitical turmoil both parallels and compounds More's malaise. The United States has moved into the fifteenth year of a war with Ecuador; race fights against race, city against city; and electoral politics has fractured between the Knotheads and the Lefts (descendants of the Republican and Democratic parties, respectively). At the start of the novel, the country is said to be on the brink of "catastrophe," falling into chaos, possibly (speculates More) as God's retribution for centuries of slavery. "The U. S. A. didn't work!" he announces in the opening chapter. "Is it possible that from the beginning it never did work? that the thing always had a flaw in it, a place where it would shear, and that all this time we were not really different from Ecuador or Bosnia-Herzegovina, just richer" (56–57).

That all this threatens our trust in normative concepts is made clear by the recurring image in the novel of a Rotary Club banner that hangs in the dining room of the motel where More is camping out. The banner is "rent, top to

---

[45] On Percy's initial conception of the novel, see Patrick H. Samway, S.J., *Walker Percy: A Life* (Chicago: Loyola, 1997), 251. On the response to the novel, see Samway, *Walker Percy*, 292–94; and Jay Tolson, *Pilgrim in the Ruins: A Life of Walker Percy* (New York: Simon and Schuster, 1992), 357–60.

[46] Walker Percy, *Love in the Ruins* (New York: Farrar Straus, 1971), 23; henceforth cited parenthetically by page number.

bottom, like the temple veil," and its questions draw attention to a now bygone language of knowledge, justice, and community:

Is it the truth?

Is it fair to all concerned?

Will it build goodwill and friendship? (9)

This vocabulary has been threatened, however, not only by the chaos of the sociopolitical landscape, but also—and here is where the parallels between *Love in the Ruins* and *Galatea* come into view—by the new sciences of the mind, and their attendant technologies. One type of technology is the "Skinner Box," enclosed units in which elderly people are "positively conditioned" by electrodes on their heads to allow them to return to society, much as Skinner's real-life "Operant Conditioning Chambers" used food dispensers and levers to shape the behavior of rodents and pigeons (121). But behaviorism was, as I've noted, losing its grip among researchers around the time *Love in the Ruins* was published, and as if to dramatize this theoretical shift, the novel spends far more time foregrounding another machine, an invention of More's that, as cognitivism had come to encourage, examines the internal constitution of the human mind. More christens it the "Qualitative Quantitative Ontological Lapsometer," and he presents it as the solution to the catastrophes crowding around him. The Lapsometer, he says in the opening pages, will redeem his increasingly directionless life and prevent the collapse of what he calls "the Christ-forgetting Christ-haunted death-dealing Western world" (3). It will do so not by solving hunger or adding to our material achievements, but by diagnosing the spiritual ills that, in his eyes, plague modernity. "These are bad times," announces More, with sicknesses that are "psychic rather than physical"; modernity has inflamed "the secret ills of the spirit" and rived "the very self from itself" (5). One particularly pressing symptom, as More sees it, is what he calls—echoing Pascal—"angelism" and "bestialism": the tendency for modern people to live either purely as mind, abstracting themselves from their condition, falling into self-consciousness, disengaging from social existence, or purely as body, embracing an entirely material existence and treating themselves merely as the loci of creaturely appetites. (Recall the "theorist-consumer," the two-pronged identity attacked in Percy's essays.) As "the first caliper of the soul" (107), "the stethoscope of the spirit" (62), the Lapsometer will provide "the very means of inoculating persons" against such extremes (5), and will "diagnose the maladies that poison the wellsprings of man's hope" (7).

The idea for the machine is double-sided. It originated, says More, in his one moment of scientific glory up to that point, a discovery he had made twenty years earlier when, following a chemical accident at Tulane University, he uncovered a direct link between Heavy Sodium or Chloride levels in people's bloodstream and sudden behavioral changes in the local populations. The Lapsometer builds on this early correlation, but now, instead of examining a patient's bloodstream, More examines the brain waves of patients to assess their attitudinal and behavioral dispositions. Using a prototype of the device (specially constructed for him by Osaka Instruments in Japan), More waves a hair-dryer-shaped receiver over the head of a patient and measures the electrical activity of "a pinhead-sized area anywhere in the brain: in the cortex, the pineal body, the midbrain—wherever" (29). The whole procedure takes about three minutes, and the results are registered on a decimal scale. So, for instance, the "deep pineal" area of Charlie Parker, the local golf pro, is measured at a phenomenally low 0.1 micromillivolts (mmv) at one point (38) but a robust 6 mmv a few weeks later (45); the Brodmann 32 area of a graduate student registers at 7.6 mmv (34); the hypothalamus of Dusty Rhodes, a local proctologist, clocks in at 7.9 mmv (86); and so forth, through all the various characters More tests (which include most people he meets). All these examinations and calculations demonstrate what More presents to us at one point as the motto of the empirical mind: "Observe, measure, verify: here's the business of the scientist" (190).

At the same time, however, Percy's narrator is, as he says, "after bigger game" than mere electrical activity, or even a set of broadly characterized dispositions. As one skeptic in the novel puts it, noting More's name for the machine, the Lapsometer is designed to "measure the uh depth of the fall" (205). Or, as a more enthusiastic patient puts it, More wants to "register the knotheadedness of the Knotheads, the nutty objectivity of the scientists, and the mad spasms of the liberals" (52). Thus when he measures the activity of the golf pro's deep pineal region, he takes himself to be computing what he calls the "site of inner selfhood" (38). The graduate student's Brodmann 32 area indicates not only 7.6 mmv of electrical activity, but also the fact that he has, in More's words, "so abstracted himself from himself and from the world around him . . . that he cannot, so to speak, enter the lovely ordinary world" (34). A young woman has an unusually high reading on her temporal lobe, which normally indicates "singular concrete historical awareness, vivid childhood memories," but she exhibits even more activity in her parietal lobe, "the site of ahistoric perceptions that are both concrete and abstract" (54). Dusty Rhodes's 7.9 hypothalamus reading is taken to indicate a "powerful, frequently satisfied, but indiscriminate sexual appetite," which reveals that he's having an illicit affair with one of his secretaries (86–87). And the pineal region of Colley Wilkes, the chief encephalographer at the hospital where More stays, elicits "good readings at layer I, little or nothing at layer II"—classic symptoms, says More, of "a self successfully playing at being a self that is not itself" (112).

The Lapsometer, then, plays the same role that Helen the neural net would play twenty-five years later in *Galatea 2.2*: It is an interpreting machine, designed to appraise physical matter in semantic terms. The Lapsometer may not be a modern computer, nor is the input processed by each machine—marks or sounds in the case of Helen, brain waves in the case of the Lapsometer—identical. But in both cases, the machine is built to translate material, quantifiable phenomena into an intentional idiom: the sense of words and sentences, the meaning of stories, the personalities of individuals, the moral conditions of souls. Using what a character in *Love in the Ruins* calls "a technique that maximizes and unites hardware and software capacities" (167), they each attempt to correlate two distinct models: the close-up views of the brain scientist or computer scientist, researchers who focus on an object's internal parts and their relations; and the broadly holistic, intentionalist views of everyday psychology and religion, where we talk about expression, intention, habits, selves, egos, and souls. In the close-up view, what matters are uncontroversially identifiable and even measurable properties: letters, sentences, brain waves, neural connections, electrical currents. In the holistic view, the stance used for understanding books and people, what matters are things like significant statements, suggestive hints, upbeat moods, or melancholic demeanors. The job of both the Lapsometer and of Helen the neural net is to correlate these two levels of description: this or that configuration of marks, sounds, or brain waves expresses this or that mood, style, condition, or—to recall John Haugeland's term—"spiritual nature." Thus psychology and morality can be brought into the scientific domain in ways that thinkers have long dreamed of doing.

Given Percy's claims about language and meaning, given his turn to Heidegger and Peirce and Catholicism, all this certainly sounds dubious. To use the terminology of his own essays, the Lapsometer confuses *signals* for *symbols*: it is constructed to record and measure moral and spiritual qualities, yet the brain waves and neural impulses it registers are wholly divorced from the various layers of context that Percy himself claims are required for interpretation. Thus, for instance, the temporal lobe of the young woman allegedly indicates "singular concrete historical awareness" *even before* More has learned the first thing about her personal, cultural, or religious background; her mental and spiritual states, that is, are imagined to be wholly independent of any behavioral, historical, or other public manifestations. The sheer tenuousness of such an enterprise leaves More himself "feeling a bit like a phrenologist" while using the Lapsometer (32), and indeed, the novel includes a number of intelligent scientists who raise thoughtful doubts about his invention. Dusty Rhodes, for instance, wonders whether correlating "wave patterns" with emotions isn't simply "subjective," and whether there isn't "a lot of room for interpretation" in drawing the body–spirit correlations More wants to draw (84). Similarly, Colley Wilkes is happy to use the machine to locate "brain tumors and such" (29), but finds More's talk of souls and spirits to be altogether "too metaphysical": "I'll stick to old-fashioned tumors and hemorrhages" (108).[47] ("Old-fashioned" is, of course, ironic; nothing is more old-fashioned than the sorts of entities—souls, spirits—that interest More.) From their perspective, the human brain—with its three pounds of dumb gray matter and trillions of firing neurons—has no obvious location for states such as "sees himself as a shadow" or "has concrete historical awareness," and there is no reason to think that even the most sensitive, exacting machine could decipher "angelism" or "bestialism." This is why these mental and moral states often look to skeptics suspiciously pre- or nonscientific, with something inexact and rough around the edges—extensions of mere "folk psychology." Like Lentz confronting Rick, the scientists in *Love in the Ruins* repeatedly confront More with the possibility that "all the meanings are yours," and nowhere is their challenge outright discredited.

The machine also suffers from guilt by association. For the character who makes the most use of the Lapsometer is not Tom More, but a comically satanic figure named Art Immelman. Immelman introduces himself to More in the middle of the novel as a coordinator between private and public funding agencies, tempting More with abundant financial support. But over the course of the novel, he grows into a deceptive Mephistophelian character, mysteriously appearing out of the blue (often accompanied by the smell of brimstone). Exploiting More's susceptibility to pride, his promises of the Nobel Prize send "a pleasant tingling sensation" down the backs of More's thighs (320), and his visions of the future focus exclusively on the sort of bourgeois well-being that Percy's writing everywhere ironizes: feeling good rather than bad, advancing science and loving women, developing one's own potential to its fullest, playing golf in knickerbockers, going bird watching.[48] Immelman claims that the

---

[47] Perhaps the most intelligent of these doctors is Max Gottlieb, who shares a name with the exemplary disinterested scientist in Sinclair Lewis's *Arrowsmith* (1925). On the connection to Lewis's text, see Lewis Lawson, *Following Percy: Essays on Walker Percy's Work* (Troy, NY: Whitsun, 1988), 165–77; and Mary G. Land, "Three Max Gottliebs: Lewis's, Dreiser's, and Walker Percy's View of the Mechanist-Vitalist Controversy," *Studies in the Novel* 15 (1983): 314–31.

[48] That More is most keenly interested in worldly glory is suggested when he compares his feeling of "Victory" at winning the Nobel Prize to Einstein's glee when one of his major theoretical claims about light was empirically confirmed. Einstein's presumed euphoria was at having achieved genuine knowledge, whereas More's anticipated delight is at earning (mere) worldly laurels and

Lapsometer will not only diagnose people's spiritual ills, but also cure them outright—and indeed, with just a slight adjustment to the device, he winds up trying just that, waving the machine over randomly chosen victims, causing massive psychological changes, and worsening the social chaos that More had hoped the Lapsometer would prevent. Far from moderating the excesses of people's disorders, the Lapsometer ignites a wildfire of sexual abandon among Immelman's victims, generating what one frightened character likens to "the St. Vitus's dance in the Middle Ages" (241).[49]

These sorts of failures lead Tom More in *The Thanatos Syndrome*, the 1987 sequel to *Love in the Ruins*, to say that his ambitions earlier in life were "grandiose, even Faustian," and that the idea of "striking pacts with the Devil to save the world" was "nuts."[50] What most undermines the legitimacy of the Lapsometer, however, is the narrative structure of *Love in the Ruins* as a whole. More expresses his highest hopes for the machine in the opening pages of the text, when he assures his fellow Americans that he will redeem them: "I can save the terrible God-blessed Americans from themselves! With my invention! Listen to me" (58). Immediately after saying this, however, More notes that he is very sleepy, and decides to take "one little catnap" (58)—which implies that the bulk of the story we subsequently read is, in fact, a dream. When More awakes toward the end of the novel, having imagined the story we've just read, things seem to have changed dramatically. He now realizes that his dissolute life of the previous five years has been a failed response to the death of his daughter, and that he has treated her death as a justification for selfishness. He has taken, he says, "a secret satisfaction" in her death, indulged a "delectation of tragedy, a license for drink, a taste of both for taste's sake," all evidence that at some level he was "not above enjoying" her suffering (374). Recalling a conversation with his daughter Samantha near the end of her life, he realizes that

---

recognition. Most of my summaries of the shallow, pleasure-seeking life here are provided by Immelman himself; see especially *Love in the Ruins* 208–18, 363–64. But the last two—playing golf in knickerbockers and going bird watching—are, in fact, activities undertaken in the novel by the African-American population when oil is discovered under their neighborhood and they become newly wealthy, adopting the mores of the oppressors.

[49] Immelman's Mephistophelian nature becomes clear at the end when More prays to Sir Thomas More to "*drive this son of a bitch hence*" and Immelman immediately "disappears into the smoke" (376–77). The sexual abandon that ensues after Immelman starts using the Lapsometer clearly is meant as a parody of the sexual revolution of the 1960s, a social change that Percy treated skeptically throughout his fiction and nonfiction. Indeed, in many respects *Love in the Ruins* deserves a place next to Saul Bellow's *Mr. Sammler's Planet* (1970) among the most mordant novels published in the immediate wake of the sixties, and it's no accident that, according to biographer Jay Tolson, Percy admired Bellow's book enormously. See Tolson, *Pilgrim in the Ruins,* 360.

[50] Percy, *The Thanatos Syndrome* (New York: Farrar Straus, 1987), 67.

he's committed "the one sin for which there is no forgiveness"—the "sin against grace," refusing to accept the mercy that God grants (373-74).

In short, *Love in the Ruins* seems in many ways precisely the novel one would expect from Percy the essayist, the thinker whose anthropology foregrounds a social theory of meaning, and who makes the second person my companion and co-celebrant of my discovery of being. It seems to fulfill Percy's call for a "quasi-prophetic" novel, mocking its narrator for his quixotic mix of dissipation and overreaching, just as it lampoons the follies permeating the culture at large. Its Swiftian satire—Percy professed his admiration for Swift's "gallows humor" not long after the book was published (*Conv.* 79)—works to expose the confusion of names and naming that pervades post-WWII culture, its substitution of expert terminologies and scientific measurements for genuinely norm-sustaining communities. Whereas *Galatea* implies the "senselessness of all stories," and suggests that even one's life story might be a "total, arbitrary construction," *Love in the Ruins* seems to point us toward the triadic relations that Percy's essays identify with naming, symbolization, and genuine Christian faith. And in reaching for this "quasi-prophetic" mode, *Love in the Ruins* seems indeed, as readers sensed, to be a departure from Percy's earlier fiction. The models behind *The Moviegoer* were two taut landmarks of late European modernism: Albert Camus's *L'étranger*, which captured Percy for the "the sparseness, the laconic brevity, and precision" of its sentences; and Sartre's *La nausée*, which taught him the value and import of a nonlinear narrative.[51] *Love in the Ruins* is by contrast ramblingly, comically dystopian, indulging in what Percy himself called a "flip-savage satirical" mode.[52] This change of direction in *Love in the Ruins*—this turn to what one reader has called an "increasing directness and insistence" in Percy's work—has been a topic of continued critical debate. Lewis Lawson, for instance, has praised the novel's effort to "go beyond realism, to use burlesque, pastiche, the absurd" in order to stretch our "range of vision" and challenge modernity's self-satisfactions. But other readers have bemoaned what they see as the "sentimentalist" lurking in the novel's "hurricane of laughter," accused Percy of selling out with easy didactic laughs, and lamented that the book "lacks the dialogic tension of Percy's earlier work."[53] Perhaps the sourest

---

[51] On his admiration for the books of Sartre and Camus, see Tolson, *Pilgrim*, 237–39. Defending *The Moviegoer* to his editor, Stanley Kaufman, Percy wrote of Sartre's book: "*Passage to India* is a much better constructed novel than *Nausea*, but *Nausea* would be wrecked by a revision" that tried to change its temporal shifts and interruptions (qtd. in Tolson, *Pilgrim*, 286).

[52] On Percy's "flip-savage" mode, see Tolson, *Pilgrim*, 260.

[53] "Increasing directness and insistence" is Desmond's phrase in *Walker Percy's Search for Community*, 3. "Sentimentalist" and "hurricane of laughter" are from V. S. Pritchett's review of the novel, quoted in Tolson, *Pilgrim*, 358. The accusation of selling out comes from Thomas LeClair, "Walker Percy's

assessment has come from Harold Bloom, who decrees *The Moviegoer* a "permanent American book," but derides Percy's later work as a "waste" of "authentic talents," "a lamentable instance of art yielding to moralism, of storytelling subverted by religious dogmas."[54]

Yet for all the shifts that Percy's third novel manifests, for all the intensification of Percy's satire, for all his occasional lack of subtlety, it's far from clear that the novel is as unequivocally prophetic as these opinions—both pro and con—suggest. Indeed, Percy himself understood his fiction quite differently, and his own self-descriptions force us to pause and ask whether *Love in the Ruins* actually represents a swerve into simple creeds and screeds. "Most of my novels," he observed in a 1980 interview, "end up more or less inconclusively," "with the hero not having his problems resolved and being in a situation not greatly different from the beginning." In his narrative works, that is, he strove to resist "a victory of eros over thanatos and life over death"—comforting endings in which characters at last achieve love, meaningful work, and a sense of identity (*Conv.* 190). "If you write a novel," he says elsewhere, contrasting his own stance with the moralism of John Gardner, "with the goal of trying to make somebody do something, you're writing a tract," merely "using literature to influence what people do" (*SSL* 380). Percy the essayist, that is, may offer a full-throated assault on machine intelligence, and may explain why the symbols instituted within a particular historical community cannot be conceived in terms of the signals used by animal bodies and machines. But Percy the storyteller, Percy the novelist, is giving us something more multidimensional. His fiction doesn't contradict his own nonfiction exactly, but it complicates it in the provocative ways that are typical—as we'll see—of the postwar sage.

For one thing, much as *Galatea*'s Helen manages to make sense of at least *some* literary texts, the Lapsometer's ways of "measuring the length and breadth of the very self" (106–7) are for a good portion of *Love in the Ruins* granted at least *some* degree of legitimacy. Dusty Rhodes, for one, does indeed seem to betray guilt about his secret affairs, and the graduate student is "abstracted" enough to have grown physically estranged from his wife. More's most striking diagnosis comes in the case of Mr. Ives, a retiree who has silently refused to participate in shuffleboard and other activities at the Golden Years Senior Settlement in Tampa. From the behaviorist point of view, expressed by one of More's hospital colleagues, Mr. Ives clearly has suffered a stroke and suffers from "senile

---

Devil," in *The Art of Walker Percy*, ed. Broughton, 157–68; the question about the novel's insufficient "dialogical" character is from Michael Kobre, *Walker Percy's Voices* (Athens: University of Georgia Press, 2000), 115.

[54] Harold Bloom, ed., *Modern Critical Views: Walker Percy* (New York: Chelsea House, 1986), 3.

psychopathy and mutism" (159), making him a prime candidate for the Happy Isles Permanent Separation Center—a euthanasia clinic. The Lapsometer, however, allows More to examine Mr. Ives's "medio-temporal region, near Brodmann 28," and to conclude that the man's "pineal selfhood" is perfectly intact and that his true problem is simply that he's "too damn mad to talk," "unable to trust you or me or anybody" (160). In an uproarious public debate with the behaviorist, More gets Mr. Ives to break out of his mutism and discuss his earlier life as a linguist, in particular his experiences deciphering a row of glyphs that belonged to a proto-Creek culture and hitherto never interpreted.[55]

Not only does the Lapsometer work quite well for much of the novel, but the text ends on precisely the "more or less inconclusive" notes that Percy identifies in his fiction generally. The conclusion of the book is a twenty-five-page epilogue titled "Five Years Later," thus long after the time when More may have been asleep and dreaming the main events of the story. Here we learn that More has returned to the Catholic rites and married his former secretary Ellen, and in the final pages, he prepares a Christmas meal for his family—all of which suggest that his epiphanies in the main narrative—about Immelmann, about his own "sin against grace"—have stuck with him.[56] But the tranquility of these pages is uneasy, fragile. The epilogue of *The Moviegoer* shifts forward a year after the main events of the plot, but in *Love in the Ruins*, the concluding leap comes even more abruptly and sends the reader even farther afield, coming without warning, and making no clearer than in the first novel what precisely has changed in the intervening time. The sociopolitical world is certainly not much altered: the apocalypse that Tom More feared throughout the text never has come to pass, the bourgeois–capitalist order has been safely restored (though now, unlike before, African-Americans are the wealthy ones playing golf, after oil was discovered under their neighborhood), and there is no sign that the normative concepts invoked by the Rotary Club banner—truth, justice, community—have found new embodiment. Nor, more strikingly, has very much decisively changed for Tom More himself. He claims, for instance, to have conquered his alcoholism, and to have not had a drink for six months; but the novel ends with him suddenly glugging down six drinks in six minutes. He goes to confession, but admits to his priest that he lacks the "firm purpose of amendment" to stop sinning, caught as always, he says, in the "spirit of the musical-erotic" (397–98).

---

[55] Desmond takes this scene with Mr. Ives to be central to the novel; see *Walker Percy's Search*, 135–36.

[56] Moreover, as Joseph Bizup points out in "Hopkins' Influence on Percy's *Love in the Ruins*" (*Renascence* 46 (1994), 250), the Lapsometer was invented on Christmas Eve, suggesting that the machine will replace the good news of Christ's arrival, but the final section of the novel takes place on Christmas Day, drawing our attention to the true nature of the good news.

Most importantly, More seems not to have learned all the lessons that Percy's own essays would want to provide about the Lapsometer. He still sees the world as "broken, sundered, busted down the middle" (382–83), and he still worries about "angelism, bestialism, and other perturbations of the soul" (390). Yet he still confidently claims that such conditions will be cured by the treatment of internal mechanisms, of "motor and sensory areas." He still believes, that is, that the Lapsometer is what will ultimately "save the world" (384) and "cure the new plague, the modern Black Death": the chronic split that "rives soul from body and sets it orbiting the great world as the spirit of abstraction whence it takes the form of beasts, swans and bulls, werewolves, blood-suckers, Mr. Hyde, or just poor lonesome ghost locked in its own machinery" (383). Indeed, however exposed the machine's limitations may have been in the first three hundred and fifty satirical pages, More still insists on using it with patients, who seem to have all the same maladies that they always have had. When at the end his priest gives More a sackcloth to wear (the Church has, according to the novel, brought back this medieval practice), he notes that Ellen gently mocks her husband and expresses doubts about the Catholic emphasis on "things, articles" (400). What he doesn't note is that Ellen—not only one of the few stable, mature, and dependable figures throughout the novel, but also a humanist with no apparent need for God to justify her selfless actions—may stand in for many of Percy's readers, enjoying More's antics without fully trusting or understanding him, even here in the final pages.

Love in the Ruins, in other words, may have more in common with *Galatea 2.2* than it seems at first blush, and Tom More may wind up at the end of the novel in precisely the position that Lentz attributes to Rick: "The maker's fate is to be a wanderer." Hostile critics of Percy's novel aren't wholly off-target: One can reasonably wonder whether this and his other later novels sometimes slip "into a nuanceless, slapdash tempo," and it's true that these books lack compelling female characters such as those of *The Moviegoer*.[57] But the complaint that his fiction is pedantic, moralizing, nondialogic, or crammed with religious dogma is overstated, and confuses the novel with Percy's essays. However heavy its satire, *Love in the Ruins* remains an instance of what Wayne Booth identified as "unstable" rather than "stable" irony—a drama of competing voices and centrifugal forces, all leaving us, to recall Percy's own self-description, in "a situation not greatly different from the beginning."[58] Hints of redemption are scattered around the conclusion, but they appear side by side with signs that little or

[57] Gail Godwin, "The Devil's Own Century," review of *The Thanatos Syndrome*, by Walker Percy, *The New York Times*, April 5, 1987. http://www.nytimes.com/1987/04/05/books/the-devil-s-own-century.html (accessed August 25, 2015).

[58] Wayne Booth, *A Rhetoric of Irony* (Chicago: University of Chicago Press, 1974).

even nothing has changed. The novel wants us to refuse the idea that the "breadth and motions of the very self"—cast in either psychological or theological terms—can be calculated down to the micromilivolt, yet it never fully illustrates what follows from this refusal. Nor does it dramatize at length how Percy's norm-sustaining community comes into being or could be maintained, and only gives us passing glimpses of Heideggerian "clearings," Peircian "triads," or Catholic "redemption." Like Percy himself, More rails against Descartes, who is said to have created the "dread chasm that has rent the soul of Western man," ripping apart mind and body (191). Yet he continues to scrutinize the "pineal body" of his patients, a goal that not only reproduces the Cartesian emphasis on the internal mechanisms of the body, but also crowds out any of the genuine answers to Descartes that Percy and his intellectual heroes develop. *Love in the Ruins* is indeed a "quasi-prophetic" novel, but only if we stress the qualifying prefix of the phrase as much as the adjective. It wants to be less skeptical than *Galatea* about the reality of our *telei*, yet its attunement to our finitude, to the limitations of our knowledge and perspective, brings readers to a comparable place. We can never be sure, the novel suggests, whether the contexts we perceive are indeed the contexts that truly matter.

V. *Fides et Ratio*

Given all this—given Percy's distance from Powers yet also the felt incompleteness of *Love in the Ruins*—an obvious last question remains. What is the rationale for Percy's project? How do we explain why he moves from form to form, or why he aspires to write both philosophical essays as well as fiction? And what does it say that these two modes should not always be tightly aligned with one another? These are questions surrounding all of the postwar sentinels that I am considering in this book, so a glance at them now will bring certain themes into clearer view.

Incongruities between Percy's essays and fiction have been noted before. And Percy's efforts to play the philosopher have drawn particular fire. Some of this fire has come, unsurprisingly, from philosophers and linguists who simply disagree with his claims.[59] But even sympathetic readers, philosophers who praise his philosophical instincts, suggest that he seems to betray his own deepest insights when turning from narrative to discursive forms. Percy displays, such critics say, a great range of imaginative talents as well as philosophical

---

[59] For a philosophical critic, see, for example, Thomas Nagel, "Sin and Significance," *The New York Review of Books* (September 18, 1975), 54–56.

expertise, and his attacks on the Cartesian tradition are unfailingly on target in the novels. But his essays, they claim, fall into the very habits that Percy wants to attack: He indulges in abstraction, seeks general theories, and uses all the terms of the philosophical tradition that he's ostensibly questioning. His nonfiction talks a great deal about specific and concrete worldly relations, yet in their language and form, it eschews local descriptions for hypothetical models, many of which Percy even charts with diagrams and arrows. Percy's vision becomes progressively more blurred as his writing grows less narrative and anecdotal, and the brilliant success of the novelist is disappointingly matched by the *systematic* (and therefore philosophically revealing confusion) of the essayist.[60]

One problem with this criticism is that it would seem to apply to any text that was not discernibly narrative in form, including that of the critic—as if discursive prose were in and of itself a symptom of Cartesian delusion. But not all reflective prose, and certainly not all of Percy's reflective prose, takes the form of proofs and arguments, just as Cartesian methods are not the only manifestation of human rationality. A second problem is that the criticism depends upon assumptions about human thought and speech that—bluntly put—Percy doesn't share. Indeed, the criticism rehearses a version of the very nominalism to which Percy objects, finding validity only in, to recall the phrase from Fredric Jameson that I cited in my introduction, "the here and now of this unique situation and this unique expression."[61] To a certain kind of Percy critic, that is, abstract thought and intellect are in and of themselves dubious, and any effort to generalize or systematize dooms one to a hopelessly blinkered abstraction. Conversely, only highly localized individuals and contexts—the kind of individuals and contexts foregrounded in modern fiction—are capable of providing the intellectual and moral resources that readers need for orienting their lives. It's a strong particularism that has sometimes been associated with the later Wittgenstein, whose distrust of theorizing has led some of his followers to prize dramatic story and character over anything that whiffs of abstraction and argument.[62]

---

[60] Here I am summarizing the criticisms of two philosophers who have read Percy with great seriousness: William H. Poteat, "Reflections on Walker Percy's Theory of Language," and Patricia Lewis Poteat, *Walker Percy and the Old Modern Age: Reflections on Language, Argument, and Telling of Stories* (Baton Rouge: Louisiana State University Press, 1985), 1–8.

[61] Fredric Jameson, *Postmodernism, or, The Cultural Logic of Late Capitalism* (Durham, NC: Duke University Press, 1991), 152.

[62] See the work of, for example, Peter Winch, Cora Diamond, Stephen Muhall, and Alice Crary, whom the footnotes of Chapter 1 discuss in passing.

But for Percy, writing stories about particular persons and situations is no more a complete and adequate response to the world and experience, is no more an expression of our human nature—no more what we as pilgrims falling prey to the world *need*—than reading stories about particular persons and situations. To emphasize only the here and now of unique situations is, in his view, just a step away from abandoning moral and religious thought *tout court*, and threatens to collapse into an aestheticism of the sort that Percy emphatically rejects. "I'm not merchandising ideas," said Percy shortly after *Love in the Ruins* appeared, but it's also true that "my interests in writing are not primarily literary." [63] Elsewhere he speaks of "the danger attendant upon literature and art," and reminds readers that "the living of one's life is not to be found in books, either the reading of them or the writing of them" (*SSL* 152). It's a danger to which, in his estimation, some of the most influential artists of the last century have succumbed. James Joyce, for instance, was a "hero of the aesthetic, seeing salvation through art and language" (*Conv.* 231), and in a frequently cited letter to Caroline Gordon, Percy declares that, though he may "kneel before the altar of Lawrence and Joyce and Flaubert, it is not because I wish to do what they did." "Actually I do not consider myself a novelist," he admitted, "but a moralist or a propagandist," for "what I really want to do is to tell people *what they must do and what they must believe if they want to live*."[64] In his own work he tried to keep in mind "the aesthetic limitations of the novel form," the way that novelists are mainly "out to give pleasure to the reader," confined as they are to the "aesthetic sphere, not the religious or even the ethical" (*SSL* 386). The scientific and technological knowledge that fascinates and sustains much of the empiricist–analytic intellectual tradition may be inadequate, as Percy's writing everywhere seeks to make clear. But one of modernity's other landmark ideas— that art is self-sufficient, self-justifying, wholly "autonomous"—is inadequate to the same degree, because art does not give ultimate purpose to our lives, does not provide the broadest contexts of meaning.

This isn't to deny, of course, that *Love in the Ruins* and other novels mattered to Percy, or that in some sense he is the strong particularist that his critics wish him to be. Like the Christian faith, he says, the novel as a genre persistently emphasizes "the value of the individual person, its view of man as a creature in trouble, seeking to get out of it, and accordingly on the move." And like Catholicism specifically, novels "confer the highest significance upon the

---

[63] Percy's remark about his interests in writing is made in "To Walker Percy, Man's Prognosis is Funny," *National Observer* (May 24, 1971), 17.
[64] Tolson, *Pilgrim in the Ruins*, 300.

ordinary things of this world, bread, wine, water, touch, breath, words, talking, listening," a world "that is a sacrament and a mystery" (*SSL* 369). But what chafes Percy is not abstraction as such but misleading or misconceived uses of abstraction: speaking as if one's words had a life of their own, as if generalities could be wholly removed from particulars and exist apart from our learning and our ongoing tacit communal agreements. In short, he's opposed not to philosophy but to philosophy that's done from the disembodied perspective that *Love in the Ruins* calls "angelism." Philosophy rightly understood and rightly practiced—as an expression of what for him is the natural human inclination toward knowledge and understanding—is no more a threat to the soul than the making of paintings, poems, or novels. (Though no less, either.)

The point can be made in the intellectual–historical terms that Percy himself was so fond of using. Percy has so regularly been associated with Kierkegaard, and so frequently invoked the Danish philosopher in essays and interviews, that it's tempting to think he's a full-fledged Kierkegaardian, committed to the fundamentally irrational nature of religious faith. Because he speaks so lucidly and often of "alienation," "despair," "subjectivity," "apostles," "indirect communication," "the aesthetic sphere"—all the great Kierkegaardian themes—it's easy to assume that he, too, regards faith as a "leap," an action of the spirit that is wholly divorced from deliberation and judgment. Such presumptions are amplified when, for instance, we see a forceful passage from Kierkegaard's *Philosophical Fragments* included as an epigraph to the title essay of *The Message in the Bottle*: "Faith is not a form of knowledge. . . .No knowledge can have for its object the absurdity that the eternal is the historical" (*MB* 119). But "The Message in the Bottle" includes a second epigraph, tellingly placed just above Kierkegaard's sentences: "The act of faith consists essentially in knowledge and there we find its formal or specific perfection" (*MB* 119). The statement comes from Aquinas, whose *Summa Theologica* Percy claimed to have read in its massive entirety (*Conv.* 153), and who in the essay itself Percy credits with defending the legitimacy of "two knowledges": "scientific knowledge, in which assent is achieved by reason," and "knowledge of faith, in which scientific knowledge and assent are undertaken simultaneously" (*MB* 145).[65] As I've suggested, the legitimacy of "two knowledges" is precisely the idea that drew Percy to Peirce, whose picture of language emphasized its status as the greatest of human cognitive

---

[65] Elsewhere, in interviews, Percy pointedly clarified this distinction between his two heroes still further. He was, he said, on Kierkegaard's "wavelength," and appreciated "his phenomenology, his analysis of the existential predicament of modern man." But Aquinas, he went on, "was right about faith. It is not a leap into the absurd, it is an act of faith, which is a form of knowledge" (*Conv.* 204).

achievements and allowed Percy to describe it in robustly "scientific"—albeit nonreductive—terms. And it's precisely the balance between these two knowledges that has driven other twentieth-century Catholic voices, such as Jacques Maritain (an early influence on Percy), Alasdair MacIntyre, and Pope John Paul, all of whom have been preoccupied with the nature of rationality and its relationship to religious belief and tradition.[66]

Most importantly for the chapters that follow, Percy's appeal to Aquinas helps explain his ambidextrous use of both philosophy and modern fiction. It explains why, for instance, he can praise contemporaries like Saul Bellow and John Updike for vividly capturing the malaise of post-World War II American culture, but then can remark that we shouldn't "leave it to the novelists" to address issues of such fundamental spiritual significance. Anything a novelist writes, he implies, must be supplemented by another form of investigation—a way of "thinking about these things rationally," of "getting some ordered discipline," a way to "make a model or develop a theory. . .of what it is to be an organism who uses language" (*Conv.* 222). Percy repeatedly insists that fiction is a cognitive matter: "it discovers and knows and tells," and possesses "insights into the way things are," much as pathologists discover and tell us about symptoms of disease (*SSL* 140, 146). But what fiction "knows" is always partial; it offers only diagnoses, not the remedies that are disclosed through a combination of rational deliberation and religious faith. *Love in the Ruins*, that is, *has* to be incomplete—has to conclude where it roughly began, has to show More spiritedly wielding his Lapsometer, has to show that the maker's fate is to be a wanderer. It has to remain only *quasi*-prophecy.

As we'll see, it's this emphasis on the incompleteness of aesthetics and literary forms that warrants Percy's inclusion among the postwar sages I'll be discussing over the next several chapters. In the twentieth century, declares Percy, as scientists and humanists were celebrating human progress, the artists saw something else: "that at a time when, according to the theory of the age, men should feel most at home they felt most homeless" (*MB* 25). At the very moment, that is, when "communication theory and technique reached its peak," poets and novelists had come to believe that we no longer communicated; when

---

[66] See, for example, Jacques Maritain, *The Degrees of Knowledge*, trans. Gerald B. Phelan (Notre Dame, IN: Notre Dame University Press, 1995); Alasdair MacIntyre, *Whose Justice? Whose Rationality?* (Notre Dame, IN: Notre Dame University Press, 1988); John Paul II, "*Fides et Ratio*," encyclical letter of September 1998 <http://w2.vatican.va/content/john-paul-ii/en/encyclicals/documents/hf_jp-ii_enc_14091998_fides-et-ratio.html?> (accessed April 22, 2016); Alasdair MacIntyre, "Philosophy Recalled to Its Tasks: A Thomistic Reading of *Fides et Ratio*," in *The Tasks of Philosophy: Selected Essays, Volume 1* (Cambridge: Cambridge University Press, 2006), 179–96.

people were massed together in larger and larger cities, true communities have been vitiated; when people lived longer and more secure lives than ever, they had become "most afraid" (*MB* 25). Percy himself often embraced this scorn for the modern scientific–bourgeois order—this "Great Literary Secession," as he calls it (*SSL* 145). It is what leads him to revere *La nausée* and *L'étranger*; and what justifies comparisons to the acerbic comedy of Pynchon, DeLillo, and others. But Percy diverges from these traditions insofar as, in his understanding of them, they have blunted their own attacks. Modern writers, he says, have "often behaved badly" and mocked modernity even while they themselves enjoyed its medical, technological, and other benefits. Most of all they have remained, in his eyes, wholly negative: for all their condemnations of modernity, for all their resistance to the era of the consumer–theorist, "the poets and artists who attacked the spirit of the age had nothing to offer in its stead" (*MB* 26). Percy believed that he *did* have something to offer in its stead—and one upshot of this belief was that he himself was not, and should not be, first and foremost an artist. The story of Tom More cannot provide this something; it offers no clear salvation, no clear redemption. Articulating our high words requires leaving artistic forms to the side, at least sometimes, and thinking of things in wholly different, more ordered and disciplined, terms.

2

THAT HOREB, THAT KANSAS

Evolution and the Modernity of Marilynne Robinson

THE VAST BREADTH of the natural world, the vast span of natural history: the recurrence of these themes in Marilynne Robinson's *Housekeeping* gives it a place among the least anthropocentric American novels of the last half-century. "The terrain on which the town built itself," says the narrator Ruth in the opening pages, speaking of Fingerbone, Idaho, "is relatively level, having once belonged to the lake. It seems there was a time when the dimensions of things modified themselves, leaving a number of puzzling margins, as between the mountains as they must have been and the mountains as they are now, or between the lake as it once was and the lake as it is now."[1] Shortly after this, Ruth returns to this lake and surveys its contents level by level, age by age:

> It is true that one is always aware of the lake in Fingerbone, or the deeps of the lake, the lightless, airless waters below. . . . At the foundation is the old lake, which is smothered and nameless and altogether black. Then there is Fingerbone, the lake of charts and photographs, which is permeated by sunlight and sustains green life and innumerable fish, and in which one can look down in the shadow of a dock and see stony, earthy bottom, more or less as one sees dry ground. And above that, the lake that rises in the spring and turns the grass dark and coarse as reeds. And above that

---

[1] Marilynne Robinson, *Housekeeping* (New York: Farrar, Straus and Giroux, 1980), 4–5; henceforth cited parenthetically as *H*.

the water suspended in sunlight, sharp as the breath of an animal, which brims inside this circle of mountains. (*H* 8)

A few chapters later, the power of such natural features and phenomena over the conscious deeds of human beings is made manifest, as several days of rain cause a flood so intense that "the houses and hutches and barns and sheds of Fingerbone were like so many spilled and foundered arks"—all further evidence, observes the narrator, that the town had always been "chastened by an outsized landscape and extravagant weather" (*H* 62).

Housekeeping began, according to Robinson, as "little bits of narrative" composed while she was in graduate school at the University of Washington, where she completed a doctoral dissertation on Shakespeare in 1977.[2] Critics have often seen it as a milestone in the development of women's fiction of the 1970s and by extension of second-wave feminism.[3] Robinson has not discouraged such a reading: her "one great objection" to the figure of the American outsider hero, she has said, is that he is "inevitably male—in decayed forms egregiously male," and the character of Sylvie in *Housekeeping* was designed in part as a corrective to that tradition.[4] But the novel's preoccupation with the sweeping canvasses of natural history marks a less noted respect in which its publication was timely. For the years surrounding the composition of *Housekeeping* saw a surge of voices claiming that human civilization should be situated within the outsized landscapes, extravagant climates, and deep cycles of natural history. Just two years before Robinson finished her doctorate, and five years before her novel appeared, the American biologist E. O. Wilson had published *Sociobiology*, which argued that all the things traditionally understood as distinctly human—religious practices, ritual, communication, altruism, ethics, aesthetics—make sense only by reference to the physical systems and behaviors that we share with other animals: hormonal responses, sensory systems, mating habits, family bonding, aggression, dominance systems, parental investment, and so on. And just a year after *Sociobiology*, the British biologist Richard

[2] Robinson interview with Thomas Schaub, *Contemporary Literature* 35.2 (1994): 231–54; henceforth cited parenthetically as *CL*.

[3] See, for instance, Paula E. Geyh, "Burning Down the House: Domestic Space and Feminine Subjectivity in Marilynne Robinson's *Housekeeping*," *Contemporary Literature* 34.1 (1993): 103–22; Karen Kaivola, "The Pleasures and Perils of Merging: Female Subjectivity in Marilynne Robinson's *Housekeeping*," *Contemporary Literature* 34.4 (1993): 670–90; Joan Kirkby, "Is There Life After Art? The Metaphysics of Marilynne Robinson's *Housekeeping*," *Tulsa Studies in Women's Literature* 5.1 (1986): 91–109.

[4] See the title essay of her collection *When I Was a Child I Read Books* (New York: Farrar, Straus and Giroux, 2012), 92; henceforth cited parenthetically as *WC*.

Dawkins published *The Selfish Gene*, which argued that what defines human life is what defines all biological life, great and small alike: the desire among genes to replicate and survive. From Dawkins's perspective, the citizens of Fingerbone may have built their houses and barns to protect their children and farm animals, but these motivations were themselves the product of unconscious prior impulses, of historically evolved imperatives among their genes to make it into the next generation.[5]

Wilson and Dawkins generated a harsh backlash in the late 1970s and early 1980s, when biologists such as Richard Lewontin and Stephen Jay Gould described sociobiology as a series of "just so" stories whose pictures of biology were almost as questionable as their likely social consequences.[6] But by the time Robinson published her second novel, *Gilead*, in 2004, claims about the biological foundations of human life and culture had regained steam, now under the banner of "evolutionary psychology." Perhaps the most ambitiously synthetic and influential defense of the new sciences of human nature has been Steven Pinker's *The Blank Slate* (2002), which appeared two years before *Gilead* and popularized the translation of Chomskyan ideas into a Darwinian idiom.[7] Darwinians always have known that human ears, tongues, and thumbs are high-level adaptations to an environment, and to this list Pinker attempts to add our language. This most elaborate of human endowments exists, argues Pinker, because of the evolved linguistic structure that underlies observable natural languages such as French or Chinese—a Language of Thought that no human ever needs to learn. *The Blank Slate* turns this argument into a polemical cluster of claims about the most encrusted problems of human life. Knowing that we are the product of replicating genes allows us to see, for instance, that aggression is partly what has allowed our species to survive, and that men are especially prone to it, given their particular role in human reproduction—which means that male violence (including rape) derives from something other than poor living conditions, pornography, or bad television (*BS* 359–71). Likewise, according to Pinker, we should accept that the different levels of power and

---

[5] See E. O. Wilson, *Sociobiology: The New Synthesis* (Cambridge, MA: Harvard University Press, 1975); Richard Dawkins, *The Selfish Gene* (New York: Oxford University Press, 1976).

[6] See Chapter 8, Part B of Stephen Jay Gould's *Ever Since Darwin: Reflections in Natural History* (New York: Norton, 1977), 251–67; Richard Lewontin, "Sociobiology—A Caricature of Darwinism," *PSA: Proceedings of the Biennial Meeting of the Philosophy of Science Association* 1976 (1976): 22–31; Lewontin, *Biology as Ideology: The Doctrine of DNA* (Toronto: Anasi Press, 1991).

[7] Steven Pinker, *The Blank Slate: The Modern Denial of Human Nature* (New York: Viking, 2002); henceforth cited parenthetically as *BS*. *The Blank Slate* was hardly the first time that this combination of Chomsky and Darwin first appeared; it has been a mark of Pinker's work at least since his book *The Language Instinct* appeared in 1994.

wealth that have typically distinguished men from women reflect not merely unjust patriarchal arrangements, but also different biological roles in propagating the species (*BS* 337–71), and that intelligence and personality are dependent less on upbringing than genetic inheritance, as studies of twins, separated twins, and adopted children suggest (*BS* 372–99). Pinker doesn't deny that our social arrangements are imperfect, and his claims are based more on statistical averages than on specific cases, but he is eager to take aim at those who ignore our universal human nature. Such deviants include thinkers who believe, with Marx, that "All history is nothing but the transformation of human nature" (qtd. *BS* 155); feminists who think, with Margaret T. Gordon and Stephanie Riger, that female fear results partly "from what women as a group have imbibed from history, religion, culture, social institutions, and everyday social interactions [as well as] social institutions like the school, the church, the law, and the press" (qtd. *BS* 365–6); and anyone naïve enough to assert, with Lyndon Johnson, that violence in modern societies is caused by "ignorance, discrimination, slums, poverty, disease, not enough jobs" (qtd. *BS* 292).

Much like Robinson's Ruth, in other words, Wilson and Dawkins and Pinker draw attention to the "foundation" of our terrestrial life, and argue that what is "smothered and nameless" in the depths of natural history has an overwhelming bearing on our current dispositions and experiences. Like her, too, the neo-Darwinian offers a "chastened" image of the human species, its barns and houses and other efforts at control all forcefully determined by the physical life of the engulfing environment. So it shouldn't be surprising that, in the years since *Housekeeping*, Robinson has taken a deep interest in what contemporary Darwinians are saying—an interest that she shares with an enormous range of thinkers, from literary critics, psychologists, and social policy researchers to high-profile newspaper columnists and powerful college presidents.[8] And yet Robinson has been relentlessly critical of this Darwinian turn. She has charged its practitioners with offering mutually incompatible claims, argued that they rely upon bad science, complained that they make unwarranted forays into

---

[8] Among literary critics, see Joseph Carroll, *Literary Darwinism: Evolution, Human Nature, and Literature* (London: Routledge, 2004); Brian Boyd, *On the Origins of Stories: Evolution, Cognition, and Fiction* (Cambridge, MA: Harvard University Press, 2009). Among columnists, David Brooks of *The New York Times* has sometimes questioned evolutionary psychology, but he's also often drawn upon its findings when it helps him make a case; see, for example, his "When the Good Do Bad," *The New York Times* (March 19, 2012). The most (in)famous case of a college president's interest in evolutionary psychology is remarks in 2005 by Larry Summers, then president of Harvard, about noncultural variability between men and women—remarks whose most committed defense in the months afterward came from Pinker.

areas of human life they don't understand, and blamed them for some of the degradation of our politics and public life. Why?

My first goal in this chapter is to unpack just what Robinson says about neo-Darwinism, and to understand why so much of her life's work has been devoted to clarifying and contesting it. One answer is that Darwinism is for Robinson what machine intelligence is to Percy: the reductive naturalism that seems most threatening to and pervasive in the culture, and that most sharply provokes her to articulate both her aesthetic and normative commitments. In Percy, the clash was with the behaviorists and cognitivists who ignore the worldly engagements, skillful naming, and broad holistic contexts that constitute our sense-making practices, and who by extension sanction the "theorist-consumer" disposition that modern nominalism fosters. In Robinson, the clash is with the work of Wilson, Dawkins, Pinker, and other thinkers who embody the "modern," as that term pejoratively appears in the subtitles of two of the works of nonfiction that she published in the years around her second novel: *The Death of Adam: Essays on Modern Thought* (1998), and *Absence of Mind: The Dispelling of Inwardness from the Modern Myth of the Self* (2010).[9] The former book opens with a forty-eight-page essay (the longest in the collection) called simply "Darwinism," and the latter reviews arguments from most of the most well-known contemporary evolutionists, including Wilson, Dawkins, and Pinker. To be "modern" in Robinson's sense is not to make, say, Kantian claims about the autonomy of aesthetic experience and the universal moral law, or to subscribe to Rousseavian beliefs about popular sovereignty and the social contract. Being modern instead means being strictly Hobbesian: to describe the universe in rigorously nonintentional terms, to examine it as extended and measurable matter that's governed by efficient rather than final causes, and to view it as non-normative motions rather than intentional actions. "Universe" here includes human beings, and reducing ourselves to various more primitive material units is what yields reliable explanations and predictions, the two essential aspirations of modern science and the source of much of the technological power that modern science has yielded. Given how conspicuous these concerns have been in Robinson's nonfiction, it is striking how seldom readers of *Gilead* have reckoned with them. It's true that the book is set in 1956, decades before the phrases "sociobiology" or "evolutionary psychology" ever circulated; and it takes place among Protestant ministers

---

[9] Marilynne Robinson, *The Death of Adam: Essays on Modern Thought* (New York: Picador, 1998), henceforth cited parenthetically as *DA*; *Absence of Mind: The Dispelling of Inwardness from the Modern Myth of the Self* (New Haven, CT: Yale University Press, 2010), henceforth cited parenthetically as *AM*. The latter was originally delivered as the 2009 Terry Lectures at Yale.

in rural Iowa, far indeed from Darwin's Galapagos Islands or the Harvard research labs of Wilson and Pinker. But Darwinism, for reasons I'll explain, haunts Robinson's fiction, and *Gilead* can be understood as giving a glimpse of the debates that Robinson pursues in her essays.[10]

My second goal, however, is to consider just how seamlessly Robinson's fiction affirms her rebuttal of Darwinian theory. In the later portions of the chapter, therefore, I'll concentrate on *Gilead*, which is important, as I understand it, not because it allegorizes the ideas on hand in her essays or summons up thinly fictionalized versions of her own analytic claims. Robinson's essays and her fiction employ different speech genres to different effect, and these purposes and effects are sometimes tellingly in conflict with one another. Like Wittgenstein's *Philosophical Investigations*, her writing amounts to an "album" of different landscapes. Readers have occasionally noticed this kind of conflict before, as when one commentator says that moving from her outspoken essays to the quiet air of her fiction is like hearing Dylan diving from folk into rock, or "as if the same author wrote Leviticus and Psalms."[11] But the exact nature and import of this conflict has been largely neglected. Just as much as Percy, Robinson in her nonfiction exemplifies what Susan Sontag has called the "directness of the essay-writing voice, the directness of its concern with opinion and argument," an "assertiveness of one kind or another" that betrays an urge to "to convert the world and everything in it" to "the reflection of an idea" which the essayist "unfolds, defends, or excoriates."[12] Robinson not only has beliefs, but has beliefs about beliefs; ideas do not "violate" the mind, to recall T. S. Eliot's remark about Henry James, but are the mind's very substance. The interesting question is not whether she commits herself to certain ideas, but what becomes of these commitments in the context of her fiction. And the direction of *Gilead*, I'll argue, is

---

[10] The issue of terminology here is complicated. Not all working biologists would accept Robinson's characterizations of evolution and Darwinism, particularly in *The Death of Adam*. The present chapter is, of course, hardly the place to decide on the correct interpretation of "Darwin," "evolution," "evolutionary psychology," and "sociobiology." In what follows I'll be using the somewhat generic terms "Darwinian," "neo-Darwinian," and "Darwinian naturalism," by which I mean the particularly reductive forms of contemporary evolutionary thought that Robinson takes herself to oppose.

[11] Todd Shy, "Religion and Marilynne Robinson," *Salmagundi* 155/6 (Summer 2007): 251. Compare William Deresiewicz's claim that Robinson the essayist is "by turns magnificent and obtuse," whereas Robinson the fiction writer is a "modern master," ruling "her fictional domain with absolute authority." See his "Homing Patterns: Marilynne Robinson's Fiction," *The Nation* (September 24, 2008) <http://www.thenation.com/article/homing-patterns-marilynne-robinsons-fiction/> (accessed January 20, 2016).

[12] Susan Sontag, "Introduction to *The Best American Essays*, 1992," in *Essayists on the Essay: Montaigne to Our Time*, ed. Carl H. Klaus and Ned Stuckey-French (Iowa City: University of Iowa Press, 2012), 149–52.

illuminating: indirect, unassertive, oblique, the novel is ambivalent about opinion and argument, receptive to the very things that the essays excoriate, and attuned to the limits of the very ideas Robinson the essayist wants to defend. Attending to both the unities and fissures of her reflective compositional strategies thus allows us to ask the central questions of this entire book—questions not only about the explanation of behavior and the status of normative concepts in contemporary culture, but also about the relation of art to argument, literature to discursive thought, the ancient quarrel between poetry and philosophy. Or so I'll be suggesting.

I. Data, Nature, and the Status of Norms

Robinson covers a remarkable range of topics in her essays, and like her touchstones Emerson and Thoreau, she is not—and never has aspired to be—an especially systematic thinker or writer. But without too much oversimplification, we can begin by isolating three interrelated themes that appear throughout her writing about "modern" thought and contemporary Darwinism.

An initial assertion concerns what counts as data in our claims about human behavior. "Data" is Robinson's own word, appropriated from the natural sciences in order to reshape our ideas of what is ontologically respectable and worth serious discussion. Neo-Darwinism, she says, embodies a "hermeneutics of condescension" that adheres "to a narrow definition of relevant data" (*AM* 15), and modern science has generally ignored the "historical data, the record we have made of our tenure on this planet," in its rush to offer "ill-founded generalizations" (*AM* xv). "History and civilization, art, science, and philosophy," are all "richer data" than anything we can say about the brain alone, and all the proof we need for "the existence of mind" (*AM* 120). The contemporary Darwinian should avoid thinking that pathological behavior lays bare the impulses that are universal, "so that any quantity of data can be refuted by a single example of behavior that would seem to illustrate his point" (*DA* 51)—and the "mass of relevant data" in such cases would be "infinitely great" (*DA* 49).

"Data," that is, is a key plank in what I would call Robinson's weak realism, and we have seen such a move already. In his account of semantics, Percy insists that we not overlook the "phenomenon of language" in our drive to be properly scientific; our shared practices of denoting are "as real as any S-R sequence, as real as H^2SO^4 to NaOH."[13] And we'll find it again in Chapter 4, when Stanley Cavell

---

[13] Walker Percy, *The Message in the Bottle: How Queer Man Is, How Queer Language Is, and What One Has to Do With the Other* (1975; New York: Picador, 2000), 39.

will occasionally put the term "data" to similar use in his early defenses of ordinary language philosophy against its positivist critics. The ordinary language philosopher, says the young Cavell, uses himself "as his subject in his collection of data," and despite the qualms of the scientific linguist, "there is nothing in that to make the data, in some general way, suspect."[14] In Robinson's case, the "data of human nature" that most needed recording include what she calls "the mind's self-awareness," the undeniable fact that "the self" "stands apart from itself," "questions, reconsiders, appraises" (*AM* 118). "Self-awareness" is part of a family of concepts that Robinson wants us to remember. Sometimes the term is "the human mind," which among Darwinists is "discounted as anomaly or delusion" (*DA* 35). Sometimes it is "the felt life of the mind," which is excluded "from the accounts of reality proposed by the oddly authoritative and deeply influential parascientific literature that has long associated itself with intellectual progress" (*AM* 35). Sometimes it is "the soul," "the self," or "inwardness," words all banished now that the "mystery of motive is solved" and we know "there are only self-seeking and aggression" (*DA* 74). Sometimes it is "human subjectivity," which exhibits "intrinsic complexity" (*AM* 16), is an "indubitable" "feature of reality" (*AM* 36), and whose "old mystery" cannot be "dispelled" (*DA* 74). In themselves these words are not always satisfying: they can evoke, if unchecked, an unwelcome residue of Cartesianism or an exaggeratedly Protestant sense of interiority. But at their core they are driven by a critical impulse that is entirely justifiable. For behind these phrases is an effort to put into question the evolutionary psychologist's frequent distinction between "proximate" and "ultimate" causes. The proximate cause of my eating chocolate is hunger and a craving for sweets, but the ultimate cause is my genetically evolved nutritional need for sweet and fat. Robinson rightly intuits that such a distinction has its limitations. Accounts of phenomena can occur at various levels, making use of different concepts and schemes of classification. And there are differences between explanations that occur within what Wilfrid Sellars called the "scientific image" of human beings and within what he called the "manifest image": between, that is, explanations that privilege entities imperceptible to the human subject (waves, particles, atoms, molecules, DNA) and explanations that privilege entities perceptible to the human senses.[15] Robinson vividly captures the spirit of Sellars's distinction in her essay "Family" when she remarks that, from a reductivist perspective, "we no longer sat in chairs after we learned that furniture

---

[14] Stanley Cavell, *Must We Mean What We Say?* (Cambridge: Cambridge University Press, 1976), 5.
[15] Wilfrid Sellars, "Philosophy and the Scientific Image of Man," *Science, Perception, and Reality* (Atascadero, CA: Ridgeview Press, 1963), 1–40.

was only space and atoms" (*DA* 91). Given that it is not always clear how to correlate different levels of explanation or translate different schemes of classification, what occurs around chairs, persons, and other features of the manifest image can sometimes, as Robinson's remark suggests, be counted as "data" as much as what occurs at the subpersonal level of waves and particles and atoms. Matisse's genes don't act generously or apply paint to canvas; *Matisse* does.[16]

Moreover, as Robinson's references to "human subjectivity" and "self-awareness" imply, Matisse is at least potentially capable of knowing when he is acting generously or applying paint to canvass. Which is to say that a central feature of the manifest image, at least when the entity under consideration is a human being, is a *first-person* point of view, what is manifest to individual consciousness. Surely I have a certain genetic makeup, but if I'm trying to decide how to act toward a stranger or staring at a blank canvas, I cannot, as Robert Pippin puts it, wait around for my highly evolved neurological machinery to recommend something. In the same way, if someone asks me why I did one thing rather than another, saying "My genes made me" will not count as a legitimate reason in most circumstances. No discovery in the neuro- or biological sciences, that is, can count as a *reason* for me to do or forbear from doing anything; a decision is fundamentally undertaken from an agent's point of view.[17] Such is the import, I think, of Robinson's claim that our idea of "the self" is elicited by the ability to "question, reconsider, appraise" (*AM* 118), and it accounts for her choice of verb when she claims that the voice of the ancient poet, saint, or visionary has "attested" to his or her sense of the holy and that their audiences have "attested to the truth" of such claims (*AM* 7). Philosophers have generally referred to such speech-acts as "avowals," but Robinson's own (Protestant-inflected) term for first-person expressions is "testimony."[18] "Modern" thought encourages us, she says, to think that "the experience and testimony of the individual mind is to be explained away" (*AM* 22). We believe we are "less and worse" than we are because "we routinely disqualify testimony that would plead for extenuation" (*DA* 27). The "power of testimony" is the power "to stand apart from ourselves, appraising" (*DA* 115–16). If by all this she means that the "data" of first-personal reports is as pertinent to the explanation of action as

---

[16] Dennett makes this Sellarsian remark in "Philosophy as Naïve Anthropology: Comment on Bennett and Hacker," in *Neuroscience and Philosophy: Brain, Mind, and Language* (New York: Columbia University Press, 2007), 76. In some recent work Dennett has implied that the distinction means less to him than it once did.

[17] Robert Pippin, "Natural and Normative," *Daedalus* 138 (2009): 38–39.

[18] On avowal, see, for example, Richard Moran, *Authority and Estrangement: An Essay on Self-Knowledge* (Princeton, NJ: Princeton University Press, 2001).

anything given by a neurologist, geneticist, or any other third-person observer, she is making a point made elsewhere by a range of Robinson's philosophical contemporaries, including Hegelians like Pippin as well as phenomenologists, Wittgensteinians, and neo-pragmatists.[19]

That Robinson doesn't entirely belong to any of these philosophical schools brings us to a second thought running through her responses to neo-Darwinians. All of these schools suggest that the proper response to evolutionary theory should be, roughly: "So what?" Biology and the other sciences, from this point of view, do get a lot right about our "nature," but the "nature" in these sciences is merely the capacities and systems that developed in the distant past—the "first nature," which has made our hearts beat in certain ways, our hair grow in certain ways, and our eyes perceive in certain ways. What matters instead, they say in various formulations, is what the Aristotelian tradition sometimes refers to as *second nature*: the deeply habitual stores of wisdom about what to say or do, the repertory of appropriate responses to a given situation, the habits that arise when character is formed and the practical intellect takes a determinative shape.[20] Practical intellect, in these terms, is defined in part by appropriate conceptual responses, what Sellars called the "space of reasons": the warranted linkage of inferences and implications and justifications that only full-fledged conceptual creatures are able to occupy. When someone says "It's pouring rain outside," one typically knows it isn't sunny.[21] But it is also defined by the acquisition of appropriate moral responses, so that when someone says "He's a wanton child-molester," we feel revulsion. Obviously such conceptual and moral responses would be impossible without our peculiarly sophisticated biological wiring, and certainly the conceptual and moral responses of second nature can over time garner what seems like the force of necessity. (We're shocked when, say, someone feels no revulsion toward a child molester.) But for these kinds of philosophers, first nature massively underdetermines the shape this second nature can acquire. It has some degree of autonomy from first nature and can be described independently, in terms with no equivalent in our accounts of the physical world: intentional agency, moral maturation, ethical deliberation,

---

[19] In this context one also could consider Robinson's discussions of "memes," another concept that raises questions as to how different levels of description (ideas circulating in a culture vs. the particular persons expressing them) are being imagined and how these levels interact. See *Absence of Mind*, 65.

[20] This formulation is drawn mainly from the work that has put the idea of "second nature" back into recent philosophical circulation, namely John McDowell's *Mind and World* (Cambridge, MA: Harvard University Press, 1994).

[21] Wilfrid Sellars, *Empiricism and the Philosophy of Mind*, ed. Robert Brandom (1956; Cambridge, MA: Harvard University Press, 1997).

tradition and its reflective modifications, *Bildung*.[22] Put negatively, failures of first nature are failures of functional teleology, failures of what's good for the organism *qua* organism, be it a tree or toad or toddler; it's what allows us to have intelligible concepts of "disability" or "disease." Failures of second nature are described otherwise: the weakening of norms, the lapse of certain responses or justifications, the dissolution of an evolved, shared social practice.[23]

This is roughly Percy's standpoint, too: symbolization, recall, is for him a "generically different" thing than anything in the universe, because what exists in the universe is simply a colossal "series of space-time events."[24] Robinson would applaud this language of agency, maturation, and *Bildung*, and would take all these terms to express the "human exceptionalism" that Darwinism "tries to discount" (*DA* 62). But she describes this exceptionalism in slightly different terms, and challenges Darwinism from a somewhat different angle. Her claim is less that the science of our genes and instincts is irrelevant than that it is simply *wrong*—or at least radically incomplete, neglecting essential features of our nature, features that don't neatly reduce to what she calls a "few simple formulae" (*AM* xvi). To say, with Pippin and Sellars and others, that science is basically irrelevant to our understanding of human life and culture is to cede too much to the crass Darwinian narrative. We must remember that "only fairly recently" did we learn "that the continents have been known to drift," or that the "biomass of the sea at middle and great depths has been fantastically underestimated," or that still today "we know almost nothing about the biology of the air." In short, we should remember that "our best information about the planet has been full of enormous lacunae" and that "every grand venture at understanding is hypothesis, not *so* different from metaphysics" (*DA* 72).

As her rebuke of a "few simple formulae" suggests, Robinson justifies this claim in part through appeals to the nonreductive sciences: the "new and truly modern physics and cosmology" developed in the early twentieth century (*AM* ix–x), the "strange ways of quarks and photons" (*AM* xiv) that show how "unknowability is the first thing about reality that must be acknowledged" (*AM* 54). This unknowability, she insists, likely extends to the human brain, which

---

[22] See McDowell, *Mind and World*, chaps. 5–6.

[23] See, on this point, Terry Pinkard, "Was Pragmatism the Successor to Idealism?" in *New Pragmatists*, ed. Cheryl Misak (New York: Cambridge University Press, 2007), 142–68. Like Pippin, whom I mentioned above, Pinkard represents the Hegelian wing of the contemporary antinaturalist coalition I'm sketching here. For other voices who have raised questions about evolutionary psychology in comparable terms, see Richard Rorty, "Philosophy Envy," *Daedalus* 133 (Fall 2004): 18–24; Christine M. Korsgaard, *The Sources of Normativity* (Cambridge: Cambridge University Press, 1996); John Dupré, *Human Nature and the Limits of Science* (New York: Oxford University Press, 2003).

[24] Percy, *The Message in the Bottle*, 153–54.

is merely "a lump of meat" to both the evolutionary psychologist and the antin-aturalist philosopher, but which in more sophisticated accounts displays "the uncanny properties of the finer textures of the physical" (*AM* 113). If, as "some people have suggested," the brain is governed by "quantum phenomena," then scrutinizing "lobes or glands" with "a primitive understanding of the brain's materiality" will not get us very far (*AM* 113). And if our longstanding mech-anistic conception of causality is indeed less plausible than it seemed before Einstein (one of Robinson's heroes), there may be room in our ontology for the spiritual and moral ideals that have seemed so resistant to physical explana-tion.[25] "Human fellow-feeling," she declares, "is demonstrably present in the world" (*DA* 68), and to understand its origins we should treat it neither as out-right "unnatural" nor as the outcome of more basic—and much darker—"natu-ral" instincts. It is built as deeply into our biology as aggression and violence, and has an equally justified place in the repertoire of human instincts.

To be sure, out-naturalizing the naturalists isn't unproblematic: the quan-tum world is still, after all, an aspect of the material world, and it's unclear why quarks and photons would yield human fellow-feeling more smoothly than lobes or glands. But the third and final claim follows from Robinson's first two, and concerns the ontological status of our normative concepts. The nominalist presumption informing all of evolutionary psychology is that our normative vocabularies are wholly reducible. The most celebrated case is the concept "altruism." If the "ultimate cause" of our behavior is to pass on our genes, how then do we explain the person who dives into the river to save the drowning child, or the worker-ants who defend the nest for the queen but who never themselves procreate? The question puzzled Darwin himself, who was well aware of the existence of neuter and sterile ants, and who proposed what came to be known as the "kin selection" theory: natural selection could give rise to such self-sacrifice if this behavior crucially aided their blood relations who *could* reproduce.[26] Nowadays the answer is typically credited to Richard Hamilton, the theoretical biologist who in the mid-1960s combined Darwin's basic insight about kin relations with contemporary work on genes (a concept Darwin, of course, never had) and the cost-benefit mathematical models that

---

[25] See Robinson's account of the public dispute between Freud and Einstein, in *Death of Adam*, 59–62. The importance of quantum explanations is raised also in Robinson's "Hysterical Scientism: The Hysterical Realism of Richard Dawkins," *Harper's* (November 29, 2006), 83–88—a combative review of *The God Delusion*, Dawkins's 2006 book.

[26] See Lee Alan Dugatkin, *The Altruism Equation: Seven Scientists Search for the Origins of Goodness* (Princeton, NJ: Princeton University Press, 2006), chap. 1. From the text of *Absence of Mind*, it is clear that Robinson's understanding of Darwinian theory is based in part on Dugatkin's book.

he had learned as a demography student at the London School of Economics. In what became known as the "Hamilton rule" (the importance of which some commentators have likened to Newton's laws of motion), Hamilton proposed that $rxb>c$—where r is the degree of relation between two animals, b is the benefit to the survival of one's genes, and c is the cost incurred by a particular act.[27] The mathematics here is complex, but the gist is not. If "fitness" refers not to the fitness of the individual person or animal but to the fitness of the gene, and if the main goal of one's genes is survival and replication, then helping one's kin—who by definition share one's genes—is almost as effective as having more offspring. And the probabilities of this "inclusive fitness" formula are quantifiable: All "benefits" being equal, I am twice as likely, in Hamilton's reckoning, to come to the aid of my own children, who share fifty percent of my genes, as I am to help my grandchildren, who share only twenty-five percent.

Hamilton's publications in the 1960s caught the eye of Wilson and Dawkins and inspired their pioneering work.[28] But for Robinson, such a view amounts to the claim that all moral behavior is at bottom an expression of calculable self-interest, and this reduction simply flies—again—in the face of the "data." Our "manifest behavior, like it or not, includes generosity" (*DA* 52), and "human fellow-feeling," to recall a remark cited earlier, is "demonstrably present in the world" (*DA* 68). August Comte's visions of universal cooperation may have been "starry-eyed," but there is indeed "something in experience that relates, however exactly, to benevolence and also altruism," and that "takes pleasure in the thought of a humane and benign social order" (*AM* 41). To say that "fellow-feeling" or "generosity" is a product of our replicating genes is not only to assume a perspective unavailable to human beings, but—just as consequentially—to diminish our confidence in these terms, to erode our trust that they identify real properties in the world. When scientists tell us that the mystery of motive is solved, politico-moral words like "kindness," "generosity," and "the general good" seem to be disposable fictions. For Robinson, understanding ourselves in these terms—as self-serving even in our most charitable moments—eventually grows into a self-fulfilling prophecy. A culture committed to reducing our normative concepts disables the practices in which these concepts have their life, grants self-interest a "seemingly unlimited power over our *moral* imaginations," and rationalizes the mistreatment of our most vulnerable citizens as "readily as

---

[27] Dugatkin, *The Altruism Equation*, x.

[28] Wilson has recently expressed reservations about the theory, saying that he now prefers something more like Darwin's kinship theory, which allows for the possibility that cooperative groups tend to fare better than competitive groups. See Jonah Lehrer, "Kin and Kind," *The New Yorker* (March 5, 2012), 36–42.

any bolder act" (*DA* 67). With the "stripping away of humane constraints" (*DA* 28), we make "resentment" respectable (*DA* 67), contribute to the "bluntly mercenary character of contemporary culture" (*DA* 73), and no longer find uses for "words like. . .courage, dignity, and graciousness; learnedness, fair-mindedness, openhandedness; loyalty, respect, and good faith" (*DA* 106). "What are 'we'," she asks, "if we must be bribed and seduced by illusory sensations we call love or courage or benevolence?" (*AM* 61). Being a nominalist about these types of words means losing more than a few quaint phrases, and more even than the practices that have, up to now, depended on them. It means, in effect, losing *us*.

II. Choosing Beauty

Summing up the claims I've just sketched, Robinson asks: "Since we do in fact have some power of choice,. . .what in the world could have moved us to choose anything so graceless and ugly?" (*DA* 59). This can sound ironic when we recall that Robinson has spent considerable energy rehabilitating John Calvin, that gray joyless preacher of determinism. But Robinson's Calvin is a far cry from the familiar picture. Calvin in her account is a deeply learned humanist, steeped in the Greek and Latin classics and a crucial inspiration for representative democracy, the abolition of slavery, and the rights of women. This Calvin remains an Augustinian—we're always estranged from God, never perfectible—but we retain something of the image of God, some (in Calvin's words) "sparks of understanding" and "some desire for truth," however "choked with dense ignorance" we may be.[29] When Calvin calls human beings "worms," Robinson claims, he isn't denying that "humankind is itself a sufficient revelation of the divine presence"; he's quoting Psalm 22, which Jesus himself recited on the cross (*DA* 183). Hence her insistence on the "data" of "generosity," "loyalty," and other normative concepts: these are "sparks" that are coeval with any instinct for selfishness or violence, and just as forceful.

However accurate it is, Robinson's image of Calvin itself constitutes a rejoinder to the idea that our visible behavior is merely a thin veneer, cloaking either a stew of aggression or an incessantly churning cost-benefit analysis.[30] But her question about our being moved to "choose" something "graceless and ugly" points to a corner of thought that I've been ignoring up to now: namely, her aesthetics. The arts are a less explicit theme in Robinson's writing than the

---

[29] Qtd. in John Passmore, *The Perfectibility of Man* (London: Duckworth, 1970), 106.

[30] On the question of how accurate her image of Calvin is, see Shy's "Religion and Marilynne Robinson."

others I've isolated, and less explicit than one might expect. Percy, for instance, writes persistently about the function and cognitive role of modern fiction, and often speaks at length of the various figures he read or admired: Sartre, Camus, Dostoevsky, Joseph Heller, Saul Bellow. Robinson, by contrast, has said remarkably little about literary texts and artworks: she has taught in a university but has never published academic criticism; she laments the "slack and underfinanced journalism" of our culture (*WC* xvi), but has seldom written reviews or literary journalism; and her references to artists and artworks consist chiefly of passing allusions.[31] Nevertheless, the question of how the arts fit into human life and culture is essential for elaborating her confrontation with contemporary Darwinism.

Darwinians have addressed the arts chiefly because they seem to flout the evolutionary narrative. As Brian Boyd says, they crystallize the question of how the human "appetite for the useful"—an appetite that clearly is at the heart of any plausible evolutionary explanation—can coexist with the many human activities that seem to have no obvious evolutionary or utilitarian payoff.[32] Some answers to this question haven't been especially illuminating, as when Pinker uses the final chapter of *The Blank Slate* to assail aesthetic modernism and postmodernism—movements that, he says, succumbed to Virginia Woolf's belief that "on or about December 1910 the nature of human character changed," encouraging artists to "cast aside" "all the tricks that artists had used for millennia to please the human palate" (*BS* 409–10).[33] But other evolutionary accounts of aesthetics have been more careful, most notably Denis Dutton's *The Art Instinct* (2009), which explores how "the existence and character" of the arts "are connected to Pleistocene interests, preferences, and capacities."[34] For Dutton, they are connected not, as Pinker implies, as mere by-products of a natural evolutionary process, a disposable "add-on" feature to our machinery. They are instead ways of *satisfying* our naturally evolved capacities and instincts,

---

[31] As when, while attacking Daniel Dennett's connection between music and the human nervous system, Robinson claims that Bach "is not to be imagined without a highly distinctive, highly elaborated conception of God, and life in a culture that invoked the idea of God by means of music" (*DA* 73).

[32] Brian Boyd, "Evolutionary Theories of Art," *The Literary Animal: Evolution and the Nature of Narrative*, ed. Jonathan Gottschall and David Sloan Wilson (Evanston, IL: Northwestern University Press, 2005), 147.

[33] Pinker in fact mangles Woolf's famous statement, rendering it as: "In or about December 1910, human nature changed." I'll avoid this problem here, but for some comments on the misquotation, see Louis Menand, "What Comes Naturally," a review of *The Blank Slate*, in *The New Yorker* (November 22, 2002), 96, which sees it as symptomatic of larger problems in Pinker's discussion.

[34] Denis Dutton, *The Art Instinct: Beauty, Pleasure, and Human Evolution* (London: Bloomsbury Press, 2009), 96; henceforth cited parenthetically as *AI*.

much as chocolate can satisfy our ancient nutritional and gustatory preferences despite our having never evolved discrete chocolate-tasting organs. Only by seeing art in these terms—as codifications of our innate interests and capacities, ways of serving and extending them—do we begin to capture the central role they have played in every human culture.

Dutton uses these basic claims to enumerate what he sees as the most salient criteria for "art" worldwide. Art objects, he says, create direct pleasure: they initiate "layered" experiences unfolding over time, and are pleasurable in their own right rather than useful or pleasurable for something else (*AI* 52). They show specialized skills and virtuosity, requiring "special talent or mastery" (*AI* 53), and have "style," made against a relatively "normal" background that allows artists to create elements of expressive surprise (*AI* 53). They involve "novelty and creativity," enabling both the "attention-grabbing function of art" and "the artist's perhaps less jolting capacity to explore the deeper possibilities of a medium or theme" (*AI* 54). They engender a language of judgment and evaluation, ranging from the shoptalk of artists themselves to the public discourse of scholars and critics (*AI* 54). They typically involve the representation of real or imaginary experiences of the world, be it in sculpture, paintings, or narratives, or sometimes even music; and they involve a "special focus," a tendency toward being "made a separate and dramatic focus of experience" (*AI* 55). To one degree or another, art is "shot through with emotion," whether these emotions are incited by what's depicted (the pathos of a painting's scene, a poem's vision of death) or the mood pervading the work itself (which may be somewhat different from the evident mood of what is being represented). Artworks typically involve "intellectual challenge," demanding that an audience stretch its perceptual and mental capacities, and partake in a culture's artistic traditions or institutions, a backdrop of historical practices. And lastly, art objects involve "imaginative experience": "All art happens in a make-believe world," a "theater of the imagination" that is "decoupled" not only from "the constraints of logic and rational understanding," but also from the very genuine novelties and virtuoso skills one might see in a chef's kitchen or an athletic competition. A Harlem Globetrotters game is a "true artistic event," designed to entertain, but the Super Bowl is sport, an activity whose considerable aesthetic attractions are secondary to what's on the scoreboard at the end of the game.[35]

Robinson wouldn't categorically object to this list. Indeed, at times she uses the term "art" in ways that, as in Dutton, align it with skills or know-how of a

---

[35] In enumerating this list, Dutton doesn't say that every artifact ever deemed "art" will completely meet every criterion, and he acknowledges the existence of many borderline cases. But he also

practical sort, part and parcel of the practices humans have developed to cope with their world. Calvin, for instance, is said to have extended the "honorable art of preaching" (*DA* 231), and contemporary people are held to assume there is "an intrinsic fraudulence in the old arts of civilization," for example, "religion, politics, philosophy, and music" (*DA* 3). But other features of Dutton's account would rankle, the clearest of which are his claims about art and human "self-domestication." The key neo-Darwinian claim here is that art can be seen as a kind of peacock's tail. As Darwin himself noted, a peacock's tail is difficult to explain in terms of adaptive survival mechanisms: biologically expensive to grow, requiring energy that could otherwise be used by the organism, and weighing the peacock down in ways that make it vulnerable to predators. But the peacock's tail is more understandable when it is seen as part of the sexual selection side of evolution, less a way for species members to cope with their immediate external environments than a way to attract one another and thus pass on their genes. This is the origin, argues Dutton, for art's association with a sense of style, uniqueness, accomplishment, intelligence, and creativity. Why are artworks everywhere so often made of rare or expensive materials? Why are they so time-consuming to create, requiring rare skills and abilities? The reason, says Dutton, is that these traits can be seen as *fitness signals*, signs that artists are mentally and physically flourishing, ripe for reproduction. Artists are (Dutton's analogy) akin to the Gilded Age conspicuous consumers whom Veblen described (*AI* 156); and their art (Dutton, again) is a "gaudy, overpowered Pleistocene home-entertainment system, devised in order that our Stone Age ancestors could attract, amuse, and bed one another" (*AI* 151). Contra Freud, the sexual component of art lies less in the alleged symbolism of a work (convex shapes standing for some tumescent body part, etc.) than the *making* of art itself, the urge to expend huge energy on "objects of the most extreme elegance and complexity" (*AI* 163). Sexual selection, claims Dutton, "explains the will of human beings to charm and interest each other" at the most fundamental level, and art is a leading—not the only, but a leading—expression of such charms and interests, a powerful forum for "self-domestication" (*AI* 163).[36]

Robinson is aware of these claims, and lampoons them by deploying, again, the distinction between first-person "testimony" and third-person

---

anticipates a host of objections, and argues forcefully that his list can accommodate works as diverse as Hindu *jyonti* paintings and Duchamp's *Fountain*.

[36] The theory of sexual selection on which Dutton bases his discussion has been questioned within the scientific community. In *The Genial Gene: Deconstructing Darwinian Selfishness* (Berkeley: University of California Press, 2009), Joan Roughgarden has pointed to a number of phenomena that seem to counteract what she regards as the dubious, politically inflected accounts of "the

explanation: "What is art?" she asks, furious tongue in cheek. "It is a means of attracting mates, even though artists may have felt that it was an exploration of experience, or the possibilities of communication, and of the extraordinary collaboration of eye and hand" (*AM* xvii). She ridicules such explanations not because she believes art is unrelated to ostensibly nonaesthetic practices. Her complaint instead derives from her sense that art has a primordial relation to *religion*—an area of culture about which evolutionary aesthetics has had relatively little to say, and about which Darwinians in general have been rather dubious, regarding it either as a "natural phenomenon" explicable through cool scientific scrutiny (Dennett) or a "delusion" meriting only educated mockery (Dawkins).[37] "It is no wonder," she says in "Darwinism," "that the major arts in virtually every civilization have centered around religion," given that "language, in its wisdom," understands that the "assigning or acknowledging of worth" is the "function of creative, imaginative behavior" (*DA* 71). Calvin's "virtuosic scholarship," she claims, "could be thought of as monumental public art, by analogy with the work of contemporaries like Michelangelo" (*DA* 199–200), and Dietrich Bonhoeffer's writing often attains the status of a "hymn": it is a "meditation" that provides further evidence that "great theology is always a kind of giant and intricate poetry, like epic or saga" (*DA* 117). Ancient literature and religion, she proposes, are unimaginable without one another, and seem even "to have come into being together, if by literature I can be understood to include pre-literature, narrative whose purpose is to put human life, causality, and meaning in relation, to make each of them in some degree intelligible in terms of the other two" (*WC* 11).

Robinson's notion of art isn't just religious; it's distinctively Protestant. Whereas the Catholic Percy emphasizes the importance of the "you" to the "Namer," as well as the overriding significance of context and relations and our shared social practices, Robinson's essays speak of "the difference I felt between the world and myself" while she attended church as a child (*DA* 235),

---

selfish gene." In many parts of nature, she claims, we don't see drab, cautious females attracted to highly ornamented, promiscuous males seeking to pass on their genes—a view that seems to naturalize selfishness, competitiveness, stereotypical sexual roles, rape, and war. Biologically speaking, what is sought in a mate is not merely sexual selection and reproduction, but what she calls "social selection," a mate that can help raise an offspring to reproductive age and in a stable infrastructure. (For a summary of Roughgarden's views, see Prescilla Long's review in *American Scholar* 78 (Spring 2009): 118–21.) Roughgarden's claims, however, change little in the current context. After all, she is still giving some account of sexual preferences and sexual attraction, the need or wish to attract members of the same species, and were such claims to be verified, Dutton could adapt them very easily to his own thesis about our instinct for art.

37 See Richard Dawkins, *The God Delusion* (New York: Bantam Books, 2006); Daniel C. Dennett, *Breaking the Spell: Religion as a Natural Phenomenon* (New York: Penguin, 2007).

and posit that the "hypertrophic bookishness of my life arose directly out of my exposure, among modest Protestant solemnities of music and flowers, to the language of Scripture" (*DA* 230). Such experiences no doubt prepared her well for William James, whose account of religious experience, she notes with admiration, emphasizes that religious emotions are felt by "individual" people in "solitude"—the "unvarying conditions of the mind," comments Robinson, "no matter the web of culture and language by which it is enabled, sustained, and limited" (*AM* 7).[38] Such a view makes art the great antidote to the "grand projects of generalization" (*AM* 22) that have marked and marred so much of "modern" thought. From Malthus and Spencer to Dawkins and Pinker, "parascientific" social and political theory has used "the science of its moment" to offer "a set of general conclusions about what our nature is and must be" (*AM* 32–33); Freudian psychology proceeds "at the highest possible level of generalization," all in order to avoid the possibility that it may merely reflect the historical context of *fin de siècle* Vienna (*AM* 81); and disciplines such as anthropology and economics "posit a human simplicity within a simple reality" (*WC* 5). Art by contrast foregrounds how "each of us lives intensely within herself or himself, continuously assimilating past and present experience to a narrative and vision that are unique in every case yet profoundly communicable" (*AM* 132). The allegedly scientific researches of game theory tell us little about "the problem of stranger altruism" that we don't all already learn from "ballads and novels and films" (*AM* 59). The greatest fiction acknowledges "the sense of the sacred, the beautiful, everything in any way lofty" (*WC* 5), and "lies outside" the "collective fiction" of our day, which operates with a "grim and minor imagination" (*DA* 77). A true modern humanism, she insists, would be one that promotes a view of the self that is "refined by exposure to things that are wonderful and difficult and imbued with what was called the human spirit," and which would rest "on the idea that people have souls, and that they have certain obligations to them, and certain pleasure in them, which arise from their refinement or the expression in art or in admirable or striking conduct" (*DA* 9).

Given these claims, it's appropriate not only that Robinson should invoke James, but also that the figures who have most shaped her fiction should be James's Transcendentalist forerunners. These affinities extend not only to Robinson's themes and style—the preference for meditation over plot, the densely packed and lyrical sentences inflected by theological language, the intimation that this natural world, if keenly enough perceived, might somehow be

---

[38] There's an irony in these invocations of James insofar as James was profoundly influenced by Darwin, Robinson's nemesis. Robinson largely ignores this connection, however.

the symbol of the divine. It also inflects her compositional methods. Much as Emerson and Thoreau pieced together their essays by splicing together their journal entries, *Housekeeping* originated from metaphors that Robinson claims to have written down over several years, and which she noticed only afterward cohered in surprising ways.[39] Emerson, Melville, Thoreau, and Dickinson use metaphor, she claims, "as a highly legitimate strategy for real epistemological questions to be dealt with in fiction and poetry," and thus provide a model for dramatizing her sense that "reality is of a piece." "It seems to me," she has said, "that reality must somehow be describable as linked through analogue," that it "has a signature quality," and that "the discovery of anything that seems communicative, that satisfies the mind, that is emblematic or that answers to the mind" should be regarded as "an opening" (*CL* 239). "A mystical experience," she has claimed, would be "wasted on me," because even the most "ordinary things have always seemed numinous": "You don't simply perceive something that is statically present, but in fact there is a visionary quality to all experience. It means something because it is addressed to you"—a feature, she says, she learned from the "individualism that you find in Walt Whitman and Emily Dickinson" (*PR*).

III. Acting On Behalf Of

The correlation between art and religion, the vindication of William James, the identification with Transcendentalism—all these are symptoms of Robinson's self-conscious distance from neo-Darwinism. There is, naturally, more one could say about Darwinian naturalism and Robinson's essayistic response to it. But I want now to move from this sketch of Robinson's aesthetics into a consideration of Robinson's art, particularly *Gilead*, which was published the same year that *Time* named Pinker one of the most influential hundred people in the world.[40] The setting and characters and overall atmosphere of the novel make it seem at first glance wholly unrelated to Robinson's nonfiction essays on

---

[39] Interview with Sarah Fay in "The Art of Fiction No. 198," *The Paris Review* 186 (2008) http://www.theparisreview.org/interviews/5863/the-art-of-fiction-no-198-marilynne-robinson (accessed January 20, 2016); henceforth cited parenthetically as *PR*. For a recent account of Emerson's particular method of splicing from journals, see Paul Grimstad, *Experience and Experimental Writing: Literary Pragmatism from Emerson to the Jameses* (New York: Oxford University Press, 2013), chap. 1.

[40] Robert Wright, "2004 *Time* 100." *Time* (April 26, 2004). <<http://content.time.com/time/specials/packages/article/0,28804,1970858_1970909_1971671,00.html>> (accessed March 27, 2016).

Darwin, an irenic retreat from the polemics of the *Absence of Mind* or *Death of Adam*. But the actual situation is more complicated.

Gilead is narrated by John Ames, a seventy-six-year-old Congregationalist minister in Gilead, Iowa, who, having been recently diagnosed with angina, begins to compose a long letter to the seven-year-old son he has with his wife, who is several decades Ames's junior. The letter begins by expressing regret for the precarious financial situation that his coming death will leave his family: "I do regret that I have almost nothing to leave you and your mother. A few old books no one else would want."[41] But, prompted by his wife, it quickly shifts into a record of what he calls his "begats" (9). After logging some basic data about his own life—"I, John Ames, was born in the Year of Our Lord 1880 in the state of Kansas, the son of John Ames and Martha Turner Ames" (9)—he turns to his family history, which is dominated by three male figures.

One is his older brother Edward, who left Gilead for college when he was sixteen, earned a doctorate in philosophy in Germany, and taught at the state college for his entire adult life. The family's voice of secular conscience, Edward wrote a dissertation on Feuerbach and is sophisticatedly defiant during his visits home, refusing to say grace at family dinners and telling his young sibling that leaving Gilead is "like waking from a trance" (26). Still more prominent in Ames's thoughts is his grandfather, a minister who saw a vision of Christ telling him to "free the captive," moved in the 1830s from Maine to Kansas to join the Free Soil Party, aided John Brown, and lost an eye in the Civil War. Ames knows the grandfather only in his old age, when he is regarded as an elderly eccentric by the townspeople and a "saint of some kind" by the young Ames, who embarrassedly watches the old man give away all the tools, food, and clothes in the Ames household in order to follow the biblical injunction "To him who asks, give" (31). The grandfather bitterly quarrels with the third looming presence in Ames family history, Ames's own father, who was also a minister but unlike his father was a resolute pacifist. Their quarrels finally come to a head when the grandfather, disgusted by what seems to him an emptily innocuous sermon, walks out of his son's church one day. Responding angrily, Ames's father retorts that the violence of the old abolitionists had "*nothing* to do with Jesus. Nothing. Nothing" (85). When the antebellum past was brought up in conversation, reports Ames, his father would simply declare that this history was "all best forgotten" (76), which gave him the impression that his grandfather had

---

[41] Marilynne Robinson, *Gilead* (New York: Farrar Straus Giroux, 2004), 4; henceforth cited parenthetically by page number.

committed "some kind of crime" and that his father was "trying to cover up for Cain" (81–82).

Even this hasty sketch suggests a few different ways *Gilead*, like Robinson's essays, distances itself from neo-Darwinian thought. One is in what I was earlier calling "data." The primary entities I have just mentioned—Ames, his older brother, his young son, his father and grandfather, John Brown—are all *persons*. An obvious point, perhaps, but next to Robinson's essays, crucial: The behavior *Gilead* is most keen to identify and track is not that of imperceptible subpersonal systems of genes or instincts, but of perceptible, embodied entities moving in complex ways through shared public space. *Gilead* is in this sense "testimony": indifferent to atoms and DNA and even brains, but fluent on the phenomenology of sitting on a porch on a summer evening and excellent at explaining the ordinary motives of parishioners visiting their minister on a weekday. "Testimony" in this sense is at the heart of what we usually call "fiction," but we should remember that Robinson didn't have to focus on this level of description, and lots of narratives can be told about other levels and other entities. In, for instance, the second chapter of *The Selfish Gene*, Dawkins tells the story of the rise of the "replicators," molecules that could copy themselves, and which emerged from the stew of other molecules floating in the primeval soup of the prehistoric seas. Over the course of hundreds of millions of years these replicators combined and recombined into ever larger stable units, until the eventual triumphs of the protozoa and fungi and eventually of reptiles and mammals.[42] The story is fascinating, its details astonishingly complex, its development full of surprises. But its key data consist of motions, causes, and things, whereas *Gilead*'s are actions, reasons, and persons. The central concern for both Dawkins and Robinson, we might say, is *inheritance*, but what inheritance means in each case—what constitutes a generation, how it transmits or receives features from its predecessors, how it might *fail* to do so—is palpably different.

A second challenge to Darwin, one less abstract and more distinctive of Robinson, is manifest in the moral and political commitments of Ames's grandfather and father. It's tempting to see these figures as poised in mutual conflict, one an emblem of antebellum revivalism and the other of late-nineteenth-century rationalism and progressivism. The grandfather, we read, was a man "afire with old certainties" (32), inspired by a vision of Jesus, and after returning from the Civil War he would stand before a congregation whose sons and

---

[42] See Dawkins, *The Selfish Gene*, 21–45.

husbands had been killed in the fighting and preach "every Sunday on the divine righteousness manifested in it all" (87). Postwar life so disappoints him that, after his final quarrel with his son, he returns to Kansas, his final words to his family alluding in prophetic tones to the Book of Proverbs: "Without vision the people perish" (85). By contrast, his son—Ames's father—began attending Quaker meetings after the war (87), "never encouraged any talk about visions or miracles, except the ones in the Bible" (48), and hurled the old man's guns into a river after his death (79). As a boy, he once encountered a U.S. soldier on the hunt for the fugitive John Brown, and the news that his own father subsequently killed this soldier seems to have instilled in him a permanent revulsion toward violence. When discussing his father's tireless work for social justice, he would often note the irony that he and his sisters were, "in a manner of speaking, left largely fatherless" (89), and reconciliation between the two men is available only after grandfather Ames's death, when Ames the younger traveled through the "godforsaken" plains (10), struggling for a month to find his father's grave.

The text, then, encourages us to see the father and grandfather in stark opposition. Seen, however, in light of Robinson's essays, their deeper commonalities come to the fore, particularly the stern challenge that both of them present to a strictly Darwinian framework. It is not immediately clear, for instance, how helping black slaves, risking his life in the Underground Railroad, constructing tunnels to hide escapees in prairie towns, and aiding one of the most wanted men in the country would yield the grandfather any straightforward evolutionary "benefit." In Hamilton's terms, he has no genetic relationship—no r—to any of these fugitives, and the violence he endorses is in no obvious way the product of any cost-benefit analysis. If anything, the novel portrays the grandfather as *inverting* the evolutionary account, showing him ready to sacrifice the well-being of his own family in order to change the plight of people to whom he has no relation whatsoever, and most of whom he will never know. The pacifism of Ames's father goes at least one step further, widening the grandfather's circle of regard into a full-fledged universalism. The humanistic ideals that animate his life are a challenge to any and all instincts for violence that humans have historically exhibited. According to his vision, one's moral concern should extend not only to the oppressed, but also to the oppressors, whose blindness deserves our sympathy rather than our vengeance. Our collective failure on this score leaves Ames's father deeply aggrieved: he dies, we learn, in 1914, "mainly from rage and exasperation" at the "celebrations" with which Europeans welcomed the start of World War I (86).

In making a radical abolitionist and a radical pacifist the central figures of the narrator's past, *Gilead* does more, in other words, than trace the history of American Protestantism from New England Calvinists to Midwestern liberal activists.[43] It also dramatizes the issue, central to Robinson's essays, of non-strategic cooperation. If altruism isn't historically specific—if it can be said to be manifest in some form at any time and any place—then it is nevertheless, *Gilead* implies, available in expansive and shrunken forms, depending on what we allow to have power over our (Robinson's term) *"moral* imagination" in any socio-historical moment (*CA* 67). These forms are tied to certain traditions and principles, all of which can wane and lose their grip over time, strengthening or fraying at different points in history. Setting the book in 1956, and granting its main characters a healthy life span, allows Robinson to evoke the fading ember of a culture that was motivated by what her essays call "compassionate imagination" and "benevolence," virtues whose "absence" forestalls the ability to understand the past in anything but "stereotyped" stories (*AM* 50). A lack of such high words leads contemporary Darwinians to warp, for instance, the story of Phineas Gage, the nineteenth-century railroad worker whose personality became suddenly surly and violent after an iron rod accidentally pierced his skull. Pinker and others cite the case to claim that rational planning and moral behavior can be localized in the brain, all the while ignoring the frustration, lost hopes, and self-loathing that also might account for the man's ensuing rage and lack of self-control (*AM* 47–50). For Robinson, a lack of "compassionate imagination" leads us likewise to simplify—and here her criticism anticipates recent work among intellectual historians—the religious traditions that generated the most significant reforms of the nineteenth century: to overlook, for instance, the social activism of the Methodists, a group Ames's grandfather greatly admires after the Civil War (88), and to drain the radicalism from the McGuffey Readers, caricaturing these nineteenth-century educational anthologies as propaganda for early American capitalism and middle-class propriety (*DA* 126–49).[44]

The Death of Adam identifies one particularly important concept that gets corroded when our naturalistic accounts draw us away from a patiently elaborated historical understanding of "altruism." *Family*, Robinson says, has many times and in many places meant "those toward whom one feels loyalty and obligation,

---

[43] A point made by a number of readers; see, for example, Betty Mensch, "Jonathan Edwards, *Gilead*, and the Problem of 'Tradition'," *Journal of Law and Religion* 21 (2005/2006): 221–41.

[44] Perhaps the most prominent intellectual historian to have studied these liberal traditions of American Protestantism is David Hollinger; see his *After Cloven Tongues of Fire: Protestant Liberalism in Modern American History* (Princeton, NJ: Princeton University Press, 2013).

and/or from whom one derives identity, and/or to whom one gives identity, and/or with whom one shares habits, tastes, stories, customs, memories"—a definition capacious enough to suggest that "the biological family. . .is, in fact, very arbitrary in its composition" (DA 87). The remark reminds us pointedly that Gilead was published in the very month that saw the reelection of George W. Bush, who many commentators, then and now, have seen as the culmination of the Religious Right and its persistent identification with militarism and "family values."[45] But the remark also draws attention to a further way that Gilead challenges evolutionary accounts of altruism—namely in its ambivalent picture of blood kinship. On the one hand, an old male's having a child with a much younger female chimes perfectly with an evolutionary account of our behavioral imperatives, and one could read Ames's warm, pedagogical letter to his son as part of his parental "investment"—to use the evolutionist's operative metaphor—in his child.[46] His affection for the small town of Gilead could likewise be read in evolutionary terms: the town is the "tribe" where his genes are mostly likely to replicate. On the other hand, however, the novel curtails this evolutionary train of thought in subtle and significant ways.

Most important are the ways that Ames's attention to his clan is portrayed as deeply problematic, not merely paternally devoted. The disruption arises with the appearance of Jack Boughton, the prodigal son of Ames's closest friend, who has returned unexpectedly to Gilead after years of estrangement. From a young age Jack was a thorn in the side of his family and of Ames, his godfather and namesake, continually getting into mischief as a boy and drinking

---

[45] For an insightful discussion of Robinson's relation to contemporary Christianity, see Christopher Douglas, "Christian Multiculturalism and Unlearned History in Marilynne Robinson's Gilead," Novel 44 (2011): 333–53.

[46] Consideration, loyalty, and long-term friendship are some of the virtues that Amy Hungerford identifies as central to the religious practices at the center of Gilead; see her Postmodern Belief: American Literature and Religion Since 1960 (Princeton, NJ: Princeton University Press, 2010), 117–18. On the metaphor of "investment," see Dupré, Human Nature and the Limits of Science, 50–54. From an evolutionary point of view, Ames would, of course, have less of an "investment" in their son than Ames's wife. But this raises the question of why, from an evolutionary point of view, she would have chosen him, an impoverished, lonely, elderly lifetime bachelor—and she is clearly depicted as the active pursuer in the relationship (see, e.g., 207–208). It's an issue clarified somewhat in Lila (New York: Farrar, Straus and Giroux, 2014), the novel about Ames's wife that Robinson published a decade after Gilead. The background that Robinson imagines there for Lila—orphaned at a young age, raised by itinerant strangers during the Depression, briefly a prostitute, then a hotel maid, and eventually drifting to Gilead, where she lives alone in an abandoned cabin—underscores the desperate state that might explain her finding the elderly Ames an attractive mate. "Somebody like me," she says to the minister shortly after they meet, "might marry someone like you just because you got a good house and winter's coming. Just because she's tired of the damn loneliness" (84–85). This hardly makes Ames into a Gilded Age baron, but for a reader like Pinker, his status as a minister in a tiny midcentury town would presumably endow him with at least a modicum of status in Lila's eyes.

and stealing as a youth. As a college student he became more ambitious in his indiscretions and permanently damaged his reputation in the town: as Ames eventually reveals, he impregnated a poor underage girl whom he then (in an act, we might note, wholly consistent with evolutionary theory) abandoned, disgracing his father and never returning to Gilead. Near the end of the narrative, however, Jack, now forty-three, privately reveals to Ames the reason for his recent return to Gilead: he has a child with an African-American woman in St. Louis, Della, whose family has objected to her marrying a white man. "We are married," observes Jack, "in the eyes of God, as they say. Who does not provide a certificate, but who also does not enforce anti-miscegenation laws" (220). After his boss caught him in a public park with his wife and promptly fired him, Jack began considering relocating his young family to Iowa, a state that, as he knows, had in the previous century been called "the shining star of radicalism" (220). Since he returned to Gilead, the precariously frail health of his aged father, Ames's friend, has made him reticent to reveal his secret to his family, and he seeks Ames's counsel in order to know if moving back permanently would be feasible with a black wife and mixed-race child.

Jack's revelation so startles Ames that he suddenly starts a new page, as if the news requires a different journal or letter altogether, and Jack's story is given almost wholly in his own words—the first time in the text that the reader hears at length a voice other than that of Ames. And these startling formal changes of direction illuminate the ways the book has been patiently, quietly calling attention to what we might call the *cost* of kinship: the forms of blindness and neglence that can arise when parochial conceptions of family are granted too much legitimacy.

With Jack's news, for instance, we may begin to reconsider Ames's frequently expressed and benign-looking love of baseball, which he played with his brother Edward. As an adult he follows the major leagues so enthusiastically on the radio that his congregation gives him a television as a gift, so he can watch some games (126). But after Jack's revelation we are forced to notice that Ames has nowhere shown any awareness of the game's tumultuous midcentury politics. One of the only stories he tells about himself and his grandfather is about the two of them going to Des Moines to watch a game involving Bud Fowler, who in the late nineteenth century was the first African-American professional player, but despite the fact that his own son wears a Dodgers cap (164), he makes no mention of Jackie Robinson, who had broken the color barrier in the twentieth century and was playing his final season as Ames writes his letter. With Jack's news, too, we recognize that Ames has made no reference whatsoever to the civil rights movement, even though he's writing his letter in the middle of the year-long Montgomery Bus Boycott, the very months when another Protestant minister, Martin Luther King, Jr. was coming to national prominence. And with Jack's news, it becomes painfully clear just how far Ames has disavowed the burning of Gilead's black church several years earlier. The book's first reference to the fire comes in a fleeting parenthetical note (36–37), and to Jack he dismisses it as a "little nuisance fire" that happened "many years ago" (231). When Jack protests this characterization by saying that the African-American community had seen the fire in more threatening terms and had left for good, Ames writes with succinct embarrassment: "Of course there wasn't much I could say to that" (231).

What seems to leave Ames speechless here is a realization of what Robinson proposes in her essays: that kinship relations can inhibit, curb, or displace altruism as much as foster and sustain it. Such relations are particularly threatening to altruism in its more expansive forms, the sort of "kinship" that refers not just to biological family but also to attachments of loyalty, obligation, habits, tastes, customs, and memories—altruism, that is, in its most demanding and politically fraught forms. "Now, the fact is," Ames pauses to note while recording Jack's revelation, "I don't know how old Boughton would take all this. It surprised me to realize that. I think it is an issue we never discussed in all our years of discussing everything. It just didn't come up" (221).[47] Such an omission may surprise readers as much as it does the narrator. Ames has routinely been read as a moral paragon: to James Wood he seems "gentle, modest, loving, and above all good," if also "a bit boring"; to Joan Acocella he is an "exceptionally virtuous person" who "nevertheless" manages to be "interesting"; to Todd Shy he is that rare literary character who exhibits "simple, complete piety."[48]

---

[47] Placed in the context of the book as a whole, Ames's word choice in this passage can be understood to elaborate this shock of self-recognition even further. Early on, Ames remarks that he will try not "to use certain words more than I ought to"—terms that, in speech, have a particular flavor but on the page might be misconstrued. One such word is "old," which, he says, "actually has less to do with age. . .than it does with familiarity," setting "a thing apart as something regarded with a modest habitual affection" (28). A second such word is "just": when people say "the sun just *shone*" or "the tree just *glistened*," "they want to call attention to a thing existing in excess of itself, so to speak, a sort of purity or lavishness, at any rate something ordinary in kind but exceptional in degree" (28). Both of these terms appear when Ames confesses how he and Jack's father have completely ignored the issue of race. Referring to his friend as "*old* Boughton" is thus a way for Robinson to highlight Ames's intimacy—his complicity—with Jack's father, and in having Ames say that race "*just* didn't come up," she is underlining the sheer magnitude of their silence on the subject of race. Their avoidance exists, horrendously, "in excess of itself."

[48] See James Wood's "The Homecoming," *The New Yorker* (September 8, 2008); http://www.newyorker.com/magazine/2008/09/08/the-homecoming (accessed January 20, 2016); Joan Acocella, "Lonesome Road," *The New Yorker* (October 6, 2014) <http://www.newyorker.com/magazine/2014/10/06/lonesome-road> (accessed January 20, 2016); Shy, "Religion and Marilynne Robinson," 251.

But this is to miss badly the depth of Ames's failure: the book presents him as being complicit with some of the worst injustices of his day. If gentleness and modesty and goodness are indeed Ames's virtues, they take a conspicuously narrow form, diminishing rather than widening his circle of moral concern and sympathy. He has, the novel implies, reneged on the broad-minded commitments of both his grandfather and father, and, by contrast, grown torpid and complacent, negligent in his single-minded emphasis on family, offspring, and local community—the very emphases that contemporary Darwinism tells us are most natural and most justifiable.

IV. Living Forward in a World Ongoing

Contemporary Darwinians might disagree with the claims I've just imputed to Robinson's novel and essays, and say that an evolutionary emphasis on offspring and family is less constrictive than it appears at first glance. Pinker, for instance, has recently scrutinized the common assumption that the twentieth century was the bloodiest in human history, that its world wars and totalitarian regimes and genocides are clear evidence that human life has grown more heartless and violent, and his conclusion is that, in the big picture that evolutionary theory allows, human beings have, in fact, grown considerably more peaceable. Maybe nothing in history can match the fifty-five million deaths in World War II, but if we take the proportional numbers rather than total numbers, the catastrophes of 1939–1945 rank a mere eighth among the military atrocities ever recorded, producing just a fraction of the dead left by the An Lushan Revolt in eighth-century China. And proportionally, the present day also sees massively fewer cases of infant sacrifice, heretic burning, and slavery, and—despite the headlines—even less rape, homicide, and persecuted minorities. With, according to Pinker, the expansion of literacy, more centralized governments, and increased global trade, humans have cultivated the better angels of our nature, thus fostering the brain's "abstract reasoning" regions, from which, in turn, we've gradually learned the benefits of strategic cooperation over instinctual aggression and violence.[49]

But Pinker's claims would only be question-begging to Robinson, who would hold that they still take moral concern beyond one's kith and kin to be a matter of "optimizing" an individual's "preferences." Pinker does not, in other words, envision a genuinely nonstrategic form of cooperation, and still views moral

---

[49] Steven Pinker, *The Better Angels of Our Nature: Why Violence Has Declined* (New York: Viking, 2011); for Pinker's ranking of death tolls, see 195.

judgments as epiphenomenal, that is, reducible to more basic drives, especially egoistic ones. Robinson would agree with the philosopher John Dupré that, although in principle the rational-choice perspective embedded in contemporary Darwinism may be capable of "encompassing any mix of self-interested and non-self-interested concerns, in practice it almost invariably reflects the assumption that the former are far more significant."[50]

Gilead, however, does something more ambitious and interesting than entering explicitly into these debates, and to see how, let us linger longer with the figure of Jack Boughton. As I've said, Jack forces on both Ames and the reader a sudden understanding of what I have called the cost of kinship, the ways that blood relationships might foster not only peace but also a dangerous degree of exclusivity and complacency. To this extent, his appearance in the text helps bring *Gilead* into line with the claims Robinson makes in her nonfiction. Yet Jack also compels our discussion into another stage. His character helps alter the fundamental stylistic and generic features of the book, and in the process forces us to reflect more carefully on the various forms of writing that Robinson undertakes. Specifically, he makes us turn back from Robinson's own essays and consider how precisely she arrives at the opinions and claims they express, and whether a certain kind of conflict arises between her two chosen generic modes.

In an insightful discussion of the novel, Jonathan Lear has suggested that Jack introduces both Freudian and Kierkegaardian ideas of illusion.[51] Freudian illusions, says Lear, are evident in Jack's very wish to return to Gilead: If, as Freud has it, an illusion is a psychological state wherein a wish causes a false belief, then Jack's idea that he could return and incorporate himself seamlessly into Gilead clearly counts as an instance. But we only recognize Jack's idea as an illusion, continues Lear, because the novel also stages a Kierkegaardian version of illusion, which is less a psychological state than a cultural or social one, a condition in which institutions, habits, and rituals are publicly endorsed but their animating force has evaporated. Gilead is, says Lear, an updated instance of the nineteenth-century "Christendom" that raised Kierkegaard's fury, and Jack represents "an occasion for others either to display or fail to display their Christian charity" (47), a "challenge" that Gilead spectacularly fails to meet. Jack's involvement with the poor white girl breaks Gilead's unspoken boundaries of class, a social transgression that Jack's father lamely tries to cover up by offering money to the girl's family; and his secret relationship with Della defies the town's unspoken boundaries of race. Neither class nor race, notes Lear,

---

[50] Dupré, *Human Nature and the Limits of Science*, 129.
[51] Lear, "Not at Home in Gilead," *Raritan* 32.1 (2012): 34–52.

would actually matter in a genuinely Christian world of love and grace. Trapped in a culture of profound self-deception, Jack is rebuked for the first relationship and never allowed to cultivate the second; he thus has no choice but to flee.

As persuasive as this description of Jack is, however, the Freudian and Kierkegaardian strands of *Gilead* extend much farther than Lear identifies. For one thing, Freudian illusions are less pronounced in Jack than they are in Ames the narrator. In a book preoccupied with fathers and sons, Ames's deepest psychological wound is having been "stranded" in Gilead by his father, who left to retire on the Gulf Coast and advised that Ames also find a "life larger than this" amid "the wonders of the larger world." The memory is mentioned early in the text but only explained at the end, after Jack's revelation, when Ames reflects anew on "the frustrations and disappointments of life"—a theme about which, he admits, "I haven't been entirely honest with you" (235–36). And this is hardly the only moment at which Ames shows himself to be less than "entirely honest." Earlier I used the term "disavowal" to describe the way Ames continually downplays the arson of the black church, and a similarly psychoanalytic characterization could be made of a number of other remarks and scenes in the book: Ames's claim, for instance, that it was just an "oversight" never to have mentioned that he has a godson and namesake to his wife and child, who are startled to hear Jack's name when he visits the family (92); or his unwillingness to probe too deeply into the recesses of his wife's past, preferring instead to speculate that she probably "experienced a good deal of sorrow in those years. I have never asked" (137). Or one thinks of Jack's visit to Ames's church one Sunday morning. Ames preaches on Hagar and Ishmael, a story that is bound to make Jack uneasy, and he deepens the discomfort by veering uncharacteristically into unscripted remarks, reflecting on how seldom the Bible depicts cruelty to children—all pretty clearly meant to taunt Jack about having abandoned his illegitimate child. But writing about it afterward, Ames resolutely denies any such motive, offering instead only a strained self-justification: "there are plenty of people whose behavior toward their children falls far short of what it should be," he remarks, "so, even when I departed from my text," it was "considerable egotism on his part to take my words as directed at him only, as he clearly did" (131). In all of these cases, Ames acknowledges a certain portion of an unwelcome reality, but minimizes its significance and ignores its full implications.[52] Indeed, his psychological evasiveness is so habitual that he himself occasionally recognizes it, confessing that

---

[52] A definition of "disavowal" provided by *The Freud Encyclopedia: Theory, Therapy, and Culture*, ed. Edward Ervin (London: Routledge, 2001), 522.

he is sometimes less candid than he seems. He can, he admits, "conceal" his "motives" from himself "pretty effectively sometimes" (147); he is even willing to "persuade" himself of the meaning of certain biblical commandments when necessary (139).[53]

That *Gilead* has a Freudian dimension would be surprising to anyone familiar only with Robinson's essays, where Freud is consistently associated with the sort of coarse materialism Robinson identifies in Darwin and contemporary evolutionists.[54] Coarse materialism is, however, precisely what Jack is there to present: his function in the text is to raise to consciousness the unsettling, undisciplined, abject, and ugly realities that the town, including Ames, has over time learned to repress. But the Kierkegaardian strands of *Gilead* are even more central to the book, and even more decisive for gauging its relation to Robinson's essays. It's certainly true, as Lear claims, that Jack's willingness to engage with society's outcasts makes him the character in the novel who remains closest to the original principle of Gilead, and in this respect he is the figure closest in spirit to Ames's grandfather. And it is certainly true, as Lear also suggests, that Jack is a "standing witness" to the town's slow rot and "corruption," a "walking legitimacy crisis for the civilization that surrounds him" (36). But *Gilead* has Kierkegaardian echoes in another sense as well, and in ways that are noticeable only when readers move beyond the novel's themes or characters and considers its aesthetics—the texture of the writing, the shifts between forms, and the elemental changes that the text undergoes.

In a sympathetic review, James Wood described *Gilead* as a "somewhat essay-istic and fiercely calm" book, "certainly a pious, even perhaps a devotional work" that proceeds at a "processional pace": its depictions of small-scale everyday occurrences make it "relatively static," given that "it is difficult to whip the don-key of dailiness into big, bucking, dramatic scenes."[55] "Less a novel than a species of religious writing," he has said of the book elsewhere, an "Emersonian essay, poised between homily and home."[56] It isn't hard to see how such impressions are garnered: the book often can feel like a piece of wisdom literature, digressive and meditative and slow-paced. Ames typically writes in short fragments, usually

---

[53] The theme appears in *Lila* as well, as when Lila is fascinated by how the Book of Ezekiel includes reference to ugly practices like prostitution. "I guess I'll have to read the whole thing over again," says Ames. "It is amazing how I always seem to be thinking about the parts I like best. And there are a lot of them. But there *is* all the rest of it" (132).

[54] See, for instance, *Absence of Mind*, 29–40; *Death of Adam*, 56–68.

[55] Wood, "Acts of Devotion," *New York Times* (November 28, 2004); http://query.nytimes.com/gst/fullpage.html?res=9E00E4DC103FF93BA15752C1A9629C8B63&pagewanted=all (accessed January 20, 2016).

[56] Wood, "The Homecoming."

between a third of a page and two pages long, and the movement between these entries is, if not wholly disconnected, then loose and associative, with threads from one fragment laced quietly into another. He quotes liberally from Metaphysical poems (Donne, Herbert), cites many biblical verses, and a passing image or memory in one passage grows into the point of focus in the next: a brief reference to the powerful preaching of his old friend Boughton leads him to explain how he himself wrote out all his sermons (18); recording the details of Boughton's aging body reminds him of his own height as a youth, which led parishioners to treat him with more respect than he deserved (38); a mention of his wife's destitute past leads to a reflection on the "holy poverty" of his grand-father (31); a comparison between listening to a far-off radio broadcast and lis-tening to a seashell leads him to record a short poem he once wrote comparing a conch and a text (44-45); and so on.

The stated aims of the letter reinforce Woods's impression. Recording "begats" is, as we've seen, one initial goal of Ames's writing, but the other is to counsel his son in how to live and what to value: "to tell you things," as he puts it, "I would have told you if you had grown up with me, things I believe it becomes me as a father to teach" (133). Thus, for instance, he judges that "there are many ways to live a good life" (3), and advises the child to control his temper in ways that Ames himself often was unable to do (6). He recommends reading Feuerbach, particularly on the subject of joy (24), and advises him to take up a religious vocation, which "helps you concentrate" (7). Among the most crucial of Ames's recommendations is that his son learn to appreciate ordinary human life and bodily existence and to recognize the beauty of the natural world and its inhabitants. "I have been thinking lately how I have loved my physical life" (69), he remarks at one point, and in fragment after fragment we find expressions of this love. We read rapturous entries devoted to the "warm little brows" of a cat that he felt when he was a boy (23), to "that feeling of a baby's brow against the palm of your hand" (56), to the "feeling of a weight of light" on an afternoon (51), and to his son's giddily blowing bubbles outside his window ("Ah, this life, this world" [9]). He revels in the laughter of the townspeople, finding it "beauti-ful" to see "the way it sort of takes them over" (5), a sign of "plain exuberance" (27). And, of course, there is the son himself, the source of Ames's most eulo-gistic writing. "If you ever wonder what you've done in your life," he says in a typical moment, remember that "you have been God's grace to me, a miracle, something more than a miracle" (52). "You're just a nice-looking boy, a bit slight, well-scrubbed and well-mannered. All that is fine, but it's your existence I love you for, mainly" (53). As one commentator has written, echoing Wood, such passages give the impression that *Gilead* "promotes . . . an aesthetic attention to the world," that it asks us to see "an experience of the divine in the immediate and the immanent: an experience that stops short of knowing through reasons and is content with simply living the experience of the miraculous in the everyday."[57]

But to focus on the "static" quality of Ames's writing, and its "processional pace," to say that it encourages only an "aesthetic attention to the world," is to give a deeply misleading impression of the text, and to overlook the ways that Ames's contemplative and discursive impulses are challenged. One challenge comes with the sheer range of figures—none unsympathetically drawn—who are worldly agents, whose uses of language are wholly different from Ames's, and who are opposed in one way or another to the serene aesthetic vision that he displays. Ames's grandfather is only the most obvious example. He was, says Ames, "the most unreposeful human being I ever knew" (49), a taciturn man who even in old age "did work just because it needed doing," splitting kindling or chopping weeds. When he puts pen to paper, his purposes are wholly practical, as when he writes letters to Washington demanding that Civil War veterans get their pensions (89). There is also the example of Ames's wife, whose reticence and work ethic align her with the grandfather: "Your mother was startled the first time I mentioned to her that she might as well not do the ironing on a Sunday evening. It's such hard work for her to stop working that I don't know what I have accomplished by speaking to her about the day of rest" (77). One thinks even of Ames's brother Edward, whose life as a scholar might initially seem to make him as unworldly as any small-town minister, but whose doctoral studies took him to Germany—which in the late nineteenth century had the most vibrant academic culture in the world. Indeed, it may not be accidental that he has left Ames a painting of a marketplace (27), an emblem of secular bustle and civic engagement. In contrast to all these examples, Ames remains an essentially speculative and narrowly private figure. The one time he considers a foray into civic affairs, his courage fails him: After the town is struck by

---

[57] Christopher Leise, "'That Little Incandescence': Reading the Fragmentary and John Calvin in Marilynne Robinson's *Gilead*," *Studies in the Novel* 41 (2009), 349. Ames's aesthetic appreciation of the world is not something that has come only with old age. Among his first anecdotes in the book is his perception of a stunning sunset he sees during his trip as a child to Kansas with his father while searching for his grandfather's grave. A full moon rises just at the moment that the sun is going down, and it seemed, he recalls, "as if you could touch" the light, "as if there were palpable currents of light passing back and forth, or as if there were great taut skeins of light suspended between them" (14). Young Ames is so struck by the sight that he even interrupts his father praying in order to show it to him; his father remarks that he is "glad to know" that the region could have such beauty (15), but Ames later says, more emphatically, that they had been "witness" to a "miracle" (48).

the Spanish flu in 1918, he writes a sermon connecting the pandemic to the town's enthusiasm for the Great War, prophetically denouncing their bloodlust, but he backs away from his plan at the last moment, choosing instead to give a comparatively innocuous sermon on the Parable of the Lost Sheep. "I seemed," he says, recalling his inner turmoil, "ridiculous to myself for imagining I could thunder from the pulpit in those circumstances" (42).

But it is the figure of Jack Boughton, the most wounded and worldly character in the book, who most vividly suggests why we should avoid focusing too exclusively on Ames as a homilist. *Gilead* may well be "static" and "fiercely calm," but only for the first third or half of the book. After this point the "processional" character of the text gradually falls away, as Jack arrives and slowly initiates a new chain of thoughts, worries, and uncertainties in Ames's narration. Jack's arrival reawakens long-buried resentments, stirred by memories of his adolescent pranks, and agonizingly revives what Ames admits has been his most frequent sin, "the old covetise" (141). He envies Jack's ability to play baseball with his son while his frail body makes him unable. He envies that his son looks at Jack "as if he were Charles Lindburgh," and that Jack calls the boy "little brother" (122). He envies that his wife and Jack, who are around the same age, seem to share a special understanding and converse in lowered tones (199). He is envious that, when Jack sits next to Ames's wife at church, they look "like a handsome young family": "the beauty of other lives" becomes once again "an offense to me" (141).

And with the arrival of Jack, in turn, we see Ames struggling to deliberate, fighting to cope with these newly stirred emotions and challenges: whether his "impulse to warn you against Jack Boughton" is justified, whether he can "trust [his] feelings on this subject," whether, "living out years I cannot foresee," "you must forgive me for warning you, or forgive me for failing to warn you" (125). As the book unfolds, it spends more and more time carefully detailing Jack's dress and gestures, anecdotes from his past, the way he sits in a chair or pew, his continual look of "sadness" (182), his ability to "see through people" (212), his mannerisms, his awkward silences and uncomfortable comments, his "meanness," and his uneasy visits with Ames and his family: the way he calls Ames "Papa," queries Ames about predestination, helps Ames's wife move furniture around the house, and poses nagging questions about Gilead's antebellum origins (171). Ames records all these things as part of a laborious effort to understand what he is seeing in front of him and what his response should be: to figure out what he should and should not tell his wife about Jack's seedy past; to grasp what Jack's designs are in returning to Gilead; to understand how Jack regards his wife, and whether their lowered tones indicates a romantic or erotic attachment; and also what he himself owes to Jack, whether he should forgive him, and if so, for what.

This is a struggle of practical reasoning, and Ames's figure for it combines biblical and abolitionist images of vulnerability and disorientation: "I have wandered to the limits of my understanding any number of times, out into that desolation, that Horeb, that Kansas, . . . leaving all landmarks behind, or so it seemed. . . . My present bewilderments are a new territory that make me doubt I have ever really been lost before" (191). Another way of putting this is to say that Jack introduces *time* and *narrative* into *Gilead*. He initiates a shift away from a meditative, essayistic, and retrospective mode and into something more open, unfinished, exposed, deeply unsettling, and tied to persons and circumstances so particularized that no general observation or broad principles would seem to apply.

The blank page that, as I noted earlier, jarringly separates Jack's revelation to Ames from the rest of the text is a visible embodiment of this shift into "new territory." As the novel advances, we as readers realize that, slowly and cumulatively, the text has moved away from the static generalizations, aesthetic reveries, and neatly framed historical anecdotes that fill the first eighty or so pages, and toward minute present-tense self-observations and present-tense assessments of motive. At various points in the book Ames recalls a time when his father and he went to a church whose steeple had been hit by lightning, and he recognizes in these memories a "sweetness" that the experience did not have at the time. The later portions of the book offer fewer and fewer instances of such tranquil recollections, and disturbingly confirm Ames's suspicion that you "never do know the actual nature of your own experience" while it is happening (95): "when things are taking their ordinary course," he observes, "it is hard to remember what matters" (102). His past-tense stories now hearken less often back to the previous century and instead recount events from the previous day, or even the previous hour; and unlike the tales of his long-dead ancestors, the actors in these later stories are figures whom Ames must make intelligible first-hand. Whereas Ames in his early entries had imagined a future in which he would be comfortably residing in heaven, missing his wife and child even as he watches over them, his later entries envision a more terrestrial and anxious future, when in his absence Jack would be capable, as he says, of doing "you and your mother harm, just because he can, just for the sly, unanswerable meanness of it" (190).

Herein, I submit, lie the truest Kierkegaardian strains of *Gilead*. At the level of theme, the novel may, as Lear argues, recall the philosopher's rebuke of a faded "Christendom," but in its form it does something much more. It embodies

Kierkegaard's famous observation about the essentially temporal character of human experience: that, though a life can only be "understood backwards," one should never forget that "it must be lived forwards."[58] In Ames's own terms, *Gilead* begins from his making a "reasonably candid testament to my better self," a devotional testimony based on the assumption that his life could be surveyed as a whole, but it gradually becomes something much more disquieting: "an old man struggling with the difficulty of understanding what it is he's struggling with" (202). Ames thus begins to confront the possibility that, as Kierkegaard puts it, "temporal life can never really be properly understood precisely because I can at no instant find complete rest in which to adopt the position: backwards" (*PJ* 161). As narrator he no longer stands securely at the end of a story, looking backward and charting his experiences, his beliefs and commitments firmly in place. He finds himself caught within what he calls "the ongoingness of the world" (191), within a story he hadn't noticed or anticipated and whose fundamentally processual nature makes it difficult to apply the concepts, paradigms, and moral orders that he has grown accustomed to using. By the end, Ames's commitments have grown unhinged; his life story murky, even to himself. The text comes to sound less and less like an inviting mixture of amateur genealogy and the Book of Psalms, and increasingly like *Nausea*—a work that Jean-Paul Sartre self-consciously used to dramatize Kierkegaardian themes, and whose diary entries enact the narrator's struggle to give coherent shape to his life. Tellingly, Ames at one point associates Jack's irksome theological questions with Sartre's text, a book that Lloyd Alexander had translated into English in 1949, seven years before Ames begins his letter to his son: his young parishioners, he laments, have used the book to articulate their "skepticism" and "the possibility of unbelief." Unremarked is that, even if the questions raised by *Nausea* have an "inevitable futility" about them (177), it is increasingly difficult to distinguish that book from the very document that we ourselves are now reading.

V. We Are All Modern Now

In my earlier sketch of Robinson's account of art, I addressed Robinson's self-conscious inheritance of American Romanticism. I didn't note then that Robinson understands this inheritance as a challenge to more than just the reductive Darwinism that she excoriates in her essays. She means also to

---

[58] Soren Kierkegaard, *Papers and Journals: A Selection*, edited and translated by Alastair Hanney (London: Penguin, 1996), 261; hereafter cited parenthetically as *PJ*.

challenge the aesthetic projects that many neo-Darwinians, including Dutton, have themselves been wont to criticize: namely, the traditions of avant-garde and experimental aesthetics associated with the early twentieth century.[59] If, she says, every human is a locus of consciousness, a center of experience that is "unique in every case yet profoundly communicable," then each of us should be regarded as "emblematic" (*CL* 237). "Emblematic," that is, as opposed to radically singular, flamelike, unrepeatable, nonappropriable, nonidentical, particularized, discontinuous—such terms that have defined the nominalist aesthetics of the last century or so, in practices that emphasize (to recall Fredric Jameson) "the here and now of this unique situation and this unique expression," and that tend toward (to recall Virginia Woolf) "the spasmodic, the obscure, the fragmentary, the failure."[60] A literary historian may wonder whether Dickinson or Whitman are really so distant from twentieth-century modernism. But the distinction clearly means something to Robinson, who refers to the latter with either deafening silence or outright disparagement. To understand ourselves as "emblematic," to see each of us as contributing to a "vast reality linked through analogue," is to diverge sharply from "the elitist model of culture" that flourished after Pound and Eliot, who believed that "democracy and cultural freedom could not accommodate each other" (*CL* 237), and who encouraged a "scorn for one's fellows," a "secular *contemptus mundi*" that legitimized the "excesses of modern European history."[61] If an "opening" to communication is indeed available to every one of us, if the "signature quality" of "reality" can be found in "some kind of conversation" (*CL* 239), then we should resist the idea—and here Robinson is presumably referring to Adorno's famous pronouncement about poetry after Auschwitz, or to the "abuse of beauty" that Arthur Danto identified throughout twentieth-century art—that when "something gives you any recognizable form of human pleasure, you've taken the easy way or you're deceiving yourself or you're engaging in nostalgia" (*CL* 244).[62]

---

[59] For Dutton's views of twentieth-century art and literature, see *Art Instinct*, 15–16, 205–206, 216–17. Pinker's views of modern literature and art are, if anything, even more simplistic; see *Blank Slate*, chap. 20.

[60] Fredric Jameson, *Postmodernism, or, The Cultural Logic of Late Capitalism* (Durham, NC: Duke University Press, 1991), 152; Virginia Woolf, "Mr. Bennett and Mrs. Brown," *Essentials of the Theory of Fiction*, ed. Michael Hoffman and Patrick Murphy (Durham, NC: Duke University Press, 2006), 35.

[61] Marilynne Robinson, "Writers and the Nostalgic Fallacy," *The New York Times Book Review* (October 13, 1985); http://www.nytimes.com/1985/10/13/books/writers-and-the-nostalgic-fallacy.html?pagewanted=all (accessed January 20, 2016).

[62] Arthur Danto, *The Abuse of Beauty and the Concept of Art* (Peru, IL: Open Court, 2003). See also Robinson's interview with Sarah Fay in *The Paris Review*, where modernism and modernists simply don't come up, with the partial exception of Nietzsche—who, she laments, gets far more attention in histories of modern thought than Lincoln.

All this helps explain why Robinson's writing can seem so unusual next to that of her contemporaries. Novelist Tom McCarthy has claimed that "the task for contemporary literature is to deal with the legacy of modernism," and as I noted in the Introduction, Mark McGurl has similarly argued that creative writing programs have pushed several generations of students to internalize the "classically modernist value of 'impersonality'" ("show, don't tell").[63] By this measure, Robinson's work seems a square peg: neither dirty-realist minimalism nor postmodern maximalism, neither "village literature" (in Toni Morrison's phrase) nor New Journalism (in Tom Wolfe's).[64] In *Gilead*, however, the issue is decidedly more complicated, and indeed the novel leaves us uncertain whether individual persons and texts are ever "emblematic" rather than obscurely failed fragments. An interviewer once asked Robinson if readers should fully trust the narrator's assertions in *Housekeeping* that reality is coherent—whether we might be skeptical of "the Emersonian analogical deeps" that the novel seems to encourage and ask whether its narrator is "engaging in wishful thinking" when she speculates that "everything that rises must unite" (*CL* 240). Robinson balked at the suggestion, and perhaps she was right to do so about that early book. But *Gilead*, as I've been arguing, is everywhere preoccupied with wishful thinking, with premature claims to hold the world in stasis.

Put otherwise, Robinson's nonfiction associates the "modern" with science, with the nominalistic expulsion of "the mind" and its intentional powers from the physical universe, but *Gilead* reminds us of another use of the term, one that Robinson's essays almost entirely ignore. This is "modern" not as natural-istic reduction, but as normative volatility and epistemic limitation: no lon-ger knowing one's convictions, what to esteem, how to act, or how we could identify these things in words that would sound anything other than embar-rassing or obscene, defaced by ages of careless usage. It's the kind of volatility and disorientation that we saw at the end of both Richard Powers's *Galatea 2.2* and, in a different way, in Percy's *Love in the Ruins*. And it's precisely what gives such power to Robinson's second novel, whose basic drama is the movement into drama itself: into tension, conflict, ongoingness, bewilderments, leaving landmarks behind, the painful deliberations of embodied characters in highly particularized situations—the very things that tended to make Freud and Kierkegaard such touchstones for twentieth-century writers.

---

[63] McCarthy's remark is quoted in David James and Urmila Seshagiri, "Metamodernism: Narratives of Continuity and Revolution," *PMLA* 129 (2014): 87; Mark McGurl, *The Program Era: Postwar Fiction and the Rise of Creative Writing* (Cambridge, MA: Harvard University Press, 2011), 23.

[64] Robinson's name appears nowhere in McGurl's *The Program Era*, though she's taught for years in the Iowa Writer's Workshop, the most influential program of all.

Which creates the complex double motion I've identified in *Gilead*. Much as *Love in the Ruins* partially defeats the vision of machine intelligence that comes under assault in Percy's essays, so, too, one strand of *Gilead* reinforces Robinson's essayistic challenge to Darwinism, whose narrowly construed notion of kinship reduces sympathy to strategic cooperation, suffocating the kind of normative concepts—altruism, courage, justice—that fostered the profoundest moral achievements in U.S. history. Yet at the same time, again as in *Love in the Ruins*, the intensifying temporality of the novel—Ames's dawning recognition that he is still "wandering," in the midst of a story as unfinished as the battle for civil rights—weakens these normative concepts from another direction. The text's move into drama challenges the authoritative, wise, and sweeping stance that Ames initially adopts and that Robinson herself typically assumes in her own nonfiction. On the ground, Ames may not know what his highly evolved neurological machinery has driven him to do, but on the ground he also lacks the perspective to confidently apply high words such as "courage," "generosity," or "justice." He cannot always know what counts as "forgiveness," "loyalty," or any of the other moral phenomena that Robinson's essays identify as "data," nor can he reliably know which path he should take to embody or achieve these virtues. In the ongoingness of the world, we come to resemble the Romans who received Paul's epistle, in a verse (Romans 1:21–22) that Ames cites after realizing the extent of his ignorance: "They became vain in their reasonings and professing themselves to be wise they became fools" (232). It's a classic scenario of the very twentieth-century traditions that Robinson disregards, complete with one of its textbook devices—the narrator whose perspective is unlinked to ours through analogue and who remains dangerously trapped by self-doubt or self-deception, too enmeshed in the events described to be fully trusted: Nick Carroway, Zeno Cosini, Jake Barnes, Quentin Compson, John Dowell, Humbert Humbert.

Robinson may not be wholly comfortable with this characterization. One sign of resistance is *Home* (2008), her third novel, which returns to Jack's story but sets it within the Boughton household rather than that of the Ameses. This novel focuses on Glory, Jack's younger sister, a minor character in *Gilead* who, like Jack, has returned to stay at her father's house. She is in Gilead to recover from an embarrassing romantic relationship, and spends the novel struggling to understand Jack, who tells her vanishingly little about both his years away from Gilead and his reasons for returning to it. With conversations stretched out and scenes dramatically enacted, *Home*'s image of Jack is in many ways more explicitly somber than in *Gilead*. We get a clearer understanding of his deep self-loathing, what Lear calls his "self-portrait of despair,"[65] and we witness up close his battles with alcoholism and even with suicide. But the narrative form of *Home* is dramatically different than that of *Gilead*, and dramatically more conventional. It is told in the third person, its language filtered primarily through the consciousness of Glory, and also is told entirely in the past tense. It is comparatively homogeneous in its voice and storytelling strategies, with fewer startling shifts between genres, modes, and styles: the extended meditations and poetic flights of both *Housekeeping* and *Gilead* are shortened or eliminated, replaced almost completely by a Jamesian scenic method. In its way *Home* is a faultless novel—its characters often compelling, its dialogues credible, and no single scene seems obviously extraneous. And it even retains *Gilead*'s elements of suspense: When Jack leaves town at the end of the novel, Della arrives unexpectedly at the Boughton house, and Glory discovers for the first time that Jack's wife is, in fact, African-American. But next to Robinson's previous novel, *Home* is a conventional and cautious work, with considerably less of the tumult and anxiety we see in Ames as a character or the artistic adventurousness of *Gilead* as a whole. Whereas Ames is placed within a narrative that he gradually comes to recognize and acknowledge, *Home*'s narrative places its events firmly in the past, allowing it to describe them as complete: They have already occurred and are now at a relatively safe distance. And whereas Ames's meditations explore—and begin to undo—a broad swath of theological, philosophical, and personal commitments, Glory's struggles to understand her brother have a more local and limited scope, a more restricted focus on character psychology and interpersonal dialogue. All this prefaces a conclusion that strikes a surprising note of finality, as Glory imagines Jack's son visiting Gilead at some point in the future:

And I will think, He is young. He cannot know that my whole life has come down to this moment.

That he has answered his father's prayers.

The Lord is wonderful.[66]

---

[65] Lear, "Not at Home," 50.

[66] Marilynne Robinson, *Home* (London: Virago, 2008), 339. A similar assessment can be made, I'd argue, of *Lila*. This novel presents the story behind the other great outcast of *Gilead*, Ames's wife. Lila is saved from life as an orphan by Doll, a woman who drifts from job to job around the Midwest, and who travels alongside other drifters throughout the Depression. The information that we get in this novel is, as in *Home*, rich and sometimes helpful for understanding *Gilead*, but as with *Home*, the form of *Lila* is dramatically more conventional. *Lila*, too, is told entirely in the third person, its language filtered primarily through the consciousness of the central character, and it, too, focuses on a character who is much less articulate and brilliantly imaginative than Robinson herself—a feature that, next to both *Housekeeping* or *Gilead*, makes it feel slender and

At first glance, *Gilead* seems to end on a comparably comforting note. Jack's confession shames Ames, who begins speaking of contemporary Gilead in terms that his father and grandfather would have for once appreciated: its "littleness" and "shabbiness," he laments, are not a "measure of . . . courage and passion," but of its being "awkward and provincial and ridiculous," a place so vacant of "truth" that it "might as well be standing on the absolute floor of hell" (233–34). At the close, however, Ames's mood seems to return to the celebratory modes of the early parts of the book. "Wherever you turn your eyes," he says seven diary entries from the end, "the world can shine like transfiguration. You don't have to bring a thing to it except a little willingness to see" (245). A page later, in a new entry, this vision extends to Gilead itself: "To me it seems rather Christlike to be as unadorned as this place is, as little regarded. . . . I think sometimes of going into the ground here as a last wild gesture of love" (46–47). Then last, in the final entries of the text, speaking directly to his son:

> I'll pray that you grow up in a brave country. I will pray that you find a way to be useful.
>
> I'll pray, and then I'll sleep. (247)

All this suggests that Robinson may have been anxious about the direction of *Gilead*, and that she wanted to return to the links, analogues, communicability, and pleasures that the novel itself had gradually lost.

Whatever Robinson's intentions, however, it would be a mistake to read the ending of *Gilead* too straightforwardly as a retreat, or as a prelude to what I just described as her later, more conventional fiction. Its final pages maintain the precariousness that the second half of *Gilead* has slowly developed, and leave the reader as uncertain as Jack Boughton himself, who in the final pages departs Iowa for good, wandering in the hopes of rejoining his wife and son. As autumn descends on the town, the novel's celebratory talk of "transfiguration" and "wild love" is poised against other, more skeptical and tenuous notes. For

---

constricted. Moreover, again like *Home*, it is told entirely in the past tense, and is strikingly homogeneous in voice and storytelling, with fewer startling shifts between genres, modes, and styles than in Robinson's first two novels. The extended meditations and poetic flights of *Gilead* and *Housekeeping* are abbreviated or eliminated, replaced almost completely by a conventional scenic method. So whereas Ames is placed within a narrative that he gradually comes to recognize and acknowledge, *Lila* and *Home* each place events firmly in the past, allowing them to describe the world as completed: their scenes have all already occurred and are now at a relatively safe distance. And whereas Ames's meditations confront a broad swath of fundamental theological and historical questions, both Glory's and Lila's struggles have a more local and limited scope, and their novels are more fundamentally interested in character psychology and interpersonal dialogue.

one thing, Ames gives up on his letter: He has, he says, "been drawn back into this world in the course of" writing, and claims that the early sections of the document—the advice to his son, the meditations on beauty and the body—sound to him now "like a kind of youthfulness" (239). For another, shattered by the intrusion of Jack, confronted anew by the limits of his own lifelong piety, Ames acknowledges that his "loyalty" to Gilead was motivated mostly by fear, by a wish "never to risk the experience" of "the wonders of the larger world." In his cautiousness he has become, unlike Jack, "one of those righteous for whom the rejoicing in heaven will be comparatively restrained" (238).

Most importantly, the language of the final entries retains a sense of ambivalence about whether our normative concepts can ever be embodied in the world. Whereas for a moment the "transfiguration" of the world was said to arrive when "you" have "a little willingness to see," the final lines emphasize the powerlessness and estrangement of human beings, prioritizing the agency of a higher power: The town, he says, "is all an ember now, and the good Lord will surely someday breathe it into flame again" (246). The courage required to be "useful," Ames continues, may perhaps arrive only through "prevenient courage," much the way that theologians say that grace is prepared by "prevenient grace"—that is, grace given wholly by God, prior to and conditioning our human choices (246).[67] And most revealing of all, the final lines of the book—the lines I just quoted above—pledge three times to perform a speech act that by its very nature takes speakers to the borders of intelligible communication: "I'll pray," "I will pray," "I'll pray." In the end, *Gilead* plaintively implies, prayer may be all we ultimately have, all we can do to identify what counts as bravery and purposeful action. If reality is "of a piece," linked through analogue, then this may be a knowledge to which we have no "opening" on our own. If appeals to our material constitution, to biology and evolution, are an inadequate justification of why we act as we do, perhaps all we have left is a desperate faith, some strained hope that our high words make sense in a divine light, even if seldom in ours. *Shantih shantih shantih*, only a god can save us: again, a posture central to the aesthetic traditions that Robinson supposedly rejects.[68] At the end,

---

[67] The significance of this remark about prevenient courage is suggested by the fact that Robinson repeats it nearly verbatim at the start of her essay "The Tyranny of Petty Coercion," in *Death of Adam*, 255.

[68] On the tone or form of prayer in modernist poetry and fiction, see Pericles Lewis, *Religious Experience and the Modernist Novel* (Cambridge: Cambridge University Press, 2010), 4–5. None of this means, of course, that all "modernists" were "actually" religious thinkers or committed to prayers of any kind; I only mean to suggest that the speech act with which Ames ends his book recall some of the modernists that Robinson ostensibly rejects.

Ames says he "can't help imagining" that his son will leave Gilead "sooner or later" (246–47), but we never learn if the boy grows up to be brave or whether he shares his father's faith in a moral order. We as readers become, in effect, Ames's son, encountering his words a half-century after he writes them, and whatever reassurances the text seems to provide, the question with which we are left is whether we ourselves have departed Gilead, and if we have, where we are wandering instead, and what now justifies our sense that our own acts are useful.

We Solemnly Publish and Declare

3

SOCIOLOGY TO THE SCIENTISTS

Ellison's Virtues

AFTER LEAVING TUSKEGEE in 1936, Ralph Ellison would spend his nights studying Ernest Hemingway, learning from him—as he often said in later interviews and essays—how to describe an action with complete fidelity and to mine the full resources of the "American language."[1] But in the mid-1940s, as he started writing what became *Invisible Man*, reservations surfaced. Hemingway had famously claimed that all modern American literature had descended from *Huckleberry Finn*: "There was nothing before. There has been nothing as good since."[2] But his reading of Twain, Ellison came to feel, suffocated the novel's true force, for what Hemingway revered about *Huckleberry Finn* was merely its "technical discoveries—the flexible colloquial language, the sharp naturalism, the thematic potentialities of adolescence." He could focus on these features, explains Ellison in "Twentieth-Century Fiction and the Black Mask of Humanity" (1946), only by ignoring the larger vision to which Twain was putting them. As Ellison saw it, Twain was the culmination of a nineteenth-century tradition that saw the "Negro as symbol of Man": "limited in circumstance but not in possibility," exemplary in his "will to possess his own labor, in his loyalty and capacity for friendship, and in his love for his wife and child." The whole point of *Huckleberry Finn*, says Ellison, lies in Huck's

---

[1] Ellison's reference to Hemingway's "American language" appears in Ellison, *The Collected Essays of Ralph Ellison*, ed. John Callahan (New York: Modern Library, 1995), 186; henceforth cited parenthetically as *CE*. For other appreciative references to Hemingway's influence, see, for example, *Collected Essays*, 57, 185, 187, 211, 394, 753.

[2] Ernest Hemingway, *The Green Hills of Africa* (1935; New York: Scribner, 1996), 22.

relationship with the slave Jim, a form of solidarity that the "conventionalized evil" of white antebellum Missouri had repressed. Hemingway, however, drove this aspect of the novel—and thus the history of slavery—"into the underground of the American conscience," reinforcing the "moral division" between black and white that Twain's book had bravely sought to scrutinize. Instead, he emphasized "technique for the sake of technique," and in the process reduced the text to "a marvelous technical virtuosity won at the expense of a gross insensitivity to fraternal values" (CE 88–91).

It wasn't just Hemingway. Ellison's complaints in the mid-1940s sum up a more general grievance against high modernism that he often expressed, even after *Invisible Man* (1952) had made him a major voice in American letters. Accepting the National Book Award in 1953, for instance, he casts doubt on "the tight, well-made Jamesian novel," whose "artistic perfection" and "good taste" makes it unfit to capture the cacophonous diversity of American life (CE 151–52). Still more damning is a 1957 essay that finds the writers of Hemingway's generation "morally diffident," turning the energy of the novel "upon itself in the form of technical experimentation" and forgetting the genre's use as a "superb moral instrument." Using the "so-called revolution of the word" as "a literary equivalent of that distraction from the realities of the moral situation provided by the material prosperity of the boom," such writers were trying to "make a highly personal morality the informing motive of an art form which by its very nature is extremely social." This impoverished "morality of craftsmanship" constitutes, says Ellison, a "tragedy" (CE 710–12), one that had gained credence in part through the apologias of Lionel Trilling and Malcolm Cowley, influential critics who likewise overlooked the realities of American culture, particularly the squalid, stubborn history of slavery and racism (CE 718–22, 724–26).

Much, then, like Walker Percy, who pitches himself as a "moralist or a propagandist," fighting the nominalist aesthetics of modern literature, Ellison locates in Hemingway's generation a certain slipperiness—moral evasion dressed up as technical prowess. And much like Marilynne Robinson, Ellison recalls the power of nineteenth-century American writers, who in their eyes are more discerning about language and American history than the elitist, regressive modernists who followed a couple generations later. As I've argued, neither Percy nor Robinson is able to sidestep the twentieth century to quite the extent that he or she hopes, and as we'll see, this is also true of Ellison. But all three authors perceive something narrow in the century's dominant aesthetic traditions, and the compulsion in their work for both art and argument—the balance they seek between narration and declaration—is one sign of their hope to chart another path.

Resemblances to Percy and Robinson don't end there. For like them, Ellison's ambivalence toward aesthetic modernism is paralleled by his even more pointed resistance to modernity's overweening naturalism. He is, in other words, troubled by the "cool" and "exact" style that Susan Sontag claims pervades techno-scientific culture as well as twentieth-century art and writing, with their resistance to "discursive explicitness."[3] In Ellison's case, anxiety wasn't caused by emerging cognitivist theories of the mind, nor did he take any interest in the neo-Darwinian theories that developed in the 1970s. What troubled him instead were the social sciences, particularly sociology, which by the mid-twentieth century had come to have tremendous authority both within public policy circles and in the increasingly rationalized research university. Ellison's nonfiction has a different texture than that of Percy and Robinson: he never dedicated entire books to dismantling the naturalist theories he rejected, and he was seldom as systematic as the Thomistic Percy or as expansively speculative as the Emersonian Robinson. But his nonfiction was not written with his left hand for a quick buck, as one commentator has said about the twentieth-century essay.[4] He studied the social sciences closely in college, read and wrote reviews of new social science publications, and made continual reference to them in his mature essays. Moreover, though his nonfiction tends to be written for specific occasions—"topical rather than timeless," in Kenneth Warren's phrase—it also exhibits an unusual degree of intellectual consistency and ambition in its claims about the social sciences. Ellison may not have been a philosopher, but he certainly had philosophical instincts, if by "philosophy" we mean simply how language, behavior, ethics, art, politics, and other broad topics hang together in the broadest sense.[5] To recall a phrase from Chapter 1, his essays sketch out an *anthropology*, a picture of our characteristic capacities, development, and limitations—what Percy would call a "general theory of man," a "study of man doing the uniquely human thing."[6] Desiccated by the "taste for

---

[3] Susan Sontag, *Against Interpretation* (New York: Farrar, Strauss and Giroux, 1966), 300.

[4] Ned Stuckey-French, *The American Essay in the American Century* (Columbia: University of Missouri Press, 2011), 5.

[5] To paraphrase a well-known definition of "philosophy" proposed by Ellison's contemporary Wilfrid Sellars: "The aim of philosophy, abstractly formulated, is to understand how things in the broadest possible sense of the term hang together in the broadest possible sense of the term." See his "Philosophy and the Scientific Image of Man," in *Science, Perception, and Reality* (New York: The Humanities Press, 1963), 1. Warren's characterization of Ellison's nonfiction is found in *So Black and Blue: Ralph Ellison and the Occasion of Criticism* (Chicago: University of Chicago Press, 2003), 3.

[6] Walker Percy, *Signposts in a Strange Land*, ed. Patrick Samway (New York: Picador, 1991), 123; Percy, *The Message in the Bottle: How Queer Man Is, How Queer Language Is, and What One Has to Do With the Other* (1975; New York: Picador, 2000), 11. As I noted in a note to Chapter one, Mark Greif also has suggested that Ellison seeks to develop a "philosophical anthropology," though how he understands Ellison's anthropology is somewhat different from what I present here. See Mark Greif,

desert landscapes" that W. V. O. Quine professed to admire, sociology and other disciplines tended for Ellison to obscure this uniquely human thing, and as much as modern aesthetics tended to stifle the sort of normative vocabularies that the "superb moral instrument" of the novel was able to utilize.

Ellison's distrust of modernity's dual scientific and artistic legacies, however, has quite a different motivation than what we see in Percy and Robinson. They write, as we've seen, as avowed theists, committed to the institutions and traditions of particular Christian denominations. For Ellison, by contrast, secularism was second nature. His mother was an intensely pious member of the African Methodist Episcopal Church in Oklahoma City, where Ralph was born and raised, but her son found magic and reverence elsewhere, namely in the music of the church's services. By high school, Ellison had grown fascinated with jazz, and among his early reviews and essays, written in the 1930s, he caustically described the "very inadequate church" that had shaped African-American life and thought.[7] Ellison, of course, knew the idiom and gestures of the black church and credited his mother's faith with being a "firm support" in his college years.[8] And a reader could perhaps—looking especially at his never-completed second novel, one of whose two main characters is a preacher—include it among what he called the *"field* of influences" shaping his work and life.[9] But this "field" was gigantic, and the vocabulary of the church appears in his writing mostly as what Mikhail Bakhtin calls the "image of a language" rather than a language itself. Much more than in Percy and Robinson, that is, the words of Christianity always have in Ellison the "taste" of a profession, party, a generation, a specific genre, and all the other things that charge it with socially bound intentions and accents.[10] His relationship to the African-American church is best summed up by a remark he made to Albert Murray in the early 1950s, recounting his visit to a college where he had been scheduled to give a lecture only to be—to his astonishment—ushered into a church service. "I know all the hymns," he

---

The Age of the Crisis of Man: Thought and Fiction in America, 1933–1973 (Princeton, NJ: Princeton University Press, 2015), 148–49.

[7] See Lawrence Jackson, *Ralph Ellison: The Emergence of Genius* (New York: Wiley, 2002), 26–29, 61, 207.

[8] Ralph Ellison, "'American Culture is of a Whole': From the Letters of Ralph Ellison," *The New Republic* (March 1, 1999): 43.

[9] For an effort to make the black church central to Ellison's writing, see Laura Saunders, "Ellison and the Black Church: The Gospel According to Ralph," in *The Cambridge Companion to Ralph Ellison*, ed. Ross Posnock (New York: Cambridge University Press, 2005), 35–55 (Ellison's phrase *"field* of influences" appears at 35).

[10] Mikhail Bakhtin, *The Dialogical Imagination: Four Essays* (Austin: University of Texas Press, 1981), 292–93.

wrote, "and the whole order of service and in spite of everything the emotions started striking past my defenses, not a religious emotion, but that of *remembering* religious feeling."[11] Religious experience, that is, was never unmediated in the mature Ellison, who liked to say that bending the knee isn't the only way to pray.[12]

In what follows I want to explore the particular normative concepts that Ellison sought to retrieve in the face of scientific and literary skepticism, and the particular archive of narratives by which he sought to illuminate them. As we'll see, the key is visible already in Ellison's criticism of Hemingway, and especially his claim, cited a moment ago, that the "marvelous technical virtuosity" of novels like *The Sun Also Rises* was "won at the expense of a gross insensitivity to fraternal values." *Fraternal*: variations on the term are scattered throughout Ellison's writing, and they suggest some of the ways that he anticipates Bernard Williams's suggestion, noted in my introduction, that we post-Christian contemporaries have more in common than we might think with the ethical world of the pre-Christian Greeks. It's a thought that will carry over into the work of Stanley Cavell and David Foster Wallace in the next couple chapters. To clarify this idea, we need to uncover, in the following section, just what Ellison finds so awry in the modern social sciences, and particularly how they understand the sources of unity structuring and defining a given social body. In sections two and three, focusing on his discussions of jazz and language and the American founding documents, I'll try to clarify the Ellisonian anthropology that generates his language of "fraternity," and specifically how it contests the vision he finds in the social sciences. From there I'll consider what happens to this vocabulary in Ellison's narrative works, first in *Invisible Man* (section four) and then in the unfinished second novel (section five), each of which, in different ways, betrays the strains that Ellison felt in archiving his highest words. These various paths of thought—the ideas that Ellison wants to defeat, the high words he sought to embody, the struggle that unfolds in practice—will allow us to map a range of concepts crucial for the remainder of this book. And in tracing them, we'll be not only casting light on a significant intellectual, creative, and normative project, but also be confronting precisely the racial history and politics that Ellison claims Hemingway and his contemporaries avoid.

---

[11] *Trading Twelves: The Selected Letters of Ralph Ellison and Albert Murray*, ed. Albert Murray and John F. Callahan (New York: Modern Library, 2000), 42.

[12] Ellison, "'American Culture is of a Whole'," 43.

I. Meaning in an Environment

Ellison's secularism places him in a long line of African-American thinkers who openly react against what E. Franklin Frazier, writing a century after emancipation, called "the most important cultural institution" of black life. As Frazier saw it, the African-American church embodied "the cultural traditions of Negroes to a far greater extent than any other institution," and while this may or may not still be the case fifty years later, it's certainly true that black churches continue to influence African-American thinkers in a way that is largely unheard of among their white counterparts: think of the openly Christian stance of, say, C. Eric Lincoln, Cornel West, or Michael Eric Dyson.[13] But the very prominence of the church has long inspired a self-consciously anticlerical countercurrent within the African-American intellectual tradition. W. E. B. Du Bois, for instance, was cool toward religious belief and institutions from a young age; the omniscient God of his Congregational youth, as Arnold Rampersad says, was displaced early on by the Unknowable of Herbert Spencer, and as Du Bois himself recalled, he turned as a student away from "religious dogmas" and toward "science and the scientific attitude," treating human actions along the lines of "those of the physical world, subject to law."[14] A generation later, Zora Neale Hurston was similarly "full of misty fumes of doubt" about Christianity": "Neither could I understand the passionate declarations of love for a being that nobody could see. Your family, your puppy and the new bull-calf, I could see. But a spirit away off who found fault with everybody all the time, that was more than I could fathom."[15] For his part, Frazier attacked what he called the "authoritarian personality and anti-intellectualism" of the African-American preacher, claiming that these "petty tyrants" have "cast a shadow over the intellectual outlook of Negroes" and damaged the black community's "education in democratic processes." And in more recent years, Adolph Reed, Jr. likewise has accused black churches of being dangerously outdated. The "antiparticipatory

---

[13] Frazier's comments originally appeared in his 1966 book *The Negro Church in America*, and are reprinted in *African-American Religious Thought: An Anthology*, ed. Cornel West and Eddie S. Glaude, Jr. (Louisville, KY: Westminster John Knox Press, 2003), 64.

[14] W. E. B. Du Bois, *Writings*, ed. Nathan Huggins (New York: Library of America, 1986), 590. Just a few years later, Du Bois would underline the point by declaring that no "chosen body of people or special organization of mankind has received a direct revelation of ultimate truth which is denied to earnest scientific fact" (*The World and Africa and Color and Democracy*, ed. Henry Louis Gates (New York: Oxford University Press, 2014), 320. Rampersad's remark appears in *The Art and Imagination of W. E. B. Du Bois* (Cambridge, MA: Harvard University Press, 1976), 19–20. For a biographical account of Du Bois's early turn from religion, see David Levering Lewis, *W. E. B. Du Bois, 1868–1919: Biography of a Race* (New York: Henry Holt, 1993), 65.

[15] Zora Neale Hurston, *Folklore, Memoirs, and Other Writings*, ed. Cheryl A. Wall (New York: Library of America, 1995), 755.

and antiintellectual [*sic*] impetus" of the black church, he argues, "deauthorizes the principle of individual autonomy, which is the basis of citizenship," and ultimately "mandates quietism, political or otherwise." No surprise that Reed's animus should be aimed as regularly at thinkers like West and Dyson as it is at post-Reagan conservatives.[16]

Like Ellison, then, Du Bois, Hurston, Frazier, and Reed each write from what the intellectual historian David Hollinger has called a "resoundingly post-Biblical stance."[17] And yet, placed next to these other figures, Ellison stands out. For unlike these others, Ellison's post-Biblical stance doesn't lead him to embrace the social sciences, be it sociology (Du Bois, Frazier), anthropology (Hurston), or political science (Reed). As a college student, Ellison was deeply drawn to the social sciences, and he took several sociology courses on African-American culture. But he quickly grew disenchanted. The watershed moment was his discovery around 1935 of a passage in *Introduction to the Science of Sociology*, the widely used 1921 textbook by Robert Park and Ernest Burgess. The Negro, Ellison read there,

> has always been interested rather in expression than in action; interested in life itself rather than in its reconstruction or reformation. The Negro is, by natural disposition, neither an intellectual nor an idealist, like the Jew; nor a brooding introspective, like the East Indian; nor a pioneer and frontiersman, like the Anglo-Saxon. He is primarily an artist, loving life for its own sake. His *métier* is expression rather than action. He is, so to speak, the lady among the races.[18]

Park and Burgess were seminal figures in the rise of "Chicago Sociology," which among other things developed the theory of the so-called "race relation cycle" in the years after their textbook appeared. According to this theory, a minority group went through four stages of "interpenetration" vis-à-vis the larger culture, a sequence that to Park seemed "apparently progressive and irreversible": First, they have *contact* with it; then comes *conflict* or *competition* between the

---

[16] E. Franklin Frazier, *The Negro Church in America* (New York: Schocken Books, 1974), 47; Reed, *The Jesse Jackson Phenomenon: The Crisis of Purpose in Afro-American Politics* (New Haven, CT: Yale University Press, 1986), 57.

[17] David Hollinger, "The Knower and the Artificer, with Postscript 1993," in *Modernist Impulses in the Human Sciences, 1870–1930* (Baltimore: Johns Hopkins University Press, 1994), 26–53.

[18] Robert Park and Ernest Burgess, *Introduction to the Science of Sociology* (Chicago: University of Chicago Press, 1921), 136. What I've quoted here is the exact passage that Ellison cites in his 1944 review of Gunnar Myrdal's *An American Dilemma* (CE 332).

groups; then the minority group achieves *accommodation* to the larger culture; and last, there is *assimilation* to it.[19] Moreover, the Chicago School was what captivated Richard Wright upon his move north in the late 1920s. When two of its younger members, St. Clair Drake and Horace R. Cayton, published *Black Metropolis* (1945), their massive study of Chicago, Wright—by then the famous author of *Native Son*, not to mention a mentor of the younger Ellison—composed a glowing introduction.[20] Ellison, by contrast, could never forget the insult he had discovered in Park and Burgess's early textbook, and refused to see Wright's writing as "a sociological case history" about a certain "simple specimen" called the Negro (*CE* 166, 139). Indeed, throughout his career, nothing provoked Ellison's venom more than an author who seemed to overestimate the social sciences. Irving Howe, for instance, belonged to the ranks of the "sociology-oriented critics" who would rather "kill a novel" than modify their political and ideological assumptions (*CE* 155–56), and LeRoi Jones's *Blues People* (1964) is similarly castigated for suggesting that blues music transparently reflects "the sociology of Negro American identity and attitude" (*CE* 279). In his 1953 National Book Award acceptance speech, Ellison insisted that we would be best off "leaving sociology to the scientists" (*CE* 153), and when he was assembling his first nonfiction collection, *Shadow and Act* (1964), he chose to close the book with his ambivalent review of Gunnar Myrdal's 1944 *An American Dilemma*, a landmark analysis of American culture and race relations by one of the preeminent sociologists in the world.

Ellison's relationship to the social sciences has been a theme among some of his most astute recent readers. Critics have examined, for instance, the gendered inflection of his anger toward Park and Burgess ("the lady of the races"), his mixed feelings toward the white-collar professionalism encouraged by Myrdal, and the inadvertent resemblances he bore to midcentury sociologists such as William Whyte and David Riesman.[21] Much of this illuminating work

---

[19] Quoted in Christopher Douglas, *A Genealogy of Literary Multiculturalism* (Ithaca, NY: Cornell University Press, 2008), 73. My understanding of the Chicago School owes a good deal to Douglas's lucid account.

[20] St. Clair Drake and Horace R. Cayton, *Black Metropolis: A Study of Negro Life in a Northern City* (New York: Harcourt, Brace, and Company, 1945).

[21] On Ellison's response to "the lady of the races," see Daniel Y. Kim, *Writing Manhood in Black and Yellow* (Stanford, CA: Stanford University Press, 2005), chap. 1; on Ellison and white-collar professionals, see Steven Schryer, *Fantasies of the New Class: Ideologies of Professionalism in Post-World War II American Fiction* (New York: Columbia University Press, 2011), chap. 2; on his relation to sociologists such as Riesman and White, see Andrew Hoberek, *The Twilight of the Middle Class: Post-World War II American Fiction and White-Collar Work* (Princeton, NJ: Princeton University Press, 2005), chap. 2. Other important recent work on Ellison's relation to the social sciences include Scott Selisker, "Simply By Reacting? The Sociology of Race and *Invisible Man*'s Automata," *American Literature* 83 (2011): 571–96; Kenneth W. Warren, *So Black and Blue*.

has suggested that Ellison may have had more affinities to early- and midcentury sociological thinking than he himself would have recognized. But when he is placed next to Percy and Robinson, with their intersecting refusals of modern naturalism, we can begin to get a sharper sense of just what Ellison found so distasteful in the social sciences, and just why we shouldn't discount the vocal objections he offered.

Ellison's most recurrent question about the social sciences is their data and what they count as real. "Real" and "data" are terms, recall, from Percy and Robinson respectively, who underscore the hard-to-deny everyday phenomena that scientistic investigators—artificial intelligence experts, philosophers of language, evolutionary psychologists—feel a professional and intellectual obligation to overlook. And like them, Ellison implicitly appeals to conceptual and explanatory pluralism: The world comprises different types of phenomena, and no one theory or scheme will be able to capture all of them convincingly. The data most typically neglected by sociologists are the remarkable creativity and joyfulness that run through African-American life. Like the researchers in *Invisible Man* who return over and over again to analyze Jim Trueblood, social scientists relentlessly fasten on the most tantalizingly horrific aspects of black life, focusing on the examples and case studies that will accommodate the researcher's drive for singular explanations and conclusions. The "sociological conditions" of black life, says Ellison in a 1961 interview, have certainly "made for misery," but they are also not the only things that make for "values which I feel I should endure and shall endure" (*CE* 80). Writing in 1959, he questions the habit among sociologists and other "serious students of culture" who, when they look back on the 1940s, speak exclusively about the riots, industrial tensions, and warfare of the decade. Such a focus overlooks "the needs of feeling" provided in the same years by a place like Minton's jazz club, a "sanctuary" that helped foster "a new key of musical sensibility" and thus "a revolution in culture" (*CE* 238–39). Similarly, Oklahoma City between the wars should have been, "according to the sociologists," an "utterly hopeless" place, bereft of "good minds or fine talent," but anyone who actually lived there at the time knew that it was "an alive community," a place where the "strength and imagination of [its] people was much in evidence," however inescapable the "harshness of slum life" sometimes seemed (*CE* 552). Researchers, says Ellison in 1965, repeatedly formulate clichés about black life—about its broken families, deviant sexuality, and so forth—but these things simply cannot "define the complexity of Harlem." Such formulae "reduce" and "abstract" the city "to proportions which the sociologists can manage" (*CE* 730).

Incomplete data inevitably generate dubious hypotheses. Yet theories can gain traction, according to Ellison, because social scientists examine African-American culture like the factory hospital doctors who place the Invisible Man in "a kind of glass and nickel box," their voices "hollow with detachment" as they prod him with questions and anatomize his body.[22] They adopt, that is, a disengaged third-person stance, describing human beings as functioning or malfunctioning bodies wholly continuous with the natural world, rather than intentional beings involved and concerned with (to use the Heideggerian idiom that Percy invokes) the world, its meanings, and our practices. At times, predictably, these outsiders are white Americans like Robert Park or Europeans like Gunnar Myrdal. Such researchers may spend enormous amounts of time studying African-American life, and they may outright reject nineteenth-century correlations between social difference and biology.[23] But whatever their advances over previous social science, these scholars tend nevertheless to see black culture as an instance of "social pathology," the unhappy outcome of having never assimilated to white culture. At other times, however, the voices of disengagement are themselves African-American. We depend too much, says Ellison in 1967, "on outsiders—mainly sociologists—to interpret our lives for us," and among these contestable "outsiders" he includes both Frazier and Kenneth Clark, two of the most prominent African-American social scientists of the mid-twentieth century. As much as Park or Myrdal, in other words, these figures present themselves as authoritative observers but, in fact, miss the celebratory and "enlarging" qualities of black experience, forcing African-Americans to "fit into the sociological terminology" (CE 751).

Such claims have earned, unsurprisingly, some pushback among social scientists.[24] But Ellison's critique of the disengaged stance, and of the explanatory monism that it encourages, can't be dismissed lightly. Its risks are perhaps best illustrated by Wright's introduction to *Black Metropolis*. One of the goals of Drake and Cayton's book, Wright claims there, is to disabuse white Americans of the belief that they actually know very much about black American lives, to give a "jolt" to white presumption. But even black Americans, in Wright's telling,

---

[22] Ralph Ellison, *Invisible Man* (1952; New York: Vintage, 1995), 233; henceforth cited parenthetically as *IM*.

[23] Robert Park, for instance, lived for almost a decade in Georgia, working as an aide to Booker T. Washington, and Myrdal took over five years to write *American Dilemma*.

[24] Jerry Gafio Watts, for instance, has accused Ellison of "folk pastoralism," a viewpoint implying that "if a subjugated people feel good about themselves, their situation is not so desperate." See Watts, *Heroism and the Black Intellectual: Ralph Ellison, Politics, and Afro-American Intellectual Life* (Chapel Hill: University of North Carolina Press, 1994), 109.

are not reliable guides to black experience. For while there is surely "a meaning in Negro life that whites do not see and do not want to see," *Black Metropolis* was written "so that Negroes will be able to interpret correctly the meaning of their own actions." Both whites *and* blacks, that is, have resisted a full-blooded presentation of "the Negro problem . . . in all of its hideous fullness, in all of the totality of its meaning." The achievement of Drake and Cayton, says Wright, is to have challenged this resistance, and to have seen race relations in their complete "political, moral, spiritual, class, and economic meaning." With this power of insight, *Black Metropolis* could potentially impact the general population as much as the Chicago School had once impacted a young aspiring writer from Natchez, Mississippi. "I did not know what my story was," says Wright, "and it was not until I stumbled upon science that I discovered some of the meanings of the environment that battered and taunted me."[25]

What stands out about the "meanings" of black life that "science" reveals for Wright is that they have until now apparently been unavailable to individual black people. Before the arrival of the social sciences, that is, African-Americans had incorrectly understood what precisely they were doing when performing this or that action, nor had they understood the full significance of the family structures, social arrangements, patterns of affiliation, schools, social clubs, taverns, government offices and programs, and other features of their everyday lives—assuming these are the types of things that Wright has in mind when speaking of the "environment" that batters and taunts. The sociologist, in Wright's picture, looks at a family, tenement, or city much as a mechanic might examine how the crankshaft links to the connecting rod of a car engine, asking whether the rod is properly operating with the piston. The crankshaft and piston don't themselves know whether they are acting correctly, but the mechanic can evaluate how such local operations contribute or fail to contribute to the goal of the machine overall—namely, combustion. Similarly, as Wright implies, the local individuals who make up a given family or tenement or city are seldom capable of knowing how their particular thoughts and actions contribute to the functioning—or malfunctioning—of the larger whole. This is the work of the sociologist, who stands back from the immediate experience of particular people in order to scrutinize the global patterns and regularities of the collective body, patterns and regularities that Wright refers to as their "meanings."

When Ellison questions the social sciences, he means above all to undercut the authority that Wright ascribes to this third-person vantage point. He's

---

[25] Wright, introduction to *Black Metropolis*, xxviii, xviii.

not rejecting the idea that environments can have meanings independent of individual agents; indeed, his essays show a sensitive awareness of the power of law, history, tradition, and the myriad other things that shape the significances that people find in the world. Nor is he denying that unknown distant strangers have done things to and in the world that will shape an individual's life, and he nowhere suggests that we can have complete knowledge of all these things and thus of ourselves. What he rejects is the idea that the teleologies and "meanings" perceptible to the agent's point of view can be *expunged* when we want to understand the "meanings" of their lives and social experiences. The fact that unknown distant strangers shape my life cannot, in itself, determine which attitude I adopt toward them, and it is the variability of such attitudes—differing levels of concern, indifference, trust, esteem, and so forth—that Ellison wants to underline. No "statistical interpretation of our lives," as he puts it, will be compelling if it is not squared with—if it cannot account for and be non-trivially correlated with—a first-person interpretation of our lives. Wright's praise of *Black Metropolis* in essence anticipates the claim of the evolutionary psychologist to have discovered the "ultimate" cause of people's behavior, the deep-down dispositions distinct from the "proximate" causes ostensibly motivating them. What remains unknowable to the average agent is, of course, different for midcentury sociologists and for late-century Darwinians: for Steven Pinker or Richard Dawkins, it is the operation of our genes, whereas for Wright, it is the motions of the "environment." But in each case, the power of the scientist comes from his or her denying the relevance of the first-person perspective. And Ellison, in turn, can be understood to anticipate the problems that I've already located in such a claim. To adapt a remark from Robert Pippin that I quoted in my discussion of Robinson, if I'm deciding how to act toward a stranger or staring at a blank canvas that I want to paint, I can't wait around for my environment to recommend something; decisions are always undertaken from an agent's point of view.[26] Thus, much as Robinson insists on the importance of "testimony," so Ellison refers to that which is "subjective, willful and complexly and compellingly human" (*CE* 731). And much as Robinson speaks of our ability to "stand apart from ourselves, appraising," Ellison speaks of becoming "conscious": of "recognizing" one's condition and making or failing to "make peace" with it (*CE* 141), of plumbing one's background "with all of the conscious thought" that one can possibly summon (*CE* 448).

---

[26] Robert Pippin, "Natural and Normative," *Daedalus* 138 (2009): 38–39.

Plumbing one's background "with all the conscious thought" is something Ellison credits to Alain Locke, but this other description of the subjective and willful—the ability to "recognize" one's situation and determine whether to "make peace" with it—appears in his early essay on Wright, the very figure who had found such sustenance in sociology. However much, in other words, Wright believed he was shaped by sociology, his actual writings display what Ellison calls "the transforming, concept-creating activity of the brain," the capacity to find significance amidst the endless "elements of experience which contain no compelling significance" (*CE* 139, 133). Wright was goaded by "the commanding and informing activity" of "the Mind," was "awoken" to the nightmare of his life that he subsequently "rejects" (*CE* 131, 142). And this is a way of making a crucial further point that we've also seen raised already in the first two chapters. Walker Percy often said that naturalistic theorists can seldom give an account of their own activity—that Darwin, for instance, can give no Darwinian account of how he came to write *Origin of Species*. Ellison is, in effect, noticing a similar slippage in social–scientific theory. "When I hear a Negro intellectual describing Negro life and personality with a catalogue of negative definitions," he says in a 1965 interview, "my first question is: How did you escape?" (*CE* 752). The very existence, that is, of a "Negro intellectual" who is able to do something as cognitively complicated as *cataloguing*—selecting what's relevant and irrelevant, placing this information in this or that order—is proof that "negative definitions" cannot be the entirety of black life and personality. It may be correct to treat the "environment" as, in Ellison's words, "the physical, the non-conscious" (*CE* 162), the realm of the nonintentional, continuous with the genes that Robinson addressed and the brain activity that preoccupied Percy. But like Robinson and Percy, Ellison is more interested in distinctions between humans and the physical world than in their continuities—what Robinson calls the "human exceptionalism" that Darwinian theory tries to discount. Continuities between us and the material world are not only obvious, given what the natural sciences have shown (the human body contains magic stuff no more than rocks or trees do), but more to the point, they are explanatorily weak. They can hardly account for the wildly various justifications that have been given both for and against our wildly various human practices—including practices such as the owning of human beings.

Such conceptual distinctions are precisely what are at stake in Ellison's review of Myrdal's *An American Dilemma*, the central question of which appears a few paragraphs from the end: Can a people—slaves and their descendants— "live and develop for over three hundred years simply by *reacting*?" (*CE* 339). "Reacting" is what environments do; it's what happens in photosynthesis or digestion or earthquakes. By contrast, human beings of African descent, like all human beings, have "helped to create themselves out of what they found around them" (*CE* 339). Obviously this "creation" hasn't been undertaken in conditions that African-Americans have themselves selected. But even in its conditions of extremity, the habits and norms of the community cannot be considered merely—in Myrdal's words—"secondary reactions" to white norms, as if whites were the only ones competent enough to institute norms, and as if everything else followed from them like a chain reaction. Black Americans *are* refused participation in white norms, but these white norms are also not the sole norms that they recognize. Excluded from much of American life, they have generated what Ellison calls "counter values," an at-times inarticulate yet nevertheless coherent set of ideals that foster a culture of "great value and rich-ness" and makes the life of African-Americans "more meaningful" (*CE* 340). With its emphasis on causality, a "sociological approach" habitually underappre-ciates just how black experience has been both "a source of creative strength as well as a source of wonder." And it tends to miss how blacks have been "a source of moral strength to America," not just in spite of the hardships they have faced but precisely *because* of them (*CE* 75). Hence the analogy Ellison draws between Wright's *Black Boy* and the blues, a folk-art form that keeps "the painful details and episodes of a brutal experience alive" while also "transcend[ing] it. . .by squeezing from it a near-tragic, near-comic lyricism" (*CE* 129)—a double-move-ment of action and motion that, tellingly, never fully made sense to Wright himself. Hence, too, Ellison's well-known complaint a few years later that Bigger Thomas, the protagonist of *Native Son*, "had none of the finer qualities of Richard Wright, none of the imagination, none of the sense of poetry, none of the gaiety" (*CE* 74). "Wright," as Ellison puts it elsewhere, "could imagine Bigger, but Bigger could not possibly imagine Richard Wright" (*CE* 162).

Critics are right, then, to suggest that Ellison remained, as Leon Forrest has said, a "race man," someone all for "building within the race" rather than ignoring race altogether.[27] But what mattered to Ellison was not just the race as such, but the capacity of the race's members to take a second-order stance on themselves: not just to *have* certain habits and beliefs, but also to reflec-tively endorse (or refuse to endorse) certain habits and beliefs, to recognize them with "conscious thought" rather than merely accepting them as givens. This rational autonomy is the heart of what I've called the Ellisonian anthropol-ogy. And one consequence of it is especially worth emphasizing. In adopting

---

[27] Quoted in Warren, *So Black and Blue*, 16–17.

second-order stances, in their capacity to plumb their experience "with all the conscious thought" that they can, human beings show themselves to be essentially *creative* beings. We always are situated in a world that pressures us in biologically and historically specific ways: we have needs and desires that parrots or protozoa do not, and life in the post-World War II United States is likewise very different than it is at other historical moments. Yet however these determinants shape our self-understanding, we have the potential to respond—not "just react"—to them in more or less inventive ways.

On Ellison's understanding, the greatest manifestation of this rational autonomy and inventiveness is, of course, art. "Negro American art style," he insists in a letter to Stanley Edgar Hyman in 1970, is not a matter of "spontaneity and lifestyle," whatever Park and Burgess liked to say about the "natural disposition" of blacks. It embodies instead "a transcendence of raw hatred or any other 'raw' emotion." Indeed, its "transcendence and sublimation" define it *as* art. Genuine art, that is, displays no "given," no spontaneous overflow of powerful emotions or—in the language of contemporary affect theory—"intensities" that escape tyrannical conceptualization. It arises from "emotional control" of the type that African-Americans have always needed to learn for survival—a discipline that "sociologists both black and white" have treated as apathy but that is, in fact, a "life-preserving measure against being provoked into retaliatory actions by those who desire only to destroy us."[28] Such layered, complexly intentional practices are things about which sociology can tell us dramatically little. As Ellison puts it in "The World and the Jug," the *locus classicus* of this argument, the "pain and ferocity" that a critic like Howe imputes to the African-American seem to be the only justifiable affects for black artists to express.[29] But art is never univocal, given that it is always composed of at least two dimensions that can sometimes seem to conflict—the subject and the form, the "jagged grain of experience" and the techniques that give it compensatory shape, the painful details of a life and the lyricism that allows one to "transcend" them.

To be sure, Ellison was not the only post-World War II writer who was hostile to the social sciences. As critics have noted, midcentury American writers often lamented the "dreary blight" (in Flannery O'Connor's phrase) that the social sciences were casting on contemporary thought and art.[30] But Ellison's

---

[28] Ellison, "'American Culture is of a Whole'," 40–41.

[29] Irving Howe, "Black Boys and Native Sons," *Selected Writings, 1950–1990* (San Diego, CA: Brace Harcourt Jovanovich, 1990), 120.

[30] O'Connor's remark and general attitudes toward the social sciences are recorded in Michael LeMahieu, *Fictions of Fact and Value* (New York: Oxford University Press, 2013), 70–71. For more on the "opposition between the literary intellectual and the sociological technocrat [that] runs

criticisms are deeper and more sustained than those of most of his contemporaries. They are also more forward-thinking, for in many ways they look ahead to the wider criticism of the social sciences that emerged in the late 1960s and beyond. Most obviously, Ellison anticipated the rise of Black Studies, which emerged from a sense that "reality has been conceptualized in terms of the narrow point of view of the small minority of white men who live in Europe and North America," and that "white concepts" must be replaced by a "new frame of reference." These are the words of the editor and historian Lerone Bennett, quoted in the epigraph of *The Death of White Sociology*, the 1973 book edited by Joyce A. Ladner.[31] Ellison's 1944 review of Myrdal's *An American Dilemma* is the oldest piece in Ladner's provocatively titled collection, and it's not hard to see a direct line between Ellison's essay and the critiques of value-neutrality and black "pathology" that dominate other chapters in the book.[32] Yet Ellison's criticism of sociology bears a family resemblance to other, less obvious strands of thought that arose around the same time. In a series of articles throughout the 1970s, culminating with the landmark *After Virtue* (1981), Alasdair MacIntyre similarly argued that human action can be understood only in teleological terms, making reference to an agent's own beliefs and understanding of what's valuable, and that the rational autonomy of human beings makes the search for law-like generalizations and predictions—as opposed to rules of thumb, proverbs, or maxims—futile. Moreover, MacIntyre agrees with Ellison about the professional incentives that often motivate and mar the social scientist's labor. Social scientists have to present their findings as lawlike and authoritative, says MacIntyre, because doing otherwise would threaten the very idea of managerial expertise, and, in turn, the grounds for employing them as expert advisers to governments or corporations. Speaking in 1965, Ellison suggests with a similarly acid glare that sociologists "are up to their necks in politics and have access to millions of governmental dollars," access that requires "propagating an image of the Negro condition which is apt to destroy our human conception of ourselves just at the moment when we are becoming more politically free"

---

throughout so much postwar fiction and literary criticism," see Schryer, *Fantasies of the New Class* (quote at 10).

[31] Joyce A. Ladner, ed., *The Death of White Sociology: Essays on Race and Culture* (1973; Baltimore: Black Classic Press, 1998).

[32] For an example in the collection of this critique of value-neutrality, see the psychologist Kenneth Clarke's discussion (drawn from his book *Dark Ghetto*) of being an "involved observer" during his study of Harlem life; *Death of White Sociology* (ed. Ladner), 399–413.

(*CE* 731). As we'll see, this is only the first of several scores on which Ellison and an Aristotelian like MacIntyre can be said to concur.[33]

II. Two Alternatives to Social Science: Engineering and Improvising

To claim that Ellison is hostile to scientific naturalism can seem an overstatement. After all, the emerging technologies of the twentieth century were among Ellison's earliest enthusiasms, and he never lost the bug. "Like so many kids of the twenties," he recalls in a 1961 interview, "I played around with radio—building crystal sets and circuits consisting of a few tubes, which I found published in radio magazines" (*CE* 63). As he grew older, this "great curiosity about the growing science of radio" (*CE* 64) was channeled into a passion for sound systems more generally, as he describes at length in the 1955 essay "Living With Music." Choosing as a young couple to "live with music" rather than "die with noise," he and his wife stuffed their apartment with "booby-trappings of audio equipment, wires, discs and tapes," and Ellison eventually took a "plunge into electronics," becoming a "compulsive experimenter," building amplifiers and record compensators that might satisfy his obsession with "the idea of reproducing sound" (*CE* 227, 233–34). And these are traits that he liberally endows to his most developed character. The Invisible Man may ultimately withdraw like Thoreau, but he's hardly a Luddite. He's enough of a gadget aficionado to have transformed a sewer hole into a lair with 1,369 lights (the expensive filament kind) and a radio-phonograph, and he plans not only to add four more stereos, but also to invent "a gadget to place my coffee pot on the fire while I lie in bed, and even . . . a gadget to warm my bed." All this puts him, as he says, "in the great American tradition of tinkers," kin to "Ford, Edison, and Franklin," a "thinker-tinker" who has built a home out of a hole in the ground (*IM* 7).

Passages such as these lead John S. Wright, for instance, to situate Ellison's writing against the background of early twentieth-century changes in electricity and communications—a history in which African-Americans, Wright shows,

---

[33] Alasdair MacIntyre, *After Virtue* (Notre Dame, IN: Notre Dame University Press, 1981), chaps. 7–8. Michel Foucault's well-known critiques of the social sciences—in books such as *The Birth of the Clinic* or *Discipline and Punish*—would be another postwar line of thought that Ellison could be said to anticipate. But as critics have often suggested, Foucault's powerful claim that psychiatry, penology, and other social sciences have been a means of social control are seldom balanced by the kind of explicit positive alternative that, as I shall suggest, both Ellison and MacIntyre take the risk of offering.

have made singular contributions.[34] But a crucial gulf separates the allegedly scientific work of the social scientist, on the one hand, and the compulsive experimentalism of Ellison and his character. For Ellison, the work of the sociologist consists primarily of data-collection and theory-building. Researchers might make policy proposals, but only after they have disengaged themselves from the phenomena they analyze. Ellison and his character, by contrast, are engaged in the *applied* sciences, *practical* arts that work with elements or forces within the material world. They enact—to recall the phenomenological terms that were so important for thinking about Percy and Richard Powers—a skillful know-how, an ingenuity and resourcefulness, that crucially extend beyond any information they might have garnered or any general principles they might have developed. What inspires Ellison and his character is not knowledge-accumulation as such, but the way that, as John Wright nicely puts it, technology can be an extension of human lives, something with personal and social meaning rather than a vast implacable force—something that "*someone* makes, *someone* owns, something *some* oppose, most *must* use, and *everyone* tries to make sense of."[35]

Let's call this engineering and worldly know-how the first of the alternatives that Ellison risks proposing in the face of the social sciences. Doing so helps make sense of a second alternative he more consistently presents, one that develops my claim above that, for Ellison, art is the mark of rational autonomy. Reminiscing on his youth in Oklahoma, he speaks of the way that he and his friends "fabricated our own heroes and ideals catch-as-catch-can, and with an outrageous and irreverent sense of freedom" (CE 53). True jazz, he writes of the Oklahoma City guitarist Charlie Christian, "is an art of individual assertion within and against the group," with "each solo flight, or improvisation" contributing to the identity of the musician; and flamenco, he discovers later in life, is an "an art of improvisation" that "allows a maximum of individual expression," embodying a "note of unillusioned affirmation of humanity" (CE 24). History shows that, "having forsaken tradition," Americans have always "improvised," "'made do' as we could" (CE 414), and such a making-do produces, among many other things, the "improvised form, the willful juxtaposition of modes" that Ellison sees crystalized one memorable afternoon on Riverside Drive: a young man of ambiguous hue wearing a cornucopian mixture of English and West African clothes, a homburg propped on the top of his enormous Afro, "his

---

[34] John S. Wright, "Ellison's Experimental Attitude and the Technologies of Illumination," in *The Cambridge Companion to Ralph Ellison* (ed. Posnock), 157–71.
[35] John S. Wright, "Ellison's Experimental Attitude," 163.

clashing of styles" sounding "an integrative, vernacular note, an American compulsion to improvise upon the given" (*CE* 510–11).

"Improvisation" might in such cases seem to imply something capricious, the random or unaccountable flash of individual genius. But the engineering analogy suggests why that's misleading. For like the good engineer, the good improviser must have a deep training and well-honed habits. (One isn't improvising when one sits at the piano for the first time; one is merely hacking away at the keys.) Like the engineer, too, the improviser solves problems for particular circumstances rather than for always and everywhere; the question isn't what *every* project needs but what *this* project needs. And like the engineer, the improviser answers these questions by drawing upon existing techniques and forms, or what one commentator has called "ready-mades": the preexisting structures, motifs, frameworks, cultural knowledge, and formal patterns that are reshaped and reformulated in a new work.[36] If, in other words, improvisational actions are by definition not carried out according to strict plans, they are not for that reason entirely formless, nor are they wholly beyond the grasp of either the individual improviser or the surrounding community. That they're executed without a clear plan doesn't mean they're executed without rationality. Moreover, they aren't the purview of an imperial individual, something carried out by the exceptional and gifted soloist. Improvisation for Ellison is the capacity of a *we*, not just an *I*. The "individual assertion" of the improviser is made, as he says, both "against" *and* "within" the group, and the definition that the improviser thus achieves is in part "a member of the collectivity and. . . a link in the chain of tradition" (*CE* 267).

So when we say, as I did earlier, that Ellison's anthropology pictures the human being as a fundamentally creative being, "creative" shouldn't be taken to mean Promethean power. Indeed, if the aesthetic domain provides for Ellison the most vibrant manifestation of rational autonomy, his descriptions of art and the artistic process tend to emphasize restraint, discretion, and discipline. Again, much as Robinson does with "data," his accounts of improvisation and aesthetics habitually appropriate terms associated with the sciences, as if to imply that art's improvisatory and expressive qualities do not compromise its cognitive dimensions. This is the case with, for instance, "reduction." A basic impulse of modern naturalism is to reduce complex descriptions of phenomena to the simplest terms possible, a goal vividly summed up when Emile Durkheim says that "only the universal is rational": The job of the social scientist is to

---

[36] R. Keith Sawyer, "Improvisation and the Creative Process: Dewey, Collingwood, and the Aesthetics of Spontaneity," *The Journal of Aesthetics and Art Criticism* 58 (2000), 157–58.

form hypotheses out of the "particular and concrete," leaving to "the poets and literary people" "things as they seem to be, without any rational method."[37] In Ellison, however, the "poets and literary people" are in the business of "reducing" particulars just as resolutely as the theorizing scientist. Writers strive for a "necessary and tragic—though enhancing—reduction" of their vision, "without reducing it to a point which would render it sterile" (CE 59). "Life could be harsh, loud and wrong if it wished," he says of his early years in New York, but when artists "expressed their attitude toward the world it was with a fluid style that reduced the chaos of living to form" (CE 229). And in a 1965 interview, just after complaining about sociological formulas that "reduce" the complexity of Harlem "to proportions which the sociologists can manage," he speaks of how writers from a particular ethnic group must "reduce" their experience "to metaphor," "convert[ing]" their sense of the world rather than allowing "our anger and our pain . . . to obscure our view of the magic forest of art" (CE 733).[38]

Other terms are similarly transplanted from scientific discourse into Ellison's aesthetic lexicon. *Law*, for example. The scientist may speak of the "laws of motion" and the "law of conservation of matter," but Ellison speaks of "the laws of art," the standards that Irving Howe forgets in his criticism of *Invisible Man*: "the laws of literary form exert their own validity upon all those who write," and it is Howe's "slighting of the formal necessities of his essay which makes for some of our misunderstanding" (CE 183). Or—as this last sentence highlights—*necessity*. The scientist may seek out causal necessities across the natural or human-made worlds, but as early as 1946, Ellison speaks of the "structural, symbolic and moral necessity" that made Twain decide to have Huck Finn rescue Jim (CE 90). Decades later, the term appears in a letter to

---

[37] Quoted in Susan Mizruchi, *The Science of Sacrifice: American Literature and Modern Social Theory* (Princeton, NJ: Princeton University Press, 1998), 8. The introduction of Mizruchi's book provides a very good overview for the play between "universal" and "particular" in turn-of-the-century social thought. On the naturalistic ideals of some social science, see Malcolm Williams, *Science and Social Science: An Introduction* (London: Routledge, 2000), 139–40.

[38] Laudatory uses of "reduce" and "reduction" are sometimes applied in Ellison's writing to things other than art, as when he claims that writing essays on different topics has provided "opportunities for me to reduce my thinking—indeed, often to discover what I *did* think—to publishable form" (CE 56). He's also, unsurprisingly, capable of using "reduce" and "reduction" in a pejorative sense to mean the erasure of particulars in favor of a simplifying universal. In the entertainment industry and in folklore, he says in the mid-1950s, "the Negro is reduced to a negative sign that usually appears in a comedy of the gross and unacceptable" (CE 103). A social-scientific model shackles our understanding of art, encouraging a "simpleminded attempt to reduce fiction to mere protest" (CE 737), and the "dismal sociological facts," together with "ideological formulas," have "sought to reduce our complex American identity to the single aspect of race" (CE 838).

Kenneth Burke, when Ellison acknowledges to his old friend that he has "always tried to turn [his] insights back to the necessities of fiction."[39]

To say that improvisational artworks strive to "reduce," that they exhibit "laws" and "necessities," is not to deny the differences between the work of the scientist and the work of the artist or human agent. One difference—to return to an earlier theme—is that the artist can reflectively endorse or refuse the reductions and laws in question. A plant doesn't ask itself how and whether to grow leaves, just as, in Robert Park's account, blacks in American cities don't evaluate whether and how to move from "contact" and "conflict" to "assimilation." These events are evidently, to recall Park's phrase, "progressive and irreversible," and for Park, the *failure* of either a plant to grow or a group to assimilate will be attributed to illness or poor environmental conditions, a disruption in the optimal set of causal necessities. By contrast, when the "necessities" of a given artistic form are not extended—when a painting shows a chevron rather than a human form, or a song is performed with electric rather than acoustic guitars—it can be attributed to the artist's "consciousness," an awareness at some level (it need not be fully articulated) that a historically shaped form has begun to die out. Our need for "reduction" and "law" hasn't diminished, but those of the past no longer seem alive, no longer have a grip.

Moreover, compared to judging whether a plant has grown, there are far fewer shared criteria for what *counts as* an effective improvisatory reduction. Certainly Ellison wasn't always convinced that the art of his contemporaries exemplified aesthetic necessities. His essays repeatedly scrutinize bebop, for instance, and for some of the same reasons they challenge Hemingway: the form shows a "near-themeless technical virtuosity, a further triumph of technology over humanism," and though Charlie Parker had "velocity, brilliance, and imagination," his playing also had "a sound of amateurish ineffectuality" that is typical of a "do-it-yourself culture" (*CE* 325).[40] It was in the older, interwar jazz—Jimmy Rushing, Charlie Christian, Duke Ellington, and above all Louis Armstrong—that Ellison found a genuine poise between form-building and form-breaking. His most common word for such poise was "lyricism," as when he says that the "lyrical ritual elements of folk jazz" embody "a superior democracy in which each individual cultivated his uniqueness and yet did not clash with his neighbors" (*CE* 325). As Paul Allen Anderson has argued, "lyricism"

---

[39] Quoted in Bryan Crable, *Ralph Ellison and Kenneth Burke: At the Roots of the Racial Divide* (Charlottesville: University of Virginia Press, 2011), 79.

[40] Parker's death at age thirty-four, says Ellison, merely confirmed the search among white audiences for a "suffering, psychically wounded, law-breaking, life-affirming hero" (*CE* 264).

sums up the centripetal and centrifugal movements in Ellison's attitude toward jazz and improvisation. He continually weighs the artist's autonomy and creativity against the equally genuine needs of his or her audience, which comes to music not only for one-off feats of genius, but also—indeed, chiefly—for collective affirmation and ritual, a glimpse of some semblance of wholeness in our lives (*CE* 275).[41]

III. Two More Alternatives: Rhetoric and Citizenship

Improvisation will return as a theme over the next couple chapters, particularly when we come to Cavell, who, like Ellison, spent his earliest years immersed in jazz, classical music, and musical composition. For now we should note—and here we come to Ellison's third alternative to the social sciences—that "lyricism" among musicians is what, apropos the arts of language, Ellison calls *eloquence*. Eloquence is what public figures and educators are said to possess, as when Ellison recalls being inspired by the "eloquence of some Negro preacher" (*CE* 53) or the way that Dr. Inman Page—the first African-American to graduate from Brown University, and later Ellison's high school principal—could move students with his "implicit authority," "wisdom and eloquence" (*CE* 596). But more frequently, Ellison applies the term to the work of the artist. Writing in 1958, for instance, he juxtaposes the presence of enduring literary archetypes with the "living human being," who must "achieve eloquence and create specific works of art" in a specific time and place (*CE* 101). "What moves a writer to eloquence," he says in his response to Irving Howe, "is less meaningful than what he makes of it" (*CE* 159), and a few pages later Ellison describes himself as "an individual who aspires to conscious eloquence" (*CE* 164). To an interviewer he modestly claims that *Invisible Man* "failed of eloquence" (*CE* 217), and in a 1981 introduction to the novel, he speaks of the obstacles facing the American novelist to endow "inarticulate characters, scenes and social processes with eloquence," a task by which, if successful, "he fulfills his social responsibility as an American artist" (*CE* 486). If today—returning to the starting point of this chapter—we read "sociology. . .more than we read novels," it may represent less a failure of readers than the fact that the novelist "has failed his obligation to tell the truth, to describe with eloquence and imagination life as it appears from wherever he finds his being" (*CE* 767).

---

[41] Paul Allen Anderson, "Ralph Ellison on Lyricism and Swing," *American Literary History* 17 (2005): 280–306.

Not "beautiful," then, and not "sublime"—those traditional terms of aesthetic appraisal—but "eloquent." Why? One answer is that, more than these other terms, "eloquence" casts the work of art as an unavoidably *public* and *rhetorical* affair, and portrays the relationship between artist and audience as one of, as Ellison puts it, "antagonistic cooperation" (*CE* 496). The theme is most extensively explored in "The Little Man at Chehaw Station" (1979), wherein Ellison describes the connoisseur of a given artistic medium who can turn up in the most unexpected places, such as, for example, an out-of-the-way train station, ready to "pounce upon" laziness or cliché. The little man symbolizes the fact that, in the United States, an audience wants not only to be entertained and moved, but also to act, "for better or worse, as both collaborator and judge" (*CE* 496). An artist, that is, may seek to shape the emotions and perceptions of the audience, playing upon its sense of experience and form, like a guest conductor confronting a strange audience. But the audience, in turn, "simultaneously cooperates and resists, says yes and says no in an it-takes-two-to-tango binary response to his effort." It engages "in a silent dialogue with the artist's exposition of forms, offering or rejecting the work of art on the basis of what [it] feels to be its affirmation or distortion of American experience" (*CE* 496). This attention to American experience is what makes the "little man" "democratically innocent of hierarchical striving," free of the "mystifications of snobbery," impatient with hard distinctions between high and low forms, elite and popular culture (*CE* 501). To ignore the "little man" is to pretend that we do not live in a restless nation, a mobile and mixed place where the artist hopes to "fashion strategies of communication that will bridge the many divisions of background and taste." It is to risk doing violence to "that ideal of cultivated democratic sensibility" endorsed by Emerson and Whitman, to withdraw into a self-secluding avant-garde, and to forget that a work of art is "an act of faith in our ability to communicate symbolically" (*CE* 503).

Like Percy, then, Ellison's picture of art and language is intensely antiformalist, emphasizing the entirety of a communicative situation, accepting the contaminations of rhetoric in a messy modern culture.[42] He emphasizes not

---

[42] Contrast, for instance, Ezra Pound's disdain for the "rhetorical din" of Victorian poetry, or T.S. Eliot's suggestion that rhetoric "may be considered bad in relation to the historical life of language as a whole," or—most famously—W. B. Yeats's belief that, "We make out of the quarrel with others, rhetoric, but out of the quarrel with ourselves, poetry." See Ezra Pound, "A Retrospect," in *Literary Essays of Ezra Pound* (New York: New Directions, 1968), 12; T.S. Eliot, "Milton I," in *Selected Prose of T.S. Eliot*, ed. Frank Kermode (London: Faber, 1975), 262; William Butler Yeats, *Per Amica Silentia Lunae* (New York: Macmillan, 1919), 29. Pound, Eliot, and Yeats are to varying degrees working off Arthur Symons, who claimed that Symbolism was an attempt "to evade the old bondage of rhetoric, the old bondage of exteriority." (See *Arthur Symons: Selected Writings*, ed. Roger Holdsworth [New York: Routledge, 2003], 83.) The relation of Modernism to rhetoric is more complicated than

only the purposes of particular speakers but also—and just as critically—the conceptual resources and environmental stimuli that they inevitably share with the audience. And this stance leads him likewise to resist what Robinson calls the "elitist model of culture" that has often been associated with aesthetic modernism, the idea that, as she puts it, "democracy and cultural freedom could not accommodate each other."[43] On Ellison's reckoning, as on Percy's and Robinson's, neither the artist nor the artwork is "autonomous" in any deep sense, and as with them, this stance leads him to a surprisingly humble conception of his own place and writing. The "cooperation" between artists and audiences may be "antagonistic," but it is cooperation all the same, not simply a matter of a decontextualized, apolitical "heroic individualist" defying the tawdry cheapness of a half-savage country.[44]

And more than just aesthetic issues are at stake here in this "cooperation." The exchange that Ellison identifies between eloquent artist and active audience is also a key step toward what I've been calling the "weak realism" of the postwar sage. The sheer instability of this exchange, suggests "The Little Man," mirrors the instability of American social relations generally, and "the fluid, pluralistic turbulence of the democratic process" can provoke feelings of isolation. What prevents this instability from plummeting into constant chaos or violence is our commitment to "principles that are abstract, ideal, spiritual," which serve as regulative ideals through even our most heated disagreements. Democracy, equality, individual freedom, universal justice: such principles are not reflections of God or Platonic Forms, but are thoroughly "man-made," "conceived linguistically and committed to paper"—the Declaration of Independence, the Constitution, and the Bill of Rights—"during that contention over political ideals and economic interests" that occurred after Americans broke away from "traditional forms of society." Yet their fundamentally historical nature doesn't weaken their force. Since they were put in place, these principles have become "sacred," and we summon them up "to name the ideal." Against the "given and amoral condition" of nature—plants, oceans, and wild animals do not act well or badly—they offer "man-made or man-imagined positives," which "nudge us toward that state of human rectitude from which, ideally, we strive." Such

---

these neat maxims imply, as Charles Altieri has argued in "Rhetoric and Poetics: How to Use the Inevitable Return of the Repressed," in *A Companion to Rhetoric and Rhetorical Criticism*, ed. Walter Jost and Wendy Olmsted (Oxford: Blackwell, 2003), 473–93.

[43] Robinson, interview with Thomas Schaub, *Contemporary Literature* 35 (1994): 237.

[44] A decontextualized and apolitical "heroic individualist" is how Watt characterizes Ellison in *Heroism and the Black Intellectual*, 55–58. "A half-savage country" and "tawdy cheapness" are, of course, well-known phrases from Pound's "Hugh Selwyn Mauberly."

"rectitude" can be achieved not only in particular individual actions, but also in our social practices and institutions, whose abstract principles "prod us ceaselessly toward the refinement and perfection of those formulation of policy and configurations of social forms of which they are the signs and symbols." They are "made flesh" "in the structures and processes of ourselves and society," as we use language "to moralize both nature" and ourselves (*CE* 505).

The guiding spirit behind these anti-nominalist claims is Kenneth Burke, the rhetorician, critic, and philosopher who is one of the key figures for understanding how the Ellisonian sage departs from that of Percy and Robinson.[45] The half-century of Ellison's friendship with Burke allowed him to absorb lessons firsthand on the time-bound and social nature of speech, a perspective that Burke developed largely out of the earthly, pre-Christian writings of Aristotle and the Roman rhetoricians.[46] Burke cast in a philosophical register much of what Ellison had already perceived in his favorite jazz and literary texts, and it was through his work that Ellison fostered much of the vocabulary that I've sketched here, including "reduction," "eloquence," and the distinction between "just reacting" and "conscious thought."[47] And it was through Burke

---

[45] Ellison first met Burke at the Third American Writers Congress in 1939, where Burke delivered a lecture on Hitler's recently translated *Mein Kampf*, and over the next few years the two men became familiar enough for Burke to write a letter of recommendation on Ellison's behalf to the Julius Rosenwald Fund, which in 1945 provided the aspiring author the respite he needed to begin what became *Invisible Man*. The most meticulous and illuminating record of the relationship between Burke and Ellison is Crable, *Ralph Ellison and Kenneth Burke: At the Roots of the Racial Divide*, which delves into the correspondence between the two men. For another extensive account, see Beth Eddy, *The Rites of Identity: The Religious Naturalism and Cultural Criticism of Kenneth Burke and Ralph Ellison* (Princeton, NJ: Princeton University Press, 2003).

[46] References to Aristotle's corpus are strewn throughout Burke's writing, and in an interview Burke credited Aristotle's exposition of the Four Causes with the development of his own so-called dramatism—as when he says that Aristotle's theories are based "upon *action*. His whole system is a *dramatistic* mode of analysis. His formula for God was 'pure act,' which of course Aquinas could take over" (qtd. in Jack Selzer, *Kenneth Burke in Greenwich Village: Conversing with the Moderns, 1915–1931* [Madison: University of Wisconsin Press, 1996], 250).

[47] Indeed, most of the major concepts that I've singled out in my sketch of Ellison's essays can be traced to Burke's corpus. The distinction, for instance, between nature as a "given and amoral condition" and "man-made, man-imagined positives," like the distinction between "just reacting" and "conscious thought," grows directly out of the Burkean division between "action" and "motion," which is central to *Attitudes Toward History* (1935) and *Permanence and Change* (1937). But many of the other, more local Ellisonian terms that I've identified also originate in Burke. "Reduction," for example, is a keyword in the book that Burke was composing when the two men met, *A Grammar of Motives* (1945), and "eloquence" appears in Burke as early as *Counter-Statement* (1931), where it is associated with the "psychology of form," a habit of mind that is different from the "psychology of information" characteristic of many nonaesthetic forms of communication. For a good account of Ellison's early reading of Burke's books of the 1930s, see Crable. Burke's refusal of behaviorism is summed up nicely in a line from *A Grammar of Motives* (1945; Berkeley: University of California Press, 1969) that both Percy and Robinson would applaud: "One cannot find a representative case of human motivation in animals if only because animals lack that property of linguistic rationalization which is so typical of human motives" (59). For a later retort to behaviorism, see Kenneth

that Ellison was able to develop his weak realism. As I noted in my introduction, Burke was keenly aware that nominalists had "failed to discover the justice" of ancient Greek realism—that, whatever the constitution of the physical
universe, we human beings *do* learn to move from particular to universal, and
do continually think and converse about general properties.[48] Whatever a reductionist might suggest, that is, the relations that are established and extended by
our use of symbols (identification, communication, rapport) are not magical or
otherworldly, ready for deconstruction or elimination. As Burke argued in his
controversial 1935 address to the American Writers Congress—and anticipating
the claims about language that I associated in Chapter 1 with Percy and West
Coast philosophy—these relations should be understood as part of a "realism of
the *act*": worldly functions that are as ontologically valid as anything described
in the propositions of science. Our concepts may look like "myths" or "illusions"
when they survive as fossils from an outdated historical situation, but when
fully alive, they provide a scheme of "allegiance," embodying the "ideal" that
humans inevitably seek.[49]

To say that Ellison was shaped by Burkean notions of eloquence, rhetoric,
and realism is not, however, to say that he absorbed Burke unthinkingly.[50] Two
issues matter most here, and taken together, they constitute the fourth and
final alternative that I want to isolate in Ellison's response to the social sciences. One issue reflects the fact that Burke generalizes the field of rhetoric
massively, and in doing so, he regularly blurs any line between persuasion and
truth, wooing and accuracy. As one critic said already in the 1960s, if rhetoric
can give effectiveness either to the truth or to the speaker, Burke's inclination is
toward the latter; keenly aware of the potency of the word, he ultimately seems
less interested in the truth than in artful presentation.[51] Thus when Burke

---

Burke, "Self-Portrait of a Person," a review of Skinner's memoir *Particulars of a Life*, in *Behavior and Philosophy* 4 (1976): 257–71.

[48] Burke, *Counter-Statement* (1931; Berkeley: University of California Press, 1968), 46–48.

[49] See Kenneth Burke, "Revolutionary Symbolism in America," in *The Legacy of Kenneth Burke*, ed. Herbert W. Simons and Trevor Melia (Madison: University of Wisconsin Press, 1989), 267–73. See also Burke's 1950 book *A Rhetoric of Motives* (Berkeley: University of California Press, 1969), particularly the section titled "Realistic Function of Rhetoric," 43–46; and 176–77, where he defends
the priority of "spirit" over "body" among symbol-using animals.

[50] Others have made this observation in different ways. Beth Eddy, for instance, has explored why
Ellison tended to talk about art in terms of the blues rather than (as in Burke) comedy, and Bryan
Crable has vividly described the various forms of evasion and envy that marred Burke's response
to his admirer, a response that Crable persuasively attributes to blind spots in Burke's understanding of race. See Eddy, *The Rites of Identity*, chap. 7; Crable, *Ralph Ellison and Kenneth Burke*. For
another effort to distinguish them, see Donald E. Pease, "Ralph Ellison and Kenneth Burke: The
Nonsymbolizable (Trans)Action," *boundary 2* (2003): 65–96.

[51] Joseph Schwartz, "Kenneth Burke, Aristotle, and the Future of Rhetoric," *College Composition and Communication* 17 (1966): 210–16.

speaks, for instance, of the various "attitudes toward history" that are available to us, it's not always clear what relationship these attitudes bear to actual historical events in the world, or what would make one human vocabulary better or worse, let alone more accurate or false, than any other. To some readers, this attention to tactics of persuasion just indicates that Burke is more interested in learning from a given text rather than pronouncing a favorable or unfavorable judgment on it. To others, however, Burke is at bottom a mere ironist, skipping briskly between different conceptual networks, exposing startling affinities and disjunctions but evading the question of which "allegiances" or "ideals" are his own, or why.[52]

Whether or not these complaints apply to Burke, they decidedly do *not* fit Ellison, who was never shy about endorsing the "ideals" to which he felt "ceaselessly prodded." Being noncommittal is a luxury more likely to be enjoyed by someone whose grandfather had *not* been born a slave. In this respect Ellison remains closer to Aristotle than Burke himself does; rhetoric for him clearly serves the truth more than the speaker. At times the norms to which he is "prodded" derive specifically from the African-American community. Recall the remark to an interviewer, cited earlier, that the "sociological conditions" of black life may have "made for misery," but they are also not the only things that make for "values which I feel I should endure and shall endure"—values that, as his essays suggest, include faith, patience, humor, a sense of timing, the "rugged sense of life and the manner of expressing it" (*CE* 79–80). And in certain moments Ellison even saw his work as a "commemoration" of these habits,

---

[52] On Burke as learner, see Herbert W. Simons's introduction to *The Legacy of Kenneth Burke*, ed. Herbert W. Simons and Trevor Melia (Madison: University of Wisconsin Press, 1989), 9. For a less flattering picture of Burke, see Austin Warren's review of Burke's *Permanence and Change*: "Perhaps all 'views' of the universe, though couched in so many series of metaphors, all, equally, afford a guide to its meaning; perhaps they play the same cosmic melody but in many keys.... The scheme is tempting, but it must be rejected if it postulates any equipollence of metaphors. Assuredly it does matter whether I think of the universe under the type of Paley's watch and Adams's dynamo or conceive of it under some more humane and spiritual guise—whether I take my start from matter or from mind, whether man or machine be my center for exploration." (*Critical Responses to Kenneth Burke*, ed. William Ruckert [Minneapolis: University of Minnesota Press, 1969], 57). The connection between Burke's views and those of post-structuralist philosophy have often been noticed, as when Timothy Crusius claims in *Kenneth Burke and the Conversation After Philosophy* (Carbondale: Southern Illinois University Press, 1999): "By 1935 Kenneth Burke already understood the intellectual situation that Jean-Francois Lyotard has called 'the postmodern condition,' part of which is a resolve to work ... without a foundation in epistemology or metaphysics, without even the aspiration for certain and comprehensive Truth that drove [modernity], especially in the Cartesian tradition.... [Burke] takes language as irreducibly metaphorical and rhetorical. For Burke subjectivity or consciousness is not the key category of philosophy, nor reason its privileged, reliable instrument, nor literal truth, faithful correspondence of word to 'reality,' its end or purpose" (1–2).

practices, and goods (*CE* 76). At other times, however, Ellison associates his avowed norms with larger currents of American society and history, which have not only shaped black culture but also, as he repeatedly argues, been shaped *by* it. His nonfiction consistently shows what Gregg Crane has called a "constitutional faith," speaking freely about the texts that are "sacred" to Americans, the documents of state that strove to provide the "original script" for American society and the conditions of its diverse reality (*CE* 412, 427).[53] This script is never rigid; as Ellison sees it, an American's identity is "tentative, controversial, constantly changing" (*CE* 499), and we are always experimenting with different names, styles, and codes. Moreover, as in any human society, an American is enfolded in a cacophonous world of greed, fear, hatred, and violence—all the social and psychological pressures that lead human beings to develop the divergent values and traditions that they have. But despite all this, Ellison speaks without irony of how our "sacred" words provoke us constantly toward "consciousness and conscience," the obligation to be "consciously aware of the ideals to which they had committed us, and conscientiously concerned with making their ideas manifest in the quality of this nation's life" (*CE* 413). In his everyday life, Burke may have accepted such concepts and claims, but in his work, he writes primarily as a *theorist*, a disinterested observer, and from this allegedly impartial perspective, the American's "sacred" texts are simply one corpus among others, a particular recent rhetorical action that seems to have caught fire (for now) in a specific communicative situation. Ellison, by contrast, spent his life face-to-face with what he called the "serpent-like malignancy" running through American history (*CE* 775), and couldn't pretend to be a coolly neutral observer. He may have seemed dispassionately aristocratic to some onlookers, but he himself confessed to being "vindictive" and "full of hate"; James Baldwin regarded him as the angriest man he'd ever met, and Norman Mailer claimed that his genius was essentially "hateful."[54] And all this separated him from his mentor. Ellison's defense of the nation's abstract principles was *indignant*, because only by not flinching could the country's "slow advance toward true equality" be realized on the "human scale," "made flesh" (*CE* 779, 782).

The phrase "true equality" brings us to the second, related distinction between Burke and Ellison, and that is their respective terminologies for describing human affiliations. In Burke, the most important words for describing a group's

---

[53] See Gregg Crane, "Ralph Ellison's Constitutional Faith," in *Cambridge Companion to Ralph Ellison* (ed. Posnock), 104–20.

[54] Quoted in Lawrence Jackson, "Ralph Ellison's Invented Life: A Meeting With the Ancestors," in *Cambridge Companion to Ralph Ellison* (ed. Posnock), 27.

shared commitments are "identification" and "consubstantiality." A is not B, he says in *A Rhetoric of Motives,* and a given person always remains "unique, an individual locus of motives." But insofar as A and B share interests, or A persuades B to join in a project, the two can be said to "identify" with one another; they can (and do) act, speak, and feel together, exhibiting a union that doesn't deny their distinctness.[55] Ellison tends to use different terms to describe such collective feelings and projects: not *identity* or *consubstantiality,* but *fraternity.* As we've seen, Hemingway seems in his eyes to have privileged "technical virtuosity" over "fraternal values," to have encouraged the "artistic segregation of the Negro" as well "the segregation of real fraternal, i.e., democratic, values" (*CE* 92). That 1946 remark reiterates a statement made the previous year at the end of "Beating That Boy" (1945), when he claims that writing since *Huckleberry Finn* has generally failed to search "for images of black and white fraternity" (*CE* 150), and a few years later, in his National Book Award Speech, he speaks similarly of having wanted to confront "the inequalities and brutalities of our society forthrightly, yet thrusting forth its images of hope, human fraternity and individual self-realization" (*CE* 153). Two decades later, he remarks to an interviewer that, even with "racial structuring of American society," with perpetual divisions between the white and black communities, "friendship and shared interests make the difference" (*CE* 803). In "The Little Man at Chehaw Station," he speaks of the "poignant, although distrusted, sense of fraternity" between blacks and whites, the sense of "intergroup familiarity" that has been threatened after the rise of "blood magic and blood thinking"—that is, the black nationalism of the 1970s. And in the 1981 introduction to *Invisible Man,* he talks of having sought "images of black and white fraternity" in the 54th Massachusetts Negro Regiment of the Civil War (*CE* 484), and of having tried to make visible to readers "the reality of black and white fraternity" (*CE* 488).

"Fraternity" may not seem very different from "identity" or "consubstantiality." And in certain ways it isn't: all these words are noticeably distant from the social scientist's vocabulary of systems, networks, and processes. "Fraternity," however, is less a piece of metaphysical jargon than "identity" or "consubstantiality." More than Burke's preferred terms, that is, Ellison's word taps into a particular stream of associations in Western political culture. "Fraternity" and "friendship" are, after all, terms that were crucial across Greek and Roman culture, as vital to Homer's heroes and Sophocles's characters as to Plato and Aristotle and later to the Epicureans and Stoics. And from these ancient

---

[55] See Burke, *A Rhetoric of Motives,* 19–29.

sources, they are laced into early modern republicanism, whose this-worldly posture foregrounds notions of citizenship and virtue, the primacy of the political over the contemplative, the actions of human beings over the actions of grace. Ellison may not have studied Machiavelli and Rousseau at length, but he returns repeatedly to the Founding Fathers, whose conceptual vocabularies have often been cited as the most developed form of the "Atlantic republican tradition." In all of these cases (and, of course, there are obvious differences between fifth-century Athens and eighteenth-century British colonies), human lives are said to be consummated not at the end of time, when the perpetual instabilities of our temporal lives are finally redeemed by a messiah. They are fulfilled in the particulars of *our* time, when, through the exercise of the virtues, a degree of individual and social stability can be imposed and maintained in the face of fortune and corruption. One comes to look upon another human being less as a suffering soul drawing toward eternal redemption or perdition, and more as a fellow citizen on whom one has a reciprocal dependence. They are objects of concern, trust, esteem, and appreciation—persons co-responsible, like me, for the welfare of the environments and institutions in which we conduct our lives. The model form of speech, in such a tradition, is not the prayer but the oration or conversation, and thought becomes less eschatological than historical, less metaphysical than practical. When the human being is essentially *zoon politikon*, a being whose nature is fulfilled by participation in the polity and (Ellison's phrase) "shared interest," *friendship* gets applied not only to the relatively narrow, relatively privatized types of intimate relationships that it often is taken to name nowadays. It also names the broader or more diffuse kinds of affiliation that mark the lives of a community's members: affiliations with a school, a fan club, a workplace, a neighborhood, a town, a region, and so forth. Accordingly, it is charged with much more than giving us pleasure or helping us pass the time; it is the model of all citizen associations. *Philia,* as Aristotle puts it, "would seem to hold cities together," for "the justice that is most just seems to belong to friendship."[56]

IV. Finding the Form of Fraternity

Walker Percy recurrently charts the communal "triads" at work in a genuine semantics, and Marilynne Robinson reflects at length on the broad cultural

---

[56] Aristotle, *Nicomachean Ethics*, VIII.ix. My sketch of republicanism in this paragraph owes much to J. G. A. Pocock's magisterial study *The Machiavellian Moment: Florentine Political Thought and the Atlantic Republican Tradition* (Princeton, NJ: Princeton University Press, 1975).

conditions needed for concepts like "courage" to find expression. But Ellison is the first figure I've discussed for whom community means *Sittlichkeit*, a form of sociality expressed in socio-civic life rather than any alleged higher order or power. And in recovering these civic–humanist traditions early in the post-World War II years, Ellison can be said to anticipate a wider movement that marked the last three decades of the twentieth century. Earlier I noted his affinity to Alasdair MacIntyre's assault on the social sciences in the 1970s and 1980s, but the other, more constructive prong of MacIntyre's project was a return to the sort of moral and political traditions that I've also just associated with Ellison. Along with Charles Taylor, Philippa Foot, and other philosophers, MacIntyre sought to recover a richer notion of the ways that friendships and communal attachments frame an individual's normative commitments, and though not all of these figures were as unflinchingly secular as Ellison (I've mentioned Taylor's religious commitments in Chapter 1), they presented powerful challenges to the reigning utilitarian and Kantian traditions of Anglophone philosophical culture. Comparable work was also undertaken around this time by intellectual historians such as J. G. A. Pocock, Quentin Skinner, and Gordon Wood, who in rich social and cultural detail excavated the civic humanist tradition of Aristotle, Machiavelli, and the American Founders. In their eyes, our accounts of the social and political culture of modernity need to include not only its strong streak of liberal individualism, but also a robust notion of purposive human affiliation.[57]

The revival of these intellectual, moral, and political traditions has drawn fire from a range of critics.[58] But it also has helped Ellison's readers draw attention

---

[57] Among the intellectual historians, see Pocock, *The Machiavellian Moment;* Gordon Wood, *The Creation of the American Republic, 1776–1787* (Chapel Hill: University of North Carolina Press, 1968); Quentin Skinner, *The Foundations of Modern Political Thought: Volume 1: The Renaissance* (Cambridge: Cambridge University Press, 1978). Among the philosophers, see Alasdair MacIntyre, *After Virtue* (Notre Dame, IN: Notre Dame University Press, 1981); Philippa Foot, *Virtues and Vices* (Oxford: Blackwell, 1978); Charles Taylor, *Philosophy and the Human Sciences: Philosophical Papers, Volume 2* (Cambridge: Cambridge University Press, 1985). See also the anthology *Virtue Ethics,* ed. Roger Crisp and Michael Slote (Oxford: Oxford University Press, 1997), which includes pieces by Elizabeth Anscombe and Iris Murdoch, who are often regarded as the first post-World War II Anglophone philosophers to put virtue ethics back on the map.

[58] To critics of a liberal and neoliberal bent, virtue ethics and republicanism can seem sentimental, unworkable in a modern technological culture, and/or dangerously indifferent to individual rights; see, for example, Stephen Holmes, *The Anatomy of Anti-Liberalism* (Cambridge, MA: Harvard University Press, 1993). To some Marxist critics, virtue ethics and republicanism can also seem unworkably sentimental, unaware of the depth of struggle and power politics needed for genuine equality to be achieved. For efforts to reconcile the Marxist and Aristotelian traditions, however, see Ruth Groff, "Aristotelian Marxism/Marxist Aristotelianism: MacIntyre, Marx, and the Analysis of Abstraction," *Philosophy and Social Criticism* 38 (2012): 775–92; Fredric Jameson, "Morality Versus Ethical Substance; or, Aristotelian Marxism in Alasdair MacIntyre," *Social Text* 8 (Winter 1983–84): 151–54.

to some of the features of his thinking that I've been discussing. Ross Posnock, for instance, has claimed that Ellison is motivated by a "notion of the political" that "recovers an almost classical sense of the word," resisting the comforts of *ethnos* for the complex ideals of *politikos*. For Posnock, the closest contemporary analogue to Ellison on this score is Hannah Arendt, who also identified the human being with the capacity for new action (what she called "natality"), and who drew explicitly on the model of the Greek *polis* as a way of reanimating a secular, worldly notion of political participation.[59] The political theorist Danielle Allen has similarly likened Ellison to Arendt, arguing that Ellison challenges the conception of modern sociopolitical life provided by Locke, Kant, and Hobbes. In all these latter figures, Allen claims, "the people" is cast as a monistic unit, public rhetoric is disdained as a perversion of interest-free speech, and disagreement is taken to be an aberration. Ellison, by contrast, replaces "oneness" with the goal of democratic "wholeness," an Aristotelian notion that implies the existence of disparate parts that may or may not be in full agreement. Within such a civic whole, different persons and groups must make sacrifices at various times for the good of everyone, and more than Hobbes and his descendants, Ellison knows that such sacrifices entail a psychological burden that can be eased only by functioning rituals and customs. And like Aristotle, Ellison knows not only that rhetoric is essential for producing trust among citizens, but also that "friendship" in such a polity is paramount—friendship understood, as Allen incisively puts it, not as "an emotion, but a practice, a set of hard-won, complicated habits that are used to bridge trouble, difficulty and differences of personality, experience, and aspiration." Ellison recognizes that a *shared* life is not the same as an *identical* life, and that our willingness to live amicably alongside our fellow citizens depends deeply on the cultivation of trust.[60]

Ellison's affinities with classical thought, in other words, go well beyond allusions to Greek and Roman literature.[61] And they help cut against the image

---

[59] See Ross Posnock, *Color and Culture: Black Writers and the Making of the Modern Intellectual* (Cambridge, MA: Harvard University Press, 1998), 9; Ross Posnock, "Ralph Ellison, Hannah Arendt, and the Meaning of Politics," in *Cambridge Companion to Ralph Ellison* (ed. Posnock), 201–16. Posnock's comparison between Ellison and Arendt is, in part, meant to highlight their differences—over, most famously, the desegregation of Little Rock schools in 1957.

[60] Danielle Allen, *Talking to Strangers: Anxieties of Citizenship Since Brown v. Board of Education* (Chicago: University of Chicago Press, 2004), 113, xxi.

[61] On Ellison and classical literature, see Patrice D. Rankine, *Ulysses in Black: Ralph Ellison, Classicism, and African-American Literature* (Madison: University of Wisconsin Press, 2006); William W. Cook and James Tatum, *African-American Writers and Classical Tradition* (Chicago: University of Chicago Press, 2010), chap. 5.

of Ellison aloofly secluding himself in the palaces of art or sinking into the "quagmire of bourgeois liberty."[62] Such an image emerged first during the Black Power movement, but in recent years it's been vividly updated by Barbara Foley, who has pored with remarkable care over Ellison's manuscripts and examined how the author of *Invisible Man* quietly erased his early commitments to Marxism. Ellison may talk, says Foley, about "black and white fraternity," and may ask about the relationship between love and politics, but the one novel he published in his lifetime, she concludes, "conveys precious little of either fraternity or love." Indeed, once we look at the characters and scenes that Ellison deleted from the novel—an affair the narrator has with a white woman, members of the Brotherhood who are sympathetically portrayed, the journal of a black activist and intellectual that he discovers at Mary Rambo's house—we can see how Ellison purged the residual memories of thirties radicalism. In such a light, *Invisible Man* comes to seem a "far less humane and antiracist novel than it might otherwise have been."[63]

The danger and lure of such a reading is the danger and lure that marked the Black Power criticisms of Ellison, namely the simplicity of the options: *either* Ellison is a political intellectual and activist, *or* he is a self-isolating subjectivist blind to the forces of history. Neither option has much place for the type of fraternity and wholeness (not oneness) that I've been tracing in Ellison's writing, much as neither full-blown determination (sociology) nor full-blown randomness (Charlie Parker) allows, in Ellison's view, a space for authentic improvisation. Indeed, it's not incidental in this regard that Foley's discussion sometimes has the flavor of Robert E. Parks and the Chicago School, insisting as she does that Ellison's psychology and biography—things, that is, about which Ellison himself might have given first-person testimony—are relatively marginal for understanding *Invisible Man,* or at least a great deal less important than what she calls the "causality operating at the level of the larger historical matrix."[64]

Foley's argument does, however, pick out something essential about Ellison's work. For she comes to her conclusions—"precious little of either fraternity or love"—after a prolonged plunge into the development of Ellison's novel rather than the nonfiction that I've been considering at length thus far. Implicit in her very methods, that is, is a sense that Ellison's essays and fiction don't always

---

[62] See Watts, *Heroism and the Black Intellectual,* 57.

[63] Barbara Foley, *Wrestling With the Left: The Making of Ralph Ellison's* Invisible Man (Durham, NC: Duke University Press, 2010), 22–23. For a much less subtle recent reading of Ellison along these lines, see Houston A. Baker, "Failed Prophet and Falling Stock: Why Ralph Ellison Was Never Avant-Garde," *Stanford Humanities Review* 7 (1999): 4–11.

[64] Foley, *Wrestling with the Left,* 17.

agreeably chime. A vocabulary of friendship extends much further than the Marxist traditions Foley explores, and these Marxist traditions are themselves hardly distinct from the civic–humanist lineage that I've been invoking.[65] But even if we recognize the full range of historical resonances of "fraternity," it *is* true that the concept is only dimly embodied in Ellison's fiction, and it remains true that *Invisible Man* is, as Foley characterizes it, "conflicted and contradictory," bearing the traces of various threads of thought.[66] On the one hand, Ellison was committed to storytelling as a form of ethical and political instruction. "For a people lacking a class with broad formal education," he wrote in 1970 to Stanley Edgar Hyman, "narrative played a special role.... [T]he Negro American's conception of himself was seldom supported by an articulate philosophy, or by conscious theology, or"—and here one detects, once again, his distaste for the social sciences—"by any of the specifically analytic forms of the mind."[67] Much as MacIntyre would say, stories are the primary embodiment of the virtues of the culture, and thus precede any particular moral arguments, decisions, or claims. On the other hand, Ellison's oeuvre exhibits precisely the push and pull between genres that we've already seen in Percy and Robinson, the persistent process of revision and modification that constitutes the Wittgensteinian "album" of the postwar sage. He was aware of art's power to move the whole person, and was wary, as he said to Albert Murray, of "presenting statements" rather than "presenting process."[68] But it would be difficult to argue that the "process" he typically presents—the temporal sequences of actions and events, the dynamic interactions he imagines between particularized individual characters—always yield clear criteria for his own keywords, even if these words have less of a theistic flavor than those of Percy and Robinson. What he "displays," in Charles Altieri's Wittgensteinian phrase, often rattles the sensibility and authority that his essays are trying to establish.[69]

The rattling is audible already in an early short story such as "Flying Home," composed in 1944 and one of the most accomplished of Ellison's early pieces. In it, a young black military pilot named Todd crashes during a training flight in an Alabama field, where he is then comforted by an elderly black man named Jefferson. Unable to move, he suffers less from the shock and pain of the crash

---

[65] On friendship and the Marxist tradition, see Daniel Brudney, "Two Kinds of Civic Friendship," *Ethical Theory and Moral Practice* 16 (2013): 729–43.

[66] Foley, *Wrestling With the Left*, 7.

[67] Ellison, "American Culture is of a Whole," 42.

[68] *Trading Twelves: The Selected Letters of Ralph Ellison and Albert Murray*, 42.

[69] See Charles Altieri, *Reckoning with the Imagination: Wittgenstein and the Aesthetics of Literary Experience* (Ithaca, NY: Cornell University Press, 2015).

than from the old sharecropper's country manner and speech, which represent for him all the retrograde aspects of Negro life that he believes he takes himself to have overcome. As Todd waits for his officers back at the base to be notified, Jefferson stirs in him long-buried feelings of racial humiliation: flying is the "most meaningful act in the world," he thinks to himself, "because it makes me less like you." At the end of the story, however, the white owner of the land arrives, accompanied by two attendants from the local psychiatric ward, angrily threatening to put the pilot in a straightjacket: The young man must be insane, the man viciously proclaims, because no black man could ever fly a plane. Jarred by the owner's racist fury, and frantic when the attendants try to pick him up, Todd suddenly recognizes Jefferson as "his sole salvation in an insane world of outrage and humiliation." When the old man eventually helps him onto a stretcher, Todd feels a hand wiping the sweat off his face, and senses that he has been "lifted out of his isolation" as "a new current of communication flowed" between the two of them.[70]

"Flying Home," then, clearly expresses the suspicion toward scientific naturalism, which, that very same year, Ellison was beginning to explore in his review of Gunnar Myrdal's book. Todd's technophilia makes him scorn the patient man who tries to comfort him rather than the piece of machinery that (cf. Icarus) has just moments earlier utterly failed him. Still more damningly, the social sciences are in the story's depiction wholly in service to the violent dominant culture: The white owner of the plantation is obviously enough in control of the psych ward that he can call on its attendants at will to whisk the black pilot off his land. At the same time, however, the story clearly has difficulty envisioning the "black and white fraternity" that Ellison would just a couple years later, in "The Black Mask of Humanity," identify with Huck and Jim. Whatever "fraternity" emerges in the text, that is, is visible between Todd and the old sharecropper whom he had at first disdained. The respect he had desperately sought from whites—the "cloudy terrain of the white man's regard," as he thinks of it early in the story (*FH* 152)—is clearly shown to be a far-off fantasy, and the story gives no indication that the technical mastery of the plane will ever be the source of dignity that he had assumed it would be.

The evolution of Ellison's career up to *Invisible Man* is the elaboration of the various movements in "Flying Home." By the time Ellison began the novel in the late 1940s, naturalism clearly had come to seem to him even more insidious and pervasive, penetrating habits of thought and cultural practices on such a

---

[70] Ralph Ellison, *Flying Home and Other Stories*, ed. John Callahan (New York: Vintage, 1996), 147–73; henceforth cited parenthetically as *FH*.

scale that only a ragged, epic-length novel could plausibly envision and confront it. Like "Flying Home," the picture of technology in *Invisible Man*—the novel is studded with images of machinery, automata, and industry—is ambivalent, but the most virulent strains of naturalism are theoretical, manifest in the social-scientific discourses that run throughout the book.[71] Indeed, the very title of *Invisible Man*, Ellison often claimed, was an inversion of a bit of social–scientific "jargon"—a play on words inspired by a "then popular sociological formulation" (*CE* 355), the "pseudoscientific sociological concept which held that most Afro-American difficulties spring from our 'high visibility'" (*CE* 482).

The critique of the social sciences begins as early as Chapter 2, with the sharecropper Jim Trueblood, who commits incest with his daughter and subsequently becomes an object of fascination for industrious researchers, as he himself explains: "Some of 'em was big white folks, too, from the big school way cross the State. Asked me lots 'bout things and 'bout my folks and the kids, and wrote it all down in a book" (*IM* 53). A few chapters later, after the narrator has moved to New York and been injured in an accident at a paint factory, he awakes under the gaze of anonymous men in lab coats who speak with "icy authority" and seek to generate, as one of them puts it, "as complete a change of personality as you'll find in your famous fairy-tale cases of criminals transformed into amiable fellows after all that bloody business of a brain operation" (*IM* 236). At first glance, the doctors would seem to be psychiatrists and neurosurgeons, but as one commentator has noted, the focus of their conversation suggests that sociology, too, is a target of Ellison's criticism. "It would be more scientific," says one of them, "to try to define the case. It has been developing some three hundred years" (*IM* 237).[72] The Brotherhood, the political party that the narrator joins and then struggles to escape in the latter half of the book, similarly prides itself on its scientific grounding, its theories of socioeconomic

---

[71] Readers have sometimes suggested that the first half of *Invisible Man* is sharply different than the second half, particularly in the way that this latter portion—revolving around the narrator's experience with the Brotherhood—grows more explicitly devoted to theorizing. Saul Bellow was one of the book's earliest champions, but in a 1955 letter claimed to "distinguish the parts of the novel that were *written* and those that were constructed as part of an argument," the latter of which are "in full cry after Meaning" and "Opinion" rather than "Creation." (See Saul Bellow, *Letters*, edited by Benjamin Taylor [New York: Viking, 2010], 138). More recently, Mark Greif has similarly claimed that the second half of the book "marks the eruption of overt theorizing," though Greif regards this transition as a fitting movement, a sign that the book is showing the narrator has begun to develop a Hegelian "theoretical consciousness" (*The Age of the Crisis of Man: Thought and Fiction in America, 1933–1973* [Princeton, NJ: Princeton University Press, 2015], 170–75.) As I'm suggesting here, this division between the first and second half of *Invisible Man* can be overstated. Theorizing, and reflection upon theorizing, is everywhere.

[72] See Selisker, "Simply By Reacting?" 573–74.

history every bit as "progressive and irreversible" as Robert Park believed his theories of assimilation to be. "There is a scientific explanation for this phenomenon," says its leader, Brother Jack, commending the narrator's spontaneous speech in defense of an old couple in Harlem. "We are all realists here, and materialists. It is a question of who shall determine the direction of events" (*IM* 307). And in the dream sequence that concludes the book's main action, the narrator imagines being castrated by all the leaders he's encountered over the course of the book—not just Brother Jack, but the college president Bledsoe, the black nationalist Ras, and others—and he mocks their efforts, crying that their efforts to neuter him are "all the history you've made, all you're going to make. Now laugh, you scientists. Let's hear you laugh!" (570).

Across the text, then—from its introductory scenes in the south and earliest scenes in New York to its long stretch with the political party and its surrealistic concluding moments—the vocabulary of social–scientific naturalism is summoned and tried with as cold an eye as it is in Ellison's essays. And much as in the essays, *Invisible Man* likewise juxtaposes these images of strict causality and necessity with alternative conceptions of human association, visions of engineering and improvisation and eloquence that recall the ad hoc performance of Peter Wheatstraw, the blues singer who pushes a cart full of blueprints around Harlem, reveling in the way "folks is always making plans and changing 'em'" (*IM* 175). These favored alternatives grow particularly prominent as the book moves into its later stages. When, for instance, Tod Clifton is shot in Chapter 20 and the Invisible Man tries to bypass the crowds that gather around his body, he uses a term that he has not used in earnest about anyone else thus far in the novel: "He's a *friend* of mine, I want to help," he says to a police officer, and to another he pleads, "I'm his *friend*" (*IM* 437–38, my italics). "Seeing nothing, my mind plunging," he then wanders into a subway, where he encounters a small band of young male friends whom he associates with "my fallen brother, Tod Clifton," and who seem expressly sent to nurture his growing doubts about the Brotherhood's theories of history and human relations. Tall and slender, swaying along the train platform, they move "like dancers in some kind of funeral ceremony," their bodies "distorted in the interest of a design." On the train they sit "as formally as they walked," communicating wordlessly like a group of jazz musicians, snapping the brims of their hats, silently sharing magazines between them, their tapping feet sending "remote, cryptic messages in the brief silence of the train's stop." History for the Brotherhood, says the narrator, "records the patterns of men's lives," documents all "things of importance," but it cannot account for such "men of transition," who speak a "jived-up transitional language full of country glamour" and who think "transitional thoughts."

In their fluency and improvisational power, they are in their own way as great an achievement as any arcane theory espoused by a political party. "Who knew," he thinks, "but that they were the saviors, the true leaders, the bearers of something precious"—a capacity for expression and mutuality that seems to place them "outside the groove of history," allows them to run and dodge the forces of history "instead of making a dominating stand." In their impudent and graceful motions, they ask whether history is more like a gambler than a "force in a laboratory experiment," "a madman full of paranoid guile and these boys his agent, his surprise!" (*IM* 439–43).

The "men of transition" are the narrator's first glimpse of collective action that is both unplanned and coordinated, lacking a tight system while still exhibiting a makeshift structure, grounded in nothing more than mutual attunement. In Chapter 21, the vision is extended when the narrator organizes Clifton's funeral in Mount Morris Park. As he watches the procession gather, an old, plaintive man's voice begins to intone the Negro spiritual "There's Many Thousand Gone," singing alone until a euphonium horn fumbles for the key and takes up the song. Soon they are joined by the older people in the procession, and eventually even the "white brothers and sisters" join in. The gradually synchronized performance is a startling adaptation of familiar materials—"I hadn't thought of it as a march before," the narrator remarks—but it also summons up a feeling that had been awaiting expression. "It was as though the song had been there all the time and he [the singer] knew it and aroused it," the narrator thinks, something "for which the theory of Brotherhood had given me no name" (*IM* 452–53).

Similarly, in the climatic Chapter 24, during the carnivalesque riot in Harlem, the narrator is saved temporarily from the chaos by a small group of looters whose "help was disinterested," and who trigger in the narrator "a surge of friendship" (*IM* 538). The men swap rumors about how the riot had started, and their deflationary laughter and easy comradery comically contrast with the theory-bound humorlessness of the Brotherhood—a contrast underlined when the unelected spearhead of the group, Dupre, appropriates one of the Brotherhood's favorite terms in his call to action: "Let's have some *organization*, y'all" (*IM* 542, my italics). Ransacking a hardware store, the men "moved in slow order," filling buckets with kerosene and bringing them together to a squalid tenement building where, we learn, they have all lived for many years. Dupre's child had died from tuberculosis in "that deathtrap," as he calls it, and as he prepares to set it all on fire, the narrator thinks that he "was a type of man nothing in my life had taught me to see, to understand, or respect, a man outside the scheme till now"—virtually the identical terms he uses for the "transitional" men on the subway. But more than those transitional men, Dupre and his gang take this capacity for improvisation in an explicitly political direction. They exemplify for the narrator the possibility that—pace the Brotherhood—strict science, expert knowledge, and careful planning are not, in fact, be the key to social and political existence. "They've done it," he thinks as they pour the kerosene. "They organized it and carried it through alone; the decision their own and their own action. Capable of their own action. . ." (*IM* 540–48).[73]

All this suggests why it's misleading to claim, with Foley, that *Invisible Man* conveys "precious little of either love or fraternity." The transitional men, the funeral marchers, Dupre's gang constitute what we might call the fraternal triangle of Ellison's text, and the heart of its latter half. But what *is* preciously little conveyed in the text, as in "Flying Home," is the specifically "black and white fraternity" described in Ellison's essays. For unlike the glances of fraternity found in Dupre and the others, the text's white characters remain too uniformly mired in the language of naturalism to achieve anything approaching friendship, restricted to seeing the world in terms of motion rather than action. It's not an accident that the social-scientific languages that I quickly canvassed above—the researchers examining Trueblood, the hospital doctors, the Brotherhood, the "scientists" condemned in the dream sequence—are virtually all deployed by white characters. And more examples could be named, for in varying ways all the whites of *Invisible Man* adopt the language of the wealthy New England philanthropist Mr. Emerson, who understands the narrator as a piece of the vast machine that will be his life's legacy. "*You* are important," he says to his young driver, "because if you fail *I* have failed by one individual, one defective cog" (*IM* 45). Unlike, that is, the transitional men, the funeral marchers, and Dupre's gang, the white figures assume that a social body is defined by its ability to behave as what Jack calls "a coordinated unit" (447). Beyond the spontaneous organization of Ellison's fraternal triangle, the world of *Invisible Man* is by and large one that seems to operate strictly according to blueprints, blind to the "unrecorded history" that takes place in everyday black life (*IM* 471), all as if the world were something "that could be controlled by science" (*IM* 381).

Two basic perspectives, then, arise in *Invisible Man*: one that identifies the cohesion of a social whole with the networks and processes of the sort described

---

[73] Posnock nicely uses this scene with Dupre to illuminate his comparison between Ellison and Arendt, the latter of whom was fascinated by participatory politics of various forms. See his "Ellison, Arendt, and the Meaning of Politics," in *The Cambridge Companion to Ralph Ellison* (ed. Posnock), 210–14.

by the Chicago School and championed by Wright, and a second that identifies such cohesion with a distinctly African-American form of comportment and affiliation—a culturalist affirmation of (in Ellison's favored term) "Negro" life. It's the power that the novel gives to this second perspective that gives contemporary critics of identity politics pause, as when one suggests Ellison's work "abetted, even as it challenged the idea of a social order defined by racial difference."[74] These competing naturalistic and culturalist strains, however, must be placed alongside a third current in the text that is every bit as crucial. "So there you have all of it that's important," opens the epilogue, or "at least you *almost* have it" (*IM* 572). Speaking from the end of the tale that he's told, the narrator reflects now on the advice that his grandfather gave from his deathbed, when the old man claimed to be a "traitor" to the public life around him: "I want you to overcome 'em with yeses, undermine 'em with grins, agree 'em to death and destruction, let 'em swoller you till they vomit or bust wide open" (*IM* 16). What follows over the next few pages is an affirmation of the power of ideals over and above the unprincipled, palpably imperfect, and often sadistic particular individuals who have coursed through American history. The old man must have known, thinks the narrator, that the principle was greater than the men, greater than the "vicious power and all the methods used to corrupt its name" (*IM* 574). By midway through the epilogue, the rhetoric has grown almost giddy, as the narrator conjures up a world of "infinite possibilities" (*IM* 576), beyond—or at least less fatally encumbered by—these sadistic men and vicious powers. Eventually the assertions grow epigrammatic: "Life is to be lived, not controlled; and humanity is won by continuing to play in the face of certain defeat. Our fate is to become one, and yet many. This is not prophecy, but description" (*IM* 577). And then, nearing the end, reflecting on his need to return to the world above:

> I condemn and affirm, say no and say yes, say yes and say no. I denounce because though implicated and partially responsible, I have been hurt to the point of abysmal pain, hurt to the point of invisibility. And I defend because in spite of all I find that I love. In order to get some of it down I *have* to love. I sell you no phony forgiveness, I'm a desperate man—but too much of your life will be lost, its meaning lost, unless you approach it

---

[74] Kenneth Warren, *So Black and Blue*, 13. Douglas's *A Genealogy of Literary Multiculturalism*, Chapter 3, raises analogous worries about Ellison's writing, comparing it with the work of Hurston and Toni Morrison, who in Douglas's eyes deploy a dubiously anthropological notion of "culture."

as much through love as through hate. So I approach it through division.
So I denounce and I defend and I hate and I love. (*IM* 579–80)

All this is a prelude to the final, famous sentence of the novel, when the speaker turns explicitly to readers and asks precisely how we have come to understand his relationship not just to Jack and Ras and Emerson and other characters within the text, but also to *us*: "Who knows but that, on the lower frequencies, I speak for you?" (*IM* 581).

Here, at last—better late than never—the language of Ellison's essays presses to the fore. The grandfather's deathbed advice rings with the nonfiction's emphasis on the force of man-made principles, and the double movement that the essays attribute to the aesthetic work—the painful details and brutal experiences that are transcended by lyricism and eloquence—finds an echo in the need to "play in the face of certain defeat." The emphasis that Ellison the essayist places on communal wholeness over "oneness" reverberates in his narrator's reference to "our fate," that we shall "become one, and yet many." And the speaker's profession of "love," like the concluding proposal that he "speaks for you," can be heard as one last-ditch effort to imagine—despite the Battle Royal of Chapter 1, the encounter with the philanthropist Norton, the manipulations of Brother Jack, and so on—the essays' vision of "black and white fraternity." If, as we should assume, Ellison aspired to reach readers across racial lines, we might say that the friendships that never materialize among black and white characters *in* the book are now meant to obtain among readers *of* the book, who are explicitly invited to enter into an "antagonistic cooperation" with the narrator and author.

Given the sentiments and substance of the epilogue, it's only appropriate that these pages have captivated the attention of the political philosopher Allen, who finds in them the "foundation for a new approach to citizenship" that our culture urgently needs.[75] Even if, however, we share Allen's aspirations, one feature of her reading is hard to miss: she treats the epilogue as an independent piece of writing, ignoring the naturalist and the culturalist threads that, as I've argued, define so much of the book. That she can do so is a testament to how strikingly different these concluding pages *sound* next to the rest of the novel, and specifically how close they veer into Allen's own intellectual and professional territory. Whereas most of the text has been a retrospective personal history, the verbs of the epilogue are overwhelmingly in the present tense, and the speaker grows

---

[75] Allen, *Talking to Strangers*, 113.

abruptly epideictic, praising the principles of the republic, exhorting himself to play a "role" in the world, and eulogizing the activities of "the *mind*" that have steadily endured throughout his underground hibernation. Whereas the novel for twenty-four chapters has presented embodied characters with proper names, and described unrepeatable actions taking place in highly particularized settings, the nouns of these declamatory final pages blossom into the unabashedly general: "the men" and "principles," "societies" and "individuals," "love" and "hate," the many parts that "a man" possesses and the "tyrant states" that one must avoid. In place of the polyphonic narrator who's written the book we hold in our hands, we now hear a moralist and rhetorician, a slightly jazzed-up Aristotle, deploying all the persuasive rhetorical talents that his admirer Allen claims are essential to the well-being of a pluralistic democracy.

Ellison often confessed to having difficulty with "transitions"; his fiction tends to be episodic, and his recurrent challenge was stitching together particular scenes convincingly.[76] But even in a book as episodic as *Invisible Man*, the leap into the epilogue is jarring, and literary critics (if not philosophers) have sensed it for decades, describing it as an unanticipated moment that is disconnected dramatically from the narrative that precedes it.[77] From the evidence of the novel's drafts and Ellison's correspondence, it's clear that the ending of the book was a site of enormous creative and editorial struggle in the final months of Ellison's composition.[78] But the textual shift represents something more than a mere malfunction on Ellison's part. It's a formal expression of the struggle that runs through the various postwar sentinels I'm describing. Percy's *Love in the Ruins*, recall, ends with an epilogue titled "Five Years After," where the narrator, suddenly unworried by the apocalypse and the sinister Art Immelman, is shown loving his new wife, settled in a domestic existence, and resuming life in the Catholic Church. And in the final pages of *Gilead*, Reverend Ames suddenly exclaims that he adores the prairie and regards Gilead as "Christlike," forgetting, it appears, that he's just admitted to finding his hometown an "awkward and provincial and ridiculous" place that "might as well be standing on the absolute

---

[76] On his difficulty with "transitions," see his 1955 interview with the *Paris Review*, when he contrasts the challenges he faces with the ease of writing among "naturalists" who "stick to case histories and sociology and are willing to compete with the camera and the tape recorder (*CE* 222). A similar point comes up in his 1974 interview with John Hersey; see *Conversations with Ralph Ellison*, 284.

[77] The earliest and most famous question in this vein is Howe, "Black Boys and Native Sons," 131; for an intelligent recent refashioning of the question, see Schryer, *Fantasies of the New Class*, 69.

[78] On Ellison's creative decisions in the final months of writing, and the circle of friends (Albert Murray, his wife Fanny, the editor Albert Erskine) who helped him bring it to a close, see Jackson, *Ralph Ellison: The Emergence of Genius*, 426–31; Adam Bradley, *Ralph Ellison in Progress* (New Haven, CT: Yale University Press, 2010), 145–208; Foley, *Wrestling with the Left*, 336–49.

floor of hell for all the truth there is in it."[79] Such sudden shifts—literary Hail Mary passes—are not damning illogical flaws, as if the texts were puzzles that the authors had created and then failed to solve appropriately. But they do generate uncertainties that we have to acknowledge, conflicting processes in which readers must participate. And the epilogue of *Invisible Man* is as uncertain a situation as we find in any of these other books. As in these other novels, the sudden movement into sanguine assertion in Ellison's book is not enough to erase the nightmares of materialism, crisis, and manipulation that the novel persistently dramatizes. Virtually no episode the narrator has recounted up to now would seem to warrant the buoyancy of his tone or the confidence that his high words will ever be incarnated. The leap of faith he offers may not be into God, but his effort to embody civic and political fraternity has all the urgency of a sacred mission. Ellison's essays juxtapose a vision of society *qua* nomological network with a vision of society *qua* active and "conscious" brotherhood, yet the novel can approach "black and white fraternity" only by rhetorically catapulting the reader out of the narrator's desolation. The unsettled condition that these exertions generate is just one reason why unbelieving readers have been liable to remain skeptical, convinced more by the data that has gradually accumulated, chapter by chapter, than in the novel's hasty final attempt to forget them.

V. Transitions After Invisibility

Let me conclude by sketching some thoughts about Ellison's career after his first novel, the overriding fact of which was his inability to finish a second. Between the mid-1950s and his death in 1994, Ellison published several pieces from his work in progress, and in 1999, his executor, John F. Callahan, published a selection of the massive unfinished manuscript under the title of *Juneteenth*. In 2010, Callahan and Adam Bradley finished editing *Three Days Before the Shooting . . . .*, an eleven-hundred page volume assembling a significant portion of the fiction that Ellison wrote toward the second novel. According to Callahan and Bradley, the most coherent segments of the manuscript are the two long parts that Ellison referred to as "Book I" and "Book II," each of which were written in the 1950s and 1960s and edited relentlessly in the years afterward; "Book II," the most polished pages, became the main source of *Juneteenth*.[80] Beyond

---

[79] Marilynne Robinson, *Gilead* (New York: Farrar, Strauss and Giroux, 2004), 234.

[80] Ralph Ellison, *Juneteenth* (New York: Random House, 1999) (henceforth cited parenthetically as *J*); Ralph Ellison, *Three Days Before the Shooting. . . : The Unfinished Second Novel*, ed. John Callahan and Adam Bradley (New York: Modern Library, 2010). This latter volume also includes scores of notes Ellison composed about the novel—ideas for plotlines and characters and symbolism—and early

the manuscript of the second novel and a couple short stories, the only narrative writing that Ellison managed to complete in these decades came in the portraits and remembrances he composed of various friends, associates, and personal heroes: Richard Wright, Duke Ellington, Alain Locke, the painter Romare Bearden, the newspaper editor Roscoe Dunjee, the conductor William L. Dawson, the Revolutionary War hero James Armistead Lafayette.

The central storyline of the second novel didn't change drastically over the decades. A black preacher and former jazz trombonist named Hickman raises a racially ambiguous boy named Bliss, whose mother abandoned him as an infant and whom Hickman eventually incorporates into his traveling revival meetings. Bliss is brought up, as Hickman recalls, in the image of Lincoln, in the hope that "a young gifted child would speak for our condition from inside the only acceptable mask," would "embody our spirit in the councils of our enemies" (J 271). But as a young adolescent Bliss discovers that the woman who may be his mother is white, and he suddenly leaves Hickman's entourage, adopting a variety of personas over the years, becoming what Ellison's notes call a "rootless American type" (J 356). In one guise he is a filmmaker who travels around the western United States with a small crew, looking for storylines and actors, but his most consequential identity is a viciously racist, rhetorically gifted U.S. senator from New England named Adam Sunraider. All versions of the novel, early and late, begin with the arrival in the mid-1950s of Hickman in Washington, DC to warn Sunraider about an impending assassination attempt. He is refused a visit with the Senator, and a few days later he and members of his church watch in horror as Sunraider is shot down while giving a speech on the Senate floor. "Book I" of the novel is narrated by a white reporter named Welborn McIntyre, who witnesses the assassination and then attempts to discover the secret history of Senator Sunraider. "Book II"—the heart of *Juneteenth*—is set in Sunraider's hospital room, as he and Hickman reflect on their distant past together. The

---

drafts of scenes, as well as the sequences that Ellison composed starting in the early 1980s, when he bought one of the first personal computers on the market. On the justification for publishing what became *Juneteenth*, see Callahan's introduction to *Juneteenth*, where he describes it as the narrative that best stands alone as a single, self-contained work, and which contained the most polished writing in the manuscript (J xv). Bradley's *Ralph Ellison in Progress* is the most complete effort at making sense of Ellison's late manuscripts, and includes insightful information about how the writer composed and what a personal computer did for (or to) his work. For Bradley, too, the material in *Juneteenth* is the late Ellison at his best: "Clearly the material that constitutes Book II is superior stylistically to the rough-hewn episodic drafts Ellison assembled in the years before and the equally unperfected sequences he produced on the computer in the years that followed." (See Bradley, *Ralph Ellison in Progress*, 31.) So although any discussion of the novel is bound to be speculative, there are good reasons to focus on *Juneteenth* when addressing Ellison's later narrative writing, as I shall largely be doing here.

question at the core of their meeting is why the young Bliss, so beloved by Hickman and so embedded in the black culture of the early twentieth century, should have not only denied the community and customs that raised him, but also have become the most vocal and maliciously bigoted member of one of the most powerful public institutions in the country.

That Ellison designed the novel to explore black and white fraternity is clear from a note he jotted while composing the book, which invokes once again Twain's exemplary pair: "Hickman is 'Jim' and Bliss is 'Huck' who cut out for the Territory" (J 362). And critics rightly have focused on the irreconcilability of Hickman and Bliss in their explanations of why Ellison never completed the book. The text, readers say, foregrounds Bliss's apostasy so intensely, and grants black identity and culture such a distinctive and self-contained quality, that Ellison had trouble squaring it with his criticism of Jim Crow, and was perhaps even expressing reservations about the belief that he spent most of his life advocating: that Negro experience held the key to claiming the full measure of our humanity.[81] But in light of what I've been saying in this chapter, the incompleteness of the second novel might be traced to different sources. Two different problems stand out—one reflecting a basic divergence between the second novel and the earlier fiction, the other reflecting a basic continuity.

The continuity is Ellison's lasting commitment to depicting individual consciousness, which at bottom reflects his resistance to the disengaged, reductionist stance of the social and natural sciences. "Flying Home," for instance, is a textbook case of free indirect discourse, its third-person voice filtered heavily through the mind of the pilot Todd, and the resolutely first-person voice of *Invisible Man* can be understood as an implicit rebuke of the third-person stance sought by the scientists who confront the narrator at every turn. But if, like Ellison the essayist, one wants to advocate for the intersubjective engagement and allegiances of fraternity, the highly particularized and contingent experiences of a single character may become as problematic as they are illuminating, their unassailable first-person standpoint always threatening to tip into solitude, separateness, or even atomism. After the experiments of high modernism, that is, first-person testimony will always suggest a degree of perspectivism and partiality, with all the risks of miscommunication and even solipsism that this implies. Precisely this threat, as I've argued, is Ellison's

---

[81] See Tim Parrish, "Invisible Ellison: The Fight to Be a Negro Leader," in *Cambridge Companion to Ralph Ellison* (ed. Posnock), esp. 149–52; and Kenneth Warren, "Chaos Not Quite Controlled: Ellison's Uncompleted Transit to *Juneteenth*," in *Cambridge Companion to Ralph Ellison* (ed. Posnock), esp. 190, 198.

obstacle in *Invisible Man*: The entire course of action in the novel arises from the narrator's epistemological limits and normative uncertainty, and the book ends with him in a state of isolation that even the charged rhetoric of the epilogue cannot fully erase.

And by the time of the second novel, "fraternity" was, if anything, even more unapologetically at the center of Ellison's normative aspirations than it had been earlier. As Adam Bradley says, the epilogue of *Invisible Man,* together with his subsequent interviews and lectures, made Ellison in the 1950s and 1960s the "most eloquent spokesman of the inextricable ties between blacks and American democracy."[82] Yet as he composed the second novel, Ellison could find no adequate aesthetic for these ties; he could never abandon the first-person singular. "Book I" is, as I've noted, narrated entirely by the reporter Welborn McIntyre, and the bulk of "Book II" and *Juneteenth* comprises long, alternating interior monologues from Hickman and Bliss/Sunraider, who sit in a hospital room wholly opaque to one another. Indeed, these resemblances to high modernism are so patent that one reviewer of *Juneteenth* suggested that they, more than anything else, are ultimately what ruined Ellison in the second half of his life.[83] The preacher is left murmuring, "Son, are you there?" while the Senator is left feeling the air stir gently across his face, unable to answer (*J* 321). Hickman's words are either kept to himself or spoken to an unconscious Bliss lying in a hospital bed, and Bliss's words are never voiced at all, surfacing (we presume) to his consciousness through the power of Hickman's tireless voice and patient pleas. The goal of their discussion seems to be mutual comprehension—"the time has come when everything has to be understood," says Hickman at one point (*J* 269)—but because their words never reach one another, it remains permanently uncertain whether the goal is ever achieved. Only once in the novel, in the seventh chapter of *Juneteenth*, do Hickman and Bliss have anything like a spoken back-and-forth, as they try to re-enact some of the call-and-response technique that they had used decades earlier during revival meetings. The fact that critics, and even Ellison himself, have treated this scene as crucial to the second novel suggests precisely the distinctive, heightened character it has within the text as a whole—the sole moment in the text when the two men achieve anything like solidarity. But even this moment, of course, is not a genuine conversation, but

---

[82] Bradley, *Ralph Ellison in Progress*, 82.
[83] See Norman Podhoretz, "What Happened to Ralph Ellison?" *Commentary* 108.1 (July 1999), 46, which says Ellison was crushed under the weight of Faulkner in particular.

the replaying of a common memory, the restaging of a performance that had been highly orchestrated and regularly rehearsed when they were younger.[84]

Ellison seems to have intuited this prolonged uncertainty in his book. Even as some notes compare Hickman and Bliss to Jim and Huck, others emphasize their estrangement. The "essence of the story," he writes at one point, "is what goes on in the minds of the characters on a given occasion. The mind becomes the real scene of the action" (*J* 352). Similarly, in another note: "They needn't talk, thus dramatizing a lack of communication, but the past is with them and in them" (*J* 352). Such observations allow us to hear in a new register Ellison's remark about having trouble with "transitions." In one sense, as I noted above, these "transitions" are clearly textual, the routes between scenes and chapters, most vividly the leap into the epilogue of *Invisible Man*. But the narrative strategies of the second novel suggest another, equally credible way of hearing it: what gave him trouble were transitions *between persons*, the kind of mutual intelligibility, shared practices, and communication that one would associate with "fraternity," the concept that his own essays repeatedly ask us to recognize and foster.[85]

---

[84] For an example of a critic focusing intensely on the scene, see Eric Sundquist, "Dry Bones," in *The Cambridge Companion to Ralph Ellison* (ed. Posnock), 217–30. The importance Ellison himself imputed to it is suggested by the fact that he chose a selection of it for one of the few public, recorded readings that he gave of the novel, in a 1966 interview that can be viewed at <<https://www.youtube.com/watch?v=LgCozZ3okh8.>>

[85] Ellison's narrative choices didn't necessarily need to erase fraternity in the way that they do. Consider, for instance, another novel published in the late 1990s, *I Married a Communist* (1998), the second of Philip Roth's so-called American trilogy, published between *American Pastoral* (1997) and *The Human Stain* (2000). Like those other books, *Communist* is narrated by Roth's sometime alter-ego Nathan Zuckerman, who one day in the summer of 1997 crosses paths with his old high school teacher, Murray Ringold, for the first time in over forty years. Over the course of several evenings, they sit together and canvass some of the most central episodes in the social and political history of the last half century: the return of the GI's from World War II, the Korean War, the gentrification of American Jews, civil rights, racial violence, "white flight," the proliferation of mass media, Watergate, and, most urgently, the McCarthy hearings, during which Murray lost his job in the Newark public school system and his brother Ira—who had befriended the teenage Zuckerman—was exposed as a communist. Most reviewers read the book as a liberal strike against the injustices of the McCarthy era, a polemical novel that reproaches the political sanctimony of a specific moment in postwar American history. But such a view overlooks the center of gravity in the text, which is less the historical events that it recounts—Ira's radio program and fame, his involvement in leftist politics, the paranoia of midcentury America—than the developing relationship between the mature Zuckerman and now-aged Murray. In the course of their conversation, each learns things that the other never knew, and thus comes to understand better the history both of his own life and of the nation. This is particularly true with Murray's stories of Ira and the period, which provide a level of historical awareness and self-knowledge that Zuckerman had never achieved. Murray sees deeper into his brother's motivations than the younger man could ever have perceived, and is aware of the long-term consequences of events that Zuckerman could have no way of knowing. In an important sense, he knows more about Zuckerman than Zuckerman himself, a thought that the narrator acknowledges when, near the start of the book, he observes that "your life story is in and of itself something that you know very little about." The contrast with Ellison's

The second underlying source of incompleteness that I want to highlight reflects how *different* this second novel is from Ellison's other writing. For in contrast to his essays and earlier fiction, what stands out about the second novel is its total lack of engagement with a virulently naturalistic culture. It's an absence felt, for one thing, in the material and technological background of the novel, which gives little hint that the narrative is set in the second half of the twentieth century. In the early 1950s, Ellison said he had "*one* Okla. book in me," and the memories recounted through text place most of the action—it would appear—in the comparatively unsettled, rough-and-tumble Oklahoma of his own childhood.[86] As such, it makes no reference to two catastrophic world wars and the machinery that made them so bloody; nor to the century's massive changes in medicine, transportation, and industry; nor any extended reference to the revolutions in communication and media that changed the way people consumed information and propaganda. To be sure, characters are sometimes shown traveling in cars and airplanes, and Bliss and his small film crew carry around camera equipment whose images are described as "a blasting of the world" (*J* 266). But other than these and a handful of other elements, *Juneteenth* could be set virtually any time in the eight decades between the end of Reconstruction and *Brown v Board of Education*. Equally striking is the book's lack of interest in the wider culture of modern naturalism, its intellectual and institutional expressions, including the social sciences that fill the pages of Ellison's essays and *Invisible Man*. The journalist McIntrye of Book I claims to have a doctorate in sociology, but he evidently didn't go into academia, and he shows no particular interest in keeping up with social-scientific scholarship.[87] *Invisible Man*'s surrealistic and allegorical strains certainly estrange it from

---

second novel is striking. Roth places Murray and Zuckerman into precisely the same scenario that Ellison places Hickman and Bliss: two elderly men sitting together for days at a time, recalling events from a distant shared past, one speaker recounting episodes that the other could never have known completely. In *I Married a Communist*, however, Murray and Zuckerman ask actual questions, exchange actual stories, and utter actual words; they carry on a conversation. Roth doesn't shirk from dramatizing mutuality, and to exhibit the rekindled friendship of Murray and Zuckerman, he not only shows them interacting with one another, but also allots them nearly an equal number of words. Entire chapters are spoken with barely a peep from Zuckerman, a man who—as we know from the rest of Roth's oeuvre—is not usually reticent about expressing his opinion or telling a tale. And entire chapters are, in turn, told almost wholly by Zuckerman. Roth never erases the difference between these co-narrators; quotation marks buttress all of Murray's speeches, even ones that last six or eight pages. But the two men are each given enormous narrative leeway, a testament to the deeply contextual and public quality of their lives and their capacity for genuine conversation and fraternity. For a fuller consideration of Roth's novel, see my "Fictions Public and Private: On Philip Roth," *Contemporary Literature* 46 (2005): 688–719.

[86] *Trading Twelves: The Selected Letters of Ralph Ellison and Albert Murray*, 44.
[87] See Ellison, *Three Days Before the Shooting. . .*, 215.

particular historical events; we never learn, for instance, the precise years in which that novel takes place, and as readers often note, the flagrantly contrived names of its characters mask any obvious links to any historical personages. Nevertheless Ellison's first novel remains a precise and ambitious chronicle of mid-twentieth-century intellectual life: social scientists researching "primitive" folk, factories run with bureaucratic efficiency, doctors experimenting on patients with the latest medical technology, political leaders wielding scientific theories of history. No comparable features appear in the second novel at all.

One effect of this absence is that the second novel crucially alters its conceptions of injustice and blame. There is no dearth of unlikable and even sinister characters in *Invisible Man*. But the hostility that readers are encouraged to feel is always dispersed. Our reproach extends beyond the individuals themselves, and is directed primarily at the large-scale cultural, political, economic, and racial systems of which they are nearly always a part. Mr. Norton speaks of the narrator as a "cog" in the machine of his philanthropic fantasies, but Norton is himself a cog, performing a well-bounded function within a network of authority and power. And the same goes for most of the other characters the narrator encounters: the doctors at the factory hospital, for instance, none of whom are named or meaningfully individuated from one another; or Lucius Brockway, the narrator's temporary foreman, who proudly describes himself as one of the most important "machines inside the machine" of the paint factory (*IM* 217); or, most vividly, Bledsoe and Brother Jack, who each make it clear where both they and the narrator stand within the particular social systems they represent (the college for one, the political party for the other). More than the doctors and Brockway, Bledsoe and Jack are able to manipulate the tightly organized collective bodies of which they're a part, controlling them for their own self-interest. But nowhere do they attempt to loosen these systems, let alone challenge or dismantle them. And the effect is that injustice is never just a matter of what any of these particular individuals do. Injustice is systemic, equated over and over again with the institutionalized tendency for scientific ideals to warp individual personalities. In a world devoted to precision, cold exactitude, and a disengaged third-person perspective, personal growth and responsibility are still achievable. But as the Invisible Man's long and tortuous story indicates, it comes only after substantial pain and struggle, every step forward matched by a step back.

The central injustice in the second novel, by contrast, is summed up in a question that Hickman poses to the unconscious Sunraider, recalling their early days together: "how after knowing such times as those you could take off for where you went is too much for me to truly understand. . . . I mean the *communion*, the coming together" (J 133). Hickman's sense of betrayal here is genuine and potent. But the absence of a powerful naturalistic culture in the text as a whole changes how we hear the question, because unlike the wrongs perpetrated by Bledsoe, Jack, and others, Bliss's particular violation is *not* portrayed as part of a massive historical and cultural development. It's presented as a personal failing. It is not, for instance, identified with an entrenched authority; as a U.S. Senator, Sunraider can obviously exercise enormous influence, but the extremism of his racism clearly makes him an outlier in the Congress of his day. Nor does Bliss's wrong reinforce, as it would in *Invisible Man*, a particular conception of knowledge: the categories governing Sunraider's thinking reflect mere selfishness and psychological denial, not something about the methods and authority of science.

And this narrowing of critique ultimately alters the reader's relationship to the text. For one thing, diminishing the stain on the practices and institutions of the culture as a whole makes it easy for us, as readers, simply to wag our finger at Bliss. In one of the extended scenes from his years as a young filmmaker—a romantic encounter one afternoon with a young African-American woman—he comes across as something of a con artist, evading questions about his past as he tries to seduce her. But as the mature Sunraider, he is something more, something outright villainous: a uncontrovertibly bigoted hypocrite who exerts terrific oratorical and political powers. More than this, however, by limiting its attention to Bliss's failure, the second novel ultimately implicates us, as readers, far less compellingly than Ellison's earlier fiction. In *Invisible Man*, the scientists may not be sympathetically drawn, but *our own* association with them is hard to avoid. In an interview, Ellison once remarked that "many of the most important issues" that motivated his first novel were "rapidly fading away" (CE 217), but even if the idea of legal apartheid might seem increasingly foreign in the twenty-first century, the culture of naturalism that the novel depicts does not.[88] However distant the *Invisible Man*'s political world might sometimes seem, that is, its doctors, university presidents, and philanthropists are *our* authorities and newsmakers as much as they are in the world of the narrator. We, too—as Percy and Robinson force us to see—diligently heed the

---

[88] Whether Ellison was right to think that the world depicted in his novel was "rapidly fading away" has been a topic of heated critical debate. At the end of *So Black and Blue*, Kenneth Warren suggests that such a fade would be a good sign, an indication that the country had begun to move beyond the Jim Crow world that the book depicts (107–8). In later work, Warren more explicitly identifies Jim Crow with African-American literature as such, and the end of legal segregation with the end of said literature; see Kenneth Warren, *What Was African-American Literature?* (Cambridge, MA: Harvard University Press, 2011).

counsels of economists, psychologists, and other social scientists. The absence of such experts and habits of thought in Ellison's second novel keeps its events at a reassuring distance, its narrative safely in the distant past, making few claims on *our* intellectual and social practices.

If, as I've argued in this chapter, science represents for Ellison the end of creativity—the reduction of the world to strictly defined positions that can be charted, the reduction of knowledge to the calculation of regular motions and events—then his career as a whole suggests that, as a fiction writer, he also desperately *needed* science. He needs an exaggerated emphasis on prediction and control in order to conjure the more fluid, unregimented, improvisational forms of action that, in his own anthropology, are the defining characteristic of the human being. Science's favored types of "reduction"—the disengaged third-person perspective, the search for lawlike processes—help him clarify the nature of his own artistic "reductions." The success of *Invisible Man* is, in part, its ability to keep these specific models in balance; the novel is in effect a dramatization of the tensions among various kinds of "reduction." In the memories of Bliss and Hickman, in their tale-telling and recollections, the second novel also wants to highlight such nondeterministic form-making. But without any extended contrast to the reductions of science, the material becomes impossible to "reduce" artistically; nothing in the text can be held in place, and scenes and actions float. At the end of *Invisible Man*, the narrator is finally released from the naturalistic pressures and institutions that have held him in place, and he leaves us by celebrating the remarkable open-endedness of his condition. Living forward more than understanding backward, he grasps that his "world has become one of infinite possibilities" (*IM* 576). In the second novel, Ellison in effect releases himself from any engagement with naturalism from the opening pages, and as a result the text itself lives forward, becoming itself radically revisable and open-ended, as unconstrained and infinite in its possibilities as Ellison's first narrator had discovered his life to be. And in taking this step, Ellison became, more than he himself recognized, an experimental writer, one whose endlessly unfolding set of presentations and fragments embody the condition of possibility for our concepts—the activity it takes to generate them, the medium in which they emerge—rather than any specific concepts themselves. Including, of course, such specific concepts as "friendship" and "fraternity."[89]

---

[89] For an account of "experimental" literature as a display of the conditions of possibility of our concepts, see R.M. Berry, "Experimental Writing," in *The Oxford Handbook of Philosophy and Literature*, ed. Richard Eldridge (New York: Oxford University Press, 2009), 199–219.

It's perhaps unsurprising, then, that the only narratives Ellison was consistently able to complete in the final decades of his life should have been portraits and tributes. In stark contrast to the sprawling novel he was struggling to fashion, such texts typically take up lives that have already been completed, and often far in the past. The tribute to Dunjee, for instance, was first presented seven years after the editor's death in 1965; the portrait of Page was written in 1979, forty-three years after Page's death; and the short essay on Lafayette appeared in 1974, almost a full century and a half after the slave and spy had passed away. The completeness of these lives allows their narrative shape—their beginnings and endings, their highs and lows—to become unmistakably visible. And with this shape available, they can without much difficulty be understood to exemplify the kind of abstract normative terms that Ellison sought to honor: Dunjee's "courage" to publish a black newspaper during Jim Crow (*CE* 459), for instance, or Lafayette's "unshakable faith" in democracy (*CE* 407). As Ellison says in a deliberately Emersonian phrase, each of these men is a "representative figure," moving onlookers with a mixture of admiration and envy, fear and respect (*CE* 596). These lives are no doubt every bit as significant as they are inspiring. But in Ellison's brief narratives, they are recounted from such a distance, and with such sparse detail—certainly nothing like the thick detail of a novel—that their representativeness can only be asserted, never fully embodied and enacted. They can be representative, that is, only when we push aside the tumultuous present in which they actually lived. Only when we ignore the ongoingness of the world can they seem clearly to incarnate the values that Ellison wants to extol. As we'll see in the next chapter, Stanley Cavell will refer to such figures—in a still more explicitly Emersonian register—as the "friends" who draw us toward our "higher self." Ellison's writing, as I've described it here, offers some of the reasons why Cavell might find appeals to such fraternity essential. But it also shows, with equal force, some of the philosophical and literary challenges that a writer might face in making these appeals more than gestures.

4

PUZZLES, PAWNSHOPS, AND IMPROVISATION

Cavell on Cavell and Others

STANLEY CAVELL WAS once hit by a car. He was a six-year-old child in Atlanta, and as he recounts in his 2010 memoir *Little Did I Know*, the resultant damage to one of his ears eventually meant that, upon finishing high school in 1943, Cavell was 4-F, and could begin work as a professional musician rather than serving in the army for the final years of World War II. A more immediate consequence of the accident was that the young Cavell was forced to stay in the children's ward of a hospital for several days and then spend a number of weeks in convalescence. Among the memories recounted in Part 1 of the memoir is that of spending "day after day" during this recovery piecing together, with the help of two uncles, a puzzle "that must actually have been made by a jigsaw," composed of several thin layers of wood and with images on both sides of the pieces. "When we had at last finished the jigsaw puzzle," says Cavell, "and I expressed satisfaction but some disappointment, the uncles reminded me that we could take our handiwork apart and solve the puzzle again with the picture on the reverse side of the pieces." Cavell recalls displaying the completed picture for several days so that visitors to his parents' home could admire it, and he then connects this early episode to some later moments of philosophical reflection:

> It was still that very puzzle I had in mind in the hours I spent some decades later speculating whether a picture puzzle was a useful image of . . . the working of language, in which the interlocking of the pieces represents syntax and the resulting picture, or pictures, represents semantics. This parable lost interest for me on considering that the solution to the puzzle

was from the beginning fixed, its only power of surprise frozen; which negates the essence of human speech.[1]

In Part 4 of the book, further along in the story of his life, Cavell recalls working as a teenager in the family pawnshop, which his father had opened after moving his wife and son across the continent to Sacramento, California. His father employed a recondite system for pricing the shop's wares—a secret code of numbers placed on each item that would inform employees how much they should ask from their customers—and the adolescent Cavell was, he reports, "charmed by these pieces of knowledge" (LD 120). But as he also notes, he "did not aspire to master" the workings of the shop or "be entrusted to make sales": "It was clear to my father that I had no such inclination, indeed that to talk people into buying something they might or might not want was a repellent idea to me" (LD 120–21). He then connects his youthful distaste for the pawnshop with two features of his later life: first, conversations with his Uncle Mendel, one of the uncles who had helped him with the puzzles, and whose success in business made him twice national president of the Printers Association of America; and second, some of his earliest encounters with philosophy, in the 1950s:

> Mendel will eventually tell me that I had an old-fashioned idea of the institution of salesmanship; he wrote books on the subject. But then his idea was, throughout the long successful years of his life . . . that selling is the essential motive of human speech. A simple difference here from Wittgenstein's vision of speech as the revelation of desire and need is that in Mendel's world we are persistently persuading others that their desires are what we desire them to be. It is I trust not difficult to imagine, from here, the creepiness I felt hardly more than half a dozen years [after working in the pawnshop], beginning the study of philosophy, to find the latest cry in moral philosophy—most notably in two volumes ubiquitous in philosophy departments at the time, A. J. Ayer's *Language, Truth, and Logic* and Charles Stevenson's *Ethics and Language*—to be the claim that moral judgment at its best, or most, was irreducibly an expression of emotion meant to move and perhaps persuade. (LD 121)

I begin with these two moments not only because they introduce two conceptions of language and human action that run through Cavell's writing generally,

---

[1] Stanley Cavell, *Little Did I Know: Excerpts from Memory* (Stanford, CA: Stanford University Press, 2010), 45–46. Hereafter referred to parenthetically as LD when the context does not make it obvious.

but also because they provide an initial justification for Cavell's inclusion in the company I'm placing him. For reasons that I'll explain, the jigsaw puzzle and the pawnshop emblematize the particular forms of naturalism that haunt Cavell's career, playing much the same role in his work that machine intelligence plays for Percy, neo-Darwinism plays for Robinson, and the social sciences play for Ellison. Cavell has often talked of feeling like a stranger in the world of Anglophone philosophy: as he puts it in the memoir, speaking of the reception of his first few books, he often had "the unmistakable sense of having said hello a number of times without anyone saying hello back" (521). And such a sentiment has led some readers—Richard Rorty, most famously—to wonder why Cavell never simply walks away from analytic philosophy, given up on it the way that he once gave up on his life as a musician and composer.[2] Part of my claim here is that he has never renounced Anglophone philosophy because it has offered an indispensable competitor and worthy adversary. At the end of Chapter 3, I suggested that Ellison's fiction grows unmoored and unworkable precisely when, in the uncompleted second novel, he no longer pays sustained attention to the social sciences. Similarly here: Anglo-American philosophy has presented some of the most deft and systematic expressions of modern naturalism ever to be produced, and thus crystallizes the nominalism and reductionism that Cavell most urgently wants to confront.

A second reason for beginning with these two moments, and a second justification for Cavell's place in this book, is the shift these passages enact between narrative and discursive modes: the jigsaw puzzle transformed into a "parable" for certain theories of language, the pawnshop made to anticipate certain theories of moral evaluation. Following Wittgenstein and Austin, Cavell's emphasis on ordinary language and its vicissitudes leads him continually to imagine and construct narratives, perspicuous representations that situate particular words in particular circumstances. And at times, as John Hollander puts it in a review of *The Claim of Reason*, Cavell's 1979 magnum opus, these "anecdotes, scenarios, little parables, and exemplary stories are better than those of most novelists."[3] It's true that these lateral generic movements are somewhat different in Cavell's case than in the others. For one thing, his longest piece of consecutive narrative comes in the form of a memoir, not a work of fiction. For another, the mingling of forms in his work is unusually intimate.

---

[2] For Rorty's frustration with Cavell's ongoing interest in analytic philosophy, see his review of *The Claim of Reason*, republished in *Consequences of Pragmatism: Essays, 1972–1980* (Minneapolis: University of Minnesota Press, 1982), 176–90.

[3] John Hollander, "Stanley Cavell and *The Claim of Reason*," *Critical Inquiry* 6 (1980), 582.

Whereas the most consistently expository writing in Percy, Robinson, and Ellison remains in their essays, Cavell's writing weaves together argument and narrative more intimately, in a way that makes them difficult to disentangle; it makes a Wittgensteinian "album" paragraph by paragraph, page by page, rather than text by text or book by book. Nowhere is this more true than in *Little Did I Know*, the 548-page book that, while patiently "telling the story of my life" (2), displays on virtually every page what Cavell calls "the delay of, or by, philosophy" (8). In the current context, however, these differences from the other postwar sages shouldn't overshadow their more fundamental similarities. Fictional and nonfictional narratives are equally apt, after all, to provide perspicuous representations, stories that can carry out a Wittgensteinian grammatical investigation, exploring the circumstances of a word's learning and use. And if the discursive and dramatic modes fluctuate *within* Cavell's texts more than *between* texts, the very phrases I just cited—"telling the story" and the "delay of, or by, philosophy"—imply some variability in the textures and purposes of his writing. Far from negating any associations he might have with the other postwar sages I'm discussing, these features simply allow us a way of grasping the different rhetorical and aesthetic powers available to the postwar sage—a further way of seeing how the figures here develop a particular stance, and how such a stance is both elucidated and complicated by a shift into character, action, and setting.

A third rationale for Cavell's inclusion here—one less explicit in the two passages I've cited—is that, like Ellison and Robinson in particular, his confrontation with bald naturalism inspires an effort to retrieve certain aspects of nineteenth-century American literary and intellectual culture. More than any major Anglophone philosopher of the last century, Cavell has championed the writings of Ralph Waldo Emerson and Henry David Thoreau, who in his eyes are not the cozily eccentric gurus of popular reputation; nor for him are they protopragmatists notable chiefly for inspiring William James, John Dewey, and other, slightly more legitimate-looking philosophers. It is Emerson and Thoreau who give the most potent expression to the sense that, as Cavell puts it (glossing Emerson), "what is wrong with empiricism is not its reliance on experience but its paltry idea of experience," and who offer the most robust form of philosophical and aesthetic reorientation.[4] This affinity with Ellison and Robinson isn't perfect alignment, of course. As we've seen, Ellison and—especially—Robinson turn to the nineteenth century as a way of sidestepping the dominant strains

---

[4] Stanley Cavell, "Thinking of Emerson," in *The Senses of Walden: An Expanded Edition* (Berkeley, CA: North Point Press, 1981), 126; henceforth cited parenthetically as *SW*.

of post-World War II thought, of evading both the (in their eyes) rampant scientism of our culture and the (in their eyes) morally and politically dubious aesthetics that emerge in modernism and beyond. Cavell's retrieval is more mixed. He is as wary as they about modern scientism and its impact on our intellectual lives, but he's also less disparaging about modern aesthetics. Indeed, as *Little Did I Know* makes clear, the young Cavell was deeply shaped by *Partisan Review* and other midcentury promoters of aesthetic modernism, and his own work includes rich, appreciative considerations of experimental modern music, Samuel Beckett, Anthony Caro, and Jackson Pollock, among others. Likewise, he has reflected openly on the way that contemporary philosophy "shares the modernist difficulty now everywhere in the major arts": its past and present are now "problematic together," its history and conventions self-consciously thematized precisely because they "can no longer be taken for granted." At the same time, however, it's perhaps not an accident that most of these discussions and observations about modernist aesthetics appear in Cavell's first two books, *Must We Mean What We Say?* (1969) and *The World Viewed* (1971). After the early 1970s, he shows less sustained interest in the art of his near-contemporaries, and his attention turns over and over to the major philosophico-literary figures of the nineteenth century—not just Thoreau and Emerson, but eventually Samuel Taylor Coleridge, William Wordsworth, Friedrich Schlegel, and George Eliot.[5] Such authors were writing, he suggests at the start of *The Senses of Walden* (1971), at a time when philosophy and literature and theology (and economics and politics) had not "isolated themselves out from one another" as they did in the early twentieth century, and reading them today "might thereby re-enact an old exchange between these traditions" (*SW* xiii–xiv). If, then, as Andrew H. Miller has suggestively proposed, Cavell should be considered a nineteenth-century sage, "incidental facts like his birth date notwithstanding," this gradual

---

[5] The most obvious exception to this generalization is Cavell's interest in film. Even with this medium, however, Cavell tends to draw on resources from the past rather than the present. After *The World Viewed*—which includes passing discussions of such then-recent films by Jean-Luc Godard and Roman Polanski—his major writing on film concentrates on, first, the "remarriage comedies" of the 1930s, and second, the "melodrama of the unknown woman," most of whose representatives appeared in the 1930s and 1940s. On Cavell's relative indifference to the fiction of his contemporaries, see my "Empiricism, Exhaustion, and Meaning What We Say: Cavell and Contemporary Fiction," in *Stanley Cavell and Literary Studies: Consequences of Skepticism*, ed. Richard Eldridge and Bernard Rhie (London: Bloomsbury, 2011), 208–23. On Emerson and Thoreau, see Cavell, *The Senses of Walden*. On Coleridge, Wordsworth, and Poe, see Stanley Cavell, *In Quest of the Ordinary: Lines of Skepticism and Romanticism* (Chicago: University of Chicago Press, 1988). On Schlegel, see Stanley Cavell, *This New Yet Unapproachable America* (1989; Chicago: University of Chicago Press, 2013). On Eliot, see Stanley Cavell, "Philosophy the Day After Tomorrow," in *Philosophy the Day After Tomorrow* (Cambridge, MA: Harvard University Press, 2005), 129–31.

reframing of allegiances—his growing openness to nineteenth-century themes and influences—is perhaps only the most obvious sign.[6]

In this chapter I want to develop this case for placing Cavell among the other postwar sages I'm discussing, treating his novelistic memoir much as I treated Robinson's *Gilead*, Percy's *Love in the Ruins*, and Ellison's *Invisible Man* and *Juneteenth*: as a sustained narrative effort to give flesh to the high words presented in his discursive moments. As my inclusion of him here in Part II indicates, Cavell presents—like Ellison before him and Wallace after—a secular sage who shows little overt commitment to religious or theological beliefs. Modernity, he suggests in his book on Shakespeare, is defined in part by a sense that "dependence upon God" is "no longer natural to the human spiritual repertory," and this is no doubt one reason why he elsewhere endorses what he calls a "(secular) perfectionist outlook": one that speaks of reaching a "higher self," but which, in probable contrast to a "religious perfectionism," never implies any endpoint to this process, any final and "true" self that one must access or contact.[7] Like Ellison, in other words, any religious impulses Cavell might have felt were channeled at an early stage toward the arts, particularly music. And as we'll see, again like Ellison, Cavell's resistance to naturalism ultimately entails an appeal to companionship between earthly agents, or what he

---

[6] Andrew H. Miller, *The Burdens of Perfection: On Ethics and Reading in Nineteenth-Century British Literature* (Ithaca, NY: Cornell University Press, 2008), 113.

[7] Stanley Cavell, *Disowning Knowledge: In Seven Plays of Shakespeare* (2nd ed.; Cambridge: Cambridge University Press, 2003), 198; Stanley Cavell, *Conditions Handsome and Unhandsome: The Constitution of Emersonian Perfectionism* (Chicago: University of Chicago Press, 1990), xix, xxxiv; henceforth cited as *CHU*. To be sure, Cavell's secularism is not single-minded or dogmatic. Commentators such as Stephen Mulhall, Peter Dula, and William Desmond are right to wonder whether his thought owes much more to religion than it might sometimes seem. (See Stephen Mulhall, *Stanley Cavell: Philosophy's Recounting of the Ordinary* [Oxford: Oxford University Press, 1994], chap. 12; William Desmond, "A Second *Primavera*: Cavell, German Philosophy, and Romanticism," in *Stanley Cavell* [ed. Eldridge], 143–71; Peter Dula, *Cavell, Companionship, and Christian Theology* [Oxford: Oxford University Press, 2011].) In an interview Cavell remarks that choosing between "Judaism and Christianity is, I suppose, still a live issue for me" (*The American Philosopher*, ed. Giovanna Borradoni [Chicago: University of Chicago Press, 1994], 136), and in the memoir he laments at one point that the distance between theology and professional philosophy has helped impoverish the latter, making it uninterested in "describing human life when it is not, or seems not to be, making sense." Theology, by contrast, is fruitfully "drenched in fallen worlds, the only ones there are, anyway the only ones that contain philosophy (or theology)" (*LD* 446). For all Cavell's sympathy, however, there are also very few references in *Little Did I Know* to anything in his own life that one would conventionally call a religious experience or religious commitment. He spends substantial time writing about his father, but relatively little time diving into the "orthodox, religious sensibility" of his father's family, whose "severity of expectation" produced "successful dentists, lawyers, and doctors, pillars of the Jewish community" (*LD* 3). And as I note later in this chapter, it's clear at several points that his father's own halfhearted yet faithful attendance at synagogue—done, it seems, more out of family tradition than spiritual dedication—left the young Cavell confused and even contemptuous.

variously terms "friendship" and "marriage."[8] My concern in what follows is not so much to provide a commentary on how Cavell's thinking arrives at these points—something that others have ably done before me. Instead, my hope is to ask how this thinking gets enacted within the narrative of *Little Did I Know.* What interests me, in other words, is not just the philosophical "content" of Cavell's work, his more-or-less paraphrasable interpretations of Wittgenstein or the startlingly sensitive, frequently compelling, often aphoristic claims he offers about language or science or aesthetic judgment, but also, and more precisely, the ways that such issues get embodied in the memoir through character, setting, action, and event. As I'll argue, it's the effort to give flesh to his normative concepts that provides a good deal of the spark in Cavell's peculiarly absorbing work, even as it forces us to ask when to trust the teller and when to trust the tale.

I. Formalism and *Fortuna*

In the rule-following sections of *Philosophical Investigations*, Wittgenstein imagines a language learner who, told to "add two" to create a series of numbers, performs the operation as we expect until he reaches 1000, at which point he continues the series by writing 1004, 1008, 1012, etc. Reflecting on this unusual scenario, Wittgenstein asks: "Whence the idea that the beginning of a series is a visible section of rails invisibly laid to infinity?"[9] What the learner exposes, in other words, is our habit of treating rules as self-applying, as an automatic process, something invariable and permanent. Once we utter a rule—"add two"—we believe that "all the steps are really already taken" (§219), and we forget, suggests Wittgenstein, the specific application that a specific speaker in a specific circumstance, and with a specific training, always has to make.

The jigsaw puzzle of Cavell's childhood can be read as a cousin of these invisible rails and the vision of absolute necessity that they embody. The location of each piece is determined by the sizes and shapes of the pieces we find in the box, and our only task as puzzle-assemblers is to discover where precisely these various pieces fit. In the "parable" Cavell entertains, different words and parts of speech would analogously lock together in predetermined ways. The intelligible unity of such concatenations, the sentences or propositions they form,

---

[8] "Companionship" is drawn from Dula's excellent *Cavell, Companionship, and Christian Theology.*

[9] Ludwig Wittgenstein, *Philosophical Investigations*, 4th edition, translated by G. E. M. Anscombe, P. M. S. Hacker, and Joachim Schulte (Oxford: Wiley-Blackwell, 2009), §218 (here and elsewhere I shall be following the longstanding custom of citing *Philosophical Investigations* by remark number (§) rather than page number.

would be constituted by the "interlocking" of existing pieces, affording no "surprise." Pieces of the puzzle fall into place the same way whether I, you, or he is solving it, and whether a child has placed it on a kitchen table or spies have traded it on an out-of-the-way park bench. And likewise, according to the parable, the meaning of a sentence—its semantics—would be evident once its syntactical structures are in place, whoever is speaking and from whichever place or time. Cavell overstates things when he implies that *no* surprise is possible in such a situation. After all, I may be startled to realize how a particular piece fits into the larger puzzle, just as I may be taken off guard by the way a particular word *must* go in a particular spot for a sentence to make sense.[10] But in either case, such local surprises will occur only a handful of times even for a child, and are not the sorts of surprises that—as Cavell's passage implies—he takes to be characteristic (or "the essence") of language.

The impetus for Cavell's mature speculations goes unnoted, and literary theorists might assume that the puzzle parable is a reference to Structuralism, which was received in the Anglo-American world in the decade that Cavell was writing the essays that became *Must We Mean What We Say?* It was Saussure, after all, who insisted that only by examining the "internal structure of [a] language," a structure that "admits no other order than its own," that we can "determine the force operating permanently and universally, in all languages, and formulate general laws which account for all particular linguistic phenomena."[11] But the connection is unlikely: though Cavell has taken the continental tradition more seriously than most Anglophone philosophers, his references to Saussure and Structuralism are fleeting. A more obvious target of Cavell's parable is what could be called Wittgensteinian conventionalism. "Obvious" because Cavell explicitly rebukes this position in his first essay on Wittgenstein, published in 1962, eleven years after the philosopher's death. At issue there is the interpretation of *Philosophical Investigations* given by David Pole, who attributed to Wittgenstein the view that language "consists of a complex set of procedures, which may also be appealed to as rule." That is, the correctness or incorrectness of a particular language-use is wholly determined by the rules of the language, and the procedures of our speech form a complete and transparent system. Much as the cut of a puzzle piece determines where it can and can't be placed—and even whether it is part of a puzzle at all—such rules and systems

---

[10] I'm thankful to Gregg Crane for noting the ways that a predetermined system *can* contain its own forms of surprise, limited though they may be.

[11] Ferdinand de Saussure, *Course in General Linguistics*, trans. Roy Harris (La Salle, IL: Open Court, 1983), 22–23, 6.

make it clear when a particular use will be in or out of bounds.[12] But such a view is, as Cavell emphatically argues, precisely what Wittgenstein is denying. Indeed, "that everyday language does not, in fact or essence, depend upon such a structure and conception of rules, and yet that the absence of such a structure in no way impairs its functioning, is what the picture of language drawn in [Wittgenstein's] later philosophy is about" (*MWM* 48). Correctness may be determined by rules and structures in a constructed, artificial language, one that operates "roughly like a calculus with fixed rules." But whether the Wittgenstein of the *Investigations* understood ordinary language in such terms "is not a question which can be seriously discussed," not least because the refusal of such a claim was a basic motivation for his rejecting his own *Tractatus* (*MWM* 48).

But the specific terms of Cavell's comparison between sentences and puzzles suggest a further set of positions, ones about which Cavell has little to say elsewhere in his writing. In particular, the idea of his parable—that the "interlocking of the pieces represents syntax and the resulting picture, or pictures, represents semantics"—is an almost exact formulation of what John Haugeland, writing in the mid-1980s, called the "Formalist's Motto" in *Artificial Intelligence*: "If you take care of the syntax, the semantics will take care of itself."[13] Such an aphorism is associated most closely with the writings of Zylon Pylyshen and Jerry Fodor, the latter of whom has credited Wittgenstein with making "a shambles out of the philosophy of language for decades," and who coauthored a scorching review of Cavell's earliest papers.[14] For these figures, tokens of symbols represent subject matter in and of themselves. The well-ordered string of marks "c-h-a-i-r" represents a chair, over and above the speaker and circumstances of use—and conceivably even as part of the hard-wiring of the brain, as part of what Fodor famously calls the "Language of Thought." And a digital computer is the most stupendously sophisticated way we have developed of combining and recombining such tokens. The power of a computer, in other words, is its unrivaled capacity to receive such representations as input, to manipulate them according to formal rules based solely

---

[12] Stanley Cavell, *Must We Mean What We Say?* (Cambridge: Cambridge University Press, 1976), 48; henceforth cited parenthetically as *MWM*.

[13] John Haugeland, *Artificial Intelligence: The Very Idea* (Cambridge, MA: MIT Press, 1985), 106.

[14] Fodor's remark about Wittgenstein is from his review of Charles Travis's *Unshadowed Thought*, "Dicing With Shadows," *Times Literary Supplement* (July 6, 2001), 7. His review (coauthored with Jerrold Katz) of Cavell's early writing was "The Availability of What We Say," *Philosophical Review* 72 (1963): 57–71. For Cavell's pained reaction to this review, see *Little Did I Know*, 442. For a fuller sense of Fodor's resistance to Wittgenstein, see his now-classic *The Language of Thought* (Cambridge, MA: Harvard University Press, 1975), where Wittgenstein is everywhere associated with the (allegedly dubious) logical behaviorism of Gilbert Ryle.

on their shapes—their syntax—and to produce more representations as their output.[15] It can perform these operations with a power and speed that most human beings could not consciously come close to replicating, and yet nothing it does goes outside any of the rules of the program. If, as Haugeland puts it, an utterance or text can be regarded as a "set of legal games," and if whatever structure they exhibit is imposed on them *by* the rules of the game, then we can conceive of language in precisely the way that Cavell's parable envisions: "if the formal (syntactical) rules specify the relevant text, and if the (semantic) interpretation must make sense of all of those texts, then simply playing by the rules is itself a surefire way to make sense."[16]

We've seen such theories before, in Chapter One, which assessed the very different ways that Walker Percy and Richard Powers respond to the question of how meaningfulness could emerge from a systematically arranged set of shapes, marks, and noises. For Cavell, two types of trouble arise in such jigsaw-puzzle theories, whatever their specific sources. One is that they reinforce the analytic philosopher's lack of interest in, as *Little Did I Know* says, "describing human life when it is not, or seems not to be, making sense" (446). To compare language to a calculus or an orderly series of inputs/outputs is to minimize how much of our lives are spent wrestling with utterances, both our own and those of others, and how suddenly words can shift between different senses or take on different implications, whether in a specific conversation or over longer stretches of history. The computer analogy constricts what Cavell calls the power of words to be "projected" into new circumstances, as when we say "feed the kitty" and in other circumstances think to say "feed the meter."[17]

Not only do the jigsaw-puzzle theories overstate the degree of transparent sense in our speech and lives, but—this is the second and larger problem with them—their emphasis on strict necessity fosters a misunderstanding about those moments when we *do* make sense. These theories miss, that is, not only the range of risks that we always run, risks of miscommunication and misunderstanding and mutual alienation, but the range of accomplishments and creativity that we show in the face of them. What enables our speech and relationships to go on in coherent ways is not the existence of strict formal conventions or syntactical sequences, but rather, as Cavell says in a well-known

---

[15] Nir Fresco, *Physical Computation and Cognitive Science* (Berlin: Springer, 2014), 107–108.

[16] Haugeland, *Artificial Intelligence: The Very Idea*, 106.

[17] On "projection," see Cavell, *The Claim of Reason: Wittgenstein, Skepticism, Morality, and Tragedy* (New York: Oxford University Press, 1979), 180–90; henceforth cited parenthetically as *CR*.

passage from that first essay on Wittgenstein, a dense mesh of reactions, habits, and skills that are both more fragile and harder to specify—namely our sharing

> routes of interest and feeling, modes of response, senses of humor and of significance and of fulfillment, of what is outrageous, of what is similar to what else, what a rebuke, what forgiveness, of when an utterance is an assertion, when an appeal, when an explanation—all the whirl of organism Wittgenstein calls "forms of life." Human speech and activity, sanity and community, rest upon nothing more, but nothing less, than this. It is a vision as simple as it is difficult, and as difficult as it is (and because it is) terrifying. (*MWM* 52)

Underlying both the conventionalism of Pole and the Language-of-Thought formalism of Fodor is a deep anxiety in the face of such a simple yet terrifying vision, a fear that nothing permanent could *ensure* the coherence of our thought and speech. The naturalism and sense of necessity that drives their claims is less an answer to this anxiety than an expression of it. ("For the crystalline purity of logic was, of course, not something I had *discovered*: it was a *requirement*" [§107].)

Nowhere in Cavell's writing is the "whirl of organism"—with its complicated mixture of fulfillment and dread, of design and *fortuna*—more vividly documented than in *Little Did I Know*. Which shouldn't be surprising. No memoir with any plausibility or any level of detail could hide the fact that one never has absolute control over one's life, or that events befall us as much as they are planned or anticipated; we are always both victims and agents. As Cavell puts it in a "recurrent surmise" following his memory of the car accident, "whatever happens," or "whatever is eventful enough for speech," can seem "from the beginning accidental, as if a human life is inherently interrupted, things chronically occurring at unripe times, in the wrong tempo, comically or poignantly." The syntax of one's life—to adopt the formalist's vocabulary—is not always fixed; the pieces that constitute the unfolding parts of my days and years, hence the semantics of my life, "is no more a matter of one action following another than the history of a culture is" (*LD* 30). Thus the persistent record of chance events that fills *Little Did I Know*, the unexpected happenings that help make up Cavell's life: a substitute English teacher who arrives when he's a high school freshman and singles him out, for the first time, as having a gift for writing (155); a new academic journal that offers to publish his response to a paper by an older, more established colleague, giving him his first lasting publication (361); his ex-wife's decision to move to the East Coast just as he's offered a job at Harvard, allowing him to keep in close contact with their young daughter (403–4); finding himself at a party "standing in a corner of a typically drab Cambridge apartment" next to Michael Fried, "having been put together" by a mutual friend who thought they should meet (406); and so on. Thus, too, the importance of "A Plea for Excuses," the Austin paper that has probably had the biggest impact on Cavell's thinking, and a text that cannily surveys our continual vulnerability to mitigating circumstances.

But just as, if "we are to communicate, we mustn't leap too far" from one another when projecting our words into new contexts (CR 192), so accident cannot be said to constitute the whole of human life. The invitation from the journal editors may have been fortuitous, but the paper that Cavell submitted was a carefully executed, meticulously argued defense of Austin and other Oxford philosophers, a paper so compelling that it remained (as Cavell often would refer to it in later years) the "first paper that I published that I still use."[18] And his ex-wife's move might have been unexpected, but Cavell took advantage of his good fortune by visiting his child Rachel regularly—often flying between Boston and New York on Fridays and Sundays to pick her up and deliver her home (LD 404). "Chronic interruption," as he says after recounting his childhood car accident, would mean "the perpetual incompleteness of human expression" (LD 30), and only the most dogmatic of theorists would deny that human disappointment is not perpetual, or that it is sometimes staved off—at least at some moments and in some places, and however fragile—by the fulfillment of human action and expression. Consider the modest achievement of a completed jigsaw puzzle, which affords the six-year-old Stanley momentary "satisfaction"; or the less modest achievement of cooking Jewish Eastern European dishes without a recipe, as his mother always did (LD 49); or, still less modestly, the poems, sonatas, and paintings that Cavell somewhat sonorously calls "the great works of the human spirit," the "inexhaustible" achievements of film and "philosophy and literature and the comparable great arts" (LD 494).

It's precisely the threat of "chronic interruption" that is thematized in the second passage I cited at the start, where Cavell traces a direct line from his father's pawnshop to his Uncle Mendel's life as a successful businessman to the moral theories he was startled to encounter as a doctoral student. As with his explorations of language, the passage underscores Cavell's persistent debates with bald naturalism, and his habit of keeping analytic philosophy always at least on the sideline of his thought. But when Cavell goes on to speak of

---

[18] Cavell, *In Quest of the Ordinary*, 153.

salesmanship and the "creepiness" of post-World War II moral philosophy, it is not an insistence on strict necessity and precise predictability that he finds objectionable in Anglophone philosophy. What he resists instead is something like the exact opposite, and the wrenching pendulum swing from one position to the other.

The swing is starkly displayed in *Language, Truth, and Logic*, the 1936 book by A. J. Ayer to which Cavell refers. At the start of Chapter 7, "Critique of Ethics and Theology," Ayer outlines his plans to "show that insofar as statements of value are significant, they are ordinary 'scientific' statements; and that insofar as they are not scientific, they are not in the literal sense significant, but are simply expressions of emotion which can be neither true nor false."[19] Ethical concepts, in this view, turn out to be "unanalysable, inasmuch as there is no criterion by which one can test the validity of the judgements in which they occur" (*LTL* 107). Such tests are well-established for statements such as "Water boils at 100 degrees Celsius" (valid) or "Venus is farther from Earth than Saturn" (invalid). But when (so the claim goes) I make a syntactically comparable statement such as "Stealing is wrong," I'm offering no "factual meaning" at all. If in response you say "Stealing isn't wrong," then you're not contradicting me; you are instead—like me, who *does* think it's wrong—giving voice to particular sentiments. In essence we're both simply exclaiming "Stealing!!!" in a tone of shock or outrage, perhaps arousing feeling and stimulating action in others, but in no way issuing a candidate for truth. Moral disagreements are thus not arguments, but a crossfire of personal preference that even in principle couldn't be settled once and for all. Because science provides us with the paradigm of rationality, anything (the claim concludes) that cannot be rendered in terms of causal laws and/or calculations is simply irrational. *De gustibus non est disputandum*, whether it's aesthetic judgments, religious beliefs, or moral conviction.

At least as much as the jigsaw-puzzle theory of language, this pawnshop theory of ethics, as I'll call it, has been a recurrent theme in Cavell's work. His most extended examination of it comes in "Knowledge and the Concept of Morality," Part III of *The Claim of Reason* and what he calls the "most thesis-bound" of that very long and dense book (*CR* xvi). The problem, he argues there—singling out Charles Stevenson more than Ayer—is that the emotivist doesn't describe what he purports to describe. To say that statements are fully psychological, that they are causal affairs, a matter of simply "influencing" another person, or that the goal of discussion is to sway attitudes—these may be descriptions of

---

[19] A. J. Ayer, *Language, Truth, and Logic* (1936; New York: Dover, 1952), 102–103; henceforth cited parenthetically as *LTL*.

certain statements, but they do *not* apply to statements made in genuine moral disagreements. Indeed, such characterizations "vitiate the concept of morality" (*CR* 275), and represent (to use one of the chapter titles within Part III) "an absence of morality" more than a recognizable account of it. In particular, they confuse the moralist with the propagandist. Whereas the former, at his or her best, attempts to use reasons that might *convince* another person, the latter thinks only of *manipulating* someone into doing something—perhaps with reasons, but just as viably by appealing to someone's fears or love of prestige, or by stoking his desire for money, or, like the tyrant, by declaring an edict and threatening those who disobey.[20] What alone matters to the propagandist, that is, is how *effective* one is in getting another person to do something. (Hence the dark irony of the Don who announces at the meeting of mobsters: "Gentlemen, let us reason together.") When, however, we're genuinely concerned with "the nature or quality of our relationship to one another" (*CR* 263), when we're treating another person as a "creature with commitments and cares" (*CR* 283), then we continually make distinctions between convincing them and manipulating them. And we appeal not merely to personal preferences or emotions ("Well, *I* think hypocrisy is just fine, no matter what you say"), but to reasons that potentially can achieve intersubjective agreement. Doing so isn't simple. At a minimum it requires attending to the reasons of others, in all their knotted complexity and nuance, but it also may require that one discover and reflect upon one's own reasons—not always a straightforward or comfortable job, given that we are often opaque to ourselves. And this work of situated dialogue and mutual clarification might not lead to perfect harmony every time. But genuine moral debate—as opposed to a war of advertising or agitprop—is always motivated by the *hope* for agreement. Contra Ayer and Stevenson, it is thus possible to have a "rational disagreement" over moral issues, one in which different parties or speakers strive, as Cavell says, to maintain the "continuance of personal relationships against the hard and apparently inevitable fact" of conflicting commitments, loyalties, and needs (*CR* 269).[21]

With its thick webs of friendship, love, familial life, institutional affiliation, and chance run-ins, *Little Did I Know* constitutes a prolonged rebuke to such theories, sketching what this hope for agreement and personal relationship might be in practice. The key figure in this regard is not Stevenson or Ayer,

---

[20] On the tyrant, see *Little Did I Know* for Cavell's record of a conversation with Thomas Kuhn about what Hitler could *threaten* one into doing, as opposed to *convincing* one to do (355).

[21] For an excellent summary of Cavell's writings on morality, including Part III of *The Claim of Reason*, see Stanley Bates, "Stanley Cavell and Ethics," in *Stanley Cavell*, ed. Richard Eldridge (Cambridge: Cambridge University Press, 2003), 15–47.

professional theorists with whom Cavell has glancing personal contact, but his uncle. Mendel appears relatively often in the memoir, in part because he is one of Cavell's favorite relations, and in part because he lives to be the oldest surviving member of the family (he turns ninety in the course of the book's writing [*LD* 43]). And with every glimpse of his life and character, Mendel seems to betray his avowed belief that, as Cavell sums it up, "selling is the essential motive of human speech" (*LD* 121). When Uncle Mendel helped young Stanley to finish the puzzle after the car accident, he was emphatically *not* trying to persuade the injured and bedridden boy to want something that he didn't want. Similarly, it is Mendel who one summer generously finds a way to get his young nephew into the swimming pool of a country club in Atlanta (126), and it is Mendel who in the same years would call Stanley to invite him for car rides to a park—moments that left Cavell feeling that his uncle "might as well have asked if I would care to visit Paradise" (137). It is Mendel who gets his nephew a job one summer in a printing plant in Sacramento (399), and it is Mendel who worries aloud when Stanley, now a young adult, gives up music and thus seems to enter "a dangerously undefined course of aspiration" (313). It is Mendel who lovingly holds the baby Stanley in an ancient photograph that Cavell's wife discovers, a picture that they have enlarged to be included in an album made for the elder man's birthday (409). And it is Mendel who, in the years after the death of his own father—Cavell's grandfather—is said to have "undertaken to become everyone's father" within the Segal house (410), a situation dire enough to have prevented him from ever attending college.

These recurring observations are more than just realistic touches, lucid little portraits of an affectionate relationship between an only child and a youthful uncle thirteen years his senior. They more broadly underline Mendel's habitual and even instinctive concern for, as *The Claim of Reason* puts it, the nature or quality of our relationship to one another. They implicitly refuse the tendency for morality to become, as Cavell says in an early essay, "politicized," a site of manipulation and mutual exploitation (*MWW* 54). Such concern and care are absent not only in Mendel's own implicit understanding of speech, but also in the emotivist's more philosophically ambitious and tortuous theories of language. For both Mendel and the emotivist, a person is always—at bottom—exposed to the manipulations and intrusions of others, who attempt to make of the self a kind of pawnshop, a random collection of other people's random preferences. Cavell is keen never to deny the sense of exposure we have to others, nor does he deny that intrusions and deceptions occur. They do, constantly. But both in our language and in our experience—in the distinctions we draw between "convincing" and "manipulating" as well as in our moral phenomenology, our near-instinctive attraction to and repulsion for certain persons, acts, and practices—such coercions cannot be "the essential" feature of speech. Nor can they define the whole of the story we would convincingly tell about our lives and the continuance of their relationships. As in Percy, Robinson, and Ellison, the issue in Cavell is how to understand our rational autonomy, how it is that we can be neither computers nor consumers, neither genetic programs nor social "cogs": how we can use words in the world, can appraise our mind's motions, can plumb our backgrounds with all our conscious thought. And as in Percy, Robinson, and Ellison, the first step in Cavell is to temper our theoretical impulses, to remain conceptual and explanatory pluralists, willing to say that our ordinary experiences provide "data" that is as dependable and "real" as anything depicted in the desert landscapes of the scientific image.[22]

II. Birthdays and Relaxed Iron

Consider now two other passages from Cavell's memoir, each focused on a different parent and each drawing out complementary aspects of how, for Cavell, humans in fact speak and act at their most genuinely human. One is the very first anecdote about his ancestors that Cavell recounts in the memoir:

> When my father was given a Jewish name in English by the immigration officer at Ellis Island, and asked for his birth date, he replied with a big smile, "It is today!". . .This story was reported by my father, who was well known in our circles, a considerably larger circle in Atlanta than in Sacramento, for his talent as a teller of Yiddish stories. If he invented this tale of giving the date of his birth, that is as interesting in its way as if it actually happened. I knew the story as early as I knew that he and his siblings did not know the exact dates, even years, of their births. I hang

---

[22] As I noted in Chapter 2, Robinson's use of "data" bears a strong family resemblance to Cavell's, particularly in some of the early papers of *Must We Mean What We Say?* The ordinary language philosopher, says the young Cavell, uses himself "as his subject in his collection of data," and despite the qualms of the scientific linguist, "there is nothing in that to make the data, in some general way, suspect" (5). "Data" also appears in Cavell's long reading of *King Lear*, when Cavell says that both literary criticism and ordinary language philosophy share the problem of "determining the data from which philosophy proceeds and to which it appeals"—specifically "of placing the words and experiences with which philosophers have always begun in alignment with human beings in particular circumstances who can be imagined to be having those experiences and saying and meaning those words" (*MWM* 270). The "usefulness," he notes elsewhere in the same book, "not to say the authority, of appeals to what we should ordinarily say, *as philosophical data*, depends upon their being met in independence of any particular philosophical position" (238).

on to this talent for improvisation as an antidote to the causes I have had for hating him. (9–10)

The second passage comes from the final pages of Part 1. Cavell has been recounting his mother's talents as a pianist, talents fostered by a demanding father and a musical family, and how, from the time she was a teenager, she could earn what she called "a man's salary" playing for theaters and cinemas (35). She took pride, says Cavell, "in beating men at their own game," and her son especially admired "her secrets of technique and strength":

> I associated the strength in my mother's hands and arms with her ability to play rapid repeated octaves delicately, as in the Liszt Sixth Hungarian Rhapsody. I think I have never heard another pianist do this as well as she. Once on my asking her how she did it she replied, "The secret is to relax." I tried following the secret, which produced mud music. She added: "But your fingers must be like iron." Relaxed iron. . . . The secret lay in knowing how to translate [such exchanges] into the motions of one's body. (52)

When Cavell refers at the end of the first passage to the "causes for hating" his father, he is alluding to his continual sense that his temperamental parent "wished I did not exist" (14–15), and the drama between the two men is one reason why, as Ross Posnock suggests, Cavell's memoir deserves a place next to the male Jewish-American *Bildungsromane* of Henry Roth and Philip Roth.[23] By contrast, he is almost everywhere affectionate when discussing his mother, who exemplifies the "artistic temperament" of her side of the family, the Segals, who had a certain "disdain for the ways of the world" (36), and who had little of the "religious, orthodox sensibility" of his father's family, where a "severity of expectation produced successful dentists, lawyers, and doctors, pillars of the Jewish community" (3).[24] But whatever the differences between his parents, the two passages share something essential, and together they constitute a rebuttal to the puzzle and pawnshop, the formalist and the emotivist.

What Cavell prizes in his father is a certain form of practical knowledge, what he here calls a "talent for improvisation," a know-how that neither

---

[23] Ross Posnock, "Fathers and Sons," *Raritan* 31 (2012), 105.

[24] The identification between Cavell's mother and the realm of art remains through the end of her life. Near the end of the memoir Cavell recounts the story of his mother's final weeks, and it is her inability to play "Blue Danube" on the piano in a home for the elderly, making of the piece a "destroyed spider's web," that gives Cavell "the greatest shock of fear, a cold thrill," and signals to him that her life was coming to an end (465).

obeys any clearly defined set of rules nor emerges from arbitrarily subjective associations. Entrance into the country requires acknowledging state power, disciplinary authority, and bureaucratic rationality, all of which are materialized in the preestablished calculus of an administrative script: assigning a name, listing that name alongside countless others, and aligning that name with a few spare and well-established biographical facts. In his response to the officer, Cavell's father doesn't quite show himself ready, with the Invisible Man's dying grandfather, to "overcome 'em with yeses, undermine 'em with grins, agree 'em to death and destruction," but his impromptu invention of his birthday is cheekily defiant, and expresses a less formulaic idea of knowledge and identity than the officer would be able to recognize.[25] Passing through Ellis Island could, after all, represent a kind of rebirth, an entrance into a substantively different life, a dramatic reweaving of one's expectations and habits and purposes. But such a figural notion of birth—such a projection of "birthday" into this new circumstance—is not something that an upright customs official would be willing or able to tally. Later in the book his father's shrewdness is thematized again when Cavell recalls his ability to tell jokes. In "the strict decorum of telling Yiddish jokes," these tales "had to be appropriate to an occasion," told with a full awareness both of the specific audience and the specific circumstances at hand. And in telling them, his father displayed, says Cavell, impeccable "timing," which "never failed to draw sharp, grateful laughter," and he had a particular "knack" for amplifying a joke's effect by playing on an audience's awareness of its corniness. The most "impressive" of the stories he told were "as long as short short stories," their punch lines "less important than the telling of the stories, making epics of out of events of unnoticeably everyday characters (everyday mostly perhaps in Bialystock eleven decades ago)" (124–25). The stories enchant the young Cavell "for the attention they held, for the mounting pleasure they constructed, and for the burst of excellent feeling they released, all depending upon the talent displayed in the telling" (124).

The passage about his mother is an apt complement to these reports on his father, recalling as it does an instance of *training*. Reflecting in a late note on the question of how we judge the "genuineness of expressions of feeling," Wittgenstein says: "Can one learn this knowledge? Yes; some can learn it. Not, however, by taking a course of study in it, but through '*experience*.'—Can someone else be a man's teacher in this? Certainly. From time to time he gives him

---

[25] Ralph Ellison, *Invisible Man* (1952; New York: Vintage, 1990), 16.

the right *tip*."[26] Cavell's mother seems like Wittgenstein to have distrusted the idea of "taking a course"—she "invariably refused to give lessons" whenever she was asked, claiming that "she hadn't the patience for it" (53)—but she makes it clear in the scene recounted here that instruction is nevertheless available, if not through "tips" then through what she calls "secrets." "Secrets," says Cavell, was one of her favorite expressions, employed not to signify forbidden knowledge but "to acknowledge, and partly explain, anything that she felt was done exactly right," such as cooking lentils with just the right unmeasurable amount of salt (49). Moreover, the second secret she tells in the passage—"your fingers must be like iron"—suggests an awareness that such "secrets" sometimes can be transmitted only through indirection and paradox. Knowledge of "correct judgments," in Wittgenstein's term, is not a "piece" of knowledge in the way that a coin is a piece of metal, and it cannot be transmitted from one person to another as a coin can pass across a counter. It requires that an audience member already be at least partially initiated into a certain form of life, and have already achieved a certain level of competence, at least enough for the "tip" or "secret" not to fall on altogether deaf ears. And it requires that listeners commit themselves to some kind of process; some type of labor must be suffered. The task of understanding the tip is akin to the labor required to understand the technique in question—how, in this case, to "translate" the figure of "relaxed iron" into "the motions of one's body." "I loved exchanges like this," says Cavell, "and regarded such descriptions as pedagogically astute and accurate" (53).

The gendered aspect of such astute and accurate descriptions becomes clear when we learn that his mother is only the first of several "accomplished, magic, judgmental women" that cross Cavell's path, figures of a sort who, in films he was later to analyze, would be played by Katherine Hepburn and Irene Dunne. But it was what he learned jointly from both parents—a capacity for improvisation, an appreciation of "experience," training, and "tips"—that initially drew Cavell to Austin's ordinary language philosophizing. In that "first paper that I published that I still use," written in response to his senior colleague, Cavell explores how our speech is deeply shaped by some notion of necessity that extends beyond the strict semantics of our sentences. If I ask you "Did you dress that way today voluntarily?" the dictionary will tell you that what's in question is your psychological or moral state: did you do so out of your own free will? But in its actual use, at least in most cases—and the fact that there

---

[26] This remark appeared in earlier editions in "Part II" of the *Philosophical Investigations*, but in more recent editions appears in §355 in *Philosophy of Psychology—A Fragment*, appended to the *Philosophical Investigations*, 4th edition.

are exceptions is not inessential—the question is implying that something is "peculiar" or "fishy" about the way you've dressed: Why, pray tell (why on earth, etc.), did you dress *that* way today? Not to know this is not to know what the expression means: what, in most cases, it *must* mean. "Must" here isn't the hard "must" of a logical or mathematical proof, but an "element of necessity" in statements "whose implications we understand" (*MWM* 9). Something's being "fishy" is, in Wittgenstein's terms, part of the grammar of "voluntarily," necessary in *this* context even if not in every other, let alone in the universe as such.

From the example of this father and mother can be traced, too, Cavell's early and ongoing attraction to philosophical aesthetics, despite his sense that, as an academic field, it has often been "fallow" (385). Obviously, the "implications" of artworks are seldom as clear as the implications of "Did you dress that way voluntarily?" But in both their creation and reception, such works depend upon an analogous set of skills, know-how, and "secrets," or what Cavell sometimes refers to as "composition." To "compose" is to "make" something that will not merely "interest and absorb" us—a crumpled handkerchief could do that much—but that will also "move us," so that we are "not merely involved with" it, "but concerned with [it] and care about" it, treating it in ways that we would otherwise do only with other people. We do this with artworks because they are "felt as made by someone," "not works of nature but of *art* (i.e., of act, talent, skill)," which explains our use of "such categories as intention, personal style, feeling, dishonesty, authority, inventiveness, profundity, meretriciousness" (*MWM* 197–98).

Such remarks are striking when we consider that the essay in which they appear was published the same year (1967) as Jacques Derrida's *Of Grammatology* and Roland Barthes's "The Death of the Author," texts that would subsequently foster such lasting and profound doubts among literary critics about the very idea of intention. But it's important to note just how *broad* Cavell's use of "intention" is here. "A work of art," says Cavell, "does not express some particular intention (as statements do), nor achieve particular goals (the way technological skill and moral action do), but, one might say, celebrates the fact that men can intend their lives at all. . .and that their actions are coherent and effective at all in the scene of indifferent nature and determined society." And essential to achieving this celebration—again, echoes of Cavell's mother and father—is the artist's capacity "for improvising and for taking and seizing chances" (*MWM* 198). Which *kind* of chances an artist takes is up to him or her, particularly if he or she is a *modern* artist: no police force or connoisseur can prevent a writer, sculptor, or musician from trying out whatever he or she wants. But artworks, too, arise against a background of prior exemplars and existing traditions of practice, and they, too, require ingenuity and resourcefulness, "virtues" that allow one "to act successfully, to follow the distance from an impulse and intention through to its realization" (*MWM* 198–99). Without these virtues, the artist's action is liable to run afoul in any number of familiar ways: distraction, "lack of preparation or foresight," a failure of one's resources, a lack of knowledge, and so on.

In a moment I'll highlight the echoes all this makes with Ellison, who, as we saw in Chapter 3, similarly insisted on nonlogical forms of necessity and the situated, improvisatory character of genuine speech and performance. But for now we should note that Cavell's mother and father are only the earliest exemplars in *Little Did I Know* of a knowledge that extends beyond a knowledge of rules, standardized forms, and sharply defined goals. The very term "improvisation" punctuates the text, used always to signal a release from constraint or an emergent openness toward the future. A first car, bought while still in high school: "From the constriction and surveillance and pummeling repetition of the pawnshop, this faithful companion meant expansion and privacy and improvisation—commodities otherwise to be found only in great cities" (27). Watching Bennie Goodman as a teenager in 1939: "To hear the familiar arrangements played live, with inevitable and enlivening alterations in the improvisations, confirmed for me as it were the knowledge of existence, in the form of, or a prophecy of, the reality of happiness [and] proof of a world beyond me" (164). "American improvisation, the ability to find common ground with any stranger," is cherished next to the closed, clubby world of Oxbridge philosophy, made known to him by his friendship with Bernard Williams (417). Part IV of *The Claim of Reason*, the piece of writing that marks for Cavell the moment "that I became confident that my writing could go on" (521), is built upon "inventions or improvisations," instants in which the "whole discussion" of Parts I to III becomes "reframed, in effect begins again" (495–96).

At other times, improvisation finds more dramatic embodiment, most startlingly perhaps in Cavell's account of his changing his name at age seventeen. Playing for a couple weeks with a band in Santa Cruz, preparing to travel with them to Chicago and to leave his family for good, he introduces himself to a young woman at the end of a show as "Stan Cavell"—a shortened version of his father's name, Kavalieruskii, changed at Ellis Island to Goldstein. Nowhere up to this point in the memoir has Cavell mentioned entertaining a change of name, let alone any specific moniker. So the reader is liable to be as surprised as Cavell's mother, who, a few days after this rendezvous, back in Sacramento, sees the name written on a note from the young woman and asks who exactly Stan Cavell is: "Deep into the imagery of escape and glamour, and both embarrassed and frightened by the question, I surprised myself by telling the truth, anyway the part of it concerning. . . .experimenting with a stage name. I began simply saying 'It's me.' And from nowhere I added, truly, and perhaps out loud, 'From now on'" (200).

Surprises and experiments that come "from nowhere" are often closely associated with music, but in *Little Did I Know*, improvisation is just as often associated with Cavell's move away from music and toward philosophy. As a music student at Berkeley and Julliard, he realizes that his life in music would be limited precisely because he "could not go on, or reliably promise, to produce worthy continuations," and whatever successes he has in the musical realm seem to him "based in some way on fraudulence" (210–11). Two moments of such fraudulence are crucial to this realization, each coming when he plays impromptu on the piano before a teacher and a group of students: first at Berkeley before Marjorie Petray (one of those "magic" women he encounters), when he stops his short audition before a difficult moment in a Liszt piece but acting "as if I could have gone on to the end were there time and need" (209); and second at Julliard, when before another teacher and a group of students "some minor deity made it possible for me" to get through an orchestral score, despite his being completely unprepared and in over his head (224). In Cavell's account, these moments are not successful improvisations but simply—that word again—"accidental": "I had little idea," he says of the latter case, "how I had arrived at a sense of lucidity as we were playing," and he came away "with no confidence that I could, on demand, present myself as capable of repeating the feat" (224). By contrast, in his first philosophy paper, written after having dropped out of Julliard and having entered the University of California, Los Angeles as a special student, he writes a paper on John Dewey that runs over seventy pages, filled

> with assertions I was impelled to voice, scarcely caring what the best-known defenses of them, or objections to them, might be, amazed by the sense of progression itself, as if the goal would take care of itself, often making an old thought interesting because of the strangeness of its apparel, but orderly enough in stretches, often turning back on itself as if that itself was integrating, to hearten me to think of myself as producing philosophy. (246)

Years later, a comparable restlessness in Cavell's lectures would lead a friend to compare them to the performances of Lenny Bruce, which Cavell understands as a reference to his "wish to keep a number of strata of ideas moving in the same direction, seeming to require perpetual modulations as well as multiple themes," "an improvisation meant to link insights that, like punch lines, can be reached no other way," even if the "cost" is "the persistent danger of abusive obscurity" (391). And several decades later, now retired, writing in response to a collection of essays on his work, Cavell describes his philosophy as "tapping the willingness to start again, to go back over one's expressions, leaving nothing standing," "to find a path, however crooked or unpredicted" (305).

The fullest instance of such a vision of language and action, however, is not any particular memory that Cavell sketches or any particular observation about his work, but the text itself, the crooked and unpredicted paths that the memoir presents to us as readers. As I noted in my discussion of Ellison, improvisations sometimes are said to depend upon the existence of "ready-mades": the preexisting structures, motifs, dramatic frameworks, cultural knowledge, and formal patterns that an artist can draw upon in undertaking an improvisation.[27] The revisions, additions, and parenthetical self-modifications of the sentences I've quoted are enough to indicate what this kind of process might mean at the level of Cavell's prose, as simple phrases are reworked, inserted, interrogated, modified, expanded, and elaborated. But consider again the passages about the jigsaw puzzle and the pawnshop, which illustrate how such patterns emerge at higher levels. If the standard trajectory of autobiography has included the growth of one's mind or the development of an identity—the emergence from childhood or youthful disorder into adult wisdom or power—then these moments "riff" on this familiar pattern in a couple different ways. For one thing, they move loosely between distant events in time, reconstructing a relatively far-off memory (assembling a jigsaw puzzle, working in his father's pawnshop) to another, slightly less remote memory (reflecting on language as an adult philosopher, talking with Uncle Mendel, encountering logical positivism). Such different moments are linked associatively through a common—often commonplace—object or emotion, suggesting that one's history might be figured more as a matter of recurrent loops than a clean line from past to present. The past is not forgotten, erased, or triumphantly overcome, but forms part of the ready-mades that our current perspective allows us to revise and reinterpret. Moreover, the passages shift not only between various moments in time, but also between narrative and non-narrative genres, creating the distinction between "telling my story" (2) and "the delay of, or by, philosophy" (8). In such movements Cavell suggests how, in the stream of our lives, our concepts are never part of

---

[27] "Ready-mades" is a term from the psychologist R. Keith Sawyer, in "Improvisation and the Creative Process: Dewey, Collingwood, and the Aesthetics of Spontaneity," *The Journal of Aesthetics and Art Criticism* 58 (2000): 157–58. On the relation of tradition to improvisation, and in a specifically Cavellian context, see William Day, "Knowing as Instancing: Jazz Improvisation and Moral Perfectionism," *The Journal of Aesthetics and Art Criticism* 58 (2000): 101.

an inhuman system, but are applied in particular circumstances in light of the particular forms of training that we receive. As we learn to speak—and in growing into the identities and existences that autobiographies typically trace—particular objects and situations become the "samples" that, as Wittgenstein suggests, embody or express the words that we learn to apply. In turn, we might project these words into other, unforeseen circumstances, which, in turn, may or may not be found appropriate—all without the knowledge that this or that authority will ensure that this process is being performed correctly.

The macro levels of the memoir similarly foreground this improvisatory "willingness to start again." For fourteen months, from July 2, 2003, when Cavell is told that doctors will need to perform a catheterization of his heart, to September 1, 2004, his seventy-eighth birthday, Cavell sets out to write in a diary format what he can recall of his life. The effect—and in this *Little Did I Know* resembles Robinson's *Gilead*, another book about parents and children—is that the book can follow what Cavell calls "a double time scheme," allowing him to "accept an invitation in any present from or to any past, as memory serves and demands to be served" (8). In fact, there are more than two time schemes, because at various points Cavell returns later on, after finishing a first draft of the book, to add observations and amplify ideas, as when, for instance, he marks "another intervention from a day of editing in 2007" (478). The point of this multiple structure, he notes, is not only to approximate "what Austin means in tirelessly demanding the context (he would often call it the story) of an utterance and what Wittgenstein means by repeatedly asking to whom an utterance is made" (60). It is also, and I think more importantly, "to refuse the already formed significance that more unified narratives would have me accept. Put otherwise, only in defeating such significance is my interest in telling my story graspable, alive for me" (60–61).

The goal of the book, that is, is not only to reanimate the events of his life for the reader, but also to reanimate his *own* sense of his own life. Improvising backward and forward through time, like riffing between narrative and philosophy, enacts Cavell's wish to avoid implying that "all that writing required was the power of unfolding implication"—laying out the syntax, as it were—"rather than that of inviting surprises, and not ones prepared by a future but ones creating the future" (95–96). This emphasis on "inviting surprises" is one reason why *Little Did I Know*, though it has a performative dimension, is not itself a "performative" in Austin's sense of the term. The speech acts that interest Austin almost always fall well within existing social and conceptual scripts: the marriage vow, the promise. Cavell's book has by contrast fewer conventional effects, is addressed to no antecedently specified persons—one writes, he says, in the hope that "one's voice has carried in certain instances beyond the circle of familiars," thus "in part, irreducibly, also for strangers" (444)—and is always open to the rebuke that its utterances are insincere or unworthy of response. It is, in short, what he calls a "passionate" as opposed to a "performative" utterance.[28] Thus Cavell repeatedly draws attention to the discoveries—the "surprises"—that the very process of writing has begun to elicit. At the end of the very first diary entry, he claims "now to glimpse a possible cause" for his having in an earlier paragraph referred to Vladimir Jankelevitch, who after the rise of Hitler forswore both German philosophy and German music (5). A few days later, after reflecting upon his father's terrible temper, he remarks that "something is already happening here that takes me particularly by surprise," namely a connection between his own "scenes of inner devastation" and Wittgenstein's claim that the *Investigations* is "destroying nothing but houses of cards" (21). And looking back on the legal difficulties of changing his name, thinking about the names adopted by different branches of his father's immigrant family, he notes that it was "not until this present writing and its attempt to peel back certain further layers in this decision" that his change of name had forged an identification between his father and his uncle, whose son, Cavell's cousin, had also changed his name (202). All of these interventions from the present suggest a stark contrast with the dissertation that he struggled to begin after his qualifying exams in the mid-1950s, when he gradually came to feel that his writing had become "mechanical, that I was repeatedly arriving at conclusions that I already knew. I could not take myself by surprise" (320). Only with the arrival of Austin and his attention to what he called "the jump of words" (323) does this absence of surprise begin to wane and Cavell begin to find his voice as a philosopher.

All this may explain what Cavell means in an early essay when he says that Wittgenstein "writes: he does not report, he does not write up results" (*MWM* 70). Reports and results are both testaments to a task completed as well as finished products in themselves, whereas the improvisations of writing are, for Cavell, part and parcel of the philosophizing itself. Moreover, the fact that writing might be less concerned with description than with discovery may be a way

---

[28] Cavell, "Performative and Passionate Utterance," in *Philosophy the Day After Tomorrow*, 155–91. Julian Baggani has suggested that philosophical autobiographies should be considered "extended speech acts," on the models that Austin provides, which encourage us to consider that "what we *do* by what we say [is] as important a philosophical issue as what we *mean* by what we say." Calling Cavell's text a passionate utterance rather than a performative utterance is a way not of disagreeing with Baggani, but of underlining the fact that, unlike in Austin's models, we may not always have any precise way of knowing or anticipating what these effects might be—and that this uncertainty is itself an essential part of the text's composition. See Julian Baggani, "Philosophical Autobiography," *Inquiry* 45 (2002): 295–312 (quotation at 298).

of grasping why Cavell's book is titled *Little Did I Know*. The phrase can sound Socratic, an owning-up, an admission that, in the end, the philosopher is ignorant. But knowing *little* is not quite knowing *nothing*, and this difference should lead us to emphasize the last term of the title more than the first.[29] Little did I *know*: my life may not be fundamentally defined by a knowledge of facts or information or propositions, nor is my story of it a matter of unfolding its implications, but I may nevertheless, at times, have been able to achieve different yet not incompatible forms of understanding—the kind of difference Cavell sometimes registers in his distinction between "knowledge" and "acknowledgement."[30] Still more specifically, the phrase suggests a moment of being *startled* by such understanding—a realization that our lives extend beyond us, into circumstances that are present all the time yet mostly obscure to us, recognized only through gradual revelation or renewed attention. Little did I know that my colleague could be so witty; little did I know when talking to him that his son had died just last year; little did I know that my next-door neighbor held those political beliefs. And little did I know the range of affiliations, unrecognized commitments, forgotten influences, and obscure desires that have constituted my life.

III. An Audience for Philosophical Memoir

Cavell's improvisatory openness to "surprise" recalls a remark Wittgenstein made to a friend in a discussion of *Philosophical Investigations*: "I was thinking of using as a motto for my book a quotation from *King Lear* 'I'll teach you differences.' [Then laughing:] the remark 'You'd be surprised' wouldn't be a bad motto either."[31] But it also should recall a pattern of themes we saw in my previous chapter. For Ellison, I argued, neither religion nor tradition can serve any longer as reflexive guides to how one should speak and behave; our ideals must be "fabricated," as Ellison says of his life as an adventurous and imaginative child, "catch-as-catch-can," with "an outrageous and irreverent sense of freedom."[32]

---

[29] In "Childhood and Philosophy," *MLN* 126 (2012), Paola Marrati makes a comparable point about the title of Cavell's memoir: "if I (or we) knew *little*, I knew enough to know there was more to know, and I knew enough to want, need, or fear to know more. In short, unlike Socrates who possessed at least the clear and reassuring knowledge that he did not know anything, we are always, constitutively, at the limits of what we know and what we do not know, neither fully ignorant nor quite knowledgeable" (957).

[30] Most extensively in "Knowing and Acknowledging," *Must We Mean What We Say?*, 238–66.

[31] M. O'C. Drury, *The Danger of Words and Writings on Wittgenstein*, ed. David Berman (Bristol: Thoemmes, 1996), 157.

[32] Ralph Ellison, *Collected Essays* (New York: Modern Library, 1995), 53; henceforth cited parenthetically as *CE*.

Ellison's vision of language, as we saw, owes a great deal to Kenneth Burke, a figure about whom Cavell has made admiring gestures, and who would applaud Cavell's insistence that understanding speech requires asking how a specific person uses "the utterly specific words he says when and as he says them" (*MWM* 269).[33] Like Cavell, too, Ellison hopes that such situated improvisations might thread the needle between the wholly necessary and the wholly arbitrary. What confronts Cavell in the image of the jigsaw puzzle confronts Ellison in claims about the "environment," "the physical, the non-conscious" realm whose overwhelming causal force makes us believe that African-Americans could "live and develop for over three hundred years simply by *reacting*" (*CE* 339). The pawnshop and emotivism that likewise haunt Cavell have their Ellisonian counterparts in the "near-themeless technical virtuosity" of Charlie Parker, showering his audience with accidental notes, and the manipulations of *Invisible Man*'s Rinehart, the shapeshifter who flatters and sways the residents of Harlem in a vast game (it seems) of manipulation. The response in both Ellison and Cavell to this double-sided threat is to conceive of the self as a dynamic back-and-forth advance, a conscious and mindful movement between established patterns and creative interventions, satisfying—in the best cases—the human being's need for both coherence and freedom.

More needs to be said about this analogy between Ellison and Cavell, but to do so, I want first to bring Cavell's project into relief by placing it alongside certain philosophical ancestors and contemporaries. Cavell is no doubt singular within philosophy, but he is not utterly without precedent or parallel. He is not, for one thing, the first American philosopher to have understood language and action in terms of improvisation and know-how, particularly as a way of avoiding the dual fantasies of perfect predictability and perfect randomness. Such a stance is a hallmark of pragmatism, a tradition about which Cavell has often expressed doubt, but which gets more appreciative words in *Little Did I Know* than in any other Cavell text. As we've seen, it was while writing a paper on Dewey that he first discovered the ferment of philosophizing, and whatever weaknesses he might later have found in it, pragmatism shows, as he says, a "restiveness with philosophy's treatments, or avoidance, or stylization, of human experience" that he still counts as "a treasured inheritance" from his earliest philosophical education (423).[34] Among classical pragmatists,

---

[33] For Cavell on Burke, see his *Philosophy the Day After Tomorrow*, 39–44; *Disowning Knowledge*, 174; *Themes Out of School: Effects and Causes* (Chicago: University of Chicago Press, 1984), 93, 201.

[34] Cavell's early sympathies for pragmatism are reflected in the fact that his first publication (one that he wouldn't reprint in later years) was a comparison of the ethical theories of Dewey and Logical Positivism; see his article (coauthored with Alexander Sesonske) "Logical Empiricism and

one thinks of C. S. Peirce, Walker Percy's hero, whose discussions of "abduction" were meant to highlight the unpredictable and inventive real-world dimensions of logic. Or one thinks of Dewey, whose conception of "art as experience" recalls Cavell's discussions of intention and composition. "A rigid predetermination of an end-product," declares Dewey, "whether by artist or beholder leads to the turning out of a mechanical or academic product. . . . Like the scientific inquirer, he permits the subject-matter of his perception in connection with the problems it presents to determine the issue, instead of insisting upon its agreement with a conclusion decided in advance."[35] Closer to Cavell's own generation, one naturally thinks of Rorty, who envisions the philosopher of the future "kibitzing" or engaged in "conversation," not prudently spelling out sound inferences or searching for the alleged foundation of truth and knowledge.[36] Or one might think of the main touchstone of Rorty's later writing, Donald Davidson, who, like Cavell, challenges the view that communication depends upon a deeply systematic, deeply shared set of regularities or conventions. Davidson doesn't use the term "improvisation," but the terms of his resistance echo both Cavell and Ellison: "There are no rules for arriving at" our actual utterances, "no rules in any strict sense, as opposed to rough maxims and methodological generalities [that are] derived by wit, luck, and wisdom from a private vocabulary and grammar, knowledge of the ways people get their point across, and rules of thumb for figuring out what deviations from the dictionary are most likely."[37]

With *Little Did I Know*, however, Cavell has gone further than any of these thinkers in elaborating the improvisations of his own life. He has not only raised questions of drama, time, and personhood in general terms and in critical commentaries, but has also composed a literary narrative of his own, one as dense and meditative as any philosophical autobiography of the last century. And his precise handling of these characteristically "American" themes—know-how, insights that take one by surprise, the import of everyday practices—comes into further focus when we place his memoir next to that of a couple other philosophers who have worked in his close vicinity. Consider, for instance, *The Time*

Pragmatism in Ethics," *Journal of Philosophy* 48 (1951): 5–17. As he moved toward Austin and then to Wittgenstein, he grew less enthused with pragmatism; for his mature views on Dewey, see *Conditions Handsome and Unhandsome*, 13–16.

[35] Dewey, *Art as Experience* (New York: Perigee, 1934), 138–39.

[36] Rorty's mention of "kibitzing" is in "Ten Years After," one of the appendices of *The Linguistic Turn: Essays in Philosophical Method*, ed. Richard Rorty (1967; Chicago: University of Chicago Press, 1992), 370.

[37] Donald Davidson, "A Nice Derangement of Epitaphs," *Truth, Language, and History* (New York: Oxford University Press, 2005), 107. Davidson's phrase for what's exhibited in this rough-and-ready process is "passing theory."

of My Life, the 1984 autobiography of Cavell's longtime Harvard colleague W. V. O. Quine.[38] The flavor of Quine's book is evident enough from the book's margins, which with dogged linearity inscribe a clear sequence of dates, beginning with "1908" (the year of his birth) on the first page and ending several hundred pages later with "1984" (the year he finishes writing). Between those two points the reader encounters a seemingly interminable series of relatively self-enclosed paragraph-sized anecdotes, each written with Quine's austerely neoclassical concision, and most, it seems, recounting this or that moment in his quest for touristic comprehensiveness: his effort to see every state in the country, or to invent diversions that he could then check off his list, or to visit every country in the world. The result, as one commentator has said, is a "relentless catalogue of travels and events," a "remarkably unengaging" book that exhibits a supreme "concern for mental order and tidiness combined with an apparent disinterest in the emotional side of life."[39] The very chapter titles of the book read like a checklist of sightseeing errands: "Italy Again" (Chapter 55), "Greece Again" (Chapter 56)," "Egypt" (Chapter 57), "Strictly By Sea" (Chapter 58), "Middletown, London, St. Martin" (Chapter 59), "Ohio, Canada, New York" (Chapter 60), "Italy, Dalmatia, Vienna" (Chapter 61), "Harvard Down, Paris Up" (Chapter 62), "Northern Climes" (Chapter 63), "Ethiopia" (Chapter 64), "Kenya" (Chapter 65), "More Africa" (Chapter 66), and so on, and so on.

At the other end of the spectrum, consider "Circumfession" (1991), the longest autobiographical piece ever published by Derrida, the continental philosopher with whom Cavell has had the most personal contact and about whom he has had the most involved discussions in print.[40] Like Cavell, Derrida explicitly sets his autobiographical writing against the model of a computer—a "programming machine" (*C* 34) that, as he puts it, would pretend to account, if not for the "totality of [his] thought, then at least the general system of that thought" (*C* 1). In Derrida's case, this formalizing aspiration isn't captured in a jigsaw puzzle or a theory of semantics and syntax, but by the careful analytic commentary on his work provided by Geoffrey Bennington, underneath which—literally, on the bottom of each page—"Circumfession" appears. Against Bennington's

---

[38] W.V.O. Quine, *The Time of My Life* (Cambridge, MA: MIT Press, 1985).

[39] Baggani, "Philosophical Autobiography," 300.

[40] Jacques Derrida, "Circumfession," in Geoffrey Bennington and Jacques Derrida, *Jacques Derrida,* trans. Geoffrey Bennington (Chicago: University of Chicago Press, 1993); henceforth cited parenthetically by page number as *C.* Cavell met Derrida as early as 1970, and over the years has come back at several points to Derrida's work, most extensively in Part 2 of *A Pitch of Philosophy: Autobiographical Exercises* (Cambridge, MA: Harvard University Press, 1994). See also his remarks on Derrida in *Little Did I Know,* 448–50, 535–38.

comprehensive and methodical explication, Derrida juxtaposes the human body at its most naked, vulnerable, and apparently incommunicable: first, his own circumcision as a baby, and second, the worsening state of his dying mother, who no longer recognizes her son, whose utterances are growing increasingly unintelligible ("I have a pain in my mother," she says at one point [C 23]), and who passes away not long after the text is completed. These raw materials are further massed together with shards of memories from Derrida's childhood (a childhood companion named Claude; being expelled from school and having his French citizenship revoked, both for being Jewish during World War II) and long quotations in Latin from Augustine's *Confessions* (particularly its descriptions of the death of Augustine's mother, Monica). Unlike Quine's drily aloof chronicle of hobbies and travel, Derrida's "duel" (C 26) with Bennington repeatedly circles back to some of the most intimate questions: guilt, innocence, trauma, religion, one's place in history and one's culture, the sheer overwhelming emotional attachments that attend one's life as a grandchild, child, and parent. And unlike Quine, Derrida writes—needless to say—with anything but austerely neoclassical concision. The text appears as fifty-nine wildly periphrastic, exhaustingly run-on sentences that break the bounds of sense. Clause is piled upon clause, each launching a slightly new memory or direction of thought, and repeatedly drawing candid attention to the present-tense circumstances of Derrida's own writing: "Santa Monica, the name of the place in California near to which I am writing" (C 19), "today is July 23, her 88th birthday" (C 125), etc. The result is a text that, as Rorty puts it in a review, can "blow us away with something we could never have expected," its juxtaposition with Bennington's "bloodless" exposition making for "as startling a textual transition as one can get."[41]

The abyss separating *Little Did I Know* and the placidly unreflective pages of Quine's memoir is hard to miss. Few authors than Quine—who as a young man did almost as much to import Logical Positivism into the United States as A. J. Ayer did to introduce it in Britain—better epitomize an assumption that writing a memoir involves, as Cavell puts it, simply "the power of unfolding implication," and Quine's lifelong devotion to cartography is an apt contrast to Cavell's mature suspicion toward jigsaw puzzles, or at least their usefulness as models of human speech and action. One could hardly find two more comically incompatible reports from men who taught in the same academic department for decades, whether the topic is the experience of graduate school, undergoing psychoanalysis, encountering Jacques Lacan, or the student movements of

---

[41] Richard Rorty, "Derrida and the Philosophical Tradition," in *Truth and Progress: Philosophical Papers, Volume 3* (Cambridge: Cambridge University Press, 1998), 328, 347.

the 1960s.[42] Whereas Cavell's text is poised between "telling my story" and the "delay of, or by, philosophy," Quine writes as an annalist, telling and telling and telling, year by successive year, never pausing for meditation or confession. It's unimaginable, to take an example almost at random, that Quine would ever confess, as Cavell does near the beginning of his own memoir, that he has struggled in his life to find "a way out the devastation" that his father "could make of his island," or his appended remark that, as a son, he has "of course" not "escaped it entirely" (19).

Yet Cavell adds, in this passage, a further confession regarding his father that crucially illuminates his differences from Derrida as well. "I have made headway," he says, "in keeping, as it were, my knack of adopting his powers of devastation separate from my own causes for despair" (19). However far Cavell may be from Quine's analytic imperturbability, "ma[king] headway" suggests that he wants to avoid expressing a "horror of understanding, either of being its subject or being its object, pinned either way"—a "horror" that he especially associates with "theorists who achieved fame as poststructuralists or postmodernists" (525). Certainly the achievement of the unexpected in "Circumfession" doesn't on the face of it coincide very often with the achievement of understanding. The text's syntactic wrenching and vertiginous swerves—from topic to topic, clause to clause, text to text—work to curtain off knowledge about both the author's past and his mother, as if the powers of the accidental were uncontainable, bursting their way into Derrida's own prose. If Quine's text consists of endless "telling," Derrida's is all "delay"; no intelligible temporal progression— between acts, events, days, years—ever comes into focus. As Rorty notes, "Circumfession" may have the power to "blow us away," but it also is bound to give to "non-fans" a "strong impression of arbitrariness as soon as they open" the book.[43] And the result is much the kind of stark dichotomy that we saw in the emotivist, who assumed that anything that couldn't be captured in scientific or logical terms must *ipso facto* be dubiously unaccountable or perhaps irrational. Quine's memoir echoes Haugeland's Formalist's Motto: If you record the syntax of your days and years, the semantics—what it all means—will take care

---

[42] For Quine on his two years as a doctoral student, see *Time of My Life*, 82–86; for Cavell on his ten years as a doctoral student, see especially Part 8 of *Little Did I Know*. For Quine on psychoanalysis, see *Time of My Life*, 190; I discuss Cavell's relation to psychoanalysis in a later footnote. For Quine on Lacan, see *Time of My Life*, 416–17; for some of Cavell's response to Lacan, see *Little Did I Know*, 447, 475–76. For Quine on the 1960s, see *Time of My Life*, 344, 351–53; for Cavell's response, see *Little Did I Know*, see 429–33 (on his involvement in the Freedom Summer of 1963) and 505–12 (on his involvement in the creation of an Afro-American Studies department at Harvard).

[43] Rorty, "Derrida and the Philosophical Tradition," 339.

of itself. "Circumfession," by contrast, recalls the emotivist, implying that the only alternative to a "programming machine" is blind chance: the random, the wholly singular, the event, or what Derrida calls a "nonknowledge" that is the "only interesting thing"—the "happening" that he will "oppose or reveal" to Bennington's totalizing analysis.

Such an assumption—that any language not attending to "facts" must be language producing only "effects" or "forces"—is just one of the ways that, as some commentators have suggested, a "latent positivism" runs through the most influential "postmodern" theories.[44] The analogy isn't perfect, of course. "Circumfession" is hardly an arbitrary splatter of words, and as Derrida says in the passage I just quoted, he does not "love nonknowledge for itself," but because it seems to suggest something "sacred," a glimpse of "something other than knowledge," much as "certain Muslims" believe that "the ink of the learned is more sacred than the blood of the martyrs" (C 142)—not terms, presumably, that Ayer or Stevenson would elect. But if Derrida's prose could hardly be confused with that of an emotivist, he is also palpably distant from Cavell, who suggestively delineates the French philosopher's peculiar power and peculiar limitations. Derrida's "astounding fluency," he writes, "seems not to describe a detour to death"—a phrase borrowed from Freud to characterize his own memoir's project—"but a wager with it, a perpetual double or nothing, as if the end, indefinable since it may look awfully like the beginning, may be permanently, or each time, deferred" (530). Much as Wittgenstein believed that "the real discovery" in philosophy is one that "gives philosophy peace," and that "different therapies" allow one to "eliminate" certain "difficulties" case by case, so Cavell's improvisational diary entries are a record of emerging moments of clarity: not infinite irony or deferral, but instances of understanding, fragile glimpses of sense, authentic discoveries. Such moments, to recall Cavell's discussion of artworks, represent impulses and intentions following the distance through to their realization. Or, as he says elsewhere of Wittgenstein's aphoristic powers, they express "completeness, pleasure, and the sense of breaking something off . . . words that epitomize, separate a thought, with finish and permanence, from the general range of experience."[45] The fact that there is no *final* authority

---

[44] "Latent positivism" is a phrase from Espen Hammer, in *Stanley Cavell: Skepticism, Subjectivity, and the Ordinary* (Cambridge: Blackwell, 2002), 152.

[45] Stanley Cavell, "The *Investigations*' Everyday Aesthetics of Itself," in *The Literary Wittgenstein*, ed. John Gibson and Wolfgang Huemer (London: Routledge, 2004), 29. On the contrast between Cavell's Wittgensteinian moments of "peace" and the endlessness thematized in German Romantic writing and in poststructuralism, see Espen Hammer, "Cavell and Political Romanticism," in *The Claim to Community: Stanley Cavell and Political Philosophy*, ed. Andrew Norris (Stanford, CA: Stanford University Press, 2005), 170–77.

for the use of a word, the fact that there is no *rigid* determination for a word's meaning in *every* case, doesn't mean we don't know how to go on with a word in specific circumstances or project it in specific cases to come. And likewise, the fact that we never arrive at complete self-understanding—if "complete" means, say, the knowledge that an omniscient God would have of us—doesn't erase our capacity to make sense of how certain parts of our lives have advanced, and hence to discover where we now find ourselves: to create a perspicuous representation for our use of a word, to clarify our cares and commitments, to reflect upon "what used to be called the state of one's soul" (*CHU* 2).[46]

To be sure, this conception of writing as improvisatory self-discovery, as a "composition" that can achieve a provisional "finish and permanence," hardly means that Cavell's writing—in the memoir or anywhere else—is transparent. He explicitly refuses, as we've seen, the "significance that more unified narratives would have me accept" (*LD* 60). One could argue, with Áine Mahon, that Cavell's work betrays a "niggling tension between recovering the obvious and *avoiding* the obvious," and an uncharitable reader would say that Cavell's own self-professed "horror of stating the obvious" (187) devolves all too often into the "competitive obscurity" that he claims to distrust in Derrida and other French theorists.[47] But not to notice any differences between *Little Did I Know* and "Circumfession" would be— to use a metaphor fitting for the musician in Cavell—tone-deaf. Derrida's work can give the impression that, as Charles Taylor has written, "nothing emerges from his flux worth affirming, and so

---

[46] An alternative way of framing this juxtaposition with Quine and Derrida would be to consider Cavell's relation to psychoanalysis, a practice that has had an enormous impact on our understanding of autobiography. Cavell immersed himself in Freud while skipping classes at Julliard, and he reports entering psychoanalytic therapy twice, "both times with a lingering, more or less implicit, idea that I might seek a path into practicing clinical work myself" (108)—first in Berkeley as his first marriage was ending and later in Boston, as he struggled to complete *The Claim of Reason*. And unlike the majority of Anglo-American philosophers, he has been deeply attuned to the conflicts and categories that preoccupied Freud. But the emphasis he gives to improvisation and practical know-how in the memoir draws attention to an important difference between Cavell and the Freudian tradition, which, according to Linda Anderson's book on autobiography, has branched roughly into two strands. One line is exemplified by Freud himself, who when writing an autobiographical sketch in the 1920s adopted the stance of the unconditional authority. Like the customs officer at Ellis Island who met Cavell's father, he sought cool detachment and scientific completeness, ignoring the familial frictions and histories that his own work had made so central. The other line is suggested by Jacques Lacan, for whom any authoritative stance is always and necessarily a delusion. The inscrutable unconscious perpetually shatters the pretention to self-knowledge, the subject is always inhabited by the Other, and one doesn't speak a language but is wholly spoken by it. (See Linda Anderson, *Autobiography*, 2nd ed. [London: Routledge, 2011], 57–66.) From what I've suggested here, it should be clear that I think Cavell avoids both of the options that Anderson lays out.

[47] Áine Mahon, "Fraudulence, Obscurity, and Exposure: The Autobiographical Anxieties of Stanley Cavell," in *The Philosophy of Autobiography* (New York: Columbia University Press, 2015), 227.

what in fact comes to be celebrated is the deconstructing power itself, the prodigious power of subjectivity to undo all the potential allegiances which might
bind it; pure untrammeled freedom."[48] Cavell's experiments are motivated, in
contrast, by the opposite hope. His goal is not to undo allegiances, but to find
them: "To arrive where others are. To achieve, that is, to participate in, a public"
(521), to satisfy "a desire to find company" (525).

"Company" returns us to the analogy with Ellison that I began to introduce
earlier. As I've said, both Cavell and Ellison conceive of improvisation as an
alternative to both the deterministic and the arbitrary, and the centrifugal and
centripetal motions of their prose and thought are intended to achieve what
Ellison calls a "lyrical" or "eloquent" expression of the self—a unity that registers, not represses, the multiple and sometimes conflicting psychological and
cultural energies that constitute us. But for both figures, such disclosures of
need and desire are not intended to alienate us as audience members, but to
invite our participation. Ellison, recall, speaks of the "antagonistic cooperation"
that artists have with their audiences, the way that they attempt to shape perceptions even as the audience "simultaneously cooperates and resists, says yes
and says no," in a "silent dialogue with the artist's exposition of forms" (*CE*
496). The avoidance of such a dialogue, implies Ellison, was the root of Charlie
Parker's failure; his individual brilliance suffocated not only the collective affirmation that audiences seek in art, but also, in the end, Parker himself. Such
a claim is, as we've seen, an extension of Ellison's more general emphasis on
fraternity, a concept that, I've argued, allows him to combat strong claims about
social or cultural necessity with an ideal of deliberative citizen activity. Such a
view, as Danielle Allen suggests, acknowledges the separateness of persons, in
all their bodily and psychological and experiential differences, and encourages
a vision of *wholeness* as opposed to *oneness*—of disparate parts that, in the best
circumstances, can be brought into workable harmony.

For Cavell, too, oneness is a fantasy, one of the various images to which human
beings are constitutionally drawn, and which—when it fails to materialize—can
propel our swings into skepticism. Indeed, his early disagreements with David
Pole and other conventionalist interpreters of Wittgenstein are driven in part
by a sense that such a picture relies on a vision of social cohesion that is not
only wildly unrealistic but also, in the modern world, pernicious. Wittgenstein's
celebrated private-language argument does not, on Cavell's reading, defeat
skepticism once and for all, but instead tries to "account for, and protect, our

---

[48] Charles Taylor, *Sources of the Self: The Making of the Modern Identity* (Cambridge, MA: Harvard
University Press, 1989), 489.

separateness, our unknowingness, our unwillingness or incapacity either to know or to be known." It signifies, that is, not only that "there is no assignable end to the depth of us to which language reaches," but also, and just as profoundly, that there is "no end to our separateness": "We are endlessly separate, for *no* reason" (*CR* 369). Hence the strong sense that, as one commentator has written, Cavell has a decidedly "more nominalistic vision of life-forms" than other Wittgensteinians, most of whom, like Pole, emphasize the role of communal rules in orienting and constraining the individual.[49]

But though Cavell repeatedly underscores our separateness, this condition is for him, as for Ellison, no more the whole story of our lives than are the powers of chance. If we are indeed as separate as Cavell's reading of the private-language argument implies, then we are to the same degree "answerable for everything that comes between us; if not for causing it then for continuing it; if not for denying it then for affirming it; if not for it then to it" (*CR* 369). The task of self-clarification that Cavell describes, the continual willingness to question and revise oneself, cannot be carried out in isolation. Because "the self is not obvious to itself," because we don't always recognize the full range of our commitments and responsibilities and cares, we require what Cavell, speaking in the memoir of a close companion from his days as a musician, calls "serious friendship," a relation in which conversation can "eventually [become] endless and [concern] getting to some depth with everything of mutual and expansive concern" (*LD* 158). Elsewhere he refers to such a relationship as "marriage," which in the films that interest him is an "allegory" of "what philosophers since Aristotle have thought about under the title of friendship, what it is that gives value to personal relations."[50] As he says of his first encounter with Fried in the Cambridge apartment, such relations encourage us to speak "at the limits, and sometimes as it were just the other side, of what we knew and could judge"; the friend is the one with whom one shares "a species of shared testing, demanding stakes of conviction. . .backed by nothing more than who we were, or thought we were, and what we could find words for and reject words for" (407). Such a friend may even act as the "higher self" to which one aspires in Cavell's later accounts of moral perfectionism—not just the comforting shoulder to cry upon, but the exemplar who shames one and calls one out of one's current habits and state of conformity. As Peter Dula argues, Cavell is no more straightforwardly opposed—on metaphysical grounds, as it were—to the notion of a collectivity

---

[49] Hammer, "Cavell and Political Romanticism," 169.
[50] Stanley Cavell, *Cities of Words: Pedagogical Letters on a Register of the Moral Life* (Cambridge, MA: Harvard University Press, 2004), 15.

than he is to the notion of authority. What he resists is certain ossified forms of collectivity and authority.[51]

As in Ellison, then, improvisation for Cavell is not merely an individual undertaking, but something we do in our relations with one another, with varying forms of harmony and varying levels of—one of his essential terms—attunement. *Little Did I Know* does not embody fraternity in as dramatically resonant a way as *Invisible Man*: There is nothing like the Invisible Man's relationship to Tod Clifton, for instance, or the self-organizing group of arsonists led by the wily Dupre. But the fragility and significance of such relations are a running theme throughout Cavell's account of his childhood, which is marked by "helpless loneliness" (55) and five disorienting cross-country trips between Atlanta and Sacramento. The first quarter of the memoir is preoccupied with moments of "bereftness and bewilderment" (3): feeling excluded in school because he was both Jewish and younger, having skipped a couple grades (55–56); being abandoned to himself many nights by his mother and father, while they worked at the theater and the pawnshop respectively (105–7); watching his parents uneasily coexist without common interests or passions, their marriage having been arranged by his mother's father (144, 152). His long accounts of friendships later in the memoir—with musicians and actors in Berkeley and New York, with Fried and Kurt Fischer and Thompson Clarke and others, with his wife Cathleen—in effect show what authentic moral relations might look like, and the recurrent appearance of some of Cavell's former students (James Conant, Arnold Davidson, etc.) is a way of embodying the friendships between older and younger people that Cavell repeatedly conjures in his writing: Socrates and his circle, the psychoanalytic therapist, Schopenhauer the "educator" in Nietzsche's essay, the men of the remarriage comedies, the unknown women of the melodramas.[52] In these latter pages of the memoir, we see the "continuance of personal relationships against the hard and apparently inevitable fact" of conflicting aspirations and commitments (*CR* 269). Such relations illuminate the contexts and histories in which genuine moral discussion actually occurs, and the actual persons who actually conduct these moral discussions, and the actual reasons they actually put forward, and the sorts of "competence" that such reason-giving ideally entails and ideally exhibits.

Like Ellison, in other words, Cavell implicitly regards his fellow human beings less as suffering souls awaiting Judgment Day than as fellow participants in the

---

[51] Dula, *Cavell, Companionship, and Christian Theology*, 68.
[52] Dula makes this point about older and younger friends in *Cavell, Companionship, and Christian Theology*, 68; he is elaborating some earlier thoughts about Cavell offered by Stephen Mulhall.

environments and institutions that we share in this temporal realm. He, too, believes with Aristotle that *philia* "would seem to hold cities together," and that "the justice that is most just" belongs not to a far-off City of God, but to our associates and fellow citizens in this world.[53] The fact that Cavell shares this basic stance with Ellison—the fact that, as he suggests, fraternity makes one more rational, more intelligible to oneself and to the world, and provokes one to further improvisatory creativity—suggests one reason why the endpoint of Cavell's memoir is the completion of a book titled not *Beyond Reason*, or *After Reason*, or *The Myth of Reason*, or *An Other to Reason*, but instead *The Claim of Reason*. Cavell was born just a few weeks before Michel Foucault, has not shied away from confronting Derrida's work, and was a colleague and friend of both Thomas Kuhn and Richard Rorty—all of whom were continually attacked throughout their careers as "irrationalists."[54] If Cavell has largely escaped these charges, it may be for his early and ongoing sense that talking of the "base" of moral conduct and judgment is not a delusion—at least insofar as this "base" comprises not something metaphysical but "a knowledge of *persons*" (CR 265): knowledge not of moral laws or universal commands or punishing deities or physiological responses, but of our fellow speakers, whom we can both acknowledge and avoid in infinitely subtle, infinitely vast ways. Whereas other philosophers of his generation stress the foundationalist (Platonist, Kantian) senses of "reason" and pummel them relentlessly, Cavell has emphasized the ways that "reason" might be a name for one's intelligibility to oneself and one's capacity to understand—not necessarily agree categorically with—other people. "The wish and search for community," he says in *The Claim of Reason*, "are the wish and search for reason" (CR 20). Such a wish, and such a search—and the sense that this wish and search are sometimes fulfilled—are the heart of Cavell's version of the weak realism that I have been identifying in all the authors discussed here.

---

53 Aristotle, *Nicomachean Ethics*, VIII.ix. For some brief comparisons between Cavell and Aristotle, see Dula, *Cavell, Companionship, and Christian Theology*, 112–13; Richard Flathman, "Perfectionism Without Perfection: Cavell, Montaigne, and the Conditions of Morals and Politics," in *The Claim to Community: Essays on Stanley Cavell and Political Philosophy*, ed. Andrew Norris (Stanford, CA: Stanford University Press, 2005), 116–20. Cavell himself addresses Aristotle only rarely, but for some thoughts on friendship in *Nicomachean Ethics*, see his *Cities of Words*, 362–69.

54 Cavell's writing has shown relatively little interest in Foucault, but the penultimate section of the memoir records a growing interest in Foucault's late notion of the "care of the self," which Cavell connects (with the help of Arnold Davidson) to his own development of the idea of moral perfectionism; see *Little Did I Know*, 479. For Cavell's relationship to Kuhn, see especially *Little Did I Know*, 352–57. Rorty is thanked in the preface to *The Senses of Walden*, and Cavell's response to Rorty's review of *The Claim of Reason* is belatedly made in "Responses" in *Contending with Stanley Cavell*, ed. Russell Goodman (New York: Oxford University Press, 2005), 158–62.

IV. The Story of an Utterance

I've been arguing that *Little Did I Know* should be seen as an extended confrontation with the bald naturalism that, as with all the main figures of this book, haunts Cavell's writing. His Wittgensteinian and Austinian emphasis on the contexts of utterances is a way of questioning both strictly formalist accounts of language as well as disembodied, decontextualized accounts of moral thought. And it makes for a memoir that continually seeks to generate "surprise," both in the author and in the reader, chronicling the forward advance of Cavell's life while also allowing his memories to lead him in unexpected directions, resonating both with one another and with the present day. Moreover, as the memoir makes clear, improvisation is a central component of what are the highest words in Cavell's lexicon, "marriage" and "friendship," terms that recall Ellison's own keyword, "fraternity."

As we've seen in each of the first three chapters, however, such high words can be difficult to embody when the postwar sage turns to particular characters, scenes, and actions. The *this*ness and *here*ness of thought and experience seep into such works, refracting the normative vocabularies that the sage wants to prevent from growing worn and hapless. And the reflective project of Cavell, as I'll begin to suggest here, is no exception. In this final section, I want to consider just how seamlessly his particular cluster of ideas and ideals holds together, and what happens to them when he turns to a longer extended narrative than he's ever tried to write before, one far more novelistic and elaborate than even, say, *The Claim of Reason*'s story of the craftsman and automaton (*CR* 403–411). At the start of his book on Shakespeare, Cavell expresses a fear that his readings of *King Lear*, *The Winter's Tale*, and other plays will be taken as "the application of some philosophically independent problematic of skepticism," that he would appear to be "impressing" Shakespeare's texts "into the service of illustrating philosophical conclusions known in advance" rather than "unsettling the matter of priority (as between philosophy and literature, say) implied in the concepts of illustration and application."[55] Whether such "impressing" is consistently avoided in Cavell's work is a matter of critical debate.[56] But certainly *Little Did I Know*, a text whose breadth and detail is matched by its philosophical ambition and "delays," seeks to "unsettle" the lines as much as any text

---

[55] Cavell, *Disowning Knowledge*, 1.

[56] Charles Altieri, for instance, argues that Cavell's readings of literary texts are marred by an "effort to anchor displays of imaginative intensities within a master plot involving the recognition of skepticism." See his "Cavell and Wittgenstein on Morality: The Limits of Acknowledgement," in *Stanley Cavell and Literary Studies: Consequences of Skepticism*, 76.

Cavell has ever composed. Such unsettling has an unusual character, however, when the narrative text in question is not someone else's play or book, but one's own life story. The blurring of lines between discursive and narrative in the memoir hardly means (as Taylor says of Derrida) that nothing worth affirming ever emerges in his work, nor does it mean that Cavell fails to make clear what kind of situations and relationships would warrant these affirmations. But their precise emergence is complicated.

The crux of the matter lies in the notion of "context" that Cavell takes over from Wittgenstein and Austin. In the memoir the theme is raised when, for instance, Cavell discusses his involvement as an undergraduate in the university's theater productions, an experience that he regards as "early, specific preparation for my eventual conviction in the interest and importance of Austin's practice of philosophizing out of a perpetual imagination of, as Austin put the matter, 'what is said when,' why a thing is said, hence how, in what context" (217). It gets raised elsewhere when he clarifies the double timeline of his memoir, which, as I've said, records not only this or that memory from the past, but also the date of each composition and whatever pertinent strains of thought might press themselves upon him in the present tense. The point of this multiple structure, to recall a remark cited earlier, is to approximate "what Austin means in tirelessly demanding the context (he would often call it the story) of an utterance and what Wittgenstein means by repeatedly asking to whom an utterance is made" (60).

As in ordinary language philosophy generally, such appeals to context no doubt complicate the priority that philosophers have traditionally accorded to the truth and falsity of statements, and they no doubt draw attention to, as Wittgenstein says, the multiplicity of tools in our language, the kinds of words and sentences we actually employ (§24). But "context" is hardly a transparent concept, and other postwar sages that we've discussed can help clarify the specific uses that Cavell seems to have in mind. Percy, for instance, also highlights the notion of "context" in his discussions of naming, and like the Wittgensteinian philosopher, he emphasizes the way that a larger community helps guide the language-learner into a particular form of life. Naming, as he says, is a form of affirmation, both of our relationship to the world and of our relationship to one another, and the Thou is, as we saw in Chapter 1, what he calls "the companion and co-celebrant of my discovery of being," enacting an "intersubjectivity" that comprises "*a triad of existents: I, the object, you.*"[57] The

---

[57] Walker Percy, *The Message in the Bottle* (New York: Picador, 2000), 281, 285.

highest institutional manifestation of this intersubjectivity for Percy is the Catholic Church, which orients us toward the "objects" of the world and leads us to the most encompassing of all contexts, the life and love of Jesus Christ. But the contexts that Percy's work envisions for our lives includes a number of other, uglier, less-glorious features as well. Narrators, for instance, who can declare: "Everything depends on the close cooperation between business and love. Never will I understand men who throw over everything for some woman. The trick, the joy of it, is to prosper on all fronts, to enlist money in the service of love and love in the service of money." Film offerings that split evenly between the "sentimental blasphemy" of schlock like *The Sound of Music* and movies where "strangers engage in sexual intercourse and sodomy on the giant, 3-D Pan-a-Vision screen." Dubious "liaisons" between "the public and private sectors" who sneakily transfer the patent rights of controversial technologies designed to integrate our personalities. Former black militants who adopt WASPy fashions—knickerbockers, English caps—on the golf course after oil companies buy their properties and catapult them into the complacent upper class. Theatrical TV talk-show hosts who, when the commercials for margarine and dog food have finished, return to discussing contemporary sexuality by welcoming their next guests, John Calvin and Confederate Colonel Pelham. Hospital interns and nurses who wear their hospital greens to nightclubs when their shifts get out, which in turn ignites a craze for nonmedical clubbers to party in wrinkled hospital greens. Neighbors in Pasadena who are both starship designers and TV personalities employed to give public relations value to their labs, and who appear on competing late-night TV talk shows to discuss their latest books, *Space and Sexuality* and *Space and Sartori*, respectively.[58]

Such mordant scenarios are extended by David Foster Wallace, whose own landscapes, starting in the 1980s, are as replete with troubling signs of the times as those that Percy imagined from the early 1960s onward: films that entrance audiences into fatal stupefaction, years that get sponsored by trash bag and soap corporations, sporting events that are plastered in advertisements for ice cream and cigarettes and fried foods, crassly sophistic radio hosts who sell on-air outrage for ratings and ad dollars, luxury cruises titillating patrons with relentless on-board "fun," lobster "festivals" built on thoughtless and dubious forms of (in every sense) consumption. We'll see Wallace's

---

[58] Walker Percy, *The Moviegoer* (New York: Vintage, 1998), 102; Walker Percy, *Love in the Ruins* (New York: Farrar, Straus, & Giroux, 1971), 19; Percy, *Love in the Ruins*, 167–69; Percy, *Love in the Ruins*, 385; Walker Percy, *Lost in the Cosmos* (New York: Picador, 1983), 52–53; Percy, *Love in the Ruins*, 23; Percy, *Lost in the Cosmos*, 66–67.

scenarios in more detail in the following chapter. The point for now is that these kinds of "contexts," the cultural practices that their work spends such time detailing—a society of fantastic competition, cupidity, corruption, and callousness—appear hardly at all in *Little Did I Know*, let alone anywhere in Cavell's more specifically philosophical work. It's true, of course, that Percy and Wallace are *satirists* in a way that Cavell is not. True but uninformative, for the question is why satire would or would not seem appropriate. And at least part of the distinction between them seems to lie in a differing sense of history, or what range or dimensions of history count as a relevant "context." Cavell's books are resolutely aware of themselves as "modern," alert always to our radical distance from previous forms of life. Recall his remark, for instance, that "dependence upon God" is "no longer natural to the human spiritual repertory," or his analogous claims that tradition and social convention no longer justify themselves as they once did. Percy and Wallace agree. But they offer visions that are far more particularized than this, more historically and culturally specified, and they don't imply that reference to Descartes, Shakespeare, or the Reformation can adequately fill in what we mean by "modern." Cavell insists on the importance of "context," yet "context" for him tends to be quite local and short-lived circumstances. Like Austin asking about what to say when I shoot your donkey (Did I do it "voluntarily" or "by accident"?), Cavell's "contexts" tend to involve two people negotiating with words and each other in intricate and often unforeseeable ways.[59] It does not mean, as it has for some philosophers (Hegel, Marx), not to mention most novelists (including Wallace and Percy), a sustained attention to a more dispersed and variable set of cultural and historical phenomena.

To be sure, the line between global and local "contexts" is hardly sharp. But one cannot help noticing, reading Cavell next to the other contemporary sages, that the narrator of *Little Did I Know* is someone who never shops or browses or purchases very much, or watches TV ads, or is confronted by glossy magazine ads for lingerie and pharmaceuticals. He does not hear Muzak in every grocery aisle and airport lounge, is not bombarded by junk mail, does not need to close pop-ups, and is nowhere shown being infiltrated by urgent news of the latest timesaving or experience-enhancing gadget. He does not know the latest source of contrived outrage among talk-show hosts or what late-night clubbers are wearing, and doesn't seem to get involved in any of the gaudier forms of American tourism or attend contemporary mass sporting events. He does not

---

[59] See J. L. Austin, "A Plea for Excuses," in *Philosophical Papers* (Oxford: Clarendon Press, 1970), 185.

seem, in short, to participate in any meaningful way in the consumer culture of post-World War II America.

And the effect is palpable. In turning his attention so intensively to his own ordinary experiences, in "telling his story," Cavell winds up revealing the chasm that, in practice, seems to separate him from the socio-historical context in which he speaks. I have in mind, for instance, the several moments when he notes that he barely knows how to use the Internet, claiming to have an "inexperienced hand" at the Web (44), performing only a "rare and primitive search" when seeking information about the Atlanta of his childhood or about his family (125), and often relying on one of his sons to do searches for him (151). Late in the memoir, he mentions ordering a book from Amazon, "a rarity for me," largely because "I both still love wandering in remaining reasonably ambitious bookstores and wish to support them" (525). In the same passage he remarks that he is "more and more reluctant to leave the house," and that when he does so, it is almost always "under duress," driven by a fear "that I might freely give in to the increasing impulse to solitude" (525). He must increasingly look at "the dateline of the morning newspaper's front page to check my alignment with events" (526). For someone who brought the study of film into the academy, and who claims to be attracted to both "high and major art and to low and minor" (539), his references to popular culture—whether musical or visual—are to works that almost never date beyond World War II. (One strand of the book's conclusion, to cite just one important example, is a meditation on Howard Hawks's 1944 movie *To Have and Have Not*.) As I've noted, the book is written between July 2003 and September 2004, and caustic references to the Bush administration are peppered through its later portions: Bush is attributed a "violent, indifferently repetitive, mind" (478), and his speeches are said to represent "a new step in self-stupefaction," a symptom of "the current process of hypnotic deformation in the public discourse of the United States" (503). But the period in which Cavell was composing his memoir also happened to be the very months when, back at the university where he once taught courses on Heidegger, Wittgenstein, and moral perfectionism, Mark Zuckerberg was in his dorm room launching Facebook. In one sense this is, of course, just a coincidence; on the well-tended paths of Harvard Yard, lots of nerdy young students stroll past lots of aging professors. And certainly I don't mean to suggest that Cavell should have done more to anticipate the creation of Facebook, let alone Twitter, Snapchat, or any other form of social media. But the juxtaposition of Cavell and Zuckerberg raises the question of what it means for the memoir of an ordinary language philosopher—a memoir that puts enormous emphasis on contextualization and the dramatization of circumstance—to have barely registered the particular technological and commercial environments that proved to be such a valuable stage-setting for an entrepreneurial member of the millennial generation, and which were put to use in such dizzyingly profitable ways.

From a certain perspective, that is, *Little Did I Know* reads much as *Gilead* would have sounded if John Ames had never been interrupted from writing a letter to his young son by the arrival of Jack Boughton, and had been allowed to withdraw into his private study, serenely recalling now-distant personal and family memories without ever being forced to confront head-on the major social changes of his day. In that novel, the narrator comes to recognize, with a shock, that the civil rights movement of his day had been one of the "contexts" in which he had been writing, wholly unbeknownst to him. Such a contrast is illuminating here because it impacts how we understand Cavell's particular descriptions of the friendship and "marriage" that, as we've seen, he thematizes so regularly in his work. In particular, Cavell's comparatively local or narrow conception of "context" raises an important question about one of his most suggestive ideas. Central to his earliest interpretations of Austin was the idea that the ordinary language philosopher's evidence for "what is said when" is *not* empirical: no polls or brain scans can tell us more than our intuitions as native speakers; no new discoveries or information could *dis*confirm our sense that you and I typically say thus-and-so in a given situation. The ordinary language philosopher puts herself forward as exemplary of this "we," aspiring toward what Kant called the "universal voice."[60] This first-person plural is never something one can *assume*—one is always vulnerable to rebukes of the form, "*I* wouldn't say that"—but is a *claim* one stakes, and the claim is valid only to the extent that others find that one's words speak for them. As Cavell fully realizes, any claim to speak for a "we" can go rebuked, unheard, or unaccepted, and in the course of the memoir he acknowledges that he is unsure whether "those who write out of a history of oppression"—women, for instance—"would be glad to adopt [the] posture" he presents, or that "men and women who sense philosophical roots beyond American culture will be moved to test my representativeness" (6). So "testing," he says, is all he is doing. But Cavell clearly wants to suggest that he might potentially, as Emerson has it, "stand here for humanity." "To know others," he says, is "to know not the things they are. . .but all the ways in which they are what they simultaneously or successively are, or partially are, or deny

---

[60] The link between the "universal voice" imagined in Kant's account of aesthetic judgment and ordinary language philosophy's use of "we" is a theme across Cavell's corpus, from the early essay "Aesthetic Problems of Modern Philosophy" (*MWM* 73–96) to "Something Out of the Ordinary," in *Philosophy the Day After Tomorrow*, 7–27.

they are" (539). Thus he is quick to observe that he has a number of "identities compacted in [his] existence"—not only that of a Jew who has wondered sometimes "in what sense the anti-Semitism punctuating European philosophical thought speaks for me" (7), but also, as he enumerates in the final pages, that of "a father, a grandfather, a son, an American, a depressed patriot, . . .a white man, a professor, knock-kneed, bald, divorced, married, temperamentally inclined to both disappointment and to joy, to solitude and to love" (539).

That such an array of identities may not be enough to "stand" for us in the present day is a question that Cavell himself raises in the opening pages of *Little Did I Know*, when he ponders whether he is "writing as an emissary from another time" (7). His response to this worry is to note that both sides of his family had been recent immigrants, people "preserving their lives in the stark freedom of America, of persisting fears and of savage ambitions and forced marriages, and of desperately preserved or rejected or rediscovered observances" (7)—the implication being that these experiences ring as true today as they did a century ago. Thus, he goes on, there's no telling that he won't be able to speak for a "young Cuban poet teaching Spanish in a community center in Buckhead," or "a middle-aged Vietnamese high school teacher, with a taste for philosophy, keeping the books for her older brother's restaurant in Allston" (7). Such a response may be what leads a reader like Ian Hacking to characterize Cavell as "a grand master of American myths."[61] But Cavell's appeal to the American immigrant narrative isn't in itself wholly unreasonable, and at any rate it is not what my contrasts with Percy and Wallace are meant to highlight. My question instead is whether, in the course of his memoir, Cavell is really responding to the specific world in which persons today—not only his poet and teacher, but also his readers—could be said to be living their lives.

Consider again Cavell's remark, cited at the start, about his frustrated spells working in the family pawnshop, and his father's justifiable sense that, in the eyes of his son, "to talk people into buying something they might or might not want was a repellent idea" (121). What repels in particular is his father's continual need for staged contrivances—the constant need to evaluate "an initial asking price" and "the taste of a stranger looking for a watch, whether it was merely by expense or sometimes aspiration, [and] whether bringing out a new object would offer a real temptation or merely dampen interest in the object in question" (120). The passage encapsulates a recurrent worry in *Little Did I Know*, namely that the author might be governed by powers—inner and outer—that

---

[61] Ian Hacking, "Conclusion: Deflections," in *Philosophy & Animal Life*, ed. Cary Wolfe (New York: Columbia University Press, 2008), 158.

he himself does not acknowledge as legitimate, and that his life might thus be in some sense *false*. In salesmanship, meaning what one says counts far less than closing the deal, and integrity far less than influence; and Cavell is disturbed by the thought that he has either bought or sold someone else's bill of goods. "The issue for me," he says, dramatically recalling his first years of graduate school, "was not to prove that this further life was better than another, but to prove that it was mine, that I was born to it, that I was born" (284). Not to be "born" in this sense is to live like his father, whose need to lure customers replicated his life as a practicing-yet-unobservant Jew, loyally attending synagogue despite not really believing. In both temple and the pawnshop, the old man performs a role and follows a set of mostly preexisting scripts, paying attention to some audience that he himself can't fully define, unconsciously treating his life as a kind of theater.

I mean "theater" here in the sense promoted by Cavell's friend Fried, who has often credited Cavell with having helped him develop the idea.[62] For Fried, "theatricality" is evident in artworks undertaken wholly in anticipation of an audience's reaction, so that they become entirely dependent upon the environment in which they're observed and on the responses of their viewers. A "theatrical" painting is, in the words of Diderot, one of Fried's critical models, like "the man who presents himself in society," "stiff and unnatural," an artificial construction created in order to impress the beholder and solicit his applause (*AT* 100). The opposite of "theatricality" is what Fried calls "absorption," a state in which the agent is oblivious to everything except the task being performed, including the painting's beholder. Thus Chardin, in the eighteenth century, "secularized the absorptive tradition" that had run through early modern religious painting, so that images of people praying or listening to Christ are now transformed into images of people reading, sleeping, playing cards, or speaking with one another, all of them turned away from the beholder's gaze, shunning us, engrossed in their activities to the point of reverie. More recently, Jeff Wall has created large-scale, tableau-sized photographs with a similar effect: pictures of window cleaners at work or draftsmen sketching laboratory specimens, each proposing an "antitheatrical" ideal, an intensified state of "mindedness" that both pushes the audience away and asks us to linger in a state of what Fried calls "passive receptivity" (*AT* 130). Of course, paintings are made to be seen,

---

[62] For Fried's influential formulations of "theatricality," see his 1967 essay "Art and Objecthood," in *Art and Objecthood: Essays and Reviews* (Chicago: University of Chicago Press, 1998), 148–72; and *Absorption and Theatricality: Painting and Beholder in the Age of Diderot* (Berkeley: University of California Press, 1980); the latter is henceforth cited parenthetically as *AT*.

and Fried is aware that both the "theatrical" and "absorptive" are each "modes of performance."[63] But artists like Chardin and Wall—or, in different ways, Anthony Caro or Adolph Menzel—bid to create the "supreme fiction" that the beholder does not exist, all in order to "defeat" the theatricality of modern culture, where agents are under increasing pressure to play for the audience and instrumentalize their social relations.[64]

Fried's terms obviously capture the powers that *Little Did I Know* attributes to art, which it repeatedly portrays as a form of religious experience. Earlier I mentioned his father's storytelling, his mother's piano playing, and his memory of watching Benny Goodman, but we also hear, for instance, how Cavell's grandfather had taught his family that "music is a religion, outlasting Judaism and socialism" (42); how, as a pupil in a Sacramento school, he met a classmate who was gifted at drawing and immediately felt "a miraculousness in this ability and an immediate conviction that such artistry meant that this boy already knew his future of clarity and happiness" (102); and how, walking into the Music Department on his first day at Berkeley, he heard an older man saying to a student, "Whenever I hear that piece, I believe in immortality"—to which Cavell immediately adds: "I had come to the right place" (205).[65] And Fried's terms likewise capture the absorptive powers Cavell seeks to depict and create in his own text. A primary goal of the book is, as we've seen, to reignite Cavell's *own* interest in his own experiences, and the diary format reinforces this aspiration: he writes not just *about* himself, but also *for* himself, as if his own achievement of meditative concentration matters as much as any approbation from us. Cavell's sentences extend this absorption to another level, their famous difficulty arising not from any specialized philosophical terminology, but from the "mindedness"—even reverie—they present, their recurring self-qualifications and self-revisions offering a sequence of moods and self-clarifications, not a staunch progression toward a conclusion or an unfolding of implications. Like so much of the post-Romantic writing that he admires, Cavell has felt, he says,

---

[63] Michael Fried, *Why Photography Matters As Art As Never Before* (New Haven, CT: Yale University Press, 2008), 41.

[64] For philosophically informed readings of Fried's work, see Robert Pippin's "Authenticity in Painting," *Critical Inquiry* 31 (2005): 575–98; Magdalena Ostas, "Kant with Michael Fried: Feeling, Absorption, and Interiority in the *Critique of Judgment*," *symploke* 18 (2010): 15–30; Walter Benn Michaels, *The Shape of the Signifier: 1967 to the End of History* (Princeton, NJ: Princeton University Press, 2004), chap. 2.

[65] One thinks also here of how a Fritz Kreisler concert struck him as a boy "as an image of total concentration," "as if music had been induced to utter itself" (53); or how a racially integrated band he joined after high school became "an image for me, even a realization, of a world adjacent. . .to the world I mostly converse with" (75).

that "the writing had cost me something, in such a way, perhaps, that it has to, and should, cost the reader something"; and as with so much of this writing, the "public response" to his work was for a long time either "silence or dismay," with critics worrying that "what I was publishing was inherently private, even secret" (442–43). It is only appropriate, given this antitheatrical spirit, that the final pages of *Little Did I Know* pause on a wartime death scene in a Hemingway novel, when a character asks his fellow soldiers to leave him alone in his dying moments because "I don't want anyone to watch" (545)—as if to be watched would be an invitation to theatricalize the most mysterious, intimate, and ineluctably personal moment of one's existence.

All these images and echoes in the memoir—Cavell's evocation of absorptive ideals, his antitheatrical visions of art and writing and speech—are a marked contrast with the state that his salesman father occupies for most of his life. And not just his father: Uncle Mendel, recall, was twice national president of the Printers Association of America, and "wrote books on the subject" of salesmanship (121), one of whose titles was *How to Sell Printing Creatively*. But glancing at the examples of Percy and Wallace, and reminding ourselves of Cavell's proximity to Zuckerberg, may push us to wonder whether something fundamentally shifted in the decades that Cavell charts, from the midcentury culture in which his father and uncle had some modest success in business to the wired, media-saturated, reductively profit-obsessed early twenty-first century world in which *Little Did I Know* is written and read. When, that is, Mendel's book was published in 1956, few people could have imagined the stupendous creativity that came to be poured into contemporary selling, the technological changes that facilitated it, and the cultural transmutations that ensued. Few people at that time could have imagined the revolutionary turn to the ironic and hip advertising diagnosed by, say, Don DeLillo, and later probed by Wallace: postwar forms of persuasion devised to adapt to a growing suspicion of authority, and made to appeal to consumers' "life styles" and perceived need for freedom and self-expression.[66] Still less could people have imagined a world where a start-up or conglomerate strives to relieve our smallest pangs of boredom with a scroll through a Facebook feed. Few could've forecasted a world in which business school students are coached to create "hooks," exploiting "internal triggers" and the brain's dopamine rewards to breed customer habits and generate higher CLV, "customer lifetime value"—the amount of money a consumer is likely to spend on a product before either switching to a competitor or dying.

---

[66] See Thomas Frank, *The Conquest of Cool: Business Culture, Counterculture, and the Rise of Hip Consumerism* (Chicago: University of Chicago Press, 1997).

To supporters, this potent brew of cognitive psychology, behavioral economics, computer science, and data analysis has meant the revolutionary flattening of the world, new glimmers of perpetual peace; at the very least it's seemed a way to help people do the things they already wanted to do but, for lack of a solution, don't.[67] To critics it has meant nothing short of devastation: reducing common life, as Hal Foster says, to shopping in the same "megastore," only in different aisles, a world of "total design and Internet plenitude." Such plenitude can seem, as Cavell's grad school friend Hubert Dreyfus puts it, an incubator of *amour proper*, gaining in extensity what it loses in intensity, diminishing speech into information, a "nowhere place for anonymous nowhere people," a domain where life is a masquerade and genuine ethical risks are unnecessary. "The shallows," as another critic has it.[68]

Perhaps such arguments, both pro and con, are overheated. The point is that one leaves Cavell's twenty-first century memoir with very little sense that these kinds of technological and economic changes have even taken place, or that the cultural shifts that have accompanied them—transformations of the sort that Percy and Wallace go a long way to intuit—have even occurred. A sensitivity to such changes may in part help explain why Percy and Wallace became novelists, Bakhtinian writers compelled to inhabit and recreate different voices, inflecting language with a tumultuous range of sociolects and speech genres; whereas the opening pages of *Little Did I Know* invoke Wordsworth, that archetype of first-person musing and the egotistical sublime (*LD* 5). And Cavell's absorptive turn may likewise account for the temporal shape of his book. As I've noted, the narrative of the text ends for all intents and purposes in 1979, with the publication of *The Claim of Reason*, a full twenty-five years before the heart surgery described in the opening paragraphs of the book—as if the intervening quarter-century had done little to color or modify the contexts in which Cavell works and writes. Contemporary media and commercial culture has peeked intermittently through Cavell's philosophical work—as when, for instance, he tries to distinguish his moral perfectionism from the hackneyed U.S. Army slogan, "Be

---

[67] See Nir Eyal's subtly titled *Hooked: How to Build Habit-Forming Products* (New York: Portfolio, 2015), 12; Eyal provides an illuminatingly exultant account of "internal triggers" and dopamine rushes.

[68] See Hal Foster, "ABCs of Contemporary Design," *October* 100 (Spring 2002): 191–99 (quotation at 198); Dreyfus's Rousseauvian–Kierkegaardian–Heideggerian denunciation of the Internet can be found in his *On The Internet*, 2nd ed. (London: Routledge, 2009); "the shallows" is Nicholas Carr's term, from his book *The Shallows: What the Internet is Doing to Our Brain* (New York: W.W. Norton, 2010). It was Dreyfus who first introduced Cavell to Derrida in the early 1970s (on their relationship, see *Little Did I Know*, 273, 449), a connection that may highlight the strikingly Dreyfusian aphorism that Cavell records having made in 1972, the year Dreyfus published *What Computers Can't Do*: "A computer has memory but no memories. Roughly like a person in a rage" (485).

All You Can Be," ubiquitous in the 1980s.[69] Yet such glances remain passing. Such intermittence will seem appropriate to most philosophical readers coming to Cavell for philosophical writing, whatever Cavell's (genuine) distance from professional philosophy. But it is harder to ignore in a memoir, a genre that, if usually narrower in range than most novels, still fixedly directs attention to the embodied settings and situations that are closest at hand. And it will in all likelihood be impossible to ignore for many contemporary literary theorists and critics reading Cavell, who for some time have worked with a different— more sociological, historical, political—notion of "context" than the one Cavell himself tends to use. From their point of view, Cavell's distance from professional philosophy is liable to seem hyperbolic, given the extent to which, as his memoir exemplifies, he re-enacts philosophy's traditional withdrawal from the world: the Academy, the Garden, Descartes by the fire, the bachelor Kant in far-off Königsberg, Heidegger's hut.

The question is not whether, by ignoring so much of contemporary life, Cavell risks growing unfashionable. The question is whether, in doing so, he weakens the perspicuous representations that his text has been presenting, the archive of images and stories from which we as readers might identify "friendship," "marriage," and other high words. The question, that is, is when "absorption" shades into self-seclusion or retreat, and whether, when it does, one will be sealing oneself off from the full range of "accidents" that are capable today of thwarting our "compositions." *Little Did I Know* may risk, that is, diminishing the range of threats to our rational improvisatory autonomy, the full swath of "interruptions" that persuade us to desire what we don't know we want, that prevent us from following the distance from an impulse and intention through to its realization. And we may, in turn, fail to ask if the aesthetic categories operable in contemporary culture have importantly shifted: if art has less religious hubris than in the past; if it is something that we are still, as Cavell put it, "concerned with" and "care about," as we are with people; or if Cavell's term "composition" is really the best word to describe (say) electro house music or GIF art or mobile games. A version of such questions was voiced in Cavell's

---

[69] See, for example, *Conditions Handsome and Unhandsome*, 16. One moment when contemporary economic shifts are registered in the memoir comes when Cavell qualifies his "undying gratitude to Harvard, or to be more specific, to the unfathomable depth of its wealth and power." Driving through the glittering Harvard Square of the early 2000s, he notes the "compounding luxuriousness of the Harvard Law School and Harvard Peabody Museum of natural history and Harvard's Fogg Museum of Art," and records finding himself "struggling against the awful awareness of irreducible arbitrariness and greediness, even where (or especially where) it is inadvertent, in such concentrated (not of course unique) advantage" (405). He does not, however, dwell on the discomfort he expresses here.

early essay on modern music; in a different tone of voice, they have also been voiced by Fredric Jameson and, more recently, Sianne Ngai; and as I've already hinted, they will be voiced in Chapter 5 by Wallace.[70] But they are not much voiced in Cavell's memoir, and the question is whether, as a result, his life will seem as "representative" as he wishes, and whether it will show the normative ideals about which it so eloquently tells. If Cavell's improvisations are meant to inspire "surprise" in both himself and others, can this surprise be available in a culture of overwhelming stimulation? As one commentator has observed, the social and technical changes of our day will surely have an impact on the way that autobiographies will come to be written: much of our lives is now captured online, and much of this online record appears in the fragmented forms of visual assemblages, blogs, tweets, digital postcards, and the like.[71] It is hard to know how Cavell's book will *sound* alongside such texts, or likewise in a culture where the concert-level pianist or virtuoso clarinetist may find that talking people into buying something isn't the "repellent" idea that the adolescent Cavell intuited it to be. Earlier I cited Cavell's passing reference to the "great works of the human spirit." Do we still talk in such terms today? If changes to the ecology of our social lives make no difference to how we interpret Cavell and his themes, can we say precisely why not? Near the end of *Little Did I Know,* Cavell describes himself as "reverse Rip Van Winkle," awakening twenty-five years after *The Claim of Reason* with a dozen more books written, and finding a newly appreciative readership, "a considerable number of strangers who apparently recognized me, or knew what I had been doing" (514). Perhaps the metaphor of sleep in this sentence is apt in ways that Cavell himself doesn't notice, and perhaps strangers do not recognize him to quite the extent that, hope against hope, he believes.

---

[70] Fredric Jameson, *Postmodernism, or The Cultural Logic of Late Capitalism* (Durham, NC: Duke University Press, 1991); Sianne Ngai, *Our Aesthetic Categories: Zany, Cute, Interesting* (Cambridge, MA: Harvard University Press, 2012). My reference here to the "hubris" of art is from Adorno, cited by Ngai at 253. The fact that Ngai's book is, in part, inspired by Austin and Cavell is obviously ironic, given what I'm saying here about Cavell's memoir.

[71] Sidonie Smith, "Narrating Lives and Contemporary Imaginaries," *PMLA* 126 (2011): 569–71.

5

THE ADVANCED U.S. CITIZENSHIP

OF DAVID FOSTER WALLACE

ACCORDING TO HIS biographer, David Foster Wallace developed his prose in part from reading the subject of my last chapter, Stanley Cavell, whose work offered a "plainspokenness" that he appreciated, a "lively, learned, but friendly approach to philosophical investigations."[1] As a description of Cavell's work, D. T. Max's characterization is flaccid, but the attraction to Cavell that he identifies in Wallace is genuine. It's an attraction expressed here and there across Wallace's earliest essays, and Cavell's presence at Harvard must have been one of Wallace's reasons for entering its doctoral program in philosophy in September 1989.[2] His fragmented semester as a graduate student there (by November he was in McLean Hospital with suicidal thoughts and a substance-abuse problem) included a course with the philosopher, and Cavell was still on Wallace's mind a few years later when he was trailed around for part of a book tour by David Lipsky, to whom he described Cavell as being "real good on, like, American film."[3]

---

[1] D. T. Max, *Every Love Story Is a Ghost Story: A Life of David Foster Wallace* (New York: Penguin, 2012), 142, 132.

[2] For mentions of Cavell in Wallace's early essays, see David Foster Wallace, "The Empty Plenum: David Markson's *Wittgenstein's Mistress*," *Both Flesh and Not: Essays* (Boston: Little, Brown, and Company, 2012), 73, 109 (henceforth cited parenthetically as *BFN*); David Foster Wallace, *A Supposedly Fun Thing I'll Never Do Again: Essays and Arguments* (Boston: Little, Brown, and Company, 1997), 141, 25, 44; henceforth cited parenthetically as *SFT*.

[3] David Lipsky, *Although Of Course You End Up Becoming Yourself: A Road Trip with David Foster Wallace* (New York: Broadway Books, 2010), 236.

A glance into the personal library that Wallace left behind at his death in 2008 confirms this sympathy. Through many years and changes of address, he kept copies of two of Cavell's books, *Pursuits of Happiness* (1981), a study of Hollywood remarriage comedies of the 1930s, and *In Quest of the Ordinary* (1988), his essays on American and European Romanticism.[4] The introduction to *Pursuits* is heavily underlined, and expressions of approval dot the margins: "Nice," for instance, when Cavell proposes that "the achievement of human happiness requires not the perennial and fuller satisfaction of our needs as they stand but the examination and transformation of our needs."[5] His notations in *In Quest of the Ordinary* are restricted mostly to one chapter, "Being Odd, Getting Even," but they suggest that this essay on Poe, Emerson, and Descartes decisively shaped his review of David Markson's *Wittgenstein's Mistress*, which was written in the spring and summer of 1989. "Markson," "*Witt's Mist*," and "Kate" (the name of Markson's narrator) are scattered in Wallace's hand throughout the margins, and indicate that he took particular interest in Cavell's reading of the *Cogito*.[6] Other marginal notes seem to anticipate "Greatly Exaggerated," Wallace's short 1992 essay on authorial intention, as when he perceptively summarizes Cavell's vexed relationship to Deconstruction: "For Decons," Wallace jots, "Cavell 'doesn't count.' He doesn't dismiss Derrideans—he dismisses himself with respect to it."[7]

Wallace's affinities with Cavell, however, are evident not only at the macro level of theme—a certain interest in Descartes, a certain stance toward literary

---

[4] Stanley Cavell, *Pursuits of Happiness: The Hollywood Comedy of Remarriage* (Cambridge, MA: Harvard University Press, 1981); Stanley Cavell, *In Quest of the Ordinary: Lines of Skepticism and Romanticism* (Chicago: University of Chicago Press, 1988).

[5] This observation is made in Cavell, *Pursuits of Happiness*, 4. Shortly thereafter, Wallace similarly jots "Cool" when Cavell observes that "There are things such as inspired times of reading or listening as surely as there are such things as inspired times of writing or composition" (13). Most of the rest of this latter sentence's paragraph is underlined, and next to Cavell's sentences about the appearance of video disks and the "changes in mere practicality" it would involve in watching films, Wallace wrote a little star and "Video→ reading films" (13).

[6] When, for instance, Cavell discusses debates over whether "I think, therefore I am" should be understood either as a performance or as an inference, Wallace writes "VITAL" and "Use for end→performative / revision / Cogito." And when Cavell summarizes Descartes's *Cogito* in a long paragraph, Wallace writes "Markson" in the margin, adding an idea about Kate, the narrator of Markson's novel: "making the world *as* language-based—Her final statement *is* cogito." In total, either "Markson" or "*Witt's Mist*" appears over a half-dozen times in the margins of the essay, as well as other comments related to the novel: "Self+Other," "Kate is real," or, next to Cavell's account of the connection between homes, rooms, and other people in the work of several American Romantics, "Markson skepticism as domestic" (*In Quest of the Ordinary*, 129).

[7] The comments on Deconstruction that inspired Wallace's remarks are in *In Quest of the Ordinary*, 131. A few pages later, when Cavell compares the response of intellectuals to Pythagoras's theories to their response to Gödel's (140), Wallace writes simply: "Nice." Cavell and Austin appear briefly in "Greatly Exaggerated," mentioned as roads too-seldom taken in contemporary literary theory.

theory—and not only at the micro level of style ("plainspokenness" or otherwise). Their affinities are also manifest at the levels that have interested me most in this book, that is, in their shared willingness to explore and exploit the resources of various prose forms. And like all the figures I've been examining, they use these various forms to question radical nominalism—to ask, as Wallace puts it in one essay, whether "service," "sacrifice," and other broad normative words "actually *stand for* something," "whether anything past well-spun self-interest might be real, was ever real."[8] Wallace's chief ancestors are routinely said (often by Wallace himself) to be Don DeLillo, Thomas Pynchon, and John Barth. But Cavell deserves a place in this catalogue of predecessors, pointing toward the experiments Wallace would undertake not only within particular works but also providing a model for the larger hopes and patterns of Wallace's career.

The generic shifts in Wallace's work are, however, more drastic than what we see in Cavell, and this may explain why Wallace had mixed feelings about his ability to handle them. *Little Did I Know* is the only extended narrative work of Cavell's career, and as I noted in Chapter 4, part of his motivation for writing it is, as he puts it, to understand "why philosophy, of a certain ambition, tends perpetually to intersect the autobiographical."[9] Wallace, by contrast, often felt disoriented by what he called the "intergeneric differences" that, "as it happens," "I know and care about as a writer" (*BFN* 302). DeLillo, Pynchon, and Barth—not to mention Cormac McCarthy, William Gaddis, and several other writers he revered—all published vastly less discursive prose than they did fiction, and this encouraged the belief the novel was, as Max puts it, "the big form, the one that mattered." "I do not know," he wrote DeLillo in 2000, "why the comparative ease and pleasure of writing nonfiction always confirms my intuition that fiction is What I'm Supposed to Do, but it does, so here I am flogging away," and he added a plea to his complaint: "if you're feeling avuncular I'd welcome gentle persuasions that people interested in writing fiction should not fuck around with essays."[10] At other times he was more optimistic about bridging the gap. Though his earliest essays, he admitted in a late interview, were written

---

[8] David Foster Wallace, *Consider the Lobster* (Boston: Back Bay Books, 2006), 166; henceforth cited parenthetically as *CL*.

[9] Stanley Cavell, *Little Did I Know: Excerpts from Memory* (Stanford, CA: Stanford University Press, 2010), 2; henceforth cited parenthetically as *LD*.

[10] Wallace's letter continues: "I never even meant to do essays in the first place—I did a couple things from Hitt and Harrison at *Harper's* hoping they'd like me and quit rejecting every story I sent them. The whole thing needs to end." Wallace letter to DeLillo, November 25, 1998 (Harry Ransom Center, University of Texas).

simply for money, he "turned out to enjoy the genre"; he was enthusiastic when approached by a publisher in 2000 to write a whole book about the concept of infinity, and he likewise found writing about the tennis player Roger Federer in 2006 to be a surprising joy.[11] But to the end, the forms did not "perpetually intersect" in the way that they seem to do for Cavell. "Both genres," Wallace said in one of his final published pieces—by "genres" he meant fiction and nonfiction—are "scary," but they involve conflicting phenomenologies: Fiction, he said, feels like it's executed over an "abyss" of "silence, *nada*," whereas "nonfiction's abyss is Total Noise, the seething stasis of every particular thing and experience, and one's total freedom of infinite choice about what to choose and attend to and represent and connect, and how, and why, & c." (*BFN* 302–3).

Such tensions haven't prevented commentators from spying a seamless body of ideas in Wallace's work, be it about radical voluntarism, surrendering one's will, the possibility of faith apart from religion, or anything else.[12] My initial goal here is to suggest that we should take seriously Wallace's own sense of conflict, and to argue that, like Wittgenstein's *Philosophical Investigations*, his work constitutes an "album" of different "landscapes." The partiality of different perspectives in his work is particularly manifest in the writing on which his reputation most rests, the period starting in the early 1990s, when he had absorbed Cavell, hit his stride composing *Infinite Jest* (1996), grew explicitly suspicious of his early fiction—the novel *The Broom of the System* (1987) and the short stories of *Girl With Curious Hair* (1989)—and moved in his nonfiction beyond the predominantly literary focus of his earliest essays, engaging more explicitly with social, political, and moral themes.[13] He is thus the culmination of the postwar

---

[11] On Wallace's admiration for writers who restricted themselves to the novel form (Max cites only DeLillo and McCarthy; I've added Pynchon and Gaddis here), see Max, *Every Love Story*, 234. For Wallace's letter to DeLillo, see Max, 260; for his "turn[ing] out to like the genre," see *Conversations With David Foster Wallace*, ed. Stephen J. Burn (Jackson: University Press of Mississippi, 2012), 154; for his reaction to being offered to write about infinity, see Max, 261; for his account of his Federer essay, see Max, 296.

[12] On Wallace as voluntarist, see Hubert Dreyfus and Sean Dorrance Kelly, *All Things Shining: Reading the Western Classics to Find Meaning in a Secular Age* (New York: Simon and Schuster, 2011), chap. 2. On Wallace and surrendering the will, see Daniel R. Kelly, "David Foster Wallace as American Hedgehog," in *Freedom and the Self: Essays in the Philosophy of David Foster Wallace*, ed. Steven M. Cahn and Maureen Eckert (New York: Columbia University Press, 2015), 109–33. On faith apart from religion, see Max, *Every Love Story*, 214.

[13] It may not be accidental that Wallace also became a bit more financially secure in this period, as he moved from short-term contracts at Boston-area colleges to a full-time position at Illinois State University and later on, in 1997, won a MacArthur "Genius" award. If, in other words, he ever felt the need to write simply for money, he would no longer have felt it the same way after around the fall of 1993. By "predominantly literary" essays early in Wallace's career I'm referring to pieces such as "Fictional Futures and the Conspicuously Young" (1988), the review of *Wittgenstein's Mistress* (1990), "E Unibus Pluram: Television and U.S. Fiction" (1990), and "Greatly Exaggerated" (1992). The earliest indication of Wallace's dissatisfaction with his postmodern ancestors is usually

sage that this book has been tracking: culmination both in a temporal sense, as the most recent incarnation of the phenomenon, and in a conceptual sense, as the most ambitious yet also the most fractured, the most naïve yet also the most disenchanted. Of the constellation of figures I've been discussing, he is perhaps the most desperate to offer readers a "moralist and pedagogue," as one commentator puts it, but he is also the most uneasy with this stance.[14]

A second goal is to investigate some of the various positions that generate this sense of strain in Wallace, and to trace some of the conflicting intellectual and historical sources that inform his work. As we'll see, much of this tension centers on the problem of "context"—why it matters, how to define it, how broad it is—that I identified in Cavell in Chapter 4. Outlining and juxtaposing the various turns of Wallace's thought will lead us to trace his relationship to several philosophical figures. These will include, in the next section, both Cavell and Wittgenstein, whose allure for Wallace has been noted before, even beyond D. T. Max, but seldom in satisfactory ways.[15] But in sections two and three, I want also to chart Wallace's relationship to two other thinkers who have been more or less ignored among his readers, namely Aristotle and John Dewey. Both Dewey and Aristotle saw major revivals in the years that Wallace came to intellectual maturity, and they came to Wallace through an influence that virtually no reader has really recognized in Wallace's work: namely, his father, the philosopher James D. Wallace. As we make our way in sections four and

---

said to be "Westward the Course of Empire Takes Its Way," the novella-length story that ends *The Girl With Curious Hair*. But this story represents nothing like the advance on his earlier work that was taken in the 1990s, and it's unsurprising that Wallace himself lost most of the pride he once took in the story, which he called a "permanent migraine." (See Larry McCaffery, "A Conversation with David Foster Wallace," *The Review of Contemporary Fiction* 13.2 [Summer 1993] << http://www.dalkeyarchive.com/a-conversation-with-david-foster-wallace-by-larry-mccaffery/>>.) In suggesting a distinction between the Wallace of the 1980s and the Wallace of the 1990s, I am diverging from critics who speak in the same basic terms about the entirety of Wallace's work. I will have relatively little to say here about his work before around 1992.

[14] Paul Giles, "All Swallowed Up: David Foster Wallace and American Literature," in *The Legacy of David Foster Wallace*, ed. Samuel Cohen and Lee Konstantinou (Iowa City: University of Iowa Press, 2012), 6.

[15] Discussions of Wallace and Cavell have been mostly impressionistic, and discussions of Wallace and Wittgenstein have tended to ignore or misconstrue the full philosophical stakes of Wallace's interpretations. On Wallace's relationship to Cavell, see Giles, "All Swallowed Up," in *The Legacy of David Foster Wallace* (ed. Coehn and Konstantinou), 8–9; Kasia Boddy, "A Fiction of Response: *Girl With Curious Hair* in Context," in *A Companion to David Foster Wallace Studies*, ed. Marshall Boswell and Stephen J. Burn (London: Palgrave Macmillan, 2013), 36–40. Wallace's relationship to Wittgenstein is a far more widely excavated subject among scholars, no doubt in part because Wallace so frequently discussed the philosopher and, in *Broom of the System*, made him a central figure. For some discussions, see Marshall Boswell, *Understanding David Foster Wallace* (Columbia: University of South Carolina Press, 2003), 21–64; Lance Olsen, "Termite Art, or, Wallace's Wittgenstein," *Review of Contemporary Fiction* 12 (1993): 199–225.

five to Wallace's fiction, particularly *Infinite Jest*, the Wallace who will emerge will look somewhat less like the offbeat guru that he has sometimes appeared since his death, and somewhat more like a sharp-eyed social critic: less the lovable, Salinger-ish big brother than a firm public moralist and political observer. Again, however, none of this will mean that the disparate currents of his work neatly converge. Wallace's writing presents us with a cacophony of voices and lines of thought, with links between the texts growing audible one moment and fading away the next. He shares with the other authors here certain grave suspicions about nominalism and bald naturalism, but as with all of them, it is a thread made of many fibers, its strength residing not in the fact that some one fiber runs through its whole length, but in the overlapping of many of them. And in Wallace's case, there are many fibers indeed.[16]

I. Looking (Not Thinking!) and the Necessities That Are Not Logical

The first thread to disentangle is the relationship between Wallace's early intellectual commitments and his turn to Wittgenstein and Cavell. By the time Wallace entered Amherst College in 1980 and began to study philosophy, the ordinary language revolution that Cavell had championed in the 1950s and 1960s had given way to a cluster of research programs that, though sometimes hostile to certain pillars of Russell's and Frege's "ideal language philosophy," recalled their early-century commitment to rigorous systematization. As I noted in my discussions both of Percy and of Cavell, the 1960s saw the widening acceptance of Noam Chomsky's Universal Grammar, including among philosophers such as Jerrold Katz and Jerry Fodor. But the formalizing impulse is also noticeable in, for instance, Donald Davidson's influential work on formal semantics, which adapted Alfred Tarski's semantic theory of truth; the appearance of Richard Montague's essays, which sought to erase the difference between natural and artificial languages, comprehending them both within a single mathematically precise theory; David Lewis's account of counterfactuals and defense of strong modal realism; and the lectures that Saul Kripke would publish as *Naming and Necessity* (1980), a book whose theories of possible worlds and rigid designation constitute, according to one admirer, "one of the great philosophical achievements of the twentieth century," inspiring insights that "are now firmly

---

[16] See Wittgenstein, *Philosophical Investigations*, translated by G. E. M. Anscombe, P. M. S. Hacker, and Joachim Schulte (Oxford: Wiley-Blackwell, 2009), §67. Here and elsewhere I will be following the custom of citing *Philosophical Investigations* by numbered remark rather than page number.

entrenched in the formal and scientific study of language, in both linguistics and philosophy."[17] These programs were hardly all identical, but when commentators speak of "the demise of ordinary language philosophy," or discuss the return of philosophy as a *Fach* with a distinctive *Wissenschaft*, or refer to Austin and Ryle as members of an "utterly discredited" midcentury school, it is these kinds of figures that they have in mind.[18]

When the young Wallace discovered his aptitude for formal logic, he was well-positioned to benefit from these disciplinary shifts. Having grown up in the Midwest "inside vectors, lines and lines athwart lines, grids," he discovered that "math at a hilly Eastern school was like waking up" (*SFT* 3), and elsewhere he would characterize himself in these years as a "hard-core syntax wienie" who felt a "click" when doing logic, a "special sort of buzz," particularly when at the end of "a gorgeously simple solution to a problem you suddenly see half a notebook with gnarly attempted solutions." Writing to Markson in the early 1990s, he ascribed part of his attachment to Pynchon to his having come from a "scientific background," and declared that *Principia Mathematica* had been "my Bible as an undergraduate," an enthusiasm that explained his immersion at the time in the autobiography of Bertrand Russell, "of whom I am in awe."[19] More frequently he would identify his lodestone in these years as Wittgenstein's *Tractatus Logico-Philosophicus*, a "mind-bending work" whose adaptation of Russell's logic was in his eyes as remarkable as its enigmatic prose (*BFN* 86–88).

Wallace's attraction to philosophical logic is understandable for at least two related reasons. First, "clicks" and "solutions" suggests that part of his

---

[17] Scott Soames, *Philosophical Analysis in the Twentieth Century, Volume 2: the Age of Meaning* (Princeton, NJ: Princeton University Press, 2005), 456, 470. For the influence of Chomsky on analytic philosophy of language at this time, see Jerrold J. Katz, *Semantic Theory* (New York: Joanna Cotler Books, 1972) and Jerry Fodor, *The Language of Thought* (Cambridge, MA: Harvard University Press, 1972). (Katz and Fodor were also among the first to review Cavell's early work, a review Cavell mentions in *Little Did I Know*: "The Availability of What We Say," *Philosophical Review* 72 [1963]: 57–71.) For Davidson's theory of meaning, see essays 1–5 of his *Inquiries into Truth and Interpretation* (Oxford: Oxford University Press, 1984). Montague's most important papers were published posthumously in *Formal Philosophy*, ed. Richard H. Thomason (New Haven, CT: Yale University Press, 1974). For Lewis's views, see his *Counterfactuals* (Oxford: Blackwell, 1973).

[18] A.P. Martinich, "Introduction" to *A Companion to Analytic Philosophy*, ed. A.P. Martinich and David Sosa (Oxford: Blackwell, 2001), 3; Richard Rorty, "Keeping Philosophy Pure: An Essay on Wittgenstein," in *Consequences of Pragmatism: Essays 1972–1980* (Minneapolis: University of Minnesota Press, 1982), 20–21; Daniel C. Dennett, "Re-Introducing *The Concept of Mind*," in Gilbert Ryle, *The Concept of Mind* (London: Penguin, 2000), xiv. (The view of Ryle et al. as "utterly discredited" is, in fact, precisely the idea that Dennett's introduction is trying to combat.)

[19] Max, *Every Love Story*, 25. On reading Russell and the *Principia* as "my Bible," see the letter to Markson of April 21, 1991 (Harry Ransom Center, University of Texas). On coming from a "scientific background," see the letter to Markson on July 29, 1990 (Harry Ransom Center, University of Texas).

fascination was logic's search for deep necessity. "All bachelors are unmarried" and "Two plus two equals four" hold no matter what else is the case: their meaning and truth are noncontingent, independent of anyone's thoughts about the world. Second, this sense of strict necessity reflects logic's wholly abstract nature, its resemblance to what J. M. Bernstein calls the "visionless medium of pure mathematics."[20] Two and a half decades after "waking up" to logic, Wallace admitted when writing *Everything and More: A Compact History of Infinity* (2003), that "the ontology and grammar of abstractions have always struck me as one of the most breathtaking problems in human consciousness," and the topic is accordingly the subject of that book's long opening meditation.[21] Philosophical logic, he says there, asks us to move from concrete particulars to abstract concepts that name these particulars, and from there to higher-order reflection on concepts as such—and so on ever higher, an ascension that brings one to the "weirdest attributes" of the human mind and elicits an "inarticulable fuguelike strain" in one's thought. Similarly, mathematical concepts—primeness, say— are powerful precisely because they have "nothing to do with the world," only with "relations between numbers": their "lack of specific real-world referents" is what allows them to "yield maximum hygiene."[22]

Such fuguelike strains and indifference to the empirical world are often colorfully on display in the philosophical programs that captivated the young Wallace. At the heart of Lewis's strong modal realism, for instance, is an ontological equivalence between the way the physical world actually is and the way the physical world *might* have been. The latter constitutes a "possible world" other than the one we happen to inhabit, furnished by entities called "ways things could have been"—none of which, presumably, would be examinable in any actually operating laboratory. For his part, Kripke has insisted that the possible-world states that he defends should not be understood "purely descriptively, as if we were looking at them through a telescope," and has admitted that he doesn't "believe in a naturalist world view" or "materialism." He also has raised serious questions about whether computers can be said to embody mental functions: given that a material entity made of gears and wires can always malfunction, the question of whether its computations are correct is never something we can know with certainty from the machine alone.[23] If, as

---

[20] J. M. Bernstein, *Against Voluptuous Bodies: Late Modernism and the Meaning of Painting* (Stanford, CA: Stanford University Press, 2006), 123.

[21] Quoted in Max, *Every Love Story is a Ghost Story*, 274.

[22] See David Foster Wallace, *Everything and More: A Compact History of Infinity* (New York: Norton Books, 2003), 25, 22–23, 31.

[23] See David Lewis, "Possible Worlds," in *The Possible and the Actual: Readings in the Metaphysics of Modality*, ed. Michael J. Loux (Ithaca, NY: Cornell University Press, 1979), 182–89; Saul Kripke,

one famous commentator once put it, the questions of logic are not about contingent laws but about necessary laws, not how we *do* happen to think but how we *ought* to think, then Wallace's philosophical education had encouraged him to hold some very counterintuitive ideas indeed.[24]

At least that's what Wallace himself came to believe. It is a well-known piece of the Wallace lore that his early infatuation with philosophical logic led him to a dead end. At the philosophical level, the possible worlds deduced by philosophical logicians seemed to him increasingly narrow, ignoring relations of time and different types of physical possibility.[25] And at the personal level, the discipline left him feeling as if he were a "98.6 calculating machine" capable only of "coldly cerebral analytic math." It's also well-known that this crisis led him to the *Philosophical Investigations*—a book that he had initially found simply

---

Naming and Necessity (Cambridge, MA: Harvard University Press, 1980), 50; Saul Kripke, *Wittgenstein on Rules and Private Language* (Cambridge, MA: Harvard University Press, 1982), 32–37. On the relationship between Lewis and Kripke, see Scott Soames, "David Lewis's Place in Analytic Philosophy," in *David Lewis*, ed. Barry Loewer and Jonathan Schaffer (Oxford: Wiley, 2015), 80–98.

[24] Immanuel Kant, *Introduction to Logic; and His Essay on The Mistaken Subtilty of the Four Figures*, trans. Thomas Kingsmill Abbott (1800; London: Longman's, Green, and Co., 1885), 4.

[25] For Wallace's account of his "midlife crisis," see McCaffery, "A Conversation with David Foster Wallace." Wallace's dissatisfaction with the possible worlds debated by Lewis, Kripke, and other logician-philosophers of the period is most elaborately expressed in the thesis he wrote in philosophy at the end of college, which was titled "Richard Taylor's 'Fatalism' and Semantics of Physical Modality" and has been published in recent years as *Time, Fate, and Language*. The goal of the thesis is to challenge Richard Taylor's logical defense of fatalism, presented in his 1962 paper "Fatalism." If, Taylor argues, you're a naval captain, you probably think that the statement, "A naval battle will occur tomorrow," is one whose truth or falsity is within your power to determine, insofar as you can choose whether to order your fleet to start a battle. But analyzing the semantics of such sentences, and using a handful of standard logical rules, generates (Taylor says) a formal argument that concludes otherwise, and that, in fact, endorses outright fatalism. In making his response to this argument, Wallace deploys some of the insights of Kripke and Montague in particular, but with some serious revisions. Kripke and Montague, Wallace notes, deal only with *logical* modalities, which means that their possible "worlds" have only synchronic relations—that is, the philosophers are blind to the diachronic relations that are actually at stake in claims about fatalism. And he uses this revision to criticize Taylor's confusion between two types of *physical* possibility: physical possibility simpliciter (what is physically possible as such) and the more time- and place-sensitive notion of possibility that Wallace dubs "situational physical modalities." The laws of nature don't prevent me from touching the wall of the Amherst College chapel, but touching the chapel is possible *at this moment* only if I am standing in front of the chapel rather than, say, sitting at a desk in Illinois. It's this latter type of possibility, the kind where one's actual coordinates in time and space *matter*, that the young Wallace claims is relevant for assessing future-tensed statements. A question Wallace does not address in the thesis is whether Richard Taylor actually *believed* the fatalist argument he was developing. According to Steven M. Cahn, Taylor was not at all a fatalist, and believed that a future-tensed statement could *become* true with the passage of time, but is not *now* true. Thus the paper against which Wallace wrote was meant as "a reductio ad absurdum argument, assuming the truth of his opponent's position, showing its unacceptable consequences, and thereby demonstrating its falsity" (*FTL* 38). Such a view presents Taylor as a kind of latter-day Kierkegaard working through "indirect communication," and suggests a literary dimension of Taylor's argument that Wallace the budding novelist would likely have appreciated.

"silly" but which, as commentators have shown, undergirds *The Broom of the System*, a frantic Pynchonian mystery novel about the granddaughter of one of Wittgenstein's protégés.[26] But we shouldn't misrepresent this turn to the later Wittgenstein. Wallace's rejection of philosophical logic was hardly linear, after all: as his letter to Markson suggests, long after college he remained "in awe" of Russell, who bemoaned Wittgenstein's post-*Tractatus* work, and in later years Wallace wrote *Everything and More*, a book that testifies to a continuing interest in high-level formal systems. But more importantly, reading the *Investigations* clearly didn't lead Wallace to jettison everything that originally had drawn him to mathematics and logic. What changed as Wallace matured was not a pursuit of the deep necessities that logic had promised, but his conviction that the visionless medium of logic and mathematics is the most legitimate means of finding it. The later Wittgenstein, in other words, offered him not a way to refuse "solutions" and "clicks," but an alternative understanding of where they might be heard.

The hallmark of the *Investigations* is its turn away from theories about our words and toward the particular worldly settings within which words are embedded. "Don't think, but look!" Wittgenstein famously cries at one point (§66), a plea that ushers from his sense that he is "talking about the spatial and temporal phenomenon of language, not about some non-spatial, non-temporal phantasm" (§108). Accordingly, some of the most celebrated images in the book reflect this challenge to the *Tractatus*: the straight regular streets that fill the new boroughs of our language, so starkly different from the maze of roads and squares elsewhere (§18); or the "slippery ice" of logic, its "perfect" smoothness preventing us from walking (§107); or the "rails invisibly laid to infinity" that we imagine a mathematical series to be (§218).[27] But what emerges from this turn toward the "rough ground"—how we use and explain numbers or colors, how we talk about 'games" or 'reading" or "being guided," how we use the verb "to know," how we follow a signpost, how we direct someone to stand

---

[26] See, for example, James Ryerson's introduction to David Foster Wallace, *Time, Fate, and Language: An Essay on Free Will*, ed. Steven M. Cahn and Maureen Eckert (New York: Columbia University Press, 2010); Boswell, *Understanding David Foster Wallace*, chap. 2. As Wallace explained to one correspondent, the grandmother of *Broom* was based on Alice Ambrose, a philosopher who taught at Smith College, near Amherst, and who had studied with Wittgenstein in the 1930s (Ryerson 19). For Wallace's assessment of the *PI* as "silly," see Ryerson's introduction, 4.

[27] One thinks also of the "despotic demand" that leads philosophers to venerate "the hardness of the logical must" (§437). Compare Austin's warning to philosophers against the *ivresse des grands profondeurs*, which leads them to obsess over majestic abstractions like "doing an action" rather than reflect on humble distinctions between sneezing, breathing, moving one's fingers, and posting a letter. See J. L. Austin, *Philosophical Papers*, ed. J.O. Urmson and G.J. Warnock (Oxford: Oxford University Press, 1961), 179.

in a certain place, how we recognize when someone is in pain—is far from a nominalist flux. We see rather that our everyday language, seemingly so loose and untidy, *can* and *does* exhibit a reliable degree of sense, and that a certain kind of realism—what I have been calling "weak realism"—is warranted. The "relations" internal to formal systems are not the only momentary stays against confusion. With proper attention, they also can be identified in the unhygienic world of everyday talk, in our habits of naming, and in our social practices.

Precisely this attention to the *sense* of the worldly and the everyday is, as we've seen, what captivates Cavell, whose work begins from the claim that, as he puts it, not all necessities are logical. When, for instance, a native speaker asks whether we dressed a certain way "voluntarily," we just *know* that he or she is issuing an insult or questioning our taste, not asking us to explain our views about free will.[28] Similarly, Cavell admires Wittgenstein's aphorisms and remarks because they exhibit the qualities of a formal proof, expressing "completeness, pleasure, the sense of breaking something off. . . words that epitomize, separate a thought, with finish and permanence, from the general range of experience."[29] And it's this worldly, engaged sense of our mutual intelligibility and shared engagement with the world that, in turn, makes Cavell so attractive to Wallace. For both of them, Wittgenstein allows us to survey the rough ground of our linguistic and cultural life: to grasp how we understand each other in practice, and to understand the various media in which such understanding is expressed.

In the next sections, I'll be highlighting several crucial differences between Cavell and Wallace, but for now, let me isolate four commonalities. The first is visible in the simple fact that Wallace's disappointment with formal logic led him to writing fiction and, eventually, criticism. As in Cavell, that is, the necessities that are not logical came for Wallace to be associated most palpably and profoundly with artworks. Artworks don't represent all that logic or mathematics are not: they aren't some non- or antilogical type of thought—some cauldron of passion, desire, or nonverbal affective "intensities." They represent instead an alternative means to the same kinds of achievement. What draws Cavell and Wallace are the normative dimensions of artistic works: the particular sense of *rightness* that they elicit, how a certain turn of phrase yields just

---

[28] Stanley Cavell, *Must We Mean What We Say?* (Cambridge: Cambridge University Press, 1976), 10–11. The voice of formal systems in this early essay is Benson Mates, a senior colleague of Cavell's at Berkeley, and a student of the logician Alfred Tarski who had questioned some of the premises of ordinary language philosophy.

[29] Stanley Cavell, "The *Investigations'* Everyday Aesthetics of Itself," in *The Literary Wittgenstein*, ed. John Gibson and Wolfgang Huemer (London: Routledge, 2004), 29.

the correct description of a given thing, or how a certain musical note sounds perfect at a particular point. The challenge comes when we want to characterize this nonarbitrary quality, and when, without the comforts of a formal proof, we want to persuade others to feel our conviction about it.

Cavell's way of talking about such conviction is not only, as I just noted, to refer to the powers of aphorism, but also to speak of "composition": a know-how that makes use of what his mother called "secrets" and which his father embodied in the "timing" and "knack" of his stories. Wallace, in a similar vein, said that the "click" he felt when doing logic was gradually replaced by the "click" he felt when reading or writing fiction.[30] He first felt it, he said, when reading Donald Barthelme's "The Balloon" as a college student, and a few years after this Barthelme-click, David Lynch's film *Blue Velvet* similarly "rang cherries" for him at a crucial moment, presenting itself as a "revelation" at a moment when his own fiction had started to seem to him "solipsistic and pretentious and self-conscious and masturbatory and bad." Lynch's film "felt *true, real*," "captured something crucial about the way the U.S. present operated on our nerve endings, something crucial that couldn't be analyzed or reduced to a system of codes or aesthetic principles or workshop techniques," and the vibrant debate that it engendered among his friends after their first viewing of it was a turning point in his conception of art's distinctive powers (*SFT* 200–201). In later years Wallace would speak in comparable ways about Kafka, whose short stories he would compare to jokes, another form that depends upon the proper use of "exformation": information that is withheld but can be evoked "in such a way as to cause a kind of explosion of associative connections within the recipient," making their impact "sudden and percussive, like the venting of a long-stuck valve" (*CL* 61).[31] Even, that is, in the most experimental traditions—traditions to which Wallace remained committed throughout his life—one finds moments of intelligibility, and when they arrive, they don't come through a set of axioms and theorems.

---

[30] "Click" is Wallace's term in his 1993 interview with McCaffery: http://www.dalkeyarchive.com/a-conversation-with-david-foster-wallace-by-larry-mccaffery/ (accessed September 26, 2014).

[31] In his introduction to the 2007 *Best American Essays* collection, Wallace returns to the theme of aesthetic judgment, and in ways that echo the remarks from Cavell that I note in the next paragraph: "Press either R. Atwan [the editor who whittled down a year's worth of essays into a manageable range of candidates for inclusion in the volume] or D. Wallace hard enough on any of our criteria or reasons—what they mean or where they come from—and you'll eventually get either paralyzed silence or the abysmal, Legionish babble of every last perceived fact and value" (*BFN* 307). Either *nothing* relevant can be said because your fellow audience member just understands the work with you, or *everything* is potentially relevant to an explanation.

A second point of contact between Cavell and Wallace is that, beyond art-works, such "clicks" and necessities are often understood in terms of the human voice, with all its inflections, invitations, and local circumstances of use. As Wallace noted in his copy of *In Quest of the Ordinary*, this issue has long put Cavell at odds with Derrida, who famously associates voice with "presence," that is, self-consciousness, completeness of intention, full control over one's words, hence full self-knowledge—all qualities that are allegedly put in question by "writing," a medium that illustratively severs inscription from intention. For Cavell, by contrast, if you've been told by your philosophy professors that genu-ine meaning is possible only in an artificial language, a language that would negate the contingencies of time and place, and if you're told that genuine knowledge is what's found in the propositions of formal logic and mathemat-ics, then the messy, uncertain, all-too-human activities of improvised everyday *talk* might actually come to seem a model of un- or antimetaphysical think-ing. Metaphysics, he writes, has in the Anglophone tradition largely "depended upon the suppression of the human voice," and it is "as the recovery of this voice (as from an illness) that ordinary language philosophy is . . . before all to be understood."[32]

A comparable "recovery" marks Wallace's work. In the 1980s he grew so enamored of Derrida's writing that he would pretentiously pester his fellow MFA students in Arizona about whether they had read him, but his mature work is defined by a Cavellian feel for everyday talk, what DeLillo in a tribute to Wallace described as the "offsetting breeze" of his "plainsong," an address that is "youthful, unstudied," and marked "by the small odd sentence that wan-ders in off the street."[33] "Language needs to find new ways to pull the reader," Wallace observed to Lipsky. "And my personal belief is a lot of it has to do with voice, and a feeling of intimacy between the writer and the reader. That sorta, given the atomization and loneliness of contemporary life—that's our open-ing, and that's our gift."[34] In his nonfiction, this "gift" is most audible in the breathlessly long sentences, where the colloquial and theoretical impishly com-mingle, subjects and verbs are scruffily distanced from one another, and heaps

---

[32] See Stanley Cavell, "The Politics of Interpretation (Politics as Opposed to What?)," in *Themes Out of School: Effects and Causes* (San Francisco: North Point Press, 1984), 48.

[33] Don DeLillo, "Informal Remarks From the David Foster Wallace Memorial Service in New York on October 23, 2008," in *The Legacy of David Foster Wallace* (ed. Cohen and Konstantinou), 23. According to Max's *Every Love Story*, Wallace discovered Derrida in a literary theory course in college (38). On his use of Derrida to intimidate his fellow MFA students, see Max, *Every Love Story*, 56–57, which includes Wallace's retrospective characterization of himself in these years: "I was a prick."

[34] Lipsky, *Although Of Course You End Up Becoming Yourself*, 72.

of conjunctions evoke the excitable mind of someone who can't get the words out fast enough—as in this attempt to summarize a moment from a Lynch film:

> And but so when Balthazar Getty's new blue-collar incarnation of Bill Pullman and Patricia Arquette's apparent blond incarnation of Bill Pullman's wife make eye-contact, sparks are generated on a scale that lends the hackneyed "I-feel-I-know-you-from-somewhere" component of erotic attraction whole new fresh layers of creepy literality. (*SFT* 159)[35]

In the mature fiction, a sense of voice arises in the recurrent use of the second person among Wallace's narrators—"Forever Overhead," the title stories in *Brief Interviews with Hideous Men* (1999), "Good Old Neon"—but even with a more traditional third-person perspective, the texts are attuned to the fits and starts and eloquence of ordinary speech. Sometimes this comes across in dialogue, as when, here, commas and subjects are elided to suggest the slangy banter of adolescent boys reviewing a grueling tennis practice:

> 'Because so that was let's see,' Struck says. . . . 'Close to let's call it an hour run for the A-squads, an hour-fifteen drills, two matches back to back.'
>
> 'I only played one,' Troeltsch injects. 'Had a measurable fever in the A.M., [Coach] de Lint said to throttle down today.'
>
> 'Folks that went three sets only played one match, Spodek and Kent for instance,' Stice says.
>
> 'Funny how Troeltsch how his health always seems to rally when A.M. drills get out,' Freer says.[36]

At other times it is heard in free indirect discourse, a mode that replicates in miniature *Infinite Jest*'s dense confluence of voices, registers, and dialects—as in this hilarious malaprop-filled moment when Randy Lenz, a resident at a drug recovery house, walks manically with another house resident through Boston,

---

[35] Elsewhere in the essays the voice is audible in the markers of time and place that habitually appear near the start of Wallace's essays, a practice that recalls Cavell's remark about Austin's "tirelessly demanding the context (he would often call it the story) of an utterance" (*LDIK* 60). "Right now," Wallace writes at the start of one essay, "it's 1:00 Saturday, 22 July 1995, on the Stadium Court of the Stade Jarry tennis complex in Montreal" (*SFT* 213); "The occasion for this article," he begins another, "is Oxford University Press's recent release of Mr. Bryan A. Garner's *A Dictionary of Modern American Usage*. . .that it is my assigned function to review" (*CL* 67–68).

[36] Wallace, *Infinite Jest* (Boston: Back Bay, 1996), 103; henceforth cited parenthetically as *IJ*.

hoping both to flaunt his worldliness and to hide the fact that he's been snort-
ing cocaine:

> Lenz tells Green how once he was at a Halloween party where a hydroce-
> phalic woman wore a necklace made of dead gulls.
>
> Lenz shares about this recurring dream where he's seated under a tropic
> ceiling fan in a cane chair wearing an L.L. Bean safari hat and holding a
> wickerware valise in his lap, and that's all, that's the recurring dream.
>
> On the 400 block of W. Beacon, . . . Lenz demonstrates for Bruce Green
> the secret akido 1-2 with which he'd demapped [a vendor], breaking the
> move down into slo-mo constituent movements so that Green's untrained
> eye could follow. He says there's another recurring nightmare about a clock
> with hands frozen eternally at 1830 that's so trouser-foulingly scary he
> won't even burden Green's fragile psychology with the explicits of it. (558)

Given Wallace's commitment to voice, it's only fitting that the most exemplary
artworks of *Jest* are the long spoken monologues of the radio DJ Madame
Psychosis, whose "outlook on the universe" seems "unironic but generally
gloomy," and whose hypnotic speech projects a "compelling beauty and light"
that recalls the "short short stories" of Cavell's improvising father: "You can
never predict what it will be, but over time some kind of pattern emerges, a
trend or rhythm" that "suggests expansion without really expanding," leading
up "to the exact kind of inevitability that it denies" (*IJ* 190-91).

A third affinity between Cavell and Wallace is how often they associate the
necessities that are not logical with states of absorption. As I argued in the last
chapter, the absorptive themes in Cavell become visible when we recall his close
association with the art historian Michael Fried, for whom "absorption" contrasts with "theatricality," and designates a state in which the agent depicted in
a painting is oblivious to everything except the task being performed, including the painting's beholder. In Cavell's memoir this dynamic appears most
obviously in the repeated images of musicians and artists immersed in their
work, but it's also expressed in the image of the writer himself, turned intently
inward—a diarist whose writing is only partly directed at us readers, the inser-
tions and extenuations of his prose following a movement of mood rather than
strict argument.

Absorption likewise punctuates Wallace's work, and two forms are particularly
prominent. The first—following up what I've just said about voice—is the act of
listening. As critics have often noted, some of the most crucial and vivid scenes
of *Infinite Jest* are its Alcoholics Anonymous (AA) meetings, where new attendees

are asked to "just sit there and listen as hard as you can" (*IJ* 343), to aim for "total empathy" and "identification" with the speaker, and to avoid the impulse to "compare" your experience with his or hers—to avoid, in essence, treating oneself theatrically, as a performer on stage next to others.[37] But beyond AA, listening is also the fundamental activity of Mario Incandenza, whose favorite moments in the day are the nightly broadcasts of Madame Psychosis: "opting for mono and sitting right up close to one of the speakers with his head cocked dog-like, . . . staring into that special pocket of near-middle distance reserved for the serious listener" (*IJ* 189). The significance of such states becomes even clearer when we come to *The Pale King*, Wallace's unfinished novel, where a man describes listening to a Jesuit priest lecture one night on the unrecognized heroism of accountancy, on the courage needed to "care" for "each detail from within the teeming worm-ball of data and rule and exception and contingency," and the fact that this task "is *a priori* incompatible with audience or applause or even the bare notice of the common run of man" (*PK* 233)—a lecture that transforms the young man from a nihilistic, pot-smoking, "wastoid" TV addict to a responsible civil servant.[38]

The other recurrent form of Cavellian absorption in Wallace's work is tennis, as it is undertaken by the serious player and watched by the knowledgeable observer. *Infinite Jest* is set, in part, at a tennis academy for high school students, and Coach Schtitt, the head trainer at the institute, is said to differ from most trainers insofar as he approached competitive tennis not as one of the "problem-solving statistical-data wonks" but a speculative wise man who understands that tennis is about "*not*-order, *limit*, the places where things broke down, fragmented into beauty" (*IJ* 81–82). Much of Wallace's own youth was spent chasing such beauty, which required entering a "kind of fugue-state" when playing, "where your concentration telescopes toward a still point and you lose awareness of your limbs and the soft shush of your shoe's slide . . . and whatever's outside the lines of the court" (*SFT* 18–19). It is a state, he says in a 1994 essay on the teenage star Tracy Austin, in which a top athlete is "totally present," when he

---

[37] Thus, for instance, the turning point for the cocaine addict Joelle comes when listening to one of the "Commitment" speakers at an AA meeting tell his life story, and when, unlike earlier in the book, she doesn't detach herself to disparage his shoddy grammar or criticize AA's "banal shibboleths and robotic piety," but instead lets "her eyes feel sandy from forgetting to blink," captivated by the man's unpretentious, harrowing narration of loss and failure (*IJ* 706–10).

[38] Absorption is likewise displayed in Chapter 46, during a conversation between an IRS employee and her colleague, the latter of whom attends intently to her long personal story "like he was merely absorbing information and adding it to himself" (*PK* 506), until, like a wise man of old, he actually levitates from the barroom chair.

or she "can proceed on instinct and muscle-memory and autonomic will such that agent and action are one," and can "withstand forces of distraction that would break a mind prone to self-conscious fear in two" (*CL* 154). "The sort of thinking involved" in tennis, he says in an essay on another professional, Michael Joyce, would stupefy even the most powerful computers, and makes it "a kind of art" (*SFT* 236), one whose "transcendent practitioner" must develop a "radical compression of . . .attention and self" (*SFT* 254). It is "the most beautiful sport there is, and also the most demanding," requiring "body control, hand-eye coordination, quickness, flat-out speed, endurance, and that strange mix of caution and abandon [that] we call courage" (*SFT* 235). No one has ever been more transcendent, suggests his last tennis essay, than Roger Federer, watching whom, Wallace says, raises "our awareness of how glorious it is to touch and perceive, move through space, interact with matter" (*BFN* 8), and whose "power and aggression made vulnerable to beauty" leaves the audience "inspired and (in a fleeting, mortal way) reconciled" (*BFN* 33).

"Even more illuminating than watching pro tennis live," Wallace writes late in the essay on Michael Joyce, "is watching it with Sam Aparicio, Joyce's coach, who knows as much about tennis as anybody I've talked to and isn't obnoxious about it," and who "helps you see things you can't see alone" (*SFT* 253). And this brings us to a fourth and final analogy between Wallace and Cavell: that the Wittgensteinian attention to worldly practices, the emphasis they place on voice and absorption, are all closely tied to the appearance of mentors, companions, fellow speakers. One's actions and ideals are shaped, writes Cavell, less by the "ought" of law or principle than by "a form of attraction, the relation to the friend," and this challenge to Kantian and utilitarian forms of moral abstraction finds its place in *Little Did I Know* in the philosopher's intimate relationships with friends such as Fried, Thomas Kuhn, and Thompson Clarke—people with whom he has had a capacity for "shared testing" (*LD* 407) and who have offered him an intimacy that is not, as he says elsewhere, "politicalized" (*MWM* 54).

In Wallace such shared testing can appear in chance encounters— meeting Sam the tennis coach—but also in the various companions who are regularly seen around the edges of the essays: the friends who debate *Blue Velvet*, the woman who joins him at the Illinois State Fair, the family and friends who accompany him to the Maine Lobster Festival or the Adult Video News awards show. But his most dramatic embodiments of companionship appear in *Infinite Jest*, whose two central settings—E.T.A., the tennis academy, and Ennet House, the recovery home—are places of trust and conversation, of characters who, in Cavell's terms, "manifest for the other another way."[39] The dialogue I cited earlier between Struck and Troeltsch about their exhausting afternoon practice typifies the camaraderie that runs through the scenes in the E.T.A. locker rooms and dormitories, and reminds us of how regularly Wallace's work envisions schools as crucial sites of character-formation.[40] Likewise, some of the most powerful passages in the Ennet House scenes describe the mutual admiration that develops between Don Gately, a resident who becomes part of the institution's staff, and Pat, the director of the rehab program. And it's both moving and wholly convincing when the residents of the house scramble outside to intervene to help Gately, caught one night in an altercation in the front yard. Indeed, this fight scene even yields the closest the novel comes to an expression of romantic love, as Gately, woozily admiring Joelle as she treats a gunshot wound to his shoulder, suddenly recognizes that she is, in fact, the DJ Madame Psychosis: "Gately's smile has reached his eyes. 'You're Madame on the FM, is how I knew you.... I knew I knew you. . . Boy do I know guys loved that show you did'" (IJ 619). All this is to say nothing of the most durable companions in the book, the elderly AA sponsors known as "Crocodiles," who preside over the AA meetings like a Greek chorus and who tutor the beleaguered, recovering Gately. In a novel that so unflaggingly investigates the phenomenology of lonely addiction, that treats solipsism and self-consciousness with such profound seriousness, that is not afraid to veer into the macabre and even the grotesquely violent, these various images of dyadic companionship stand out, and seem Wallace's own answer to his famous call for writing that would risk sentimentality and softness, that would "treat of plain old untrendy human troubles and emotions in U.S. life with reverence and conviction" (SFT 81). The absence of manipulation in these relationships, and the sheer pleasure that they afford in the face of horror, is clearly meant as a model for our own relationship with Wallace's book, and is surely one reason why it has won such fierce loyalty among its readers.

II. Portrait of the Artist as a Young *Zoon Politikon*

Earlier I observed that Wallace enrolled in a graduate seminar with Cavell, and I used this as an indication of sympathy for the philosopher's work—a sympathy

---

[39] Stanley Cavell, *Conditions Handsome and Unhandsome: The Constitution of Emersonian Perfectionism* (Chicago: University of Chicago Press, 1989), 31.

[40] See, for example, "The Soul Is Not a Smithy" or "Good Old Neon," both in *Oblivion* (Boston: Little, Brown, and Company, 2004).

that I've just now been tracking through portions of his work. What I've deferred noting, however, is just how sour Cavell's seminar left him. According to Max, Wallace found Cavell to encourage a fawning attitude among his students, and to speak only to himself and his initiates. One fellow student remembers a frustrated Wallace, a "snarl" on his face, interrupting Cavell to ask him to "make himself intelligible please," and another member of the class recalls encountering Wallace after one of their seminars, collapsing on a couch in the philosophy department lounge and wondering whether he would ever manage to understand what Cavell was talking about. It wasn't too long, it seems, before Wallace simply stopped attending.[41]

Once again the marginalia in Wallace's library underscores these reports. The introduction of his copy of *Pursuits of Happiness* may be heavily underlined, as I noted earlier, but the markings stop on page twenty-five, and there's no sign that Wallace read a line of Cavell's analyses of any particular film. And though "Being Odd, Getting Even" gets keen attention in Wallace's copy of *In Quest of the Ordinary*, his annotations grow increasingly ironic the further he reads. When, for instance, one of Cavell's sentences indulges even more than usual in the first-person singular, Wallace underlines the several appearances of "I" and quips in the margins, "He exists, that Stanley." When, a couple pages later, Cavell identifies a connection between skepticism and melodrama, Wallace pithily summarizes the point in the margins ("Melodrama—fiction's favorite threat to forms of marriage"), but when Cavell concludes his claim by remarking, "This is said on tiptoe," Wallace finds him precious: "This is cool and irritating." And when Cavell loquaciously explains, in the opening sentences of a later essay in the book, that he has taken the opportunity to "fit together into some reasonable, or say convivial, circle a collection of the main beasts in my jungle or wilderness of interests," Wallace charges him with simple narcissism: "Very American—He cannot speak but of himself." This is the final annotation in the book.[42]

---

[41] Max discusses Wallace's time at Harvard—not only his seminar with Cavell, but also a class with John Rawls and Wallace's strained relationship with his grad student cohort—in *Every Love Story*, 132–34. The memory of Wallace flopped on a couch is from the musicologist Dmitri Tymoczko, who sheepishly continues: "Taking pity on a lost soul, I deigned to translate a few of Cavell's sentences into ordinary English. ('It's just a language,' I said; 'you get used to it eventually.') The student, I am embarrassed to say, was David Foster Wallace, perhaps the most brilliant writer of his generation and certainly one of Cavell's most original and interesting descendants." See Dmitri Tymoczko, "Dear Stanley," *Journal of Music Theory* 54 (2010), 7. Wallace's father James describes his son's experience at Harvard this way: "The students did their professors' laundry and clustered around them, and he thought it was just ridiculous. He was a published author and expected to be treated as an equal" (Max 314).

[42] The remarks that I've cited in this paragraph are found on pages 128, 130, and 158 of Wallace's copy of Cavell's *In Quest of the Ordinary*.

These annotations push us to reflect on the differences between Wallace and Cavell—differences in interest and inclination that get shortchanged if, as I've been doing, we fixate on their commonalities. It's these differences that will interest me in this and the next section, both of which unpack the various ways that Wallace responds to the questions I raised at the end of Chapter 4: namely, what's overlooked in Cavell's emphasis on dyadic relations, and what's lost in his avoidance of the specifically contemporary world.

As a way into this issue, let me return to Wittgenstein and the particular escape from formal philosophy that he offered both Cavell and Wallace. Both men were puzzled at first by the philosopher's later work—Wallace, as I've noted, found the *Investigations* merely "silly" at first, whereas Cavell thought it was just an "unsystematic pragmatism."[43] But when they warmed up to the book, they understood it in markedly different terms. Competing interpretations of Wittgenstein may seem like an arcane point of entry here, a way of overemphasizing intellectual as opposed to psychological, generational, or historical differences. But both Cavell and Wallace make it tough to distinguish what is and what isn't an "intellectual" problem, and their vying perceptions are a way of drawing attention to other influences and tendencies that readers have generally failed to appreciate.

Cavell's memoir, as I argued in my last chapter, challenges what it sees as two misleading conceptions of language and human action. One is a formalistic habit of focusing on the rules, syntax, and other structural aspects of language, and the other suggests that any language use outside of logic, math, and science is just random activity, a matter of sounds and reactions occurring without any purposive guidance or genuine meaning. Against these pictures, Cavell understands language as a form of improvisatory know-how, a fragile and moment-to-moment performance—something he claims to find in' *Philosophical Investigations*. Wittgenstein's late writing, he says in an early essay, is governed by the idea that language "does not, in fact or essence, depend upon" a well-defined "structure and conception of rules, and yet that the absence of such a structure in no way impairs its functioning" (*MWM* 48). Such a reading emphasizes the literary qualities of Wittgenstein's writing, its baffling layers of voices and moods, and eventually finds expression in the memoir that Cavell writes late in his life, with its emphasis on "surprise" and its refusal of the idea that writing entails "unfolding implications."

A different Wittgenstein—more systematic, more thesis-bound, more conventionally philosophical—emerges in Wallace's writing. A hint of this image

[43] See the interview "Stanley Cavell in Conversation with Paul Standish," *Journal of Philosophy of Education* 46 (2012), 156.

is found already in his undergraduate philosophy thesis on fatalism, when he dismisses the notion that appeals to ordinary language could offer strong arguments against fatalism. The ordinary language philosopher, says the undergraduate Wallace, is concerned with "how we use language in ordinary ways," "*sociological* claims" that do not actually touch the true fatalist, since he or she probably believes that our everyday talk is "in need of some metaphysically-motivated revision" (*FTL* 154–55, emphasis mine). A few years later, this "sociological" theme is implicit in Wallace's review of Markson's novel when he says that the major task of *Philosophical Investigations* is to show that "the existence, nay the very *idea* of language depends on some sort of communicative *community*"—an idea that constitutes, he says, "the most powerful philosophical attack on skeptic-/solipsism's basic coherence since the Descartes whose *Cogito* Wittgenstein had helped to skewer" (*BFN* 109). A few years still later, in a 1993 interview, Wallace reiterates the point when he praises the later Wittgenstein—his "conclusions seem completely sound to me, always have"—but suggests that the *Investigations* leads us to the same quicksand as post-1960s literary theory. The older Wittgenstein, he says there, shows that language "must always be a function of relationships between persons," but though this makes language "dependent on human community," we are unfortunately, he says,

> still stuck with the idea that there is this world of referents out there that we can never really join or know because we're stuck in here, in language, even if we're at least all in here together. . . . If the world is itself a linguistic construct, there's nothing "outside" language for language to have to picture or refer to. This lets you avoid solipsism, but it leads right to the postmodern, post-structural dilemma of having to deny yourself an existence independent of language.[44]

And six years later, in a seemingly less anxious tone, he writes in "Authority and American Usage," a long review of a book on modern language use, that "language is by its very nature public," clarifying his point with a lengthy footnote that once again emphasizes the sociological dimension of Wittgenstein's thought:

> [As] Mr. L. Wittgenstein's *Philosophical Investigations* proved in the 1950s, words actually have the meanings they do because of certain rules and verification tests that are imposed on us from outside our own subjectivities,

---

[44] See McCafferey, "A Conversation with David Foster Wallace."

viz., by the community in which we have to get along and communicate with other people. Wittgenstein's argument centers on the fact that a word like *tree* means what it does for me because of the way the community I'm part of has tacitly agreed to use *tree*. (*CL* 87)

Such statements do more than offer a different picture of Wittgenstein than that conjured by Cavell. They articulate the exact view that Cavell's interpretation of Wittgenstein is designed to dismantle. From Cavell's point of view, to treat the *Investigations* as a high-level work of sociological theory—to insist on the primacy of "the public," or that language is "imposed upon us from outside our own subjectivities"—is to treat "the community" as if such an entity were singular, clearly bounded, and fully knowledgeable about its own words. It is to exaggerate the agreement between speakers, to overlook what Cavell calls our continual *disappointment* with our shared criteria, and thus to reintroduce, in a sociological or cultural form, the surprise-less systems of the formal semanticist. That I continually get into muddles, that I grow unsure how to project my words, is the main reason why suprapersonal entities such as "language" or "community" hardly ever even appear in Cavell, and when they do, they are pictured as fundamentally vulnerable, fragile things. Our shared language emerges, he writes in an early essay, within a "whirl of organism," a flurry of human activity and speech that allows nothing to be "insured" and which is as "difficult" to recognize "as it is (and because it is) terrifying" (*MWM* 52). In the opening chapters of *The Claim of Reason*, this lack of insurance appears in his sense of being "at odds with those who understand Wittgenstein to begin with, or to assert thesis-wise, the publicness of language, never seriously doubting it, and in that way to favor common sense."[45] To the extent that we share our words, they are shared like "pitches and tones, or clocks, or weighing scales, or columns of figures": entities that require constant attention, care, and monitoring if they are ever to function harmoniously. Wittgenstein is indeed motivated, Cavell notes, by a "perception of the attunement of one human being's words with those of others," but "another part of his motivation"—dramatized most vividly in the intrusive questions of his interlocutor—"is a perception that they sometimes are out of tune, that they do not agree." Appeals to shared criteria do not settle facts in any ordinary sense. They put our isolation on display, and are made when our "separate counts and out-calls of phenomena" no longer seem to have the "assurance of conventions" (*CR* 32–36).

---

[45] Stanley Cavell, *The Claim of Reason: Wittgenstein, Skepticism, Morality, and Tragedy* (New York: Oxford University Press, 1979); hereafter cited parenthetically as *CR*.

Wallace, by contrast, reads *Philosophical Investigations* as a straightforwardly argumentative text, something that "proves" how words get their meanings, and in the process he planes away most of the literary qualities that draw Cavell. This may be a curious strategy for a novelist, but it chimes with a longstanding and powerful tradition of Wittgenstein interpretation. In particular, it allows Wallace to stress Wittgenstein's affinities with what John Haugeland has wittily called "socialist phenomenology." From such a perspective, claims Haugeland, the "fundamental pattern" relevant to discussions of meaning and intention are found not in the individual's brain or body, but in "a culture or way of life, with all its institutions, artifacts, and mores," where "ritual objects, customary performances, and tools . . .occupy determined niches within the social fabric," and these niches "define" them as what they are. What matters in this view is how the "mutual attraction among the behavioral dispositions of the different community members" generates a robust sense of normativity, enabling everything from chess and conversation to social customs and legal systems.[46]

Such an interpretation of Wittgenstein has long been defended by social scientists.[47] But it also recalls the orthodox reading of his work that developed among philosophers in the 1950s and 1960s, when commentators such as Norman Malcolm—to name just one of the figures whose reading of Wittgenstein is rebuked in *The Claim of Reason*—argued that the fundamental aim in the later Wittgenstein is to undermine skepticism. According to this line of argument, we usually take inner states like "pain" to be something that I know about "immediately," as a visceral something-or-other inaccessible to anyone else; but Wittgenstein shows that the concept of "pain" is learned in a public setting, not on my own but as part of a custom instilled by my family and society; therefore (this orthodox argument continues) my "inner" or "private" life is knowable not through language-less "introspection," but through our linguistico-cultural training, which establishes the shared criteria for the

---

[46] John Haugeland, "The Intentionality All-Stars," in *Having Thought: Essays in the Metaphysics of Mind* (Cambridge, MA: Harvard University Press, 1998), 147–49. The conceit of Haugeland's essay is that positions in the philosophy of mind can be imagined as positions on a baseball field, with "neo-Cartesians" (Fodor, Hartry Field) at first base, "neo-behaviorists" (Daniel Dennett, W. V. O. Quine) at second base, and "neo-pragmatists"—his other name for "socialist phenomenology"—at third base. Haugeland's leading third-basemen are Martin Heidegger, Wilfrid Sellars, and Robert Brandom; he also indicates (166) that this is where his own sympathies lie. Presumably as a testament to both to Wittgenstein's stature and the difficulty of aligning him with any clear position, Haugeland pauses in his survey of the infield to submit the simple sentence: "Wittgenstein might have been a shortstop" (147).

[47] See, for instance, the work of David Bloor, Jeff Coulter, Christopher C. Robinson, and Gavin Kitching.

application of our words.[48] As Wallace sums up the idea (recalling, perhaps, some memories of his own teenage years), "if I am an angst-ridden adolescent pot-smoker who believes that there's no way I can verify that what I mean by *tree* is what anybody else means by *tree*," then "*tree* has ceased really to 'mean' anything at all," because I have no way of knowing whether *I myself* am using the term in a way that's consistent with my own definition (*CL* 87–88). Both the Cavellian Wittgenstein and the communitarian Wittgenstein appeal, against the logician, to the manifest world of embodied creatures, to our temporal and contingent social practices rather than the abstract realm of logical relations. The difference between them is that (1) on the communitarian interpretation that Wallace favors, this manifest world comprises a much more diffuse, extended set of associations and social phenomena; and (2) on this communitarian picture, appeals to such social practices are definitive and conclusive, a form of assurance that determines once and for all what one means when one says something.

If, then, despite one commentator's claim, a "late-Wittgensteinian faith in language as a public phenomenon" is precisely what Wallace could *not* have found in Cavell's work, where exactly did he pick up his reading of Wittgenstein?[49] Why, for all his affinities with Cavell, would he have remained unmoved by, or simply not have noticed, the philosopher's literarily sensitive account of the *Investigations*? And what would have shaped his understanding of the later Wittgenstein ("Wittgenstein's conclusions seem completely sound to me, always have") for it to remain so conventionally communitarian?

An answer comes, I think, if we consider a philosophical elder other than Cavell, a figure often overlooked in discussions of Wallace, but with whom he had a far more intimate relationship—who even, in fact, first introduced him to philosophy as a teenager. This is the elder who earns a footnote in the review of Markson, when Wallace cites an authority characterizing Wittgenstein as "this clearheaded & intellectually honest man" who "was hopelessly at odds with himself." "Dr. James D. Wallace," reads the footnote, "unpublished response

---

[48] Malcolm's reading of Wittgenstein is summarized in his essay "Wittgenstein's *Philosophical Investigations*," which along with articles by P.F. Strawson and Rogers Albritton—other figures who are questioned in *The Claim of Reason*—was helpfully gathered in *Wittgenstein: The Philosophical Investigations—A Collection of Critical Essays*, ed. George Pitcher (Notre Dame, IN: University of Notre Dame, 1966). Cavell also challenges Malcolm's reading of Wittgenstein in "Knowing and Acknowledging," in *Must We Mean What We Say?*, 238–66.

[49] A "late-Wittgensteinian faith in language as a public phenomenon" is what Kasia Boddy claims Cavell offered to Wallace; see her "A Fiction of Response: *Girl With Curious Hair* in Context," in *A Companion to David Foster Wallace Studies*, ed. Marshall Boswell and Stephen J. Burn (London: Palgrave Macmillan, 2013), 37.

to his son's cries for help with *Wittgenstein's Mistress* and *Tractatus Logico-Philosophicus*" (*BFN* 96).[50]

James D. Wallace finished his doctorate in philosophy in 1963, two years after Cavell finished his own Ph.D., and he worked for decades thereafter at the University of Illinois in Urbana-Champaigne, teaching courses in aesthetics, ethics, moral philosophy, bioethics, and ancient philosophy. Like Cavell, Wallace Sr. was a product of the midcentury ordinary language revolution, and had a comparably blue-chip resumé. Whereas Cavell had studied briefly with J. L. Austin, Wallace Sr. studied at Cornell, which at the time was the "premier center for Wittgenstein studies" in the country; and his dissertation ("Pleasure: Its Objects and Its Relation to Action") was written under Norman Malcolm, one of Wittgenstein's closest friends from the 1930s onward and author of one of the first biographical sketches of the philosopher—and moreover, as I noted a moment ago, one of the very philosophers whose influential understanding of Wittgenstein Cavell has spent much of his life challenging.[51] Wallace Sr. never wrote extensively about Wittgenstein, but it's clear that he absorbed his adviser's interpretations of *Philosophical Investigations*. His writing regularly invokes Wittgenstein to shore up important claims, and these references invariably indicate that he understands the *Investigations* to be speaking for socialist phenomenology, rejecting the Cartesian subjectivism of modern philosophy through appeals to "culture," "form of life," and related concepts. Thus, for instance, the rebuke that he issues in one book to William James, whose introspective psychology argued that fear and other emotions were identical to the bodily symptoms of which one is "immediately" aware: "Wittgenstein," writes Wallace Sr. bluntly, "shows that a wide variety of psychological phenomena—understanding, meaning, intending, etc.—must be understood as features of

---

[50] James Wallace says that, after his adolescent son asked what philosophy was about, they read Plato's *Phaedo* together. David's grasp of the dialogue was immediate, and made his father realize for the first time how brilliant his son was, his mind faster than that "of any undergraduate I have ever taught" (Max, *Every Love Story*, 11). One commentator who has looked at the influence of Wallace's father on Wallace is Thomas Tracey, "The Formative Years: David Foster Wallace's Philosophical Influences and *The Broom of the System*," in *Gesturing Toward Reality: David Foster Wallace and Philosophy* (London: Bloomsbury, 2014), 157–75. As his title indicates, however, Tracey sticks close to Wallace's first novel, and for reasons that will become clear, I find it a bit simplistic to say that Wallace was in his fiction willing or able to "manipulate and reconfigure" philosophical concepts that he found in his father's work (157).

[51] Norman Malcolm, *Wittgenstein: A Memoir* (Oxford: Oxford University Press, 1958). On Cornell as the center for Wittgenstein studies in the United States, see Hans-Johann Glock, "The Influence of Wittgenstein on American Philosophy," in *The Oxford Handbook of American Philosophy* (New York: Oxford University Press, 2008), 384–85.

forms of life that are fundamentally social and public."[52] Thus, too, the attack Wallace Sr. makes on the claim that moral judgments are made by the "intuitive weighing up of reasons." What precisely, he asks, is the difference between my intuitive "weighing up" and my *arbitrarily* selecting one reason over another—a question he fortifies with §258 of *Philosophical Investigations*, on the need for public standards: "In the present case I have no criterion of correctness. One would like to say: Whatever is going to seem right to me is right. And that only means that here we can't talk about 'right'."[53]

That Malcolm's interpretation of Wittgenstein trickles down from Professor Wallace to David Wallace is more than speculation. "Authority and American Usage" makes the genealogy explicit when, in the footnote crediting "Mr. L. Wittgenstein" with having "proved" that language is inexorably public, Wallace openly summons his father's *Doktorvater*: "Because *The Investigations'* [sic] prose is extremely gnomic and opaque and consists largely of Wittgenstein's having weird little imaginary dialogues with himself, the quotations [he's been providing] are actually from Norman Malcolm's definitive paraphrase of L. W.'s argument" (*CL* 88). But if this assumption that Malcolm is "definitive" helps generate Wallace's "sociological" picture of the *Investigations*, the issue of Wittgenstein is, as I've suggested, really only a first pass onto assessing his distance from Cavell, and to explain how, I want to wade a bit deeper into the work of his father. For though Wallace Sr.'s communitarian vision of the *Investigations* aligns him with larger currents of Wittgenstein interpretation, it plays only a secondary role in his thinking. And his primary concerns—the uses to which he puts Wittgenstein, so to speak—are equally illuminating. Literary scholars have observed that Wallace's father was a philosophy professor almost as reflexively as they've observed Wallace's own fascination with logic, but seldom have they asked about the *content* of this philosophical work. And though to many readers Wallace Sr.'s work will have the dryly workmanlike tone of most analytic philosophy, it grows more colorful when we see how it anticipates many of the themes and perspectives that his son's writing came to explore.

James Wallace's first book, *Virtues and Vices* (1978), appeared a year before *The Claim of Reason*, and like Part III of Cavell's book, it offers a critique of non-cognitivist conceptions of our ethical lives. But far more than Cavell, Wallace Sr. argues specifically for a species-wide notion of human "flourishing," one explicable through an account of well-defined and "fairly fixed traits of character"—self-restraint, benevolence, honesty, fairness, truthfulness, generosity—and the social conventions that help develop them. Whatever massive variations exist between cultures, it would be hard, according to Wallace Sr., to find a society that *doesn't* want to encourage these virtues in some form or another. Indeed, they are so obligatory that we should even posit strong analogies between notions of moral or psychological "health" on the one hand and biological "health" on the other. Both biology and social philosophy, as Wallace Sr. puts it, study "what it is for certain kinds of creatures to live well" (*VV* 19): In other words, a society in which benevolence is waning or honesty no longer prized would be comparable to a body losing its oxygen. Which means—he declares in sentence that aggressively challenges the logical systems of Kripke or Lewis—that "normative data are found in nature": when we talk about what, for example, a horse is, we are talking about a *healthy* horse, a "normal, non-defective individual of its kind," living "the mode of life characteristic of an organism of a certain kind" (*VV* 18–19). It's an idea that he credits to Aristotle, who recognized that humans are biological creatures, able to thrive or decline like any other organic matter, but who also argued that our health depends on features absent in other creatures. Unlike with the horse, our goods are expressed and developed in our conventions, where specific intellectual and moral virtues can be cultivated. Indeed, our communal structures play such an overwhelmingly large role in an individual human life that we should consider our particular *ergon*—Greek for "task," "deed," or "employment"—to be "social life informed by convention," as opposed to "activity in accordance with *logos*" as Aristotle himself sometimes implied (*VV* 37). If self-restraint, benevolence, and other virtues are insufficiently assembled in a large group of people, then we could never achieve this *ergon*, could "not live together the sort of life characteristic of human beings." "This is not to say that a good human being invariably flourishes," concludes Wallace Sr. in his final sentences, but it is to say that "the more good people there are in a community, the better life in general in that community is apt to be." The wide differences between conventions in different communities "do not affect these points that are firmly grounded in the nature of things" (*VV* 161).

Such claims place *Virtues and Vices* squarely within the revival of Aristotle and virtue ethics that arose in the late 1970s and through the 1980s, and which in Chapter 3 I suggested was anticipated in essential respects by Ellison. And Wallace Sr.'s second book, *Moral Relevance and Moral Conflict* (1988), is timely in a similar way, tapping discreetly into another philosophical revival that was underway in the period—this time the revival of American pragmatism. The touchstone here is less Aristotle than John Dewey, whose 1922 book *Human Nature and Conduct* is said to be the "one worked-out version of" the view Wallace Sr. defends (*MR* 56).[54] As in Dewey, Wallace Sr.'s project is to elucidate what he calls "our practical educations" (*MR* 57), the way our earliest imitative and unthinking behaviors eventually develop into an ability to adapt to complex and fluid new situations. Our capacity to cultivate such a "plasticity of response" is what he calls—using terms that saturate Dewey's work—"intelligence" and "understanding," capacities that are developed as we become self-conscious and self-critical, revising our responses to unforeseen circumstances.

Moral Relevance and Moral Conflict reiterates two points from *Virtues and Vices* that are worth noting here. One is the distinctively *public* dimension of moral training and assessment. Humans, Wallace Sr. argues, must acquire "from other people a variety of ways of doing various things, thus reaping the benefit of other's knowledge of living and coping with the world" (*MR* 55). "Private moralities," in other words, yield only "peripheral cases of moral considerations," for morality is predominantly "connected with techniques for solving problems arising from the peculiarly social dimensions of human life" (*MR* 61). Second, like *Virtues and Vices*, this later book attacks what it calls an "atomistic conception of value" (*MR* 116), a view whereby one good or value is found by a "decision procedure, an algorithm" (*MR* 4) and then takes precedence over all others. What's needed instead is a continual balancing of goods, an awareness of how one set of valued activities connects to or supersedes another set of activities within the larger context of an entire life. How are such connections and priorities properly established? To this question Wallace Sr. invokes a passage from Hilary Putnam's *Reason, Truth, and History* (1981), a central work of the pragmatist revival that challenges Bentham's famously reductive claim that, "Prejudice apart, the game of push-pin is of equal value with the arts and sciences of music and poetry." Leveling all of our interests and activities, says Putnam, means overlooking not only the genuine benefits that a "higher" activity such as poetry provides, but also its intricate connections to other aspects of our

---

[54] Another pragmatist who influenced Wallace Sr. is Frederick L. Will. During his 1997 appearance on *The Charlie Rose Show*, Wallace described his father's relationship to Frederick Will in the following terms: "When Dad first came [to the University of Illinois], Fred Will, who's now I think in his 70s, was maybe in his 40s or 50s, and was a guy of major stature, and he was nice to Dad. I think most junior academics, this is what happens, you find older people in the department whose intellectual approach is congenial to you and who are nice to you, and you kind of become friends with them." The fact that a selection of Frederick Will's essays—*Pragmatism and Realism*, ed. Kenneth R. Westphal (Lanham: Rowman & Littlefield, 1996)—includes a foreword by Alasdair MacIntyre is one way of underlining that James Wallace's move from an Aristotelian to a Deweyan framework did not represent a startling change of direction.

lives: its enlargement of our imagination, its contributions to our repertoire of images and metaphors, its ability to reshape our mundane perceptions and attitudes. Push-pin and other games, concludes Wallace Sr., have no such essential relation to our lives as a whole; they could vanish from our culture without any grievous damage to our individual or collective health. Poetry, by contrast, celebrates our language as a whole, and thus has an importance that no piddling diversion ever could.

Again, as in Cavell, all of these claims emerge not from logical or mathematical reflection, but from Wallace Sr.'s attention to a range of historical and cultural practices. Professor Wallace's touchstones, Aristotle and Dewey, are unashamedly earthly thinkers who are unafraid to question the other-worldly inclinations of their philosophical ancestors (Plato for the one, German Idealism for the other). Unlike Cavell, however, their schemes of concepts include a strong notion of communities and social goods, and they foreground the concept of *citizenship* in a way that Cavell tends to downplay. James Wallace, that is, could not brook Cavell's fierce awareness of modern skepticism, of how we grow perpetually "out of tune" with one another in large and small ways; by the same token, the very idea that morality would be a "technique" used in the "peculiarly social dimensions of human life" would be no more convincing to Cavell than the claim that "normative data" are found "in nature." Another way of saying this is that, unlike in Cavell, the traditions that matter most to Wallace Sr. take "companionship" to refer to more than dyadic relations, treating humans as what Aristotle famously called a *zoon politikon* and engaging openly with what Dewey called "the public and its problems." The line between Aristotle and Dewey isn't indirect. As I observed in my discussion of Ellison, the human being for Aristotle is always rooted in a form of social life, and the idea that, in Alasdair MacIntyre's words, one occupies "a set of roles each of which has its own point and purpose"—"member of a family, citizen, solider, philosopher, servant of God"—is revived by the civic humanists of the early modern period, eventually shaping the republicanism of the American Founding Fathers. And as various intellectual historians have argued, it comes from Jefferson, Adams, et al., to shape the Progressives at the turn of the twentieth century, most importantly Dewey, Wallace Sr.'s hero, whose vast output is, as Putnam says, informed by one concern: the "meaning and future of democracy," the belief that "we don't know what our interests and needs are or what we are capable of until we actually engage in politics."[55] Dewey may have disdained Aristotle's

---

[55] Alasdair MacIntyre, *After Virtue: A Study in Moral Theory*, 2nd ed. (Notre Dame, IN: University of Notre Dame Press, 1984), 58–59. For a classic account of this tradition as it descends from Aristotle

aristocratic and essentialist tendencies, but no more than the ancient philosopher did he treat terms like the "common good," "the public interest," and "community" as if they were insubstantial projections. Cavell doesn't dismiss such words outright, but his skeptical instincts largely inhibit him from using them, and the social relations that have the most weight for him remain those that are "personal," not "politicized." It's no coincidence that he has shown little interest in Aristotle generally, voiced reservations about modern-day communitarianism and virtue ethics, and often raised serious questions about Dewey and his followers.[56]

III. Wear a Button, Accrete with Others

This hastily drawn intellectual–historical backdrop helps answer a question that has remained largely unasked among Wallace's readers: Just how familiar *was* Wallace with his father's philosophical work, and how aware *was* he of the traditions his father was extending? The answer is: very. There's little firsthand evidence that he read his father's first book (he would have been a young adolescent when it was written), but in college he grappled seriously with the writings of Philippa Foot, whose most celebrated book—also titled *Virtues and Vices*, and also published in 1978—touches many of the themes that Wallace *père* defended, and which Wallace *fils* kept until the end of his life.[57] Several essays in his copy of Foot's book are heavily marked up, and though there are fewer chatty or provocative marginalia of the sort that Wallace would

---

to early modern Florence to the American colonialists, see J.G.A. Pocock, *The Machiavellian Moment: Florentine Political Thought and the Atlantic Republican Tradition* (Princeton, NJ: Princeton University Press, 1975). On the line from civic humanism to Pragmatism and Progressivism, see James T. Kloppenberg, *The Virtues of Liberalism* (New York: Oxford University Press, 1998). Putnam's claim about Dewey is found in *Renewing Philosophy* (Cambridge, MA: Harvard University Press, 1992), 180, 188–89. For a different famous Pragmatist talking about similar themes, see Richard Rorty, *Achieving Our Country: Leftist Thought in Twentieth-Century America* (Cambridge, MA: Harvard University Press, 1998); Richard Rorty, "The Priority of Democracy to Philosophy," *Objectivity, Relativism, and Truth: Philosophical Papers 1* (Cambridge: Cambridge University Press, 1991), 175–96.

[56] In *Cities of Words: Pedagogical Letters on a Register of the Moral Life* (Cambridge, MA: Harvard University Press, 2005), Cavell acknowledges that he has read Aristotle over the years mainly "out of dutifulness" rather than "pleasure," despite the many similarities between Aristotle and Cavell's hero Austin (352–54). For Cavell's ambivalence about virtue ethics, see his remarks on Murdoch and others in *Conditions Handsome and Unhandsome*, xviii–xix. On Dewey and pragmatism, see *Conditions Handsome and Unhandsome*, 13–16.

[57] Philippa Foot, *Virtues and Vices: And Other Essays in Moral Philosophy* (Oxford: Oxford University Press, 1978). I've surmised here that Wallace read this book in college because, as with some other texts in his collection, he printed his name and campus address in the top-right corner of the inside cover: "D. Wallace/Box 444."

later make while reading Cavell, he is sensitive to the ways her claims fit into the larger landscape—asking, for instance, how Foot's ideas compare to J. M. Mackie's *Inventing Right and Wrong* (1977), an influential contemporary defense of emotivism, and a copy of which Wallace also kept in his personal library, equally dog-eared. His grasp of his father's Deweyan pragmatism is even harder to dispute. By the time *Moral Relevance and Moral Conflict* appeared, Wallace had a double BA in English and philosophy, a well-received first novel, and applications underway for doctoral programs in philosophy, so it is unsurprising to find his name among the various people thanked in the preface of the book for having read and commented on the manuscript. One of Wallace's late short stories borrows its title from Rorty's *Philosophy and the Mirror of Nature*, probably the best-known text of neopragmatism, and in a letter to DeLillo, written in late 1999 or early 2000, he said that he could "heartily recommend" Putnam's *Reason, Truth, and History*, the very book that *Moral Relevance and Moral Conflict* enlists to rebuke Benthamite and atomistic ideas of value.[58]

One effect of inheriting these traditions, I want to argue, is that Wallace is able to take a more consistent—and consistently critical—interest than Cavell in what we might call the public conditions of absorption. As with his father, Wallace's Aristotelian–Deweyan impulses entail a deep attention to the practices of contemporary culture as a whole. Such attention makes much of his work an exercise in what one of his essays calls "advanced US citizenship"—a phrase that can seem "corny" today (*CL* 166), can "make your eyes glaze over" (*CL* 224), but that we cannot smirk away. So again and again he asks us to think about the kind of sociopolitical world within which absorption seems an intelligible goal, something valued or even (as in Cavell) divine. The question he asks is whether too much weight can be given to absorption, and whether such an emphasis might sometimes be a symptom of some sickness, a sign that, as James Wallace puts it, a "private morality" has become more than a "peripheral" case of "moral consideration."

---

[58] Wallace's story "Philosophy and the Mirror of Nature" appears in *Oblivion*, 182–89. Wallace's recommendation to DeLillo comes in the context of a review of films from a letter dated March 21: "Plus also the single best movie I've seen in the last year—and I cringe to admit that this includes foreign art movies—the Wachowski Bros.' "The Matrix" (now on video), which yes is commercial postmodernism with a capital C, and yes has Keanu Reeves, and yes owes much to the Campbell-grade mythopoeia in ways that are about as subtle as a croquet mallet across the back of your head, but the movie is also an incredible evocation of what's creepy and powerful in Descartes' first two *Meditations on First Philosophy* (no kidding) and Hilary Putnam's "Brains in a Vat" (which if you don't know Putnam I heartily recommend "Reason, Truth and History")." (The year of this letter is unnoted, but since *The Matrix* was released in cinemas on March 31, 1999, and on DVD in September 1999, I'm inferring that it was written at some point in the months around the turn of the millennium.)

Thus, for instance, virtually every tribute Wallace pays to the absorptive powers of tennis is matched by an observation about the economics of the sport, about the "uncontainable" (*BFN* 157) barrage of commerce that surrounds professional matches, from the billboards and sponsors to the marked-up concession prices and the high-end fashion of the fans in the expensive seats. This is most crassly true of the U.S. Open, a spectacle that prompts Wallace to say in "Democracy and Commerce at the U.S. Open" (1996) that, although tennis "always gets called an international sport," "it would be more accurate to call it a *multinational* sport: fiscally speaking, it exists largely as a marketing subdivision of very large corporations" (*BFN* 134–35). But the same barrage surrounds the more modest Canadian Open, where, as Wallace notes in a two-page catalogue halfway through "Tennis Player Michael Joyce's Professional Artistry" (1995), a spectator can buy Spanish peanuts and fudge and all manner of fried foods, pay to have the speed of one's own serve clocked, gape at semipornographic billboards selling ice cream, and visit a mini-mall inside the stadium hawking tennis gear and vitamin drinks (*SFT* 247–49). And the consumerism of the big tournaments and stadiums only parallels the Darwinian financial arrangements of the professional tennis circuit itself, which Wallace is also keen to delineate. Whereas the most glamorous and highly seeded players receive money ("guarantees") simply for entering some tournaments, the rest of the tour's players—themselves all astonishingly gifted athletes, and who all sacrificed their childhoods just to get to the tour—struggle every week just to cover the cost of travel and training. Given "the distorted standards of TV's obsession with Grand Slam finals and the world's top-five," these second-tier players live largely unseen lives, "a couple of plateaux away from true fame and fortune," and survive only by equipping themselves psychologically not to get "exercised about things you can't control," like how much money Andre Agassi has received just for showing up (*STF* 221–22). In a word, serious tennis is also serious business, not just the "most beautiful sport there is," but also a fantastically, obscenely lucrative consumer good.

A similar chastening occurs with the other absorptive activity that Wallace prizes, namely attentive listening. I said earlier that the monologues of the DJ Madame Psychosis are the least ironized artworks in *Infinite Jest*, the trends and rhythms of her voice forming a "compelling beauty and light" that captivates Mario Incandenza, the book's most "serious listener." But Madame Psychosis works for a nonprofit college radio station, WYYY, out of the Massachusetts Institute of Technology, a far cry from the crudely corporate world detailed in "Host" (2005), the long profile of the Los Angeles-based talk-radio personality John Ziegler that concludes *Consider the Lobster*. Talk radio, "Host" argues, is motivated not at all by ideology, as liberals often assume, but by the exact same thing that drives professional tennis—"maximum profits," which in this case means "high Arbitron ratings, high ad rates" (*CL* 290). And this is, as Wallace explains, a deeply historical phenomenon rather than the nature of broadcasting *an sich*. In the early years of radio, regulators demanded that stations show a consistent level of "symmetry," requiring them to balance their airtime among various political perspectives. That goal had arisen from a conviction that, as Wallace puts it, "the airways belong to everyone" and that broadcasters had "some special obligation to serve the public interest" (*CL* 313). But when the Reagan administration deregulated the industry, commercial radio became "just another for-profit industry," and hosts such as Ziegler could abandon any need to "meet a higher standard of social responsibility"; they could ignore fussy old distinctions between "the public interest" and "what interested the public" (*CL* 313–14). Such transformations account for the industry's particular patois, the way the minutes available in a show are reduced to "inventory" (*CL* 300), or the way radio executives are riveted by "Ratings," "Shares," "Cumes," "AQHs," and "TSLs," that is, by various indices for measuring their listenership (*CL* 307). More than that, such legal transformations explain the shift in tone on the airwaves since the 1980s, and why "anger, outrage, indignation, fear, despair, disgust, contempt, and a certain kind of apocalyptic glee" (*CL* 279) now dominate the medium: these are the emotions that will most absorb listeners. In such a world, explains Wallace, the talk-show host's job is not to be a conscientious journalist, striving to be "responsible, or nuanced, or to think about whether his on-air comments are productive or dangerous, or cogent, or even defensible." He has "exactly one on-air job, and that is to be stimulating" (*CL* 281–82).

Nowhere in Cavell is there anything as historically particularized as these succinct accounts of professional tennis and broadcasting, domains whose level of commodification Cavell never would have witnessed in Mendel, the dear uncle who, like the emotivist philosopher, believed that "selling is the essential motive of human speech" (*LD* 121). As I noted in Chapter 4, *The Claim of Reason* and other books are deeply "modern" in a certain sense, alert to the gulfs that separate us from the centuries before, say, Descartes or Shakespeare. Wallace, by contrast, writes closer to the rough ground of our contemporary practices, and it's just this historical sensitivity that generates the pun in the title of "Host": if Ziegler is a "host" in the sense of being an on-air radio personality, he is in another sense—and here one recalls Wallace Sr.'s proposed analogy between moral and physical health—only a conduit, an unconscious carrier infecting or contaminating the wider population.

But the term "stimulating" in Wallace's description of Ziegler (he has "exactly one on-air job, and that is to be stimulating") introduces an additional cluster of issues. At first glance the word seems to equate talk radio with pornography—another industry that, as Wallace knows, uses its own densely specialized jargons (e.g., *CL* 23), exhibits its own comical levels of "obtuseness" and *"unabashedness"* (*CL* 32, 44), and has become "big, big business" by embracing the *"vulgar"* and disdaining the *"pretentious or snobby"* (*CL* 8). But pornographers and radio producers are, in fact, capitalizing on different dispositions in their audiences, or different aspects of a similar disposition. Outlaw Video, Vivid Video, and the other porn producers in "Big Red Son" depend upon a weakening of what Wallace's father, in *Virtues and Vices*, calls "self-restraint": the virtue of temperance that, as Aristotle had it, allows one to desire something in the right way, and that constrains the most self-indulgent bodily appetites, particularly those of taste and touch—a point that Wallace underlines when he compares pornography to drug addiction (*CL* 19).[59] But a different kind of indulgence is fostered by contemporary radio, at least as "Host" describes it. A key to this difference lies in the arrows that plaster the essay, appearing above or below a word or phrase in the body of the text and leading us to boxes of notes in the margins, stuffed with clarifications and qualifications and questions. It's a dizzying layout, juxtaposing several thoughts side by side, leaving us uncertain where we're supposed to look next and forcing us to ask how a particular thought refracts the one sitting just above, below, or next to it. The marginal notes, in other words, intensify the effect achieved elsewhere by Wallace's famous footnotes: they challenge not our senses of taste or touch, but our habits of inference-making.[60] They reinforce, that is, the essay's suggestion that what's lost in talk radio is an epistemic virtue vital to pragmatism from Peirce to Putnam: a sense of fallibilism. What Ziegler lacks is a sense of self-restraint that harnesses not the indulgences of the body but those of the mind—an awareness that there is always more background to a story than what we immediately notice, and that one's own initial understanding is not the end of inquiry.

What defines Ziegler both on and off the air, says Wallace, is his "unflagging industry, broad general knowledge," and "mordant wit," but most of all, his "extreme conviction" (*CL* 280)—conviction about what he knows, conviction

---

[59] Aristotle, *Nicomachean Ethics*, book III, chapter 10.

[60] On the variety of uses to which Wallace put his footnotes—to amuse, to criticize, to offer second thoughts, to confirm research, to substantiate information, to justify his own fractured consciousness—see Ira B. Nadell, "Consider the Footnote," *The Legacy of David Foster Wallace* (ed. Cohen and Konstantinou), 218–40.

about his moral insight, and conviction about his country's "moral clarity" in the post-9/11 world.[61] He is not, in other words, merely an agile, manipulative, contemporary Gorgias professing not to believe anything at all. Indeed, just the opposite: he believes all too strongly. However ugly, that is, Wallace finds the content of Ziegler's beliefs, it's the sheer belligerent tenacity of their hold over him that the essay finds most troubling. When, for instance, Ziegler and other radio hosts repeatedly declare that a man in a high-profile legal case was obviously guilty of killing his wife, Wallace asks readers to pause: "On the surface, there's something ballsy and refreshing about someone who'll flatly state 'I know the bastard's guilty', but this is only if you don't really think about it. The truth is that the hosts do *not* know whether Scott Peterson is guilty" (*CL* 326). And when one night Ziegler confronts an African-American caller about the O. J. Simpson trial, insisting that his own intense hatred for Simpson has nothing to do with Simpson's being African-American, Wallace similarly focuses on his outsized self-assurance: "Again, it's nothing so simple as that he doth protest too much; but it would be less discomfiting if Mr. Z didn't feel he could so totally *assure* [the caller] of this—i.e., if Mr. Z weren't so certain that his views are untainted by racism" (*CL* 334). The final lines of the essay underscore the lack of warrant behind Ziegler's epistemic confidence, as an interview with O. J. Simpson unfolds across the TV screen while the show's crew is preparing for an evening's show. With a "snort" Ziegler announces that even Simpson's own children are convinced that their father is guilty: "They know, and he knows they know, that he did it." To which Wallace responds by asking readers not to mock or condemn the host, but to feel "compassion, empathy": "Because one can almost feel it: what a bleak and merciless world this host lives in—believes, nay, knows for an absolute *fact* he lives in. I'll take doubt" (*CL* 343).

"Doubt" in this abrupt concluding sentence doesn't mean paralyzing self-criticism. Just as the boxes girdling the margins of "Host" are linked by arrows, not arbitrarily strewn across the page, so "doubt" should be read less as an aporia of radical skepticism than a readiness to temper our certainties, to reflect upon what we know and find reasonable. It's the attitude that allows us to stand back from the massive array of sweet foods at the Illinois State Fair or the sheer brutality of the Golden Glove boxing matches that go on there. It's the reflective distance we need to question the "titillation," the "constant activities, parties, festivities, gaiety, and song" that are forced upon one during a luxury cruise (*SFT* 264), and to interrogate the cheap "essay" penned by a famous author that

---

[61] As Wallace knows and indicates, "moral clarity" was a phrase that in the mid-2000s often was associated with George W. Bush and his decision to start the Iraq War.

the cruise company uses in its advertising (*SFT* 285–90). And it's the posture we need to meditate on our consumption of animals, to "Consider"—think about, reflect upon, not be complacent about—"the Lobster," the title of an essay that asks how close our usual eating habits are to "something like a Roman circus or medieval torture-fest" (*CL* 253).

The temperance and fallibilism that I've been highlighting in Wallace thus far are supplemented by at least two other virtues that can be said to reflect his basic affinity with his father James. They are most fully thematized in "Up, Simba," Wallace's report on his week with the presidential campaign of John McCain in 2000. At one level "Up, Simba" is clearly a eulogy for the heroic virtues that McCain's personal history has embodied: "service," "honor," "duty," and commitment to something beyond self-interest. These are the qualities that Wallace repeatedly asks us in the opening pages to pause and imagine in the young John McCain, trapped for over five years in a brutal North Vietnamese prisoner of war camp. And the dominant question in the essay is whether these virtues are still credible for "Young Voters," or whether the McCain who was so legendarily courageous as a youth has devolved into an aging politician lost irretrievably to the televisual salesmanship of a presidential campaign. But what's less in question, particularly as the essay moves into its middle sections, is Wallace's reverence for the more intellectual virtues of *techne* and *phronesis*: the knowledge of craft or art on the one hand, and practical wisdom on the other.

Techne comes to the fore when we notice how little interaction Wallace has with the campaign operatives that he is ostensibly there to follow, and who are the obsessive focus of the high-profile journalists who trail them around. His "one and only journalistic coup" for the article, he claims, is to have met the network news' tech specialists, the cameramen and sound engineers who work behind the scenes. The "almost occult talent" that one cameraman shows— "always finding the perfect place to set up his ladder and film at just the right angle for what his HQ wants" (*CL* 205)—is typical of the know-how that all of the techs exhibit, and Wallace clearly treasures their mastery of their craft. Indeed, one might even say that it's their *techne* that Wallace himself is seeking to emulate on the page, taking his title as he does from one of their running jokes. ("It is Jim C.'s custom," he notes at one point, "always to say '*Up, Simba*' in a fake-deep bwana voice as he hefts the camera to his right shoulder" [*CL* 208].) But this *techne* is, with the news techs, more than just the mastery of isolatable skills, the way one might be able to bake a cake or play push-pins in isolation from everything else. In their case, *techne* is an avenue to a broader practical wisdom. This *phronesis* becomes manifest in the intelligence the techs bring to the political landscape that they cover. They speak, notes Wallace, without the "political self-interest of the McCain2000 staff," yet also without the "raging egos" of the print and TV journalists who depend upon the politician's handlers (*CL* 204). So they are particularly helpful for evaluating the political decisions that campaigns are forced to make on the fly—as when, for example, the Bush campaign suddenly airs "negative" TV ads about McCain. The senator, his aides, and the network newsmen are all said to "agonize" over what the campaign's response can or should be, but the techs seem to know perfectly well, and over the course of several pages, Wallace traces their shrewd reasoning, informed conversation, and nuanced analysis as they evaluate McCain's various options—evaluations that, as Wallace records things, are promptly borne out: "It turns out to be enough just getting to hear the techs kill time by deconstructing today's big news, because events of the next few days bear out their analysis pretty much 100 percent" (*CL* 211). Michael Joyce's tennis coach, recall, "knows as much about tennis as anybody I've talked to and isn't obnoxious about it" (*SFT* 253), and the techs embody something similar: they are not just first-rate cameramen, but also "more astute and sensitive political analysts than anybody you'll read or see on TV" (*CL* 204).

An analogous esteem for *techne* and *phronesis* runs through "Authority and American Usage," which lauds the author of *A Dictionary of Modern American Usage*, Bryan A. Garner, for having discovered a distinct alternative to the stale claims of both linguistic "Prescriptivism" and linguistic "Descriptivism." The former is singlemindedly driven to instill and spread "correct" English; the latter is a cool, value-neutral enterprise that tries to record how actual English-speakers actually talk. (A dichotomy familiar from Ellison and Cavell: an appeal to social convention versus an appeal to science, as if either option explains why we care about our language in the first place.) In Wallace's view, Garner fully recognizes that, in our actual existing economic and social institutions, we constantly distinguish between "good" and "bad" English, but he doesn't allow his own distinctions and recommendations to depend simply on elitist appeals to tradition, or by disdaining "considerations of persona or persuasion" (*CL* 120). Instead, like the news techs who've come to their insights through years of unglamorous experience on the road, his work consists "in *establishing* [the] authority" required to make lexicographical evaluations, judgments that would be "not just accurate and comprehensive but *credible*" (*CL* 122). To do so, Garner recasts the voice of the Prescriptivist in a way that presents him "not in an *autocratic*" light "but in a *technocratic*" one, "not as a cop or a judge but as more like a doctor or lawyer" (*CL* 122)—a "palatable image of authority" who is "immune to the charges of elitism/classism" that Americans so viscerally abhor. The "genius" of his book lies in his ability to embody "the Democratic Spirit," a combination of "rigor and humility," a "passionate conviction plus a sedulous respect for the convictions of others" (*CL* 72). He works "quietly and steadily" at the task before him, "always informed by the larger consensual purposes" that Standard Written English is "meant to serve." Unlike the Descriptivist, Garner is fully aware that his claims about appropriate words and grammar amount to evaluative judgments, but unlike the Prescriptivist, he supports them with habits and attitudes that make his judgments hard to dismiss: passionate devotion and accountability; exhaustive, up-to-date research; an even and judicious temperament; and a "humble integrity" that "transmits the reverence for English that"—and here Wallace's analogy is telling—"good jurists have for the law, both of which are bigger and more important than any one person" (*CL* 124).

Garner and the news techs epitomize Jonathan Franzen's observation that Wallace was always fascinated by the "arcana" of people's work.[62] But in both cases, a knowledge of arcana is important chiefly because mastering a local field instills the skills and dispositions required to achieve a wider range of goals and purposes. Behind this view is a belief that, once again, echoes his father's Aristotelianism: that a failure of justice damages not just the oppressed, but also the oppressor, who poisons himself by refusing to strive for the good. Garner and the news techs do excellent work not simply because it will earn them more money; they do it because they want to achieve excellence. "I would like my generation to realize," Wallace said to an interviewer in 1996, "that it would be way better for us, like inside, . . . to be willing to pay higher taxes, to be able to shelter and feed poor people—not for their sake, but for ours. So that we would be the sort of culture that doesn't let people die."[63] Absent such virtues, public discourse corrodes. Contemporary debate in the United States, Wallace said in another interview, is a "bloodsport" in which "everything's relentlessly black-and-whitened": How can the oversimplifications and combat of our public discussions "possibly help me, the average citizen, deliberate about whom to choose to decide my country's macroeconomic policy," or think about

---

[62] Jonathan Franzen, "Informal Remarks from the David Foster Wallace Memorial Service in New York on October 23, 2008," in *Legacy of David Foster Wallace*, ed. Cohen and Konstantinou, 177. Wallace's deep respect for practical know-how isn't restricted to "Authority" and "Up, Simba." When, for instance, a young producer described in "Host" fills in for a colleague and turns out to be "a veritable blur of all-business competence and technical savvy," Wallace honors the man with a striking metaphor: his transformation from a "slackerish stoner" into an energetic technician is, he says, like "when you place a fish back in the water and it seems to turn electric in your hand" (*CL* 340).

[63] Wallace, interview with Christopher Lydon on "The Connection," WBUR Boston, February 1996 (statement at 24:43).< http://radioopensource.org/david-foster-wallace-chris-lydon/> (accessed April 8, 2016).

other "gray and complicated" issues? "Maybe at least," he went on, "we can help elevate some professional political journalists" who are polite, well-informed, and relatively neutral.[64] Perhaps we can "as a polity and culture" start "paying attention and start handling information in a competent grown-up way," honoring writing and reporting that exhibit "integrity in their handling of fact" and an "absence of dogmatic cant" (*BFN* 315–16). And, ultimately, we can *act*—participate, get involved, get out the vote. "My own plan in the coming fourteen months," he told Dave Eggers in the fall of 2003, "is to knock on doors and stuff envelopes. Maybe even to wear a button. To try to accrete with others into a demographically significant mass" (*LI* 76–77).

IV. Why Wantons Are Bad Citizens

I began by outlining Wallace's affinities with the later Wittgenstein and Cavell, particularly the ways that they locate meaningfulness less in pristine logical orders than in the intricately fastened, overlapping threads of a community's everyday speech and practices. It's by looking here that we can be weak realists about our normative terms. I then suggested that, however broad these affinities may be, Cavell and Wallace differ radically on the question of how stable and firm a "community" can be, and that Wallace's version of "socialist phenomenology" makes him a literary offshoot of the Aristotelian and pragmatist revivals that were occurring in the years when he reached intellectual maturity. But the concepts that these traditions help us identify in Wallace—"self-restraint" or temperance, fallibilistic "doubt," technical skill, practical wisdom—are worth emphasizing not only for the contrast they make with Cavell. They also diverge from the popular image of Wallace himself, who has most usually been associated with the normative keywords of "E Unibus Pluram"—*sincerity, conviction*—or his Kenyon speech—*compassion, empathy*. None of these words are incompatible with those I've been highlighting, but they're also not identical. "Sincerity" and "conviction" pertain chiefly to the mood of an utterance, not to its content: one can be sincere or convinced about *any*thing. And though "compassion" and "empathy" do name social virtues, they pertain chiefly to the private or dyadic relations that, as I'm claiming, Wallace is frequently trying to see beyond. As one Thai philosopher has said, writing about Buddhism, they are traits for a "personal way of life" more than a stance on rights, liberty, freedom,

---

[64] *David Foster Wallace: The Last Interview and Other Conversations* (Brooklyn: Melville House, 2012), 76; henceforth cited parenthetically as *LI*.

fairness, and other characteristics of a modern liberal democracy.[65] Again, Wallace knows that such antinominalism about "advanced US citizenship" can make one skittish: It sounds embarrassingly close to "old men grumbling about the vulgarity of modern mores" (*CL* 79), a "controlling, condescending, nanny-state" attitude (*CL* 314). But we should also, he says, learn when to "suck it up" (*CL* 224). We need to "hear clichés as more than just clichés," and to consider, to recall a remark I quoted at the start, what normative terms "might really refer to, like whether the words actually *stand for* something" (*CL* 166).

But my evidence for Wallace's civic humanism has, of course, been drawn up to now entirely from his interviews and nonfiction—and this hasn't been accidental. For one thing, the journalistic thrust of his essays makes them the clearest place to see his willingness to probe the embodied, temporal things of the material world, over and against his early attachment to philosophical logic. His father's work may reject the abstractions of the philosophical tradition, and may look to biology and social theory for its models of human flourishing, but "Tennis Player Michael Joyce," "Host," and other essays descend deep into the sludge of empirical and social life, ascending to higher-altitude themes only after giving fine-grained descriptions of particular agents, actions, and institutions. More than that, the essays are the clearest place where he adopts a stance toward the texture and social practices of contemporary culture. Commentators have sometimes compared Wallace as a journalist to the participant-observers of the New Journalism, someone "stupider and schmuckier than I am," as he once put it, who enters a foreign territory to report on the local tribe.[66] But the analogy risks suggesting that his essays are value-neutral anthropological studies. They're not. They are not dispassionate scientific reports any more than

---

[65] Somparn Promta, quoted in Owen Flanagan, *The Bodhisattva's Brain: Buddhism Naturalized* (Cambridge, MA: MIT Press, 2011), 122. That this remark about compassion is drawn from a book on Buddhism is appropriate in this context. As Wallace was aware, "compassion" and "empathy" are absolutely central to Buddhist traditions, and his library includes a 1995 Barnes and Noble edition of Swami Paramananda's *A Practical Guide to Buddhist Meditation*. Moreover, as Max notes, he responded with warm curiosity when Buddhist readers claimed a deep interest in his work (see *Every Love Story is a Ghost Story*, 181, 291). But as Flanagan has suggested, though Buddhism is a tradition that overlaps very deeply with the Western tradition of virtue ethics, it also tends to be "very weak in the political philosophy department, overrating compassion and underrating the need for institutions that enact justice as fairness" (xii).

[66] On Wallace's relation to the New Journalism, see Josh Roiland, "Getting Away From It All: The Literary Journalism of David Foster Wallace and Nietzsche's Concept of Oblivion," in *The Legacy of David Foster Wallace*, 40, 48. Roiland claims that "The literary journalists whom Wallace most closely resembles are Hunter S. Thompson and Joan Didion" (40), an assessment that would've left Wallace himself uneasy. Though he professed admiration for Didion, he openly disdained Thompson; see the interview with *Le Nouvel Observateur*, collected in *Conversations With David Foster Wallace*, ed. Burn, 153–54. On his "stupider and schmuckier" essay persona, see Lipsky, *Although Of Course You End Up*, 41–42.

they are the record of a drifting tourist floating between exotic locales to compile "interesting" personal "experiences." Wallace's yarns always contribute to a larger, sober examination, an investigation into the tasks that we contemporaries undertake and the deeds that express our conceptions of the good life. And they take a stance on these tasks and deeds, exhibiting, to recall Susan Sontag's description of the essay genre, an "assertiveness" and a "directness of . . . concern with opinion and argument."[67]

To turn from Wallace's essays to his fiction is to feel immediately just how central these civic-humanist impulses are. Cavell writes an intimate personal memoir; Wallace writes *Infinite Jest*, a book whose sheer girth is only the most palpable sign of his effort to encompass the full range of the public and its problems.[68] The looking-glass minimalism of Barthelme's short stories may have been what first drew Wallace to fiction, but he was obviously most captivated by the maximalist powers of the modern novel, with its historical ties to the epic and its ambitions to take account of the entire social expanse. But an Aristotelian or Deweyan reader like Wallace's father could appreciate more specific aspects of *Jest* as well. As, for instance, the fact that so much of the novel is set at a tennis academy, a world in which a commitment to *techne* is at a premium. In their time at E.T.A., the adolescent players encounter many incarnations of Sam Aparicio, coaches who help you see things you can't see alone, and they must develop many of the virtues that Bryan Garner displays in *A Dictionary of Modern American Usage*: passionate devotion, accountability, a prudent temperament, and a humble integrity that makes them aware of practices that are bigger than any one person. Most obviously James Wallace would appreciate the philosophical dialogues that punctuate the text between Rémy Marathe and Hugh Steeply. As readers have noted, these spies are essentially glossing Isaiah Berlin's 1958 essay "Two Concepts of Liberty," with the American Steeply defending "negative" freedom and the Quebecois separatist Marathe

---

[67] Susan Sontag, "Introduction to "*The Best American Essays*, 1992," in *Essayists on the Essay: Montaigne to Our Time*, ed. Carl H. Kraus and Ned Stuckey-French (Iowa City: University of Iowa Press, 2012), 29.

[68] Not all readers have welcomed this encyclopedic quality, of course. Countless more people have started the book than have finished it, and those that do sometimes view it, with James Wood, as one of the "perpetual-motion machines" of contemporary writing, its "glamorous congestion" seeking to "abolish stillness." That's probably too harsh, but Wood is obviously correct to suggest that the novel is something other than a tidy character study. See James Wood, "Human, All Too Inhuman," *The New Republic* (July 24, 2000); <http://www.newrepublic.com/article/61361/human-all-too-inhuman; accessed August 22, 2014). A version of this high-profile piece was republished in Wood's *The Irresponsible Self: On Laughter and the Novel* (New York: Farrar, Straus and Giroux, 2004) as "Hysterical Realism."

speaking for "positive" freedom.[69] "There are no choices without personal freedom, Buckeroo," argues the American Steeply, as if channeling the radio host Ziegler or the porn producers of "Big Red Son" (*IJ* 320). But in a book whose other characters are so debilitatingly lonely, the French-Canadian Marathe gets most of the best lines, even if his English is less than elegant. To Steeply's claim that "one cannot be human without freedom," Marathe asks whether "freedom" has only one dimension: "Your freedom is the freedom-*from*: no one tells your precious individual U.S.A. selves what they must do.... But what of the freedom-*to*? . . . How for the person to freely choose?" And in a moment that recalls James Wallace's confident emphasis on training and education, on acquiring "from other people a variety of ways of doing various things," Marathe asks: "How to choose any but a child's greedy choices if there is no loving-filled father to guide, inform, teach the person how to choose? How is there freedom to choose if one does not learn how to choose?" (*IJ* 320).[70]

All this, as I've been saying, has comparatively little place in Cavell's voluminous writing, and the fact that the conversations between Marathe and Steeply were among the earliest pieces of *Infinite Jest* to be written—Max suggests drafts of them were written in the 1980s—indicates just how longstanding these themes were in Wallace's mind.[71] But as significant as these scenes in the novel are, and as much as they make explicit the overarching themes of the text, *Jest* is full of other voices and moments that pull against them, tugging the reader in radically different directions. Versions of this tension have been seen in the other postwar sages I've discussed, whether it's the five-year leap that ends Percy's *Love in the Ruins*, or the present-tense voice that disrupts the reflective retrospection of *Gilead*, or the difficulty Ellison shows in embodying fraternity in *Invisible Man* and his unfinished novel. In *Jest* we see a similar centrifugal movement. The text is not only at odds with certain central aspects

---

[69] See Isaiah Berlin, "Two Concepts of Liberty," in *Four Essays on Liberty* (New York: Oxford University Press, 1969), 118–72. On the place of Berlin's essay in Wallace's novel, see Adam Kelly, "Development Through Dialogue: David Foster Wallace and the Novel of Ideas," *Studies in the Novel* 44 (2012), 274–77.

[70] One could argue perhaps that Marathe doesn't fully believe his own arguments: he is, after all, secretly colluding with Steeply's government in order to get medical aid to his fragile, horrendously disfigured wife. But this conflict only adds a complexity to Marathe's character that the glib and manipulative Steeply generally lacks, and does little to undermine his claims. Marathe's struggle is not over whether he is constituted in essential ways by his relations to others, but which particular relations are most critical in this constitution. His conflict is over not whether, as he puts it, loving something "bigger than the self" "enlarges the heart" (*IJ* 107), but which particular type of love—which type of affinity, which type of "freedom-to"—should take precedence. And this is a conflict that a modern civic humanist would acknowledge as wholly legitimate, and could praise *Infinite Jest* for dramatizing.

[71] See Max, *Every Love Story*, 159.

of Cavell's work, including the Cavellian glimpses of friendship and absorption that I sketched in Chapter 4. In its orchestration of voices and perspectives, it is also deeply in conflict with Wallace's own hunger for a modern civic humanism.

A first source of conflict returns us to the themes of education and training stressed, as I just noted, by both James Wallace and Marathe, and this concerns the character of Mario Incandenza. Mario is the slightly older brother of Hal, but he will seem to most readers the younger of the siblings, because he is disabled in various ways that have hindered his mobility, impaired his capacity to learn, and restricted his social life. The first thing we hear about him is that "Mario didn't drill [at tennis] and couldn't play, and needed all the sleep he could get" (*IJ* 32), and over the next several hundred pages we gradually get a fuller picture of his condition: the diminutive size ("somewhere between elf and jockey"), the withered-looking arms, the "*block* feet" and inwardly curved spine, the one eyelid that hangs low, the "khaki-colored skin" that gives him "an almost uncannily reptilian/dinosaurian look," the "refracted" mind that is "ever so slightly epistemically bent," that is "just a little off and just taking a little bit longer" (*IJ* 314). And yet for all these physical obstacles—or rather, because of them—Mario is a towering moral force in Hal's life. People who have suffered like Mario, we read, either "curl up in their fire, or else they rise"—and in Hal's eyes, Mario "floats" (*IJ* 316). It's Mario who forces uncomfortable questions about what Hal feels "inside" when he plays tennis, whether he believes in God, and whether their mother was truly aggrieved when their father died (*IJ* 39–42). And it's Mario who perceives that the residents crying and talking about God are what make Ennet House "real," just as he recognizes that the melancholy of Madame Psychosis—her interest in "stuff about heartbreak and people you loved dying and U.S. woe"—makes her radio program "valid art" (*IJ* 591–92). His "Panglossian constitution" makes him unable to detect fabrications or deception in others (*IJ* 772), and in a novel that cherishes the capacity for listening, Mario is "basically a born listener," someone whose endurance, humility, and visible disabilities allow others to reveal "deep beliefs," "diary-type private reveries" (*IJ* 80).

As Timothy Jacobs has noted, such descriptions are plainly meant to recall Alyosha of *The Brothers Karamazov*, a book that Wallace revered and which parallels *Infinite Jest* in a number of ways.[72] In a culture of disbelieving Ivans, Mario

---

[72] See Timothy Jacobs, "The Brothers Incandenza: Translating Ideology in Fyodor Dostoevsky's *The Brothers Karamazov* and David Foster Wallace's *Infinite Jest*," *Texas Studies in Literature and Language* 49 (2007): 271–75. Wallace's own fascination with Dostoevsky is recorded in "Joseph Frank's Dostoevsky" (1996), included in *Consider the Lobster*, 255–74.

stands apart as the "idiot" child whose paternity is unclear, whose patience is saintly, who is free from cynicism, and who is joyfully open to religious belief and charity.[73] Yet it's precisely this "valorization of children," in Jacobs's term, that makes this strand of *Jest* so hard to reconcile with Wallace's civic humanism. Perhaps this valorization betrays a latent Christian longing in Wallace, a hope that a little child shall lead them; perhaps it's a Romantic intuition that the child is father to the man.[74] Whatever its source, it is deeply at odds with Aristotle, Dewey, and James Wallace, all of whom implicitly view the ideal individual as a mature adult, a citizen who has had the right kind of practical education and who exhibits "understanding" and "intelligence." (Indeed, according to Wallace Sr., Aristotle's term for the self-indulgent person was *akolastos*, a word that the Greeks originally used to mean "the ways of small children" or "undisciplined children").[75] Their exemplar is a fully developed person whose existence as a natural creature both shapes and is shaped by the conventions of the culture, and who has learned how to reflect broadly on the peculiarly social dimensions of human life. Such a presumption has caught Cavell's eye, and informs his resistance to pragmatism in particular: "the speech of children," Cavell has said, "hardly appears" in Dewey's writing, driven as he is to "correct" us, "as though the world into which he is drawn to intervene suffers from a well-defined lack or benightedness."[76] But the corrections of the adult perspective are everywhere in Wallace's call for "advanced US citizenship": explicitly in his hope that we will handle information "in a competent grown-up way" (*BFN* 313), that we'll consider "what free, informed adulthood might look like in the context of Total

---

[73] Walker Percy puts Dostoevsky's novel to identical use in *The Moviegoer*, a novel that Wallace also knew very well. Indeed, Hal's relationship to Mario is virtually identical to Binx's relationship with his suffering, earnest, devout stepbrother Lonny. According to Max's biography, Wallace read Percy while in rehab, an experience that he reported gave him "the creeps" (Max, *Every Love Story*, 152). But among the books left behind after his death is a copy of *The Moviegoer* that is as heavily marked up as any of the books in his library. It has the feel of a teaching copy, with purple marks instructing himself to "Do epigraph" or 'Do pp. 10–14 Search." It also has phrases from *The Moviegoer* itself that Wallace seems to have appreciated ("warm and solid as roast beef," "a thin, hump-shouldered girl," "a gelid hush"), as well as remarks about "Atwater," who became a major character in *The Pale King*: "Atwater as manipulator—he set up a certain complicity" / "Atw. has feeling that the last 12 yrs of his life were but a sojourn between Indiana afternoons" / "Mrs. Atwater said her son Cletis wore his soul in his eyes."

[74] Elsewhere in *Infinite Jest*, the condition of childhood is much less valorized but still regarded as essential, the core of any person's true being, in explicitly Freudian ways: "Hal. . .theorizes privately that what passes for hip cynical transcendence of sentiment is really some kind of fear of being really human, since to be really human (at least as he conceptualizes it) is probably to be. . .in some basic interior way forever infantile, some sort of not-quite-right-looking infant dragging itself anaclitically around the map" (*IJ* 695).

[75] Wallace, *Virtues and Vices*, 82.

[76] Stanley Cavell, "What's the Use of Calling Emerson a Pragmatist?" in *Emerson's Transcendental Etudes* (Stanford, CA: Stanford University Press, 2003), 218.

Noise" (*BFN* 317), and more tacitly in his respect for the linguist Bryan Garner and the network news techs. Mario's sincerity and empathy are no doubt crucial elements of a polity, but as I've just suggested, these norms are only marginally political. And this inevitably invites questions about Wallace's sentimentalism. Whereas Hal, for instance, claims to have "administrative bones to pick with God," whose "laid-back management style I'm not crazy about" (*IJ* 40), Mario's nighttime prayers are said to "take almost an hour and sometimes more and are not a chore," and sound from the outside "like a conversation" (*IJ* 590). And similarly, the last Incandenza-related story we read in the novel describes a life-saving gesture that Mario provides to a total stranger on the street, a gesture he's not "worldly or adult" enough to know not to make (*IJ* 971). Such passages reinforce William Deresiewicz's suggestion that Wallace tried to solve "the problem of American adolescence"—the need to escape the cage in which Hal feels caught—"not by advancing to adulthood but by regressing to childhood."[77] This is incomplete, as I've been suggesting: Wallace *is* capable of describing mature adulthood. But not here, not in the venerated figure of Mario, who leads us away from the norms traced and endorsed elsewhere in Wallace's work.

Yet adulthood is refracted in *Infinite Jest* in other ways, as we see when we reflect on the conceit that runs through the text. As readers know, the connecting thread of the novel's tangled plot is a film that is so powerfully riveting, so consuming, that viewers are unable to look away from it. They want only to play it over and over, craving that it never end, and in doing so they ignore hunger, thirst, and other bodily needs until eventually they weaken and die. The film is the object of an intense hunt by competing political factions—including Marathe's Quebecois nationalists—who refer to it simply as "The Entertainment," and who seek to use it as a weapon against their enemies. One way to read the film is as another of Wallace's challenges to Cavell, insofar as it instantiates the diseased forms of absorption that I noted earlier: absorption not as a heightening of subjectivity and attention but as what the novel calls "spectation," a state that consists of "private watching" (*IJ* 620) and that cultivates "the appetite to choose death by pleasure" (*IJ* 319)—the "rapt, mindless fascination" with the visual object that Fredric Jameson, in a sentence Wallace knew, finds definitive of contemporary culture generally.[78] It's precisely

---

[77] William Deresiewicz, "The Children's Hospital: On David Foster Wallace," *The Nation* (June 15, 2011); <http://www.thenation.com/article/161456/childrens-hospital-david-foster-wallace> (accessed August 22, 2014).

[78] Fredric Jameson, *Signatures of the Visible* (New York: Routledge, 1990), 1; Wallace cites this line in a footnote of "Authority and American Usage" (*CL* 115). Wallace quotes the line as an instance of how arcane and irrelevant academic writing about the arts has become, but as I'm suggesting here, he was, in fact, much more attuned to Jameson's claim than his criticism suggests.

this threat of "spectation," and the socioeconomic conditions that make it constitutive of our moment, that my last chapter argued seems largely absent in Cavell's work.

But we can be more exact. To use the favored terms of both the Peircian Percy and the Burkean Ellison, what matters most about the conceit is that, in thoroughly naturalist fashion, it transforms an intentional *act*—watching a film, making intelligible the characters and actions that it depicts, understanding the formal techniques and gestures it displays—into a strictly nonintentional *motion*. When the narrator says of the film, about halfway through the novel, that "whoever saw it wanted nothing else ever in life but to see it again" (*IJ* 548), the "wanted" should be heard in a radically attenuated sense. It's the "want" of simple first-order desires: viewers "want" to watch the film only in the sense that a thermometer "wants" to measure the temperature, without ever considering whether such measurements are themselves desirable, whether they will achieve some end, are praiseworthy, or are something with which it should identify.[79] Or, to change the image—one that recalls the pun in the title of "Host," and that is closer to the events of the novel—viewers "want" to watch the film the way that a virus "wants" to penetrate a membrane, and they can no more look away from what they see than an immune system can decide whether to react to a foreign body. A short catalogue of the film's victims gives a sense of its force: a film-scholar and his partner in Berkeley who were "now lost to meaningful human activity henceforward," along with all the police, paramedics, and technicians sent to rescue them, seventeen people in all; an audience at an avant-garde film festival in Arizona, felled by the "lethal" film, their lives saved only by a custodian who cut the power to the building; a Middle Eastern medical attaché (the first person in the novel shown viewing it), along with his wife and "a dozen incidentals in Boston." This is nothing less than a public health crisis:

> These persons now all in wards .... The persons' lives' meanings had collapsed to such a narrow focus that no other activity or connection could hold their attention. Possessed of roughly the mental/spiritual energies of a moth, now, according to a diagnostician out of C.D.C. (*LJ* 548–49)

---

[79] The classic formulation of this point is Harry G. Frankfurt, "Freedom of the Will and the Concept of a Person," in *The Importance of What We Care About* (Cambridge: Cambridge University Press, 1988), 11–25.

Aesthetic works always have a sensory dimension, an impact on our ears or sight, but the conceit of the novel is to conflate the shaped sensuality of the artwork with the raw materiality of the physical object. The film is presented as if a work were *only* matter, and as if it could trigger specific reactions as predictably as particles of the Ebola virus trigger specific symptoms when attached to human cells.

Like the figure of Mario, then, the film produces a stark contrast to the vocabularies I've been identifying elsewhere in Wallace. From its inception, the language of civic humanism has been a language of self-determination and self-governance. Against the Christian vision of a City of God, against the monarchical vision of a ruler maintaining a domain, the earliest civic humanists understood the republic as a whole to be the responsibility of its citizens, the product of their collective will. And, in turn, they conceived of the citizen as an individual who could influence the directions that this collective will takes, a rational agent whose experienced deliberation and appropriate emotional responsiveness grants him (it was, of course, usually a "him") the right to elect leaders and sway policy through public discourse. These complementary forms of agency—their social and individual modes—have often put civic humanism at odds with, for instance, Marxism, at least in the structural versions of it that view history as a "process without a subject." But Aristotle and his descendants never confused agency with omnipotence: *fortuna* always lurks, both in individual lives and in human culture generally. The point was that such agency could be trained in better and worse ways, and if cultivated, could be a partial constraint on chance, a way of anticipating and coping with *fortuna*, even if never eliminating it.[80]

The starting point of *Infinite Jest*, by contrast, is a condition of self-governance annihilated. It's "a diagnostician out of C.D.C." who treats the Entertainment-watchers, not a film critic assigned to challenge their interpretations, much as a "voter spasm," not a series of informed deliberations, gets the ex-crooner and germophobe Johnny Gentle elected president (*IJ* 382). The degree to which meaners are made into matter, persons into bodies, makes the novel the most concentrated exploration of bald naturalism in Wallace's oeuvre. All the various

---

[80] History as a "process without a subject" is an oft-cited phrase from Louis Althusser, *Lenin and Philosophy and Other Essays*, trans. Ben Brewster (New York: NLB, 1971), 122. That civic humanists never equated agency with omnipotence is one reason why it's distrusted as much by liberals as it is by Marxists. For two standard accounts of the civic humanist's challenge to chance and corruption, see J.G.A. Pocock, *The Machiavellian Moment*, chap. 4; Quentin Skinner, *The Foundations of Modern Political Thought, Volume 1: The Renaissance* (Cambridge: Cambridge University Press, 1978), 94–101.

stages of his thought—the attraction to the "maximum hygiene" of formal logic, the engagement with Wittgenstein and Cavell, the broadly Aristotelian-Deweyan impulses of the essays—are designed to overcome it. As readers have noted, the effects of the Entertainment are modeled on mid-twentieth-century experiments by James Olds, who claimed to have found the pleasure-center of rats' brains, but if the behaviorism that undergirded these experiments was largely discredited by the 1990s, Wallace was nevertheless writing at a moment when totalizing causal explanations of human behavior seemed to be just over the horizon. The evolutionary psychology that so piques Marilynne Robinson, for example, first boomed in the 1990s, with major books by Leda Cosmides and John Tooby, Steven Pinker, and Daniel Dennett. Still more obvious are the advances in computer science and neuroscience of the sort dramatized in Powers's *Galatea 2.2*, which was published just a year before *Jest*. As Stephen J. Burn has observed, the gestation of Wallace's novel coincides with what President George H. W. Bush declared to be "the Decade of the Brain," and the novel was written alongside the emergence of the Internet, whose distributed systems and decentering energies have long been said to inform *Jest*.[81]

Infinite Jest never dwells at length on such theories or disciplines, and unlike some of his contemporaries (Richard Powers, John Banville, Ian McEwan) Wallace spends no time in the novel dramatizing the working lives of working scientists. But the reductionism that such theories exploit, their transformation of intentional judgments into triggered symptoms, appears on virtually every page and in every plot line. Most forcibly it appears through the characters who are said to live on the "repetitive gerbil-wheel of addiction," who struggle with "the Disease," and who thus recall the afflictive compulsions of characters we have seen in earlier chapters: Jack Boughton of *Gilead*, Tom More of *Love in the Ruins*. These include the father of Hal's father, who in the chronologically earliest scene of the novel—a monologue delivered in the winter of 1960 "B.S." (Before Subsidization)—preaches a fusion of mind and body, but who offers whisky and car keys to his ten-year-old son James, his adult sense

---

[81] Stephen J. Burn, *David Foster Wallace's* Infinite Jest: *A Reader's Guide* (2nd ed.; New York: Continuum, 2012), 50–51; on the experiments of James Olds, see 105. For examples of influential scientific writing around the years of *Jest*, see Steven Pinker, *The Language Instinct: How the Mind Creates Language* (New York: William Morrow, 1994); Daniel Dennett, *Darwin's Dangerous Idea: Evolution and the Meanings of Life* (New York: Simon & Schuster, 1995); Leda Cosmides and John Tooby (ed.), *The Adapted Mind: Evolutionary Psychology and the Generation of Culture* (New York: Oxford University Press, 1992). The analogy between *Jest* and the Internet's distributed systems and "decentering energies" is from Sven Birkerts's review of the novel, "The Alchemist's Retort," *The Atlantic* (February 1, 1996) <http://www.theatlantic.com/magazine/archive/1996/02/the-alchemists-retort/376533/>> (accessed April 11, 2016).

of discrimination patently compromised. In this novel of fathers and sons, the gerbil wheel also comes to include James himself, who undergoes a "very gradual spiral into the crippling dipsomania of his [own] late father" (*IJ* 64), becomes "one of those profound-personality drinkers," unpredictably extreme in his moods (*IJ* 379), and who winds up existing chiefly as a "figurant" among his own family, "furniture at the periphery of the very eyes closest to him" (*IJ* 837). And the wheel includes Joelle, a.k.a. Madame Psychosis, whose cocaine addiction is described as "this cage, this unfree show" (*IJ* 223), and who, on the night that she overdoses in a friend's bathroom, gives voice to Wallace's early fascination with the *Tractatus*: "The back of the toilet is lightly sheened with condensation of unknown origin. These are facts. This room in this apartment is the sum of very many specific facts and ideas. . . .Deliberately setting about to make her heart explode has assumed the status of just one of these facts" (*IJ* 239).

The conflation of meaning and matter is most richly imagined through the novel's two central characters, the teenage Hal and the 28-year-old burglar Don Gately. In certain respects their stories move along contrary tracks, their dependencies traced from different directions: Hal is in the midst of his "devolution from occasional tourist to subterranean compulsive, substance-wise" (*IJ* 270), whereas Gately, after years of addiction and a stint in jail, is finally learning to live sober. The construction of their narratives, however, emphasizes the deep parallels between the two characters, both associated with the gradual loss of expressiveness, with the objecthood and causal necessities that the film-watching conceit of the novel literalizes.

Consider, for instance, the opening pages of the text, where Hal, in a calmly neutral voice, describes sitting in an admissions office at the University of Arizona, being interviewed by a small group of administrators for an athletic scholarship. His introduction of the scene focuses entirely on the material constitution of his surroundings, reducing his environment—much like Joelle in the bathroom—to a universe of inanimate physical objects: "I am seated in an office, surrounded by heads and bodies. My posture is consciously congruent to the shape of my hard chair. . . .Three faces have resolved into place above summer-weight sportcoats and half-Windsors across a polished pine conference table" (*IJ* 3). It's the first detached *Tractarian* vision of the novel, and one that Hal clearly experiences as threatening. As he sits speechless, unable to answer questions about his unusual application essays and test scores, the administrators wonder aloud how the university could avoid "just using" him "simply as an athletic asset," "using a boy just for his body, a boy so shy and withdrawn he won't speak up for himself" (*IJ* 8, 10). Finally Hal talks, delivering a eulogy to his rational freedom that rebuts the claim, voiced by his grandfather many pages later, that "you are a machine a body an object" (*IJ* 159):

> 'My application's not bought,' I am telling them. . . . 'I am not just a boy who plays tennis.' . . .
> 'I *read*,' I say. 'I study and read. I bet I've read everything you've read.'
> '. . . I'm not a machine. I feel and believe. I have opinions. Some of them are interesting. I could, if you'd let me, talk and talk. . . .I believe the influence of Kierkegaard on Camus is underestimated. I believe Dennis Gabor may very well have been the Antichrist. . . .I believe, with Hegel, that transcendence is absorption. I could interface you guys right under the table,' I say. 'I'm not just a creātus, manufactured, conditioned, bred for a function.' (*IJ* 11–12)

The constructions are simple, the tone composed, but the verb tense is a clue to a worrying undercurrent: a retrospective narrator would be assumed to have made at least minimal sense out of events, whereas Hal's present tense indicates a future beyond the speaker's control. And beyond his control it turns out to be. For the administrators hear Hal's words not as meaningful utterances, but merely as "sounds." However inscrutable his allusions to holography, philosophy, and Latin may have been, the bigger obstacle is that his words are "undescribable" "noises," only "marginally mammalian," even "*sub*animalistic" (*IJ* 14–15). Hal may, in other words, have a fantastically bright "inner" life, but to the rest of the world, he has already become "a machine a body an object," material infected by a virus, and the scene ends with him being taken into the emergency ward of a hospital, his limbs strapped to a stretcher.[82] The anaphoric conclusion of his monologue presents a drifting catalogue of what to readers are phantasmagorically random observations that we have no way of understanding at this early point in the text:

---

[82] The strapping of Hal to a stretcher anticipates the fate of his brother Orin, who, in a passage that recalls the hospital scene of *Invisible Man*, is at the end of the book trapped under a giant "bathroom-type tumbler" by the Quebecois nationalists, who examine him like a lab specimen and press him for the master copy of the Entertainment (*IJ* 971–72). In Orin's case, such treatment is only poetic justice, given the clinical stance that he, too, takes throughout the novel: his references, for instance, to his many romantic partners as "Subjects" (e.g., *IJ* 43, 47, 251), or his view of sex as, in Hal's words, "different configurations of limbs," "organs going in and out of other organs, emotionless, terribly lonely" (*IJ* 956–57). Part of Hal's description here is from his account of the infidelities of their mother, whose various sexual infidelities he imagines as "somehow generic, mostly a matter of athleticism and flexibility. ...the mood one more of cooperation than complicity or passion" (*IJ* 957).

I think very briefly of the late Cosgrove Watt. I think of the hypophalan-
gial Grief-Therapist. I think of the Moms, alphabetizing cans of soup in the
cabinet over the microwave. Of Himself's umbrella hung by its handle from
the edge of the mail table just inside the Headmaster's House's foyer. ... I
think of John N. R. Wayne, who would have won this year's What-a-Burger
[Tennis Tournament], standing watch in a mask as Donald Gately and I dig
up my father's head. There's very little doubt that Wayne would have won.
(*IJ* 16–17)

Infinite Jest plays with *discours* and *récit* in all the ways that narratologists have
taught us to notice, and as we eventually learn, this scene is the chronologically
latest scene of the novel: the remaining 950-plus pages are in effect the background to Hal's being strapped to the stretcher. And his assertion to the administrators that he is "not just a boy who plays tennis" is an initial indication that
his objecthood has long been in the works. Wallace's essays on the U.S. Open
and Tracy Austin may raise questions about tennis, but nowhere is he more
damning of the sport than in *Jest*, whose young players refer to the professional
game as "The Show" and are considered by the academy administrators to be
"by intension training also to be entertainers" (*IJ* 188). Moreover, *Infinite Jest*
includes no detailed description of any match or even many points in a match,
and although there are a couple players at the institute—including Hal—who
have a shot at making the pro tour, it includes no Roger Federer, no "transcendent practitioners" of the game. What dominates the tennis scenes in the novel
instead is the systematic, mentally repressive, and physically exhausting regi-
men that the young players endure: *techne* reduced to technique. (Recall the
dialogue cited earlier about sprints and drills.) Learning to play with "no wasted
motion, egoless strokes, no flourishes or tics or excesses of wrist" (*IJ* 110), is not
a matter of individuals coming to flourish through munificent *Bildung*, but of
honing a manner that is "less alive than undead" (*IJ* 263), allowing the "repetition" of the training to "sink and soak into the hardware" (*IJ* 117), and becoming
one of the "grim machines" (*IJ* 483), someone whose very respiration exhibits
"no waste, complete utilization of each breath" (*IJ* 957).[83]

Yet in a circular narrative, in a text where the end is the beginning, any drama
that the tennis narrative of *Jest* may have engendered—whether Hal will escape
the academy's militaristic training, whether he will develop enough to make it to
the pros, etc.—is eradicated. Hal is, as it were, pinned to his future by his own

---

[83] See also the sharp distinction Schtitt makes between (a) the inner world of intention and engaged
competition and (b) the outer world of weather and other "conditions" (*IJ* 458–59).

narrative, his fate as an object appearing to us from the start as an inevitability. As we work through the text, it is wholly foreseeable that he should spend more and more time in a dark common room watching his father's films, immobile on a couch; and we are likewise unsurprised to see him grow unwilling or unable to converse with classmates. The epitome of this degeneration comes as Hal gradually loses control over his facial expressions in the final section of the book. "Shoot, are you crying? What's the matter?" he is asked suddenly by one of his classmates one morning, when Hal himself had believed his voice had been merely "neutral" (IJ 865); elsewhere he has to feel his own face to verify whether or not he is as "doubled over" and "*mirthful*" as another student observes (IJ 875–76). It's a telling shift, given how intimately the movements of our eyebrows, lips, and so forth are tied to our lives as expressive creatures. Objects may convey emotions or ideas, and animals may communicate altering moods, but as thinkers from Hegel to Wittgenstein to Levinas have noticed, neither has anything like the capacity for subtle, variegated, significant expression that the human countenance does. Our final glimpse of Hal in the novel comes through an unnamed E.T.A. student, as if immediate access to Hal's thoughts had begun to close off—a suspicion underlined when the narrator reports that Hal is "acting weird" in the locker room before a match, his face assuming "various expressions ranging from distended hilarity to scrunched grimace, expressions that seemed unconnected to anything that was going on" (IJ 966).[84]

The questions raised in Hal's narrative are only magnified in the narrative of Gately, the working-class pill addict. Gately is associated from the earliest stages of the book with his massive body and physical capacities. He is "almost twenty-nine and sober and just huge," a man of "intimidating size" and "a massive square head made squarer-looking by the Prince Valiantish haircut he tries to maintain himself in the mirror" (IJ 277), with a physical strength that has made him a high school football star, a bookie's enforcer, and now, in the rehab center, a live-in staff member who keeps the other residents under control. But all of Gately's physical capabilities are expunged in section 28 of the novel—the last and longest of the book, around 180 pages—which focuses on him lying in a hospital bed, motionless, unable to talk, struggling to recover from the gunshot wound that he suffers during his fight on the lawn of Ennet House. As in "Host" and the film-watchers of the novel, a healthy body has been penetrated

---

[84] Wondering aloud whether his actions are real, Hal is said to ask whether anyone else believed that "all this had been done and said so many times before it made you feel it was recorded, they all in here existed basically as Fourier Transforms of postures and little routines, locked down and stored and call-uppable for rebroadcast at specified times"—but "also, as a consequence, erasable" (IJ 966).

and weakened, only this time the penetration is neither metaphorical nor sur-really allegorical: the bullet is, a doctor reports, an "invasive foreign body" that creates a "massive infection" (*IJ* 814–15). In a series of scenes, Gately is vis-ited by several figures from Ennet House, who speak to him as a "huge empty confessional booth" (*IJ* 831), and he likewise experiences a string of hallucino-genic dreams that recall Hal's scrambled thoughts at the end of his opening monologue.[85]

But over time Gately's passivity descends to still another, deeper level, for in order to prevent himself from taking the painkillers that are continually offered to him by the hospital staff, he begins to meditate on his personal his-tory, attempting to "Abide via memory" (*IJ* 918). And this meditation takes us into most terrifying depths of isolation and paralysis in the entire book. As section 28 proceeds, Gately recalls an event from his darkest days as an addict, when his fellow "operative" Gene Fackelmann steals some money from their boss and asks Gately to join him on a binge. The two men hole themselves up in an empty apartment and proceed to ingest huge amounts of drugs, "on a hell of a tear, cooking up and getting off and eating M&M's when they could find their mouths with their hands, moving like men deep under water" (*IJ* 934). As the days pass, "the Substance seemed inexhaustible," and the mountain of pills they had piled up on the floor "changed shape but never really much shrank that they could see" (*IJ* 936). When their boss gets other henchmen to break into the apartment, they bring a circus of strange and threatening accomplices, and the prose begins to sound like a drowsy, drunken ramble, the redundan-cies and syntactic strains of its sentences evoking an increasingly nightmarish atmosphere: a woman is carried in by two men, "one leg out and a white stick of bone protruding from her shin, which her shin was a serious mess" (*IJ* 975); the room "smelled like Dilaudid and urine and Gately's vomit and Fackelmann's bowel movement and the red leather girl's fine leather coats" (*IJ* 976); two "fags" fill "the Graphix's huge party-bowl with grass from the Glad bag, which contained grass" (*IJ* 978); everybody "was drinking out of their square bottle, standing around the sunny room in the awkward postures of way more people than seats" (*IJ* 978). Gradually the scene comes to resemble a grotesque revision of earlier moments in the book, as if Gately's descent is the hellish endpoint awaiting most of the novel's other characters. The foul smell of the room recalls the odor that is said to fill the room of the medical attaché sitting "very still

---

[85] The most important of these visitors is a "figurant" who sounds decidedly like the late James Incandenza, a man Gately has never met, and who tells him of his struggles to communicate with his withdrawn youngest son.

and attentive" before the Entertainment (*IJ* 87), and Gately and his partner are reduced to the kind of blankly inarticulate state that Hal presents to the college administrators in the opening scene: "His whole front side of him was cold from lying on the wet floor. Fackelmann around somewhere behind him was mumbling something that consisted totally of *g*'s" (*IJ* 974). Most gruesome of all is the retribution taken upon Fackelmann, an act of punishment that parallels Hal's gradual loss of control over his facial expressions: "Fackelmann started screaming. The scream's pitch got higher as it drew out. When Gately could look away from the stuff going on, he saw [someone] was sewing Fackelmann's eyelids open to the skin above his eyebrows. As in they were sewing poor Count Faxula's eyes open" (*IJ* 979). Once again meaners have become matter, and a distinctive site of human expressiveness shrunk to a manipulable piece of flesh.

To be sure, this final scene is chronologically far from the end of Gately's story: we know that he survives this ravaging binge and eventually gets clean in the recovery house, realizing that the "quilted-sampler-type cliché" offered by AA can, in fact, be "masking something ghastly deep and real" (*IJ* 446). Wallace himself often offered such redemptive lessons in interviews and essays, not only in the pieces of civic humanism that I've described, but also when he famously speaks at the end of "E Unibus Pluram" about art that shows "reverence and conviction," that risks seeming "backward, quaint, naïve, anachronistic" (*SFT* 81). But as Burn notes, *Infinite Jest* is keen everywhere to disrupt our sense of temporal progression, its "antiteleological spirit" infecting the entire novel, "refusing or parodying the notion of resolution or goal-reaching."[86] Like Hal's narrative, Gately's is essentially circular, ending almost where it began, its forward progress defeated by its continual movements backward in time. Gately's story may gesture toward Aristotelian self-governance,[87] but as a narrative, it concludes with him lying on his back in an utterly static condition, constrained two times over—once in the present tense of the hospital, suspended between sobriety and addiction, and once in the remembered past of the binge. It's a collapse that concludes with the harrowing polysyndeton of the book's final sentences:

the last thing Gately saw was an Oriental bearing down with the held square and he looked into the square and saw clearly a reflection of his

---

[86] Stephen J. Burn, "'Webs of Nerves Pulsing and Firing': *Infinite Jest* and the Science of Mind," in *Guide to David Foster Wallace Studies*, ed. Burn and Boswell, 61.

[87] See, most notably, the joyful drive he takes around Boston midway through the book, cruising in his boss's car to buy groceries for Ennet House.

own big square pale head with its eyes closing as the floor finally pounced. And when he came back to, he was flat on his back on the beach in the freezing sand, and it was raining out of a low sky, and the tide was way out. (*IJ* 981)

Some early readers found this conclusion frustrating, but Wallace's justifications were shrewd and, in the present context, revealing. It was meant, he explained to his discomfited editor, as "an almost Artaud-ish blackout-type ending," one that "might look truncated or even violently ablated," but which resonates with "themes of stasis, annulation, paralysis, undecidability, clarification of questions > solutions to questions, etc."[88] All very far, in other words, from the redemptive vision that springs suddenly from the final pages of *The Brothers Karamazov*, Wallace's ostensible model, and all very similar to the themes offered in the opening scene with Hal in the hospital: action broken and unachieved, a central character lying immobile, floating backward in time rather than deliberating on the future, shards of a traumatic personal history whirling through his thoughts.

Infinite Jest is, of course, hardly the first novel to have imagined the evaporation of rational autonomy, the transformation of persons into bodies, and actions into motions. Such deterioration runs through all the authors I've discussed, not to mention a great deal of science fiction and postmodernism.[89] But Wallace's book adds a further dimension to this deterioration, one that comes into focus only when, as I've been doing, we set the text against the Aristotelian and Deweyan strains of his nonfiction. Recall the remark, in

---

[88] Quoted in Max, *Every Love Story*, 193. Among the early readers who were puzzled by the ending was Michiko Kakutani of the *New York Times*, who criticized the book for leaving the "old-fashioned reader who harbors the vagues expectations of narrative connections" "suspended in midair and reeling from the random muchness of detail and incident." Quoted in Max, 217.

[89] In my discussion of Percy and Powers in Chapter 1, I mentioned Pynchon's *V.*, where the growing inanimacy of the mysterious shape-shifting title character coincides with her increasing attraction, from the turn of the century to World War II, to extreme right-wing ideologies across Europe and beyond. The encroachments of objecthood among the characters in Wallace's novel parallel the election to the presidency of the Reagan-ish (or, as of the election of 2016, Trumpian) Johnny Gentle, "lounge singer turned teenybopper throb turned B-movie mainstay, for two long-past decades known unkindly as the 'Cleanest Man in Entertainment'" (*IJ* 381). Encouraged by sinister advisers, striving for "the advent of a Tighter, Tidier Nation" (*IJ* 382), Gentle oversees the massive expansion of advertising and of "self-selected" television viewing, and he also engineers the annexation of both Canada and Mexico, a move that creates a sprawling nation called the Organization of North American Nations (known, naturally, as "O.N.A.N."). Given the cartoonishness of these political developments, it's only appropriate that readers learn about them primarily through a filmed version of a puppet show made by Mario, whose "openly jejune version" of the story "unfolds in little diffracted bits of real news and fake news and privately-conceived dialogue" over the course of dozens of pages (*J* 385).

Virtues and Vices, that informs so much of James D. Wallace's vision of moral and political life: "normative data are found in nature," in our understanding of healthy, "normal, nondefective individual[s] of a certain kind" leading "the mode of life characteristic" of this kind (*VV* 18–19). The essays of *Supposedly Fun Thing* and *Consider the Lobster* echo Wallace's father insofar as they seek in the particulars of the empirical world a range of available normative concepts: the *techne* of the news techs, the judiciousness of the language specialist, and so on. The fundamental questions of *Infinite Jest*, by contrast, are whether such virtues are actually perceptible in our contemporary "mode of life," and whether, given the power of "nature," given the overwhelming force of the nonintentional, any kind of "normative data" can actually be discovered there.[90]

"Nature" here means, in part, the natural world; the novel's setting is, after all, full of poisoned bodies and toxified space.[91] But "nature" here more pressingly means the nature of human beings, or human beings *qua* natural organism as James Wallace understands them. It's tempting to say that *Infinite Jest* is fundamentally about akratic action, weakness of the will. The stories of Hal and Gately, of the Ennet House residents, of the people viewing the Entertainment—all these narratives seem to thematize the ancient question of how someone who is capable of mature deliberation could go against his or her better judgment in specific cases. But talking of *akrasia* is misleading. For as Aristotle first noted, incontinence is attributable only to beings who have general ideas, who have a set of goals or projects, because only a creature who understands these things can be said to *fail* to live according to them.[92] As I've been suggesting, these are precisely the capacities that *Infinite Jest* so radically diminishes. The diminishment is most melodramatic in the public health crisis unleashed by the film, but it is also on offer in the narrative of Hal on the hospital stretcher, of Gately on the freezing sand, and even of Mario sitting

---

[90] For a philosopher who raises comparable questions about James Wallace's work, see Ronald de Sousa's review of *Virtues and Vices*, in *Noûs* 16 (1982): 161–65.

[91] "Poisoned bodies" and "the toxification of space" are phrases from Heather Houser, "*Infinite Jest's* Environmental Case for Disgust," in *The Legacy of David Foster Wallace*, ed. Cohen and Konstantinou, 128. Houser's essay is, in part, an extension of one of the earliest essays on the novel, N. Katherine Hayles's "The Illusion of Autonomy and the Fact of Recursivity: Virtual Ecologies, Entertainment, and *Infinite Jest*," *New Literary History* 30 (1997): 675–97.

[92] Aristotle's explanation is given in Book VII of the *Nicomachean Ethics*, and hinges on his claim about practical action's (tacit) syllogistic structure. If, for instance, we say that everything sweet must be tasted, and then perceive a particular thing that is sweet, the unhindered person will act on this perception. Beasts, however, are neither continent nor incontinent because they have no universal supposition, only appearances and memory of particulars. A gerbil, that is, has no concept of "everything sweet," let alone "sweetness" as such; it has only the perception and memory of specific sweet items in the world, and thus can't act counter to its will.

before the radio. These are not akratic actors, but what Harry Frankfurt has classified as "wantons": creatures who not only have no control over their wills, but who do not *care* about their wills, whose desires move them to do certain things without their ever wanting to be moved by them. Like nonhuman animals or small children, they all lack the capacity to reflect upon their first-order desires, unable to evaluate their desires and motives, and they pursue whatever course of action their inclinations demand, all without asking how desirable their particular inclinations are.[93] Mario's first-order desires may be pure and innocent, and lead to patient and benevolent actions, whereas the first-order desires of the film-watchers, Hal, and Gately may lead to self-destructive paralysis. But structurally, these behaviors are all identical. None of them arises from someone achieving what Ellison would call "conscious thought," or being able, as Robinson would say, "to stand apart from themselves, appraising." The characters are thus akin to the feral hamsters and feral infants who are said to roam the overfertilized areas of what had once been Quebec: creatures who may have conflicting desires but who cannot solve these conflicts by reflecting upon and ranking their preferences—and who thus, at least on Frankfurt's reckoning, may not even qualify as full-blooded persons. A person is an entity whose agency may be fragmented or partial, but it is doubtful that these figures could be said to have any agency to fragment or lose.

All this helps explain why Wallace's fiction often is said—often by himself—to have extended DeLillo's major interests and themes: the fading of the autonomous self in a culture defined by an accelerating specialization of knowledge, large-scale geopolitical movements, looming ecological threats, rapidly advancing information systems, and so forth.[94] But what I've been arguing here points to a less commonly discussed aspect of *Infinite Jest* that it inherits from DeLillo. To recall a notorious phrase applied to DeLillo's *Libra* (1988) by an old family friend of the Wallaces, the pundit George F. Will, *Infinite Jest* is in many ways

---

[93] Frankfurt, "Freedom of the Will and the Concept of a Person," in *The Importance of What We Care About*, 16–17.

[94] This characterization is partly drawn from Tom LeClair's account of DeLillo in *In the Loop: Don DeLillo and the Systems Novel* (Urbana: University of Illinois Press, 1987)—one of the few books of literary criticism that Wallace kept till the end of his life, and which he marked up heavily. His notations consist mostly of heavy underlining, particularly in the introduction and the chapters on *Great Jones Street*, *End Zone*, and *Ratner's Star*. (There is no underlining in the chapters on *White Noise* or *Black Dogs*, and only a few lines in the chapters devoted to *The Names* and *Americana*.) The introduction includes several handwritten notes about systems theory, including a "Nice" at the top of page 12, next to a passage in which LeClair discusses the relationship between long novels, media, and uncertainty. For LeClair's early reading of *Infinite Jest*, see his essay "The Prodigious Fiction of Richard Powers, William Vollmann, and David Foster Wallace," *Critique: Studies in Contemporary Fiction* 38.1 (Fall 1996): 12–37.

an act of "bad citizenship."⁹⁵ At the very least it's a book preoccupied with bad citizenship—with the forces that degrade our rational reflection on the common good and that prevent us from believing that our normative concepts "actually *stand for* something." The attention to these forces in *Jest* reminds us that one of the first novels to captivate the young Wallace was *McTeague*, Frank Norris's great naturalist work about San Francisco at the turn of the century and a key work for *Broom of the System*.⁹⁶ But given the intellectual framework in which I've placed Wallace, one might go still further back in time, well beyond DeLillo and George Will and Norris, and identify these forces and conditions with an even more august group of bad citizens. For in a novel that so consistently focuses on human powerlessness, that is so full of references to Narcissus and Heracles and other ancient myths, that so seldom treats Christianity as a live option for most of its characters, that seems so ambivalent about what human beings have achieved and how they might live, its truest predecessors might, in fact, be Aeschylus or Sophocles, the tragedians whose focus on the supreme power of fate and accident was partly what provoked Aristotle a few decades later to prize the rational autonomy and civic virtues that he did. For all its high-tech experiments and near-future settings, in other words, *Infinite Jest* gives us another way of dramatizing Bernard Williams's claim that, in our ethical situation, we contemporaries may be more like human beings in antiquity than any Western people have been in the meantime. Like the tragedians, the novel envisions life not as an education in the virtues or as training for the *polis*. It nowhere views human beings achieving control over contingencies, or our ethical relations to the world as fully intelligible. It sees us instead as driven by forces we never fully grasp, as living in a world that cannot be made safe either for individuals or collectively: beings caught in a deadly undertow.⁹⁷ Had

---

⁹⁵ George F. Will, "Shallow Look at the Mind of an Assassin," *The Washington Post* (September 22, 1988), A25. George Will is the son of Frederick Will, the pragmatist who, as I noted in an earlier footnote in this chapter, heavily influenced James D. Wallace. So when DeLillo addressed the "bad citizenship" comment in a profile in *The New Yorker*, Wallace was quick to salt his praise with some personal reminiscences, in a 1997 letter/postcard: "If you're interested, G.W. is a towering peckerhead in person. His Dad & mine were colleagues at Illinois for decades; Will used to come to dinner parties [at our house], behave churlishly, and leave without saying thank you to my Mom, thereby earning her irremediable hatred—she buys cherries with the *Times* every Sunday so she can spit pits at GW when he appears on *Brinkley*" (Harry Ransom Center, University of Texas at Austin).

⁹⁶ For Wallace's response to *McTeague*, see Max, *Every Love Story*, 39.

⁹⁷ Bernard Williams, *Shame and Necessity* (Berkeley: University of California Press, 1993), 164–67. The phrase "deadly undertow" is taken from Mary K. Holland, whose reading of *Jest* as a struggle with narcissism accords with my own sense—and contrary to a heavily influential way of reading it—that the novel doesn't entirely fulfill Wallace's stated ambitions; see her *Succeeding Postmodernism: Language and Humanism in Contemporary American Literature* (London: Bloomsbury, 2013), 68. On the place of Greek myth in the novel, see Burn, *David Foster Wallace's Infinite Jest: A Reader's Guide*, 60–63. On the Greek philosophers' response to the heavy emphasis on *tuchē*

Wallace wanted an epigraph for the novel, he might have done worse than the chorus's lines in *Antigone*: "When a god drives him, and deceives, / a man will decide / what is bad is good / and lives only a brief while / outside disaster."[98]

V. You're Talking Like a Civics Class

Infinite Jest may be comparable to an ancient tragedy, but we shouldn't lose sight, of course, of the specific social and ethical world that Wallace is describing. Ancient tragedians were typically using narratives that had existed already for hundreds of years, and the plays were typically about characters whose specific, metaphysically inflected social stations guided their actions to one degree or another, even if they could become conflicted about how to act in a given case. Antigone's orientation as a citizen and her orientation as a sister didn't necessarily conflict, until suddenly they did. Wallace, by contrast, is self-consciously writing in and about an age when such ethical orientations have withered to almost nothing. He speaks in and of an era that, in Lukács's famous words, is no longer "integrated," where "the structures made by man for man" are no longer "his necessary and native home," and at a moment when, as Bakhtin says, "the speaking subjects of high, proclamatory genres—of priests, prophets, judges, leaders, patriarchal fathers, and so forth—have departed this life."[99]

To Bakhtin such departures were liberating, as they obviously were at some level for Wallace, and it's fitting that critics have linked the two.[100] Mathematics and logic, the early passions that gradually waned for Wallace, epitomize the "monologic" systems that raised Bakhtin's ire: a timeless and unified realm separate from the "unfinished, still-evolving contemporary reality (the openended present)," and sealed off from the laughter and grotesquerie that both he and

---

(chance) in earlier Greek culture, see Martha Nussbaum, *The Fragility of Goodness: Luck and Ethics in Greek Tragedy* (Cambridge: Cambridge University Press, 1986). It may be worth underlining that Williams's comparison between us and the ancients is not meant to deny the obvious differences, particularly our powerful inheritance of Judaism and Christianity. "I am not," Williams remarks, "denying that the modern world is through and through different from the ancient world. I am not suggesting either, that we should feel sorry for ourselves because we are not Homeric or tragic or Periclean people." His goal is instead more modest and pragmatic: "if we find things of a special beauty and power in what has survived from that world, it is encouraging to think that we might move beyond marveling at them, to putting them, or bits of them, to modern uses" (166–67).

[98] Sophocles, *Antigone*, trans. Richard Emil Braun (New York: Oxford University Press, 1973), 46.

[99] Georg Lukács, *The Theory of the Novel*, trans. Anna Bostock (Cambridge, MA: MIT Press, 1971), 64; Mikhail Bakhtin, "From Notes Made in 1970–71," *Speech Genres and Other Late Essays*, trans. Vern W. McGee, ed. Caryl Emerson and Michael Holquist (Austin: University of Texas Press, 1986), 132.

[100] On Bakhtin and Wallace, see, for example, Boddy, "A Fiction of Response," *A Companion to David Foster Wallace Studies*, 36–39; Catherine Nichols, "Dialogizing Postmodern Carnival: David Foster Wallace's *Infinite Jest*," *Critique* 43.1 (2001): 3–16; Kelly, "Development Through Dialogue."

Wallace found so definitive of human life.[101] But Wallace was also Lukácian, viewing modernity and its exemplary literary genre—the genre that seemed "What I'm Supposed to Do," as he said to DeLillo—with ambivalence, even mourning. As an essayist he may side with his father and Aristotle and Dewey, calling us to the virtues and asking us to believe that our normative words might actually "*stand for* something." Yet his fiction is everywhere marked by a nominalist skepticism about these words, and a sense that, as Lukács says, "the extensive totality of life is no longer directly given," that the "problematic individual" struggles painfully with "the absence of any manifest aim."[102] Indeed, the very idea of an "extensive totality of life" seems in Wallace's fiction to have grown obscured in a historically singular way. Lukács was writing, after all, about texts that were sometimes centuries old, which implies at least some continuity between them and the moment of his own composition. *Don Quixote* still mattered when he sat at his desk in 1914. By contrast, the almost total absence in Wallace's work of any historical event predating his own birth suggests that the transformations of our own volatile day—including the forms of nominalism and bald naturalism that have concerned me throughout this book—make us historically unique: no other culture has been so skeptical toward normative languages and judgment. More even than Lukács, Wallace sensed that the "primaeval images" of good and evil have lost "their objective self-evidence for us," that "everything that falls from our weary and despairing hands must always be incomplete," because we are always conscious that our purposes have been diminished to mere "ideals," "subjective facts."[103] Thus the

---

[101] Mikhail Bakhtin, *The Dialogic Imagination: Four Essays*, trans. Caryl Emerson and Michael Holquist, ed. Michael Holquist (Austin: University of Texas Press, 1981), 7.

[102] Lukács, *Theory of the Novel*, 62.

[103] Lukács, *Theory of the Novel*, 34, 80. As I'm suggesting, the tension that Lukács identified in classic novels is heightened in Modernism and its afterlife, when the onslaught of "what is" empirically seems further and further from "what should be," artistically and morally. Thus, for instance, T.S. Eliot's famous mixture of apocalypse and voluntarism in his claims about *Ulysses* and its way of "controlling, of ordering, of giving a shape and a significance to the immense panorama of futility and anarchy which is contemporary history." Compare Michael André Bernstein's felicitous formulation of the modernist's predicament: "Their task was not really commensurate with the efforts of even their most ambitious predecessors, in part because the category of the whole had become essentially arbitrary. One could accept, in other words, the abstract principle of a *Gesamtkunstwerk*, but since there was no longer cultural agreement on what constituted a coherent totality in the first place, each artist was compelled to work out his own, particular, and thus necessarily idiosyncratic selection. The logic of a representative masterpiece makes any acknowledgment of its arbitrariness inadmissible, however, so the text must not only select its *materia poetica* from a range of possibilities and with an absence of generic guidelines hitherto unthinkable, but it must also do so in such a way as to make that selection appear simultaneously inevitable and complete." See Michael André Bernstein, "Making Modernist Masterpieces," *Modernism/Modernity* 5 (1998), 7–8.

irony that Lukács recognized in the novel as a genre becomes a singular obsession in Wallace. *Not* to be "weary and despairing" about this condition is to be James Incandenza, Hal's father, who for most of his filmmaking career shows disastrously little remorse that his own created forms—"technically gorgeous" yet "oddly hollow, empty" (*IJ* 740–42)—are "subjective facts" wholly without "objective self-evidence." But to go to the opposite extreme, to be *only* "weary and despairing" about our forms, is to risk getting lost: to become a wanton, to succumb to the tragic undertow.

I raise these issues of belief and genre here because they provide a fitting way both to conclude my discussion of Wallace and to bring this book as a whole toward an end. For *The Pale King*, the sprawling novel that Wallace never finished, brings to a head many of the basic dilemmas faced by the postwar sages I've been discussing. The novel (or what we have of it) is clearly in line with Wallace's nonfiction as I've described it. As Marshall Boswell has noted, most early reviewers, as well Wallace's editor, understood the book to be fundamentally concerned with monotony, or what Wallace's notes refer to as "Paying attention, boredom, ADD," and "people performing mindless jobs." But the bigger themes of the book are, in fact, political, and *civics* is one of its guiding keywords: "Being individual" as the same notes put it, "vs. being part of larger things—paying taxes, being 'lone gun' in IRS vs. team player" (*PK* 547).[104] As Boswell notes, *The Pale King* is a sort of genealogy of contemporary civic life and public policy. It is the first *historical* novel in Wallace's oeuvre, and uses the early-to-mid-1980s to present a genealogy of contemporary civic life, particularly the wide-ranging impact of Reagan's "trickle-down economics"—a model whose simplemindedness fostered a political culture that, as Wallace said to an interviewer, is "childish, and totally unconducive to hard thought, give and take, compromise, or the ability of grown-ups to function as any kind of community."[105]

---

[104] Marshall Boswell, "Trickle-Down Citizenship: Taxes and Civic Responsibility in David Foster Wallace's *The Pale King*," *Studies in the Novel* 44 (2012): 465.

[105] Ibid., 466, 470. Boswell's emphasis on Wallace's criticism of Reagan's simpleminded economic models is meant in part, justly, as a criticism of readers who fixate on Wallace's appreciation of simple clichés—an interpretation that he associates with Hubert Dreyfus and Sean Dorrance Kelly in *All Things Shining*. It seems to me less right to imply, as Boswell does, that boredom and taxes are separate themes in the novel, the one simply overshadowing the other. The boredom theme is, in fact, put in the service of the civics theme, and the acceptance of boredom itself—the capacity to cope with and understand boredom—is pictured as a civic virtue. The remark Boswell cites about what is "childish, and totally unconducive to hard thought" is taken from Wallace's interview with Eggers, republished in *Last Interview*, 75.

Much as it echoes Wallace's essays, so, too, *The Pale King* often echoes *Infinite Jest*. Most obvious is its epic sweep: As in *Jest*, the sheer number of characters and (nascent) plotlines is a testament to the book's ambition, its effort to encompass the entirety of the republic. As in *Jest* as well, it makes prominent use of the philosophical dialogue, particularly in discussions over competing conceptions of freedom. The clearest example is §19, where *Jest*'s debates between Marathe and Steeply over positive and negative liberty are expanded by several unnamed characters who are caught in an elevator, debating the history and ontological status of "civic virtue," "selfishness," "duty," "responsibility," "honorable," and other broad normative concepts.[106] Moreover, as elsewhere in Wallace's oeuvre, *The Pale King* shows a deep interest in the arcana of people's labor and institutional life, though the work and settings of this novel (accountancy, IRS offices) required far heavier research on his part than did tennis, schools, or rehab houses.[107] And, much as the stories of Poor Tony or Gately and Fackelmann lead *Jest* into dark and violent subcultures that are

---

[106] Beyond returning to the themes of Isaiah Berlin's "Two Concepts of Liberty," the scene is also very much a retelling of Wallace's argument in "E Unibus Pluram" about the confluence of postmodernism and capitalism. "But if I'm getting DeWitt's thrust," says one character, "the fulcrum was the moment in the sixties when rebellion against conformity became fashionable, a pose, a way to look cool to the others in your generation you wanted to impress and get accepted by.... [T]hat's when corporations and their advertisers can step in and start reinforcing it and seducing people with it into buying the things the corporations are producing" (*PK* 147). In "Development Through Dialogue," Adam Kelly makes two points about these scenes that are worth noting. First, both the Steeply–Marathe debates of *Jest* (which occur primarily on a mountain top in Arizona) and the elevator debates of *Pale King* are set in elevated places, "as if such elevation allows the characters a survey of the territory" (268). Second, one wouldn't want to equate Marathe and the main speaker (Glendenning) in the elevator: Marathe's arguments are complicated by the way he "dabbles in psychological games" with Steeply, working as a double- or triple- or quadruple-agent, whereas Glendenning "seems unconcerned to wield power over others," "admitting confusion about the accuracy and tightness of his arguments" (277–78).

[107] Max sketches Wallace's research on taxation in *Every Love Story*, 291–92. His research on the subject led him to query his father, James, in one of the few e-mails held in his papers at the Random Center, dated October 18, 2005:

Long shot, I know, but do you happen to be familiar with any scholarship in ethics regarding taxation—i.e., the ethical problems involved in taxation, in paying or not paying taxes, in evading taxes for selfish, pecuniary reasons vs. withholding taxes for moral or political reasons (tax evasion vs. tax protest?)?

If so, can you give me some references?

—ton fils

To which his father responded on the same day (in a less casual and playfully familiar tone):

Dear David,

The things that come to mind are discussions of taxation that are embedded in some sort of theoretical context—Nozick arguing that taxes on income is theft, Walzer arguing for a negative income tax. There must be straightforward discussions of the ethics of paying taxes but I don't know of them off hand. You might look up the entry on taxes in Lawrence Becker et al, eds., The Encyclopedia of Ethics. If there is such an entry, it would have a bibliography.

—Dad

very far removed from the white-collar world that Wallace intimately knew, so *The Pale King* includes (using an odd pastiche of Cormac McCarthy) chapters devoted to Toni Ware, whose childhood in trailer parks is darkened by sexual abuse in much the way that her own unmarried mother is haunted and stalked by unstable men. Last but not least, as in the earlier novel, *The Pale King* is powerfully drawn to the figure of the wanton: here, Chris Fogle, who at the start of his long monologue in §22 describes himself as having been, as a teenager, "the worst kind of nihilist—the kind who isn't even aware he's a nihilist." Growing up in the 1970s, he says (in a parody of a thought experiment attributed to Wittgenstein) he was "like a piece of paper on the street in the wind, thinking 'Now I think I'll blow this way, now I think I'll blow that way'. My essential response to everything was 'Whatever'" (*PK* 156).[108] Only years later, after untold hours spent watching soap operas and smoking pot and moving aimlessly between colleges, does he claim—as if channeling Wallace the essayist—to have "put away childish things" and to have developed "some initiative and direction in my life" (*PK* 174).

Fogle's particular "initiative and direction," however, suggests some of the crucial differences between *Jest* and *The Pale King*—and some reasons, I think, why Wallace ran aground with his third novel. The "dramatic event" that suddenly changed Fogle is said to have occurred during an Advanced Tax review class that he accidentally attends at DePaul University one evening (he had planned to attend a review for a course in American Political Thought), when he hears a lecture on accounting by an "unmellow" Jesuit. I suggested in passing earlier that the scene represents a moment of Cavellian absorption, but just as important as the immersive experience is the actual content of the priest's lecture and what it impels Fogle to undertake. The Jesuit lecturer sees in accountancy a form of moral greatness, but a type of greatness that's very far from what Fogle's generation had been encouraged to seek. "True heroism," the priest announces, "is *a priori* incompatible with audience or applause or even the bare notice of the common run of man." It is instead, he continues, the ability "to attend fully to the interests of the client and to balance those interests against the high ethical standards of FASB and extant law—yea, to serve those who care not for service but only for results. . . . Effacement. Sacrifice. Service" (*PK* 232–33). The intensity and purposiveness of the priest shames Fogel, who recognizes him as "the first genuine authority figure I ever met, meaning a figure

---

[108] See Elizabeth Anscombe, *Intention* (Oxford: Blackwell, 1957): "I once saw some notes on a lecture of Wittgenstein in which he imagined some leaves blown about by the wind and saying 'Now I'll go this way . . . now I'll go that way'" (6).

with genuine 'authority' instead of just the power to judge you or squeeze your shoes from their side of the generation gap" (*PK* 229). Not long after the end of the lecture—"Gentlemen, you are called to account," intones the priest (*PK* 235)—Fogel decides to visit an IRS recruiting station, realizing for the first time a truth that his post-1960s generation had failed to grasp, and which he credits to the man who became his boss at the Agency: "Real freedom is freedom to obey the law" (*PK* 195).

The key term in this maxim is "the law." For Marathe in *Infinite Jest*, "freedom" is belonging to a community—a matter of "what we worship," "what we invest with faith," "attachments," "love of your nation, your country and people" (*IJ* 107). But to obey the law is quite different from loving these various other things. For unlike a community, modern law is an institution, with demarcated boundaries, systematic rules, and a legitimacy that is understood to derive from its impersonality and universalism. Laws are typically put in print, apply to all citizens, are defended by coercive power that is recognized as rightful, and are designed to embody, in Max Weber's famous phrase, a "rational" form of authority rather than a "traditional" or "charismatic" one. In such a regime, Marathe's words—"worship," "faith," "attachments," "love"—become officially irrelevant, replaced by the chillier language of "contract," "rights," "principles," and "obedience." And from these words it is, of course, only a short step to the image of the modern state as a merely formal apparatus, what Hegel called "a *dead, cold letter* and a *shackle*": a machine of impersonal procedures grinding out impersonal decisions, a network of regulations rather than a narrative of shared experiences that inspire identity and devotion. Whether or not such a view reflected, as Hegel believed, "superficial philosophy," the ambitious writers who preceded and followed him recognized its profound effects.[109] For most novelists, that is, neither I nor anyone else is especially responsible for the legal systems that shadow our lives, and many of the characters who have provided the best material for new stories—the young people newly loosened from family, village, and church, hunting for opportunity in the quickly expanding cities or the increasingly colonized territories—are either indifferent or hostile toward modern political institutions.[110] (Think of *Bleak House*, *The Scarlett Letter*, Kafka's trials and penal colonies, *1984*.) Such texts are the ancestors to the farcical and the dystopian images of government that fill contemporary fiction and

---

[109] G.W.F. Hegel, *The Philosophy of Right*, trans. H.B. Nisbett, ed. Allen W. Wood (Cambridge: Cambridge University Press, 1991), 16–17.

[110] The classic claim about the importance of *youth* in modern fiction is Franco Moretti, *The Way of the World: The* Bildungsroman *in European Culture*, trans. Albert Sbragia (London: Verso, 1987).

popular media, where façades of legality cover up paltry self-interest and party apparatchiks calculate how to execute the directives of their glib, smiling leaders. (Think of *Jest*'s Johnny Gentle.) And this is to say nothing of the long tradition of fiction that envisions that most problematic arm of the modern state, the military, as a den of careerist administrators and cold-blooded rationalizations. It's become commonplace to associate the decade of the 1960s with a resistance to what Toni Morrison has called "statist" language, or what Foucault referred to as "statutory" politics; and to identify those years with a heady brew of libertarian and communitarian hopes, a growing suspicion toward government institutions, and a distaste for official forms of dispute and negotiation.[111] But if such anxieties about our legal institutions were radicalized in these years, they were in themselves hardly new. They pervade recent literary and cultural history, part and parcel of a broader dissatisfaction with modern bourgeois culture that has been expressed repeatedly over the last two and a half centuries.

As a genre, that is, the novel seems predisposed to associating the modern state with something very much like the reductionism that streams through *Infinite Jest*. So the dilemma that Wallace faced in finding a "click" for the pieces of his third book was not just that boredom is an impossibly difficult theme to dramatize. It was also that the civic institutions whose types of boredom the text explores—the civic institutions whose clichés about the common good we should take more seriously, that decide our macroeconomic policy and other gray issues—can be difficult to dramatize compassionately in the literary form that he felt compelled to use. From Quixote and Sancho onward, the novel genre has always been able to foreground friendship, and as critics have always noted, it's been particularly preoccupied with bourgeois marriage. But friendships and marriages are wholly embodied relations, affiliations between specific persons who can sit and walk and talk with one another in specific settings, who can discuss and reflect upon specific personal histories, and who can express beliefs, preferences, and desires in the form of letters, conversations, gestures, or text messages. By contrast, modern governments and their agencies are— by design—too abstract and disembodied to perform these fragile, nuanced actions, and they're made to be anonymous in all the ways that one's friends and spouses are not. Their functions are meant to be implemented by any individual regardless of his or her experiences, tastes, and family backgrounds. And

---

[111] For an especially sharp expression of this view, see Sean McCann and Michael Szalay, "Do You Believe in Magic? Literary Thinking After the New Left," *The Yale Journal of Criticism* 18 (2005): 435–68 (Morrison's "statist" quotation at 449).

its leaders have all and only the legal powers that their predecessors had. Meet the new boss, same as the old boss.

The Pale King may, in other words, have been trying to move beyond the overthrow of a particular personality type, the ironist; and it may have been thinking about solving the specifically structural and institutional causes of postmodern suffering. But one reason for its failure might be that it's very hard to say just what "solving" such "structural and institutional" problems would really look like in a novel.[112] Novels characteristically attend to relationships that are anything *but* universal, yet *The Pale King* wants us to commit ourselves to institutions whose structures have been assembled to act as mechanically as possible. It wants us to conceive of a government agency not as "a corporate entity" but as a "*moral* one" (*PK* 545), and like the Founding Fathers—those "geniuses of civic virtue"—it wants us to be "rational, honorable, civic-minded," with "at least as much concern for the common good as for personal advantage" (*PK* 136). And in the story of Chris Fogle and elsewhere, *The Pale King* is trying to imagine characters who understand their role in staggeringly large bureaucracies not as a job but as a vocation, a calling, and whose leaders are worthy of (Bakhtin's phrase) proclamatory genres. The result is a text that, as Wallace himself worried, often falls prey to the deflationary reproach leveled at one of the speakers caught on the elevator, solemnly preaching about one's "duty" to others and one's "duty" to be a certain sort of person. "You're talking," says a colleague, "like a civics class" (*PK* 133).

Wallace's dilemma recalls nothing so much as Bakhtin's explanation for why Gogol, having finished *Dead Souls*, struggled to carry out his plan for a trilogy based on the *Divine Comedy*. "The tragedy of Gogol," Bakhtin writes, "is to a very real extent the tragedy of a genre": of trying to install "distanced and positive images" into a form that tends by and large toward "familiar contact" and the "spontaneity of the inconclusive present." Working in the "zone" of the novel, he says, Gogol "could not manage the move from Hell to Purgatory and then to Paradise with the same people and in the same work; no continuous transition was possible."[113] If *Infinite Jest* is Wallace's *Inferno*, its meaners condemned to a state of matter, then the difficulty of completing *The Pale King* suggests

---

[112] Here I am disagreeing with Lee Konstantinou's very interesting essay on Wallace's relationship to various avant-garde or experimental traditions, "No Bull: David Foster Wallace and Postironic Belief," *The Legacy of David Foster Wallace* (ed. Cohen and Konstantinou), 106, 110. Konstantinou's essay ends with an apt contrast between Wallace and Dave Eggers, who has championed Wallace's will to believe but who, unlike Wallace, mixes an "offbeat aesthetic with a laudable urge toward philanthropy and the active construction of alternative institutional structures" (106).

[113] Bakhtin, *Dialogic Imagination*, 28.

just how blurry our high words have become, and how ferociously difficult it is, in turn, to write a novelistic *Paradiso*. It's not hard to see why some image of government would help contribute to the comprehensive, large-scale canvass that Wallace is drawn to make: governmental structures are one expression of a collective, both embodying and orienting the sorts of practices and character that a society wants to promote. But the particular governmental structures that interest Wallace, *our* governmental structures, are both in theory and in practice a bewilderingly dense, impersonal bureaucratic network, and it has been difficult for novelists to present these complex webs as something other than an object of mocking hilarity or heated attack. Wallace wants to be proclamatory about them, and the fact that it's a priest who emboldens Fogle to join the IRS is one indication of the way he wants not only to treat the agency as a *"moral"* entity, but even to re-sacralize a notion of the "common good." But Johnny Gentle can't be forgotten so easily; he, not the earnest boss who identifies freedom with obeying the law, has been the more natural image of official or state authority in Wallace's chosen genre. Whatever its shortcomings as a work of fiction, then, *The Pale King* winds up summarizing a great deal of Wallace's life's work. Wallace the essayist was hoping that I as a reader might see my connection to other persons as a matter of solidarity—a manifestation of who I am and what I value, not merely as an external constraint on my liberty. But Wallace the novelist was keenly attuned to the forces that have kept his contemporaries from "sucking it up." He knew the literary, historical, and cultural powers that have kept us from full conviction. It's a tension that can seem scary, even tragic, and can leave one stranded on the freezing sand, the tide way out.

The abstractionist and the materialist thus mutually
exasperating each other
EMERSON, "Montaigne"

AFTERWORD

Words to Go On

THE YEAR THAT *Philosophical Investigations* appeared, the year that *Invisible Man* won the fourth annual National Book Award, the economist Milton Friedman made a claim about our disagreements over economic and public policy. In the Western world, he said, our differences are almost always about the most efficient means of achieving agreed-upon ends, and most disagreements boil down to conflicting predictions. We all want, for example, everyone to have a living wage, but we clash over whether a legal, enforceable minimum wage can effectively make that happen. What we're *not* disagreeing over in such cases are "fundamental differences in basic values"—differences, Friedman says, "about which men can ultimately only fight."[1]

A year after Wallace's suicide, a year before Cavell's memoir, the philosopher Alexander Rosenberg made a claim about fermions and bosons. The universe, he said, consists of them and "everything that can be made up of them, and nothing that can't be made up of them." Which means there is no room for a set of free-floating, independently existing norms or values (or facts about them) that humans are uniquely equipped to discern and act upon. Evolution *did* give a firm place in our makeup to "niceness"—cooperation, altruism—but we shouldn't thereby think that this "moral core" is anything other than a convenience for our genes, allowing them to survive into the next generation. Analogously, there's no sense (in all senses of "no sense")

---

[1] Milton Friedman, *Essays in Positive Economics* (Chicago: University of Chicago Press, 1953), 5.

in discussing things like "the meaning of a work of art" or "the meaning of an action," let alone the notion of a self, soul, enduring agent, or subject of the first-person pronoun. The astonishingly complex neural firings of our brains don't, after all, operate on beliefs or any other intentional states, and the meanings we find in people, artifacts, religions, and history are simply "diverting stories, *post hoc* explanations, and very short term expectations about the human future." In the end, human life and history is really just "a nested series of arms races that never attain more than a temporary and unstable equilibrium."[2]

When I set out to write this book several years ago, my goal was to consider how the baldly naturalistic drive propelling these kinds of statements—the taste for desert landscapes, in W. V. O. Quine's phrase—had penetrated various regions of the humanities, particularly literary studies. I planned to look at the recent rise of Darwinian criticism, cognitivist poetics, and the versions of affect theory indebted to neuroscience, as well as older influential theories that had (and have) a positivistic thrust, such as structuralism and narratology. Several threads, I planned to show, united these various literary theories with the claims of a Friedman or a Rosenberg. Most obvious is a wariness toward intentionality—either talking of it at all or talking of it in something other than scientific terms. Meanings, on such a view, are either dubious posits that won't survive in a completed account of the physical universe (Rosenberg's view), or they are attributed to various allegedly systematic, causally operating entities that perform tasks over and above the agent: language, culture, society, genes, the brain, the nervous system. Two things, I planned to argue, follow from such wariness. One is that interpretation comes to be seen as a sign of limitation in a field of inquiry, thus something to be overcome. "What troubles people about interpretation," Hilary Putnam has written, "is not its lack of methodology, but its lack of *convergence*."[3] When, that is, a discipline is pervaded by disagreement, it hardly seems a discipline, and the response is either to dismiss it as a cluster of differences over which we can only fight (as Friedman says), or to erase the disagreements with the vocabularies and techniques of modern science, which seem to have such a sound record of settling quarrels. The second consequence is strong nominalism. To think that one could competently use a normative

---

[2] Alexander Rosenberg, "The Disenchanted Naturalist's Guide to Reality," http://nationalhumanities-center.org/on-the-human/2009/11/the-disenchanted-naturalists-guide-to-reality/ (accessed April 17, 2016).

[3] Hilary Putnam, *Realism with a Human Face*, ed. James Conant (Cambridge, MA: Harvard University Press, 1992), 130.

concept is essentially naïve, because "courage," "fraternity," and comparable words either don't name anything at all (certainly nothing like fermions and bosons) or are wholly the product of those prior, systematic, casually operating systems—the only respectable objects of analysis for any field that wants to make a claim to knowledge. The aim of my book was to argue that none of these three ideas—the wariness toward intentions, the skepticism toward interpretation, and the strident nominalism about normative concepts—is as persuasive as it may look, and should be abandoned if literary and humanistic study is going to have any continued interest and relevance in the twenty-first century. My plans for this project began to alter when I gradually realized that there was a constellation of contemporary American authors who had not only developed versions of such criticisms already, but who had done so in more compelling, provocative, and lasting terms than I myself would be able to muster. As I began to see, Percy, Robinson, Ellison, Cavell, and Wallace are all deeply familiar with scientific or positivistic claims that closely mirror the ones that I had begun to track in contemporary literary studies. And in all five figures, as I also came to see, the starting point is a sense that the unchecked use of scientific models—not scientific models per se, but their manipulation and misapplication—can genuinely impoverish human life and even threaten it. The writing they produce can at times feel repetitive, hyperbolic, self-involved, weakly imagined, and/or clumsily scolding. But it is also richer—more ambitious, illuminating, significant—than my analysis of contemporary criticism was likely to be, and after a few trial-balloon essays, I eventually turned my attention more exclusively to what I had come to think of as the postwar sage.[4]

Four things stand out about the postwar sages I've discussed over the course of the previous chapters—four things that they help draw to our attention, or at least have drawn to mine. One is that the nominalism of Friedman, Rosenberg, and the naturalistic tradition generally isn't restricted to the scientists and the theorists who explicate or imitate them. A parallel skepticism about normative vocabularies—toward concepts of ought and ought-not—has been a mark of literary writing from high modernism onward, as critical histories of "renunciation" and "show, don't tell" suggest.[5] Thus, in all the authors I've discussed

---

[4] See Robert Chodat, "Is Narrative a Something or a Nothing?" in *Wittgenstein on Aesthetic Understanding*, ed. Garry Hagberg (London: Palgrave Macmillan, forthcoming); "Is Style Information?" *Partial Answers* 11 (2013): 133–62; "Evolution and Explanation: Biology, Aesthetics, Pragmatism" *Contemporary Pragmatism* 7.2 (December 2010): 155–92.

[5] Ross Posnock, *Renunciation: Acts of Abandonment By Writers, Philosophers, and Artists* (Cambridge, MA: Harvard University Press, 2016); Mark McGurl, *The Program Era: Postwar Fiction and the Rise of Creative Writing* (Cambridge, MA: Harvard University Press, 2009).

here, the rejection of modern naturalism has gone hand in hand with a certain ambivalence toward modern aesthetics, with its emphasis on what Ellison called "technical virtuosity" and what Wallace saw as its self-protective formalism. The analogy between the nominalism of modern science and the nominalism of modern art doesn't erase the differences between these domains. But it does highlight a frequently overlooked convergence. There's a reason that Susan Sontag—to recall a remark I quoted in the introduction—could say that the twentieth century had seen "the creation of a new (potentially unitary) kind of sensibility," one that makes no firm "divorce between science and technology, on the one hand, and art, on the other," and that this "cool," "exact" art eschews the "moral journalism" of the "Matthew Arnold notion of culture."[6] And there's a reason that her ex-husband, Philip Rieff, could with far less ebullience say that twentieth-century art shares with modern naturalism the "gaiety of being free from the historic Western compulsion of seeking large and general meanings for small and highly particular lives." In achieving, he said, "an impersonality no less impressive than that achieved by modern science," the modern artist has "augured the emancipation from the classical moral demand system, rejecting the person as an object of aesthetic interest and concentrating on the self-fulfilling function of the work of art itself."[7]

Second, though the sentinels I've discussed recognize precisely the convergence between art and science that Sontag and Rieff identify, they avoid either one-dimensional glee or one-dimensional rage. Strict nominalism, they suggest, is unintelligible in theory and—even more—in practice. Made of matter, we live with a sense of what matters, a sense that requires some use of abstracting judgments, some capacity to regard a particular thing *as* some species of thing. And we cannot, they also suggest, occupy a position from which we could see *all* such matterings and *all* such judgments as projections onto meaningless reality. Thus they are willing to entertain the "large and general meanings" that Rieff finds in so much traditional culture, and to risk trafficking in the sort of "moral journalism" that Sontag derides. Hence, I've argued, the undisguised discursive strands of their writing. As essayists, they may be less dispassionately systematic than most post-World War II Anglophone philosophers, but simply listing their keywords—"courage," "fraternity," "marriage," "fallibilism"—is enough to indicate that they're working within traditions that extend back to the origins

---

[6] Susan Sontag, "One Culture and the New Sensibility," in *Against Interpretation* (New York: Farrar, Straus and Giroux, 1966), 296–97, 300, 302.

[7] Philip Rieff, *The Triumph of the Therapeutic: The Uses of Faith After Freud* (Chicago: University of Chicago Press, 1966), 59, 258. For a fresh assessment of the relationship between Sontag and Rieff, see Posnock, *Renunciation*, 217–33.

of philosophical and religious reflection. Yet these argumentative, earnest, high-minded essayists are at the same time novelists and memoirists, inclined in their narrative works to "small and highly particular lives." Nominalism may be hard to credit, but no harder than the high words that we struggle to articulate, imagine, and give material embodiment. As I've argued, the result is an ambidextrous movement between dramatic and expository forms, art and argument. In some cases—Robinson, Ellison, Cavell—this generic mobility reflects a self-conscious affinity to nineteenth-century American intellectual culture. But all the authors here move between the discursive progression of ideas and the sequential progression of actions and events. And in doing so, they are recalling and extending traditions that foreground know-how over quantification, practical reasoning over misplaced demands for exactitude.

Third, the postwar sage is not just an overlooked category in recent literary and cultural history, and isn't just a throwback to certain older (in certain respects premodern) intellectual currents. For the back-and-forth movements of their writing in many ways anticipate and parallel some of the—in my view—most promising positions to have emerged in humanistic study over the last few decades. For one thing, the postwar sage can be read as enacting the wish in recent literary studies to revise, rebuke, and/or expose overstretched claims about aesthetic "autonomy." Little that these authors write is intended to be wholly self-fulfilling, detached either from other parts of their work or from all the various things that their work is about. They are, in this sense, antiformalists, acting as their own contextualists, making explicit to readers and critics at least some of the psychological themes, historical contingencies, and normative assumptions that are pertinent to an understanding of their works. By the same token, the extended grammatical investigations these authors undertake can be taken as an actualization of the wish among certain strands of recent philosophy to read literary texts more patiently and respectfully, to step down from abstract theories and principles and work closer to the ground of our actual psychology, social practices, institutional and natural environments, and moment-to-moment experiences. Like Hannah Arendt, the postwar sages philosophize, but always with a sense that "nothing perhaps is more surprising in this world of ours than the almost infinite diversity of its appearances, the sheer entertainment value of its views, sounds, and smells, something that is hardly ever mentioned by the thinkers and philosophers."[8] Like Martha Nussbaum, they range widely over philosophical, moral, political,

---

[8] Hannah Arendt, *The Life of the Mind* (New York: Harcourt, Inc., 1978), 20.

and social issues, but they understand that literature is more "disturbing" than purely analytic modes, that it "puzzles and disconcerts" in ways that engage the imagination and reveal the limits of more abstract habits of thought.[9] And like Kwame Anthony Appiah, they want to defend broad normative concepts such as "honor," but they also recognize that such terms are best explored by "seeing [them] in action in the lives of individuals and communities," a conviction that leads us to reflect less upon abstract arguments than on far-reaching histories, biographies, and other narrative forms.[10]

Two correctives, then: a salutary dose of contextualism to our aesthetics, a salutary dose of particularism to our philosophy. But if the postwar sages parallel some recent turns both in professional literary studies and in professional philosophy, they also complicate these turns. This is the fourth, final, and most vexing aspect of their projects that I've wanted to highlight—the one that makes writing about them so difficult, and the one that most urgently forces us to reflect on our own habits and desires as readers and scholars. For in moving so insistently between the discursive and the literary, in pursuing reflective composition on such a broad scale, they are able, more than both the revisionary critics and philosophers, to display the *fissures* that such a movement can generate. There comes a moment, in all the narrative works I've described, when the general and abstract come into conflict with the *this*ness and *here*ness of a life ongoing, when characters or readers find themselves newly hesitant in the present moment, and when the future stretches out before us in such a way as to make appropriate concepts seem hard to find. Perhaps the moment is marked by a sudden change of tone or style; perhaps it arrives in the ending, where a mood of affirmation unexpectedly emerges through the doubts and confusions of earlier stretches of a text. Such moments recall a remark that I cited from Bernard Harrison in my introduction: that narratives are ultimately about the particular sayings and doings of particular people in particular circumstances in a particular world, and that the intensity of this particularism places under pressure the tissue of confident generalities—"this story tells us something general about . . ."—that we feel tempted to offer.[11] And such moments are a corrective not only to the authors themselves, but to us as readers. They suggest how the particulars of a literary work can frustrate not only the abstractions

---

[9] Martha Nussbaum, *Poetic Justice: The Literary Imagination and Pubic Life* (Boston: Beacon Press, 1995), 5–6.

[10] Kwame Anthony Appiah, *The Honor Code: How Moral Revolutions Happen* (New York: W.W. Norton, 2010), xix.

[11] Bernard Harrison, *Inconvenient Fictions: Literature and the Limits of Theory* (New Haven, CT: Yale University Press, 1991), 58–59.

that these authors themselves use in their essays, but equally the kind of broad psychological, sociological, cultural, political, or historical explanations that contemporary literary scholars often strive to offer. Analogous stumbling blocks face the literary-minded philosophers. The sheer ambiguities and instabilities running through the narratives I've described underscore the ways that, in Arendt's terms, the "infinite diversity" of the world's appearances might in some sense *negate* the "thinkers and philosophers" altogether, including herself; that literature might "puzzle and disconcert," as Nussbaum says, to such an extent that little uncontroversial or undogmatic can be inferred from it; and that scrutinizing the lives of individuals and communities, in Appiah's phrase, can in many ways *hamper* our developing a general account of normative concepts. As Emerson says of Montaigne—two ancestors of the writers I've described at length in this book—the "abstractionist" and the "materialist" continually exasperate one another. Such exasperation, however, is liable to arise not only between individuals, but also *within* individuals and scholars, within *us*, pushed and pulled as we are between the streams of embodied events and actions, on one side, and the high words to which we and others have aspired on the other. An album of landscape sketches may be all we can manage, both collectively and individually.

The permanence of this restless back-and-forth movement makes ending a discussion of these authors oddly challenging. In Chapter 4, I briefly noted the moment in Wittgenstein's reflections on rule-following when he considers how we "go on" with a sequence of numbers. His question there is what happens—how to explain, how to correct—when a student is told to "add two," performs it skillfully up to 1000, and then begins to (as we would say) add *four*. The suggestion seems to be that even such basic words, so simple that even a small child can use them, are not self-applying, though we routinely regard the predictable-looking series 2, 4, 6, 8, 10 as "a visible section of rails invisibly laid to infinity" (§218). But as Wittgenstein knew, our competence with basic arithmetic forces upon us a larger question: If an action as straightforward as adding two numbers can begin to look strangely ungrounded, how much more unsettled is our use of other words, particularly those hard-to-wield moral and political concepts that we often feel compelled to apply, faced with one or another a staggeringly layered, blurrily bounded situation? In such cases, we are searching for words to go on—words to depend upon, to count on, to articulate our sense of what matters, to guide and orient our actions and decisions. But how to go on with such honored words is hardly obvious; that's one lesson from the last five chapters. No more than with "add two" does applying "courage" or "fraternity" come mechanically to an end. Certainly, no end apart from the previous examples we have observed, or the customs, usages, institutions, and shared human behavior that forms the massive, unfixed background of all our speech and action. We do manage to go on, at least much of the time, just as we often manage to add numbers blindly, without effort or interpretation. But uncertainty with our highest words—finding ourselves in a muddle, caught in a world ongoing, confronted with a reality that's circuit-blowingly huge and complex, with a life that can be harsh and loud and wrong if it wished—is always a standing threat. In the face of such conditions, wisdom seems to lie in pressing on, circling from particular to general, general to particular, all without any assurance ahead of time that our labors will be rewarded. So here, as this book concludes. The high words of the postwar sage may not always be our own, and their efforts to embody them in story, character, and style may not always be achieved or achievable. Their writing sometimes fragments, goes silent, incomplete. But in their stubborn efforts to make their words flesh, to find words that they can solemnly declare, they offer contemporary readers perspicuous examples, patterns of thought and reflection that might make sense of our own lives and provoke us to find our own ways to go on.

Bibliography

Acocella, Joan. "Lonesome Road." *The New Yorker* (October 6, 2014) http://www.newyorker.com/magazine/2014/10/06/lonesome-road. Accessed January 20, 2016.

Adorno, Theodor. "The Essay as Form." In *Notes to Literature, Volume 1*, translated by Shierry Weber Nicholsen, 3–23. New York: Columbia University Press, 1991.

Allen, Danielle. *Talking to Strangers: Anxieties of Citizenship Since Brown v. Board of Education*. Chicago: University of Chicago Press, 2004.

Althusser, Louis. *Lenin and Philosophy and Other Essays*. Translated by Ben Brewster. New York: NLB, 1971.

Altieri, Charles. "Cavell and Wittgenstein on Morality: The Limits of Acknowledgement." In *Stanley Cavell and Literary Studies: Consequences of Skepticism*, edited by Richard Eldridge and Bernard Rhie, 62–77. London: Continuum, 2011.

———. *Reckoning with the Imagination: Wittgenstein and the Aesthetics of Literary Experience*. Ithaca, NY: Cornell University Press, 2015.

———. "Rhetoric and Poetics: How to Use the Inevitable Return of the Repressed." In *A Companion to Rhetoric and Rhetorical Criticism*, edited by Walter Jost and Wendy Olmsted, 473–93. Oxford: Blackwell, 2003.

Ammon, Theodore, ed. *Interviews with William H. Gass*. Jackson: University Press of Mississippi, 2003.

Anderson, Linda. *Autobiography*. 2nd ed. London: Routledge, 2011.

Anderson, Paul Allen. "Ralph Ellison on Lyricism and Swing." *American Literary History* 17 (2005): 280–306.

Angus, Lynne E., and John McLeod, ed. *The Handbook of Narrative and Psychotherapy: Practice, Theory, and Research*. London: Sage, 2004.

Anscombe, Elizabeth. *Intention*. Oxford: Blackwell, 1957.

Appiah, K. Anthony. *The Honor Code: How Moral Revolutions Happen*. New York: W. W. Norton, 2010.

Arendt, Hannah. *Lectures on Kant's Political Philosophy*. Edited by Ronald Beiner. Chicago: University of Chicago Press, 1982.

———. *The Life of the Mind*. New York: Harcourt, Inc., 1978.

Aristotle. *Nicomachean Ethics*. Translated and edited by Roger Crisp. Cambridge: Cambridge University Press, 2000.

Austin, J. L. *Philosophical Papers*. Oxford: Clarendon Press, 1970.

Ayer, A. J. *Language, Truth, and Logic*. 2nd ed. New York: Dover, 1952.

Bacon, Francis. *The Works of Francis Bacon, Volume 4*. Edited by James Spedding et al. London: Longman and Co., 1858.

Baggani, Julian. "Philosophical Autobiography." *Inquiry* 45 (2002): 295–312.

Baker, Houston A. "Failed Prophet and Falling Stock: Why Ralph Ellison Was Never Avant-Garde." *Stanford Humanities Review* 7 (1999): 4–11.

Bakhtin, Mikhail. *The Dialogic Imagination*. Translated by Michael Holquist and Caryl Emerson. Austin: University of Texas Press, 1984.

———. "From Notes Made in 1970–71." In *Speech Genres and Other Late Essays*, translated by Vern W. McGee, edited by Caryl Emerson and Michael Holquist, 132–58. Austin: University of Texas Press, 1986.

Banfield, Ann. *The Phantom Table: Woolf, Fry, Russell and the Epistemology of Modernism*. Cambridge: Cambridge University Press, 2000.

Barkow, Jerome, Leda Cosmides, and John Tooby, ed. *The Adapted Mind: Evolutionary Psychology and the Generation of Culture*. New York: Oxford University Press, 1992.

Barthelme, Donald. *Not-Knowing: The Essays and Interviews*. Edited by Kim Herzinger. New York: Vintage, 1999.

Bates, Stanley. "Stanley Cavell and Ethics." In *Stanley Cavell*, edited by Richard Eldridge, 15–47. Cambridge: Cambridge University Press, 2003.

Bellow, Saul. *Letters*. Edited by Benjamin Taylor. New York: Viking, 2010.

Benjamin, Walter. "The Storyteller." In *Selected Writings, Volume 3: 1935–1938*, edited by Howard Eiland and Michael W. Jennings, 143–66. Cambridge, MA: Harvard University Press, 2002.

Berger, Kevin. "Richard Powers, The Art of Fiction No. 175." Interview with Richard Powers. *The Paris Review* 164 (2002-3). http://www.theparisreview.org/interviews/298/the-art-of-fiction-no-175-richard-powers. Accessed October 2, 2016.

Berlin, Isaiah. "Two Concepts of Liberty." In *Four Essays on Liberty*, 118–72. New York: Oxford University Press, 1969.

Bernstein, J. M. "Aesthetics, Modernism, Literature: Cavell's Transformation of Philosophy." In *Stanley Cavell*, edited by Richard Eldridge, 107–42. Cambridge: Cambridge University Press, 2003.

———. *Against Voluptuous Bodies: Late Modernism and the Meaning of Painting*. Stanford, CA: Stanford University Press, 2006.

Bernstein, Michael André. "Making Modernist Masterpieces." *Modernism/Modernity* 5 (1998): 1–17.

Berry, R. M. "Experimental Writing." In *The Oxford Handbook of Philosophy and Literature*. Edited by Richard Eldridge, 199–219. New York: Oxford University Press, 2009.

Birkerts, Sven. "The Alchemist's Retort." *The Atlantic* 277 (1996): 106–13.

Bizup, Joseph. "Hopkins' Influence on Percy's *Love in the Ruins*." *Renascence* 46 (1994): 247–59.

Blake, William. *The Complete Poetry and Prose of William Blake.* Edited by David V. Erdman. New York: Random House, 1965.

Bloom, Harold, ed. *Modern Critical Views: Walker Percy.* New York: Chelsea House, 1986.

Boddy, Kasia. "A Fiction of Response: *Girl With Curious Hair* in Context." In *A Companion to David Foster Wallace Studies*, edited by Marshall Boswell and Stephen J. Burn, 23–41. London: Palgrave Macmillan, 2013.

Boler, John. "Peirce and Medieval Thought." On *The Cambridge Companion to Charles Sanders Peirce*, edited by Cheryl Misak, 58–86. Cambridge: Cambridge University Press, 2004.

Booth, Wayne. *A Rhetoric of Irony.* Chicago: University of Chicago Press, 1974.

Borradoni, Giovanna, ed. *The American Philosopher: Conversations With Quine, Putnam, Nozick, Danto, Rorty, Cavell, MacIntyre, and Kuhn.* Translated by Rosanna Crocitto. Chicago: University of Chicago Press, 1994.

Boswell, Marshall. "Trickle-Down Citizenship: Taxes and Civic Responsibility in David Foster Wallace's *The Pale King.*" *Studies in the Novel* 44 (2012): 464–79.

———. *Understanding David Foster Wallace.* Columbia: University of South Carolina Press, 2003.

Boyd, Brian. "Evolutionary Theories of Art." In *The Literary Animal: Evolution and the Nature of Narrative*, edited by Jonathan Gottschall and David Sloan Wilson, 149–78. Evanston, IL: Northwestern University Press, 2005.

———. *On the Origins of Stories: Evolution, Cognition, and Fiction.* Cambridge, MA: Harvard University Press, 2009.

Bradley, Adam. *Ralph Ellison in Progress.* New Haven, CT: Yale University Press, 2010.

Brandom, Robert. *Articulating Reasons: An Introduction to Inferentialism.* Cambridge, MA: Harvard University Press, 2000.

Brooks, Cleanth. *The Well-Wrought Urn: Studies in the Structure of Poetry.* New York: Harvest/ HBJ, 1947.

Brooks, David. "When the Good Do Bad." *The New York Times.* March 19, 2012. A27.

Brouwer, René. *The Stoic Sage: The Early Stoics on Wisdom, Sagehood, and Socrates.* Cambridge: Cambridge University Press, 2014.

Browning, Oscar. *Life of George Eliot.* London: Walter Scott Ltd., 1892.

Brudney, Daniel. "Nineteenth-Century Ideals: Self-Culture and the Religion of Humanity." In *The Cambridge History of Philosophy in the Nineteenth Century (1790–1870)*, edited by Allen W. Wood and Songsuk Susan Hahn, 731–59. Cambridge: Cambridge University Press, 2012.

———. "Two Kinds of Civic Friendship." *Ethical Theory and Moral Practice* 16 (2013): 729–43.

Burke, Kenneth. *Counter-Statement.* 2nd ed. Berkeley: University of California Press, 1968.

———. *A Grammar of Motives*, 2nd ed. Berkeley: University of California Press, 1969.

———. *Permanence and Change*, 3rd ed. Berkeley: University of California Press, 1984.

———. "Revolutionary Symbolism in America." In *The Legacy of Kenneth Burke*, edited by Herbert W. Simons and Trevor Melia, 267–73. Madison: University of Wisconsin Press, 1989.

———. *A Rhetoric of Motives*, 2nd ed. Berkeley: University of California Press, 1969.

———. "Self-Portrait of a Person." *Behavior and Philosophy* 4 (1976): 257–71.

Burn, Stephen J., ed. *Conversations With David Foster Wallace.* Jackson: University Press of Mississippi, 2012.

———. *David Foster Wallace's Infinite Jest: A Reader's Guide.* 2nd ed. New York: Continuum, 2012.

———. "'Webs of Nerves Pulsing and Firing': *Infinite Jest* and the Science of Mind." In *Guide to David Foster Wallace Studies*, edited by Stephen Burn and Marshall Boswell, 59–85. London: Palgrave Macmillan, 2013.

Caputo, John D. *The Prayers and Tears of Jacques Derrida: Religion Without Religion*. Bloomington: Indiana University Press, 1997.

Carlyle, Thomas. *A Carlyle Reader: Selections from the Writings of Thomas Carlyle*. Edited by G. B. Tennyson. Cambridge: Cambridge University Press, 1984.

Carr, Nicholas. *The Shallows: What the Internet is Doing to Our Brain*. New York: W. W. Norton, 2010.

Carroll, Joseph. *Literary Darwinism: Evolution, Human Nature, and Literature*. London: Routledge, 2004.

Cavell, Stanley. *Cities of Words: Pedagogical Letters on a Register of the Moral Life*. Cambridge, MA: Harvard University Press, 2004.

———. *The Claim of Reason: Wittgenstein, Skepticism, Morality, and Tragedy*. New York: Oxford University Press, 1979.

———. *Conditions Handsome and Unhandsome: The Constitution of Emersonian Perfectionism*. Chicago: University of Chicago Press, 1990.

———. *Disowning Knowledge: In Seven Plays of Shakespeare*. 2nd ed. Cambridge: Cambridge University Press, 2003.

———. *In Quest of the Ordinary: Lines of Skepticism and Romanticism*. Chicago: University of Chicago Press, 1988.

———. "The *Investigations'* Everyday Aesthetics of Itself." In *The Literary Wittgenstein*, edited by John Gibson and Wolfgang Huemer, 21–33. London: Routledge, 2004.

———. *Little Did I Know: Excerpts from Memory*. Stanford, CA: Stanford University Press, 2010.

———. *Must We Mean What We Say?* Cambridge: Cambridge University Press, 1976.

———. *Philosophy the Day After Tomorrow*. Cambridge, MA: Harvard University Press, 2005.

———. *A Pitch of Philosophy: Autobiographical Exercises*. Cambridge, MA: Harvard University Press, 1994.

———. *Pursuits of Happiness: The Hollywood Comedy of Remarriage*. Cambridge, MA: Harvard University Press, 1981.

———. "Responses." In *Contending with Stanley Cavell*, edited by Russell Goodman, 149–76. New York: Oxford University Press, 2005.

———. *Themes Out of School: Effects and Causes*. Chicago: University of Chicago Press, 1984.

———. *The Senses of Walden: An Expanded Edition*. Berkeley: North Point Press, 1981.

———. *This New Yet Unapproachable America*. 2nd ed. Chicago: University of Chicago Press, 2013.

———. "What's the Use of Calling Emerson a Pragmatist?" In *Emerson's Transcendental Etudes*, 215–23. Stanford, CA: Stanford University Press, 2003.

Cavell, Stanley, and Alexander Sesonske. "Logical Empiricism and Pragmatism in Ethics." *Journal of Philosophy* 48 (1951): 5–17.

Cavell, Stanley, and Paul Standish. "Stanley Cavell in Conversation with Paul Standish." *Journal of Philosophy of Education* 46 (2012): 155–76.

Charon, Rita. "Narrative Medicine: A Model for Empathy, Reflection, Profession, and Trust." *Journal of the American Medical Association* 286 (October 17, 2001): 1897–902.

Chénetier, Marc. *After Suspicion: New American Fiction Since 1960*. Translated by Elizabeth A. Houlding. Philadelphia: University of Pennsylvania Press, 1996.

Chodat, Robert. "Empiricism, Exhaustion, and Meaning What We Say: Cavell and Contemporary Fiction." In *Stanley Cavell and Literary Studies: Consequences of Skepticism*, edited by Richard Eldridge and Bernard Rhie, 208–23. London: Continuum, 2011.

———. "Evolution and Explanation: Biology, Aesthetics, Pragmatism." *Contemporary Pragmatism* 7.2 (December 2010): 155–92.

———. "Fictions Public and Private: On Philip Roth." *Contemporary Literature* 46 (2005): 688–719.

———. "Is a Narrative a Something or a Nothing?" In *Wittgenstein on Aesthetic Understanding*, edited by Garry Hagberg. London: Palgrave Macmillan, forthcoming.

———. "Is Style Information?" *Partial Answers* 11 (2013): 133–62.

———. *Worldly Acts and Sentient Things*. Ithaca, NY: Cornell University Press, 2008.

Churchland, Patricia S. *Braintrust: What Neuroscience Tells Us About Morality*. Princeton, NJ: Princeton University Press, 2011.

———. Preface to W. V. O. Quine, *Word and Object*. Cambridge, MA: MIT Press, 2013.

Churchland, Paul M. *The Engine of Reason, the Seat of the Soul: A Philosophical Journey into the Brain*. Cambridge, MA: MIT Press, 1996.

———. "Toward a Cognitive Neurobiology of the Moral Virtues." In *Neurophilosophy at Work*, 37–60. Cambridge: Cambridge University Press, 2007.

Claybaugh, Amanda. *The Novel of Purpose: Literature and Social Reform in the Anglo-American World*. Ithaca, NY: Cornell University Press, 2007.

Clark, Andy. *Mindware: An Introduction to the Philosophy of Cognitive Science*. Oxford: Oxford University Press, 2001.

Clarke, Lindsay. "Going the Last Inch: Some Thoughts on Showing and Telling." In *Creative Writing: A Workbook with Readings*, edited by Linda Anderson, 487–91. New York: Routledge, 2006.

Cohen, G. A. *If You're an Egalitarian, How Come You're So Rich?* Cambridge, MA: Harvard University Press, 2001.

Collins, John. "Meta-Scientific Eliminativism: A Reconsideration of Chomsky's Review of Skinner's *Verbal Behavior*." *The British Journal for the Philosophy of Science* 58 (2007): 625–58.

Conrad, Joseph. *The Nigger of the 'Narcissus'*. New York: Dover, 1999.

Cook, William W., and James Tatum, *African-American Writers and Classical Tradition*. Chicago: University of Chicago Press, 2010.

"Court Lifts Ban on 'Ulysses' Here." *The New York Times*. December 7, 1933. https://www.nytimes.com/books/00/01/09/specials/joyce-court.html. Accessed April 12, 2016.

Crable, Bryan. *Ralph Ellison and Kenneth Burke: At the Roots of the Racial Divide*. Charlottesville: University of Virginia Press, 2011.

Crane, Gregg. *Race, Citizenship, and Law in American Culture*. Cambridge: Cambridge University Press, 2002.

———. "Ralph Ellison's Constitutional Faith." In *Cambridge Companion to Ralph Ellison*, edited by Ross Posnock, 104–20. Cambridge: Cambridge University Press, 2005.

Crary, Alice. *Beyond Moral Judgment*. Cambridge, MA: Harvard University Press, 2007.

Crawford, Hugh. "Modernism." In *Routledge Companion to Literature and Science*, edited by Bruce Clarke and Manuela Rossini, 508–17. London: Routledge, 2011.

Crisp, Roger, and Michael Slote. *Virtue Ethics*. Oxford: Oxford University Press, 1997.

Crusius, Timothy. *Kenneth Burke and the Conversation After Philosophy*. Carbondale: Southern Illinois University Press, 1999.

Danto, Arthur. *The Abuse of Beauty and the Concept of Art*. Peru, IL: Open Court, 2003.

————. *After the End of Art*. Princeton, NJ: Princeton University Press, 1998.

Dasenbrock, Reed Way, ed. *Literary Theory After Davidson*. University Park: Pennsylvania State University Press, 2001.

Davidson, Donald. "A Nice Derangement of Epitaphs." In *Truth, Language, and History*, 89–108. New York: Oxford University Press, 2005.

Davidson, Donald. *Inquiries into Truth and Interpretation*. Oxford: Oxford University Press, 1984.

Dawkins, Richard. *The God Delusion*. New York: Bantam Books, 2006.

————. *The Selfish Gene*. New York: Oxford University Press, 1976.

Day, William. "Knowing as Instancing: Jazz Improvisation and Moral Perfectionism." *The Journal of Aesthetics and Art Criticism* 58 (2000): 99–111.

DeLillo, Don. *Cosmopolis*. New York: Scribner's, 2003.

————. "Informal Remarks From the David Foster Wallace Memorial Service in New York on October 23, 2008." In *The Legacy of David Foster Wallace*, edited by Samuel Cohen and Lee Konstantinou, 23–24. Iowa City: University of Iowa Press, 2012.

Dennett, Daniel C. *Breaking the Spell: Religion as a Natural Phenomenon*. New York: Penguin, 2007.

————. *Darwin's Dangerous Idea: Evolution and the Meanings of Life*. New York: Simon & Schuster, 1995.

————. "The Logical Geography of Computational Approaches: A View from the East Pole." In *Brainchildren: Essays on Designing Minds*, 215–34. Cambridge, MA: MIT Press, 1998.

————. "Philosophy as Naïve Anthropology: Comment on Bennett and Hacker." In *Neuroscience and Philosophy: Brain, Mind, and Language*, 73–96. New York: Columbia University Press, 2007.

————. "Re-Introducing *The Concept of Mind*." In *The Concept of Mind*, by Gilbert Ryle, xii–xvii. London: Penguin, 2000.

DePietro, Thomas, ed. *Conversations with Don DeLillo*. Jackson: University Press of Mississippi, 2005.

Deresiewicz, William. "The Children's Hospital: On David Foster Wallace." *The Nation* (June 15, 2011); http://www.thenation.com/article/161456/childrens-hospital-david-foster-wallace. Accessed August 22, 2014.

————. "Homing Patterns: Marilynne Robinson's Fiction." *The Nation* (September 24, 2008) http://www.thenation.com/article/homing-patterns-marilynne-robinsons-fiction/. Accessed January 20, 2016.

Derrida, Jacques. "Circumfession." In *Jacques Derrida*. Translated by Geoffrey Bennington. Chicago: University of Chicago Press, 1993.

————. "The Law of Genre." *Critical Inquiry* 7 (1980): 55–81.

————. *Of Grammatology*. Translated by Gayatri Chakravorty Spivak. Baltimore: Johns Hopkins University Press, 1976.

Desmond, John F. *Walker Percy's Search for Community*. Athens: University of Georgia Press, 2004.

Desmond, William. "A Second *Primavera*: Cavell, German Philosophy, and Romanticism." In *Stanley Cavell*, edited by Richard Eldridge, 143–71. Cambridge: Cambridge University Press, 2003.

Dewey, John. *Art as Experience*. New York: Perigee, 1934.

Dos Passos, John. "Against American Literature." On *Modernism: An Anthology of Sources and Documents*, edited by Vassiliki Kolocotronic et al., 334–37. Chicago: University of Chicago Press, 1999.

Douglas, Christopher. "Christian Multiculturalism and Unlearned History in Marilynne Robinson's *Gilead*." *Novel* 44 (2011): 333–53.

———. *A Genealogy of Literary Mutliculturalism*. Ithaca, NY: Cornell University Press, 2008.

Drake, St. Clair, and Horace R. Cayton, *Black Metropolis: A Study of Negro Life in a Northern City*. New York: Harcourt, Brace, and Company, 1945.

Dreyfus, Hubert. *On The Internet*. 2nd ed. London: Routledge, 2009.

———. *What Computers Still Can't Do: A Critique of Artificial Reason*. Cambridge, MA: MIT Press, 1992.

Dreyfus, Hubert, and Sean Dorrence Kelly. *All Things Shining: Reading the Western Classics to Find Meaning in a Secular Age*. New York: Simon and Schuster, 2011.

Dreyfus, Hubert, and Paul Rabinow. *Michel Foucault: Beyond Structuralism and Hermeneutics*. Chicago: University of Chicago Press, 1982.

Dreyfus, Hubert, and Charles Taylor. *Retrieving Realism*. Cambridge, MA: Harvard University Press, 2015.

Drouin, Jeffrey S. *James Joyce, Science, and Modernist Print Culture*. London: Routledge, 2015.

Drury, M. O'C. *The Danger of Words and Writings on Wittgenstein*. Edited by David Berman. Bristol: Thoemmes, 1996.

Du Bois, W. E. B. *The World and Africa and Color and Democracy*. Edited by Henry Louis Gates. New York: Oxford University Press, 2014.

———. *Writings*. Edited by Nathan Huggins. New York: Library of America, 1986.

Dugatkin, Lee Alan. *The Altruism Equation: Seven Scientists Search for the Origins of Goodness*. Princeton, NJ: Princeton University Press, 2006.

Dula, Peter. *Cavell, Companionship, and Christian Theology*. Oxford: Oxford University Press, 2011.

Dupré, John. *Human Nature and the Limits of Science*. New York: Oxford University Press, 2003.

Dutton, Denis. *The Art Instinct: Beauty, Pleasure, and Human Evolution*. London: Bloomsbury Press, 2009.

Eddy, Beth. *The Rites of Identity: The Religious Naturalism and Cultural Criticism of Kenneth Burke and Ralph Ellison*. Princeton, NJ: Princeton University Press, 2003.

Eldridge, Richard. *Leading a Human Life: Wittgenstein, Intentionality, and Romanticism*. Chicago: University of Chicago Press, 1997.

Eliot, T. S. "Arnold and Pater." In *Selected Essays, 1917–1932*, 346–57. New York: Harcourt, 1950.

Eliot, George. *The Writings of George Eliot: Essays and Leaves from a Note-book*. Edited by John Walter Cross. Boston: Houghton Mifflin, 1908.

———. *Selected Prose of T. S. Eliot*. Edited by Frank Kermode. New York: Harcourt, 1975.

Ellison, Ralph. "'American Culture is of a Whole': From the Letters of Ralph Ellison." *The New Republic*. March 1, 1999.

———. *The Collected Essays of Ralph Ellison*. Edited by John Callahan. New York: Modern Library, 1995.

———. *Flying Home and Other Stories*. Edited by John Callahan. New York: Vintage, 1996.

———. *Invisible Man*. New York: Vintage, 1995.

———. *Juneteenth*. Edited by John Callahan. New York: Random House, 1999.

———. *Three Days Before the Shooting. . .The Unfinished Second Novel*. Edited by John Callahan and Adam Bradley. New York: Modern Library, 2010.

Ervin, Edward, ed. *The Freud Encyclopedia: Theory, Therapy, and Culture*. London: Routledge, 2001.

Eshel, Amir. *Futurity: Contemporary Literature and the Quest for the Past*. Chicago: University of Chicago Press, 2013.

Eyal, Nir. *Hooked: How to Build Habit-Forming Products*. New York: Portfolio, 2015.

Fant, Joseph L., and Robert Ashley, ed. *Faulkner at West Point*. Jackson: University Press of Mississippi, 2002.

Faulkner, William. *As I Lay Dying*. New York: Vintage, 1990.

Fay, Sarah. "Marilynne Robinson, The Art of Fiction No. 198." *The Paris Review* 186 (2008). http://www.theparisreview.org/interviews/5863/the-art-of-fiction-no-198-marilynne-robinson. Accessed October 2, 2016.

Fenellosa, Ernest, and Ezra Pound, *The Chinese Written Character as a Medium for Poetry: A Critical Edition*. Edited by Haun Saussy et al. New York: Fordham University Press, 2008.

Ferry, Luc. *Homo Aestheticus: The Invention of Taste in the Democratic Age*. Translated by Robert De Loaiza. Chicago: University of Chicago Press, 1994.

Fitzpatrick, Kathleen. "The Exhaustion of Literature: Novels, Computers, and the Threat of Obsolescence." *Contemporary Literature* 43 (2002): 518–59.

Flanagan, Owen. *The Bodhisattva's Brain: Buddhism Naturalized*. Cambridge, MA: MIT Press, 2011.

Flathman, Richard. "Perfectionism Without Perfection: Cavell, Montaigne, and the Conditions of Morals and Politics." In *The Claim to Community: Essays on Stanley Cavell and Political Philosophy*, edited by Andrew Norris, 98–127. Stanford, CA: Stanford University Press, 2005.

Flynn, Thomas R. *Sartre, Foucault, and Historical Reason, Volume 2*. Chicago: University of Chicago Press, 2005.

Fodor, Jerry. "Dicing With Shadows." *Times Literary Supplement*. July 6, 2001. 7.

———. "Having Concepts: A Brief Refutation of the Twentieth Century." *Mind & Language* 19 (2004): 29–47.

———. *The Language of Thought*. Cambridge, MA: Harvard University Press, 1975.

Fodor, Jerry, and Jerrold Katz, "The Availability of What We Say." *Philosophical Review* 72 (1963): 57–71.

Foley, Barbara. *Wrestling With the Left: The Making of Ralph Ellison's* Invisible Man. Durham, NC: Duke University Press, 2010.

Foot, Philippa. *Virtues and Vices: And Other Essays in Moral Philosophy*. Oxford: Oxford University Press, 1978.

Foster, Hal. "ABCs of Contemporary Design." *October* 100 (Spring 2002): 191–99.

Foucault, Michel. *The Foucault Reader*. Edited by Paul Rabinow. New York: Vintage, 1984.

———. *The History of Sexuality, Volume 1: An Introduction*. New York: Vintage, 1990.

Frank, Thomas. *The Conquest of Cool: Business Culture, Counterculture, and the Rise of Hip Consumerism*. Chicago: University of Chicago Press, 1997.

Frankfurt. Harry G. "Freedom of the Will and the Concept of a Person." In *The Importance of What We Care About*, 11–25. Cambridge: Cambridge University Press, 1988.

Franzen, Jonathan. "Informal Remarks from the David Foster Wallace Memorial Service in New York on October 23, 2008." In *Legacy of David Foster Wallace*, edited by Samuel Cohen and Lee Konstantinou, 177–81. Iowa City: University of Iowa Press, 2012.

Frazier, E. Franklin. *The Negro Church in America*. New York: Schocken Books, 1974.

Fresco, Nir. *Physical Computation and Cognitive Science*. Berlin: Springer, 2014.

Fried, Michael. *Absorption and Theatricality: Painting and Beholder in the Age of Diderot*. Berkeley: University of California Press, 1980.

———. *Art and Objecthood: Essays and Reviews*. Chicago: University of Chicago Press, 1998.

———. *Why Photography Matters As Art As Never Before*. New Haven, CT: Yale University Press, 2008.

Friedman, Milton. *Essays in Positive Economics*. Chicago: University of Chicago Press, 1953.

Frow, John. "'Never Draw to an Inside Straight': On Everyday Knowledge." *New Literary History* 33 (2002): 623–37.

Gendler, Tamar. *Intuition, Imagination, and Philosophical Methodology*. Oxford: Oxford University Press, 2010.

Geyh, Paula E. "Burning Down the House: Domestic Space and Feminine Subjectivity in Marilynne Robinson's *Housekeeping*." *Contemporary Literature* 34.1 (1993): 103–22.

Gibson, John. *Fiction and the Weave of Life*. New York: Oxford University Press, 2007.

Giles, Paul. "All Swallowed Up: David Foster Wallace and American Literature." In *The Legacy of David Foster Wallace*, edited by Samuel Cohen and Lee Konstantinou, 3–22. Iowa City: University of Iowa Press, 2012.

Gillespie, Michael Allen. *The Theological Origins of Modernity*. Chicago: University of Chicago Press, 2008.

Gladstone, Jason, Andrew Hoberek, and Daniel Worden, ed. *Postmodern/Postwar—And After*. Iowa City: University of Iowa Press, 2016.

Glock, Hans-Johan. "Concepts: Where Subjectivism Goes Wrong." *Philosophy* 84 (2009): 5–29.

———. "The Influence of Wittgenstein on American Philosophy." In *The Oxford Handbook of American Philosophy*, edited by Cheryl Misak, 375–402. New York: Oxford University Press, 2008.

Godwin, Gail. "The Devil's Own Century." Review of *The Thanatos Syndrome*, by Walker Percy, *The New York Times*. April 5, 1987. http://www.nytimes.com/1987/04/05/books/the-devil-s-own-century.html. Accessed August 25, 2015.

Goodman, Russell B. *Wittgenstein and William James*. Cambridge: Cambridge University Press, 2002.

Gould, Stephen Jay. *Ever Since Darwin: Reflections in Natural History*. New York: Norton, 1977.

Greenberg, Clement. "Modernist Painting." In *Modern Art and Modernism: A Critical Anthology*, edited by Francis Frascina and Charles Harrison, 5–10. New York: Harper and Row, 1992.

Greif, Mark. *The Age of the Crisis of Man: Thought and Fiction in America, 1933–1973*. Princeton, NJ: Princeton University Press, 2015.

Grimstad, Paul. *Experience and Experimental Writing: Literary Pragmatism from Emerson to the James*. New York: Oxford University Press, 2013.

Groff, Ruth. "Aristotelian Marxism/Marxist Aristotelianism: MacIntyre, Marx, and the Analysis of Abstraction." *Philosophy and Social Criticism* 38 (2012): 775–92.

Habermas, Jürgen. *The Theory of Communicative Action*. Translated by Thomas McCarthy. Boston: Beacon Press, 1984.

Hacking, Ian. "Conclusion: Deflections." In *Philosophy & Animal Life*, edited by Cary Wolfe, 139–72. New York: Columbia University Press, 2008.

Hadot, Pierre. *Philosophy as a Way of Life*. Edited by Arnold I. Davidson. Translated by Michael Chase. Oxford: Blackwell, 1995.

Hammer, Espen. "Cavell and Political Romanticism." In *The Claim to Community: Stanley Cavell and Political Philosophy,* edited by Andrew Norris, 164–85. Stanford, CA: Stanford University Press, 2005.

——. *Stanley Cavell: Skepticism, Subjectivity, and the Ordinary.* Cambridge: Blackwell, 2002.

Harrison, Bernard. *Inconvenient Fictions: Literature and the Limits of Theory.* New Haven, CT: Yale University Press, 1991.

Haugeland, John. *Artificial Intelligence: The Very Idea.* Cambridge, MA: MIT Press, 1985.

——. *Having Thought: Essays in the Metaphysics of Mind.* Cambridge, MA: Harvard University Press, 1998.

——, ed. *Mind Design: Philosophy, Psychology, and Artificial Intelligence.* Cambridge, MA: MIT Press, 1981.

——, ed. *Mind Design II: Philosophy, Psychology, and Artificial Intelligence.* Cambridge, MA: MIT Press, 1997.

Hayles, N. Katherine. *How We Became Posthuman: Virtual Bodies in Cybernetics, Literature, and Informatics.* Chicago: University of Chicago Press, 1999.

——. "The Illusion of Autonomy and the Fact of Recursivity: Virtual Ecologies, Entertainment, and *Infinite Jest.*" *New Literary History* 30 (1997): 675–97.

Hegel, G. W. F. *The Philosophy of Right.* Translated by H. B. Nisbett. Edited by Allen W. Wood. Cambridge: Cambridge University Press, 1991.

Hemingway, Ernest. *A Farewell to Arms.* New York: Scribner, 1995.

——. *The Green Hills of Africa.* New York: Scribner, 1996.

——. *The Sun Also Rises.* New York: Scribner's, 1926.

Henry, Holly. *Virginia Woolf and the Discourse of Science: The Aesthetics of Astronomy.* Cambridge: Cambridge University Press, 2009.

Hobbes, Thomas. *Leviathan.* Edited by C. B. MacPherson. London: Penguin, 1982.

Hoberek, Andrew. "Introduction: After Postmodernism." *Twentieth-Century Literature* 53 (2007): 233–47.

——. *The Twilight of the Middle Class: Post-World War II American Fiction and White-Collar Work.* Princeton, NJ: Princeton University Press, 2005.

Holdsworth, Roger, ed. *Arthur Symons: Selected Writings* New York: Routledge, 2003.

Holland, Mary K. *Succeeding Postmodernism: Language and Humanism in Contemporary American Literature.* London: Bloomsbury, 2013.

Hollander, John. "Stanley Cavell and *The Claim of Reason.*" *Critical Inquiry* 6 (1980): 575–88.

Hollinger, David A. *After Cloven Tongues of Fire: Protestant Liberalism in Modern American History.* Princeton, NJ: Princeton University Press, 2013.

——. "The Knower and the Artificer, with Postscript 1993." In *Modernist Impulses in the Human Sciences, 1870–1930,* edited by Dorothy Ross, 26–53. Baltimore: Johns Hopkins University Press, 1994.

Holloway, John. *The Victorian Sage: Studies in Argument.* London: Macmillan, 1953.

Holmes, Stephen. *The Anatomy of Anti-Liberalism.* Cambridge, MA: Harvard University Press, 1993.

Houser, Heather. "*Infinite Jest's* Environmental Case for Disgust." In *The Legacy of David Foster Wallace,* edited by Samuel Cohen and Lee Konstantinou, 118–42. Iowa City: University of Iowa Press, 2012.

Howe, Irving. *Selected Writings, 1950–1990.* San Diego, CA: Brace Harcourt Jovanovich, 1990.

Hulme, T. E. *Speculations.* Edited by Herbert Read. London: K. Paul, 1924.

Hungerford, Amy. *Postmodern Belief: American Literature and Religion Since 1960.* Princeton, NJ: Princeton University Press, 2010.

Hunter, J. Paul. *Before Novels: The Cultural Contexts of Eighteenth-Century English Fiction.* New York: Norton, 1990.

Huyssen, Andreas. *After the Great Divide: Modernism, Mass Culture, Postmodernism.* Bloomington: Indiana University Press, 1987.

Hurston, Zora Neale. *Folklore, Memoirs, and Other Writings.* Edited by Cheryl A. Wall. New York: Library of America, 1995.

Izenberg, Oren. "Confiance au Monde; or, The Poetry of Ease." *nonsite* 4 (2011); http://nonsite.org/article/confiance-au-monde-or-the-poetry-of-ease. Accessed September 1, 2016.

Jackson, Lawrence. "Ralph Ellison's Invented Life: A Meeting With the Ancestors." In *Cambridge Companion to Ralph Ellison,* edited by Ross Posnock, 11–34. Cambridge: Cambridge University Press, 2005.

———. *Ralph Ellison: The Emergence of Genius.* New York: Wiley, 2002.

Jacobs, Timothy. "The Brothers Incandenza: Translating Ideology in Fyodor Dostoevsky's *The Brothers Karamazov* and David Foster Wallace's *Infinite Jest.*" *Texas Studies in Literature and Language* 49 (2007): 265–92.

James, David, and Urmila Seshagiri, "Metamodernism: Narratives of Continuity and Revolution." *PMLA* 129 (2014): 87–100.

James, Henry. *The Critical Muse: Selected Literary Criticism.* Edited by Roger Gard. New York: Penguin, 1987.

———. *The Awkward Age.* Edited by Ronald Blythe. New York: Penguin, 1987.

James, William. *Writings, 1902–1910.* Edited by Bruce Kuklick. New York: Library of America, 1988.

Jameson, Fredric. *Late Marxism: Adorno, or, the Persistence of the Dialectical.* London: Verso, 1990.

———. "Morality Versus Ethical Substance; or, Aristotelian Marxism in Alasdair MacIntyre." *Social Text* 8 (Winter 1983–84): 151–54.

———. *Postmodernism, or, The Cultural Logic of Late Capitalism.* Durham, NC: Duke University Press, 1991.

———. *Signatures of the Visible.* New York: Routledge, 1990.

Janik, Allan, and Stephen Toulmin, *Wittgenstein's Vienna.* New York: Simon and Schuster, 1973.

John Paul II. "*Fides et Ratio.*" Encyclical letter of September 1998; http://w2.vatican.va/content/john-paul-ii/en/encyclicals/documents/hf_jp-ii_enc_14091998_fides-et-ratio.html?. Accessed April 22, 2016.

Kaivola, Karen. "The Pleasures and Perils of Merging: Female Subjectivity in Marilynne Robinson's *Housekeeping.*" *Contemporary Literature* 34.4 (1993): 670–90.

Kant, Immanuel. *Critique of Judgment.* Translated by Werner S. Pluhar. Indianapolis, IN: Hackett, 1987.

———. *Introduction to Logic; and His Essay on The Mistaken Subtilty of the Four Figures.* Translated by Thomas Kingsmill Abbott. London: Longman's, Green, and Co., 1885.

Katz, Jerrold. *Semantic Theory.* New York: Joanna Cotler Books, 1972.

Kaufman, R. Lane. "The Skewed Path: Essaying as Unmethodical Method." In *Essays on the Essay: Redefining the Genre,* edited by Alexander J. Butrym, 221–40. Athens: University of Georgia Press, 1989.

Kelly, Adam. "Development Through Dialogue: David Foster Wallace and the Novel of Ideas." *Studies in the Novel* 44 (2012): 267–83.

Kelly, Daniel R. "David Foster Wallace as American Hedgehog." In *Freedom and the Self: Essays in the Philosophy of David Foster Wallace*, edited by Steven M. Cahn and Maureen Eckert, 109–33. New York: Columbia University Press, 2015.

Kenner, Hugh. "On Man the Sad Animal." *National Review*. September 12, 1975. 1000–1003.

Kim, Daniel Y. *Writing Manhood in Black and Yellow*. Stanford, CA: Stanford University Press, 2005.

Kirby, Joan. "Is There Life After Art? The Metaphysics of Marilynne Robinson's *Housekeeping*." *Tulsa Studies in Women's Literature* 5.1 (1986): 91–109.

Klaus, Carl H., and Ned Stuckey-French, ed. *Essayists on the Essay: Montaigne to Our Time*. Iowa City: University of Iowa Press, 2012.

Kloppenberg, James T. *The Virtues of Liberalism*. New York: Oxford University Press, 1998.

Kobre, Michael. *Walker Percy's Voices*. Athens: University of Georgia Press, 2000.

Konstantinou, Lee. "No Bull: David Foster Wallace and Postironic Belief." In *The Legacy of David Foster Wallace*, edited by Samuel Cohen and Lee Konstantinou, 83–112. Iowa City: University of Iowa Press, 2012.

Korsgaard, Christine M. *The Sources of Normativity*. Cambridge: Cambridge University Press, 1996.

Kripke, Saul. *Naming and Necessity*. Cambridge, MA: Harvard University Press, 1980.

———. *Wittgenstein on Rules and Private Language*. Cambridge, MA: Harvard University Press, 1982.

Ladner, Joyce, ed. *The Death of White Sociology: Essays on Race and Culture*. Baltimore: Black Classic Press, 1998.

Land, Mary G. "Three Max Gottliebs: Lewis's, Dreiser's, and Walker Percy's View of the Mechanist-Vitalist Controversy." *Studies in the Novel* 15 (1983): 314–31.

Landow, George. *Elegant Jeremiahs: The Sage From Carlyle to Mailer*. Ithaca, NY: Cornell University Press, 1986.

Laugier, Sandra. "Hadot as a Reader of Wittgenstein." *Paragraph* 34 (2011): 322–37.

Lawrence, D. H. *Studies in Classic American Literature*. London: Penguin, 1990.

Lawson, Lewis. *Following Percy: Essays on Walker Percy's Work*. Troy, NY: Whitsun, 1988.

Lawson, Lewis, and Victor A. Kramer, ed. *Conversations with Walker Percy*. Jackson: University of Mississippi Press, 1985.

———, ed. *More Conversations with Walker Percy*. Jackson: University of Mississippi Press, 1993.

Lear, Jonathan. "Not at Home in Gilead." *Raritan* 32.1 (2012): 34–52.

LeClair, Thomas. *In the Loop: Don DeLillo and the Systems Novel*. Urbana: University of Illinois Press, 1987.

———. "The Prodigious Fiction of Richard Powers, William Vollmann, and David Foster Wallace." *Critique: Studies in Contemporary Fiction* 38.1 (Fall 1996): 12–37.

———. "Walker Percy's Devil." In *The Art of Walker Percy: Stratagems of Being*, edited by Panthea Reid Boughton, 157–68. Baton Rouge: Louisiana State University Press, 1979.

Lehrer, Jonah. "Kin and Kind." *The New Yorker* (March 5, 2012): 36–42.

Leise, Chrisopher. "'That Little Incandescence': Reading the Fragmentary and John Calvin in Marilynne Robinson's *Gilead*." *Studies in the Novel* 41 (2009): 348–67.

Leiter, Brian. *Nietzsche on Morality*. London: Routledge, 2002.

LeMahieu, Michael. *Fictions of Fact and Value*. New York: Oxford University Press, 2013.

Lewis, David. "Possible Worlds." In *The Possible and the Actual: Readings in the Metaphysics of Modality,* edited by Michael J. Loux, 182–89. Ithaca, NY: Cornell University Press, 1979.

Lewis, David Levering. *W. E. B. Du Bois, 1868–1919: Biography of a Race.* New York: Henry Holt, 1993.

Levenson, Michael. *A Genealogy of Modernism: A Study of English Literary Doctrine, 1908–1922.* Cambridge: Cambridge University Press, 1984.

Lewis, Pericles. *Religious Experience and the Modernist Novel.* Cambridge: Cambridge University Press, 2010.

Lewontin, Richard. *Biology as Ideology: The Doctrine of DNA.* Toronto: Anasi Press, 1991.

———. "Sociobiology—A Caricature of Darwinism." *PSA: Proceedings of the Biennial Meeting of the Philosophy of Science Association* 1976 (1976): 22–31.

Leys, Ruth. "The Turn to Affect: A Critique." *Critical Inquiry* 37 (2011): 434–72.

Lipsky, David. *Although Of Course You End Up Becoming Yourself: A Road Trip with David Foster Wallace.* New York: Broadway Books, 2010.

Locke, John. *Essay Concerning Human Understanding.* Edited by Roger Woolhouse. New York: Penguin, 1998.

Lodge, David. *Consciousness and the Novel: Connected Essays.* Cambridge, MA: Harvard University Press, 2002.

Lovibond, Sabina. *Realism and Imagination in Ethics.* Minneapolis: University of Minnesota Press, 1983.

Lukács, Georg. *The Theory of the Novel.* Translated by Anna Bostock. Cambridge, MA: MIT Press, 1971.

Lydon, Christopher. Interview with David Foster Wallace. *The Connection.* WBUR. http://radioopensource.org/david-foster-wallace-chris-lydon/. Accesssed October 2, 2016.

MacIntyre, Alasdair. *After Virtue: A Study in Moral Theory.* Notre Dame, IN: Notre Dame University Press, 1981.

———. *Whose Justice? Whose Rationality?* Notre Dame, IN: Notre Dame University Press, 1988.

———. "Philosophy Recalled to Its Tasks: A Thomistic Reading of *Fides et Ratio.*" In *The Tasks of Philosophy: Selected Essays, Volume 1,* 179–96. Cambridge: Cambridge University Press, 2006.

MacLeish, Archibald, "Ars Poetica." http://www.poetryfoundation.org/poetrymagazine/poem/6371. Accessed January 29, 2014.

Mad Men. "Smoke Gets in Your Eyes." *Mad Men: Season One.* Directed by Alan Taylor. Written by Matthew Weiner. (2007), DVD.

Mahon, Áine. "Fraudulence, Obscurity, and Exposure: The Autobiographical Anxieties of Stanley Cavell." In *The Philosophy of Autobiography,* edited by Chrisopher Cowley, 217–36. New York: Columbia University Press, 2015.

Malcolm, Norman. *Wittgenstein: A Memoir.* Oxford: Oxford University Press, 1958.

Maritain, Jacques. *The Degrees of Knowledge.* Translated by Gerald B. Phelan. Notre Dame: Notre Dame University Press, 1995.

Marrati, Paola. "Childhood and Philosophy." *MLN* 126 (2012): 954–61.

Martinich, A. P., and David Sosa. *A Companion to Analytic Philosophy.* Oxford: Blackwell, 2001.

Max, D. T. *Every Love Story is a Ghost Story: A Life of David Foster Wallace.* New York: Penguin, 2012.

McCaffery, Larry. "A Conversation with David Foster Wallace." *The Review of Contemporary Fiction* 13.2 (Summer 1993); http://www.dalkeyarchive.com/a-conversation-with-david-foster-wallace-by-larry-mccaffery/.

McCann, Sean, and Michael Szalay. "Do You Believe in Magic? Literary Thinking After the New Left." *The Yale Journal of Criticism* 18 (2005): 435–68.

McClure, John. *Partial Faiths: Postsecular Fiction in the Age of Pynchon and Morrison.* Athens: University of Georgia Press, 2007.

McDowell, John. *Mind and World.* Cambridge, MA: Harvard University Press, 1994.

———. "Virtue and Reason." In *Mind, Value, and Reality*, 50–73. Cambridge, MA: Harvard University Press, 1998.

McGann, Jerome. *Black Riders: The Visible Language of Modernism.* Princeton, NJ: Princeton University Press, 1993.

McGurl, Mark. *The Program Era: Postwar Fiction and the Rise of Creative Writing.* Cambridge, MA: Harvard University Press, 2009.

McHale, Brian. *Postmodernist Fiction.* London: Routledge, 1987.

Menand, Louis. "What Comes Naturally." *The New Yorker.* November 22, 2002.

Mendelsohn, Daniel. "The Man Who Loved Chekhov." *The New York Times.* July 6, 2004. http://www.nytimes.com/2003/07/06/books/the-man-who-loved-chekhov.html?pagewanted=all. Accessed August 17, 2015.

Mensch, Betty. "Jonathan Edwards, *Gilead*, and the Problem of 'Tradition'." *Journal of Law and Religion* 21 (2005/2006): 221–41.

Michaels, Walter Benn. *The Shape of the Signifier: 1967 to the End of History.* Princeton, NJ: Princeton University Press, 2004.

———. *The Trouble with Diversity: How We Learned to Love Identity and Ignore Inequality.* New York: Henry Holt & Co., 2006.

———. Review of *The Message in the Bottle*, by Walker Percy. *The Georgia Review* 29 (1975): 972–75.

Miller, Andrew H. *The Burdens of Perfection: On Ethics and Reading in Nineteenth-Century British Literature.* Ithaca, NY: Cornell University Press, 2008.

Mizruchi, Susan. *The Science of Sacrifice: American Literature and Modern Social Theory.* Princeton, NJ: Princeton University Press, 1998.

Moi, Toril. *Henrik Ibsen and the Birth of Modernism: Art, Theater, Philosophy.* New York: Oxford University Press, 2006.

———. "'They practice their trades in different worlds': Concepts in Poststructuralism and Ordinary Language Philosophy." *New Literary History* 40 (2009): 801–24.

Montague, Richard. *Formal Philosophy.* Edited by Richard H. Thomason. New Haven, CT: Yale University Press, 1974.

Moran, Richard. *Authority and Estrangement: An Essay on Self-Knowledge.* Princeton, NJ: Princeton University Press, 2001.

Moretti, Franco. *The Way of the World: The* Bildungsroman *in European Culture.* Translated by Albert Sbragia. London: Verso, 1987.

Mulhall, Stephen. *Stanley Cavell: Philosophy's Recounting of the Ordinary.* Oxford: Oxford University Press, 1994.

Mullarky, John. *Post-Continental Philosophy: An Outline.* London: Continuum, 2006.

Murdoch, Iris. *Existentialists and Mystics: Writings on Philosophy and Literature.* Edited by Peter Conradi. New York: Penguin, 1999.

Murray, Albert, and John F. Callahan, ed. *Trading Twelves: The Selected Letters of Ralph Ellison and Albert Murray.* New York: Modern Library, 2000.

Nabokov, Vladimir. *Lectures on Literature.* Edited by Fredson Bowers. New York: Mariner, 2002.

———. *Strong Opinions.* New York: Vintage, 1990.

Nadell, Ira B. "Consider the Footnote." In *The Legacy of David Foster Wallace,* edited by Samuel Cohen and Lee Konstantinou, 218–40. Iowa City: University of Iowa Press, 2012.

Nagel, Thomas. "Sin and Significance." *The New York Review of Books.* September 18, 1975. 54–56.

Ngai, Sianne. *Our Aesthetic Categories: Zany, Cute, Interesting.* Cambridge, MA: Harvard University Press, 2012.

Nichols, Catherine. "Dialogizing Postmodern Carnival: David Foster Wallace's *Infinite Jest.*" *Critique* 43.1 (2001): 3–16.

Nietzsche, Friedrich. *Beyond Good and Evil.* Translated by Walter Kaufmann. New York: Penguin, 1966.

———. "On Truth and Lying in a Non-Moral Sense." In *The Birth of Tragedy and Other Writings*, edited by Raymond Geuss and Ronald Speirs, 139–54. Cambridge: Cambridge University Press, 1999.

———. *Twilight of the Idols.* Translated by Richard Polt. Indianapolis, IN: Hackett.

Nussbaum, Martha. *The Fragility of Goodness: Luck and Ethics in Greek Tragedy.* Cambridge: Cambridge University Press, 1986.

———. *Poetic Justice: The Literary Imagination and Public Life.* Boston: Beacon Press, 1995.

Olsen, Lance. "Termite Art, or, Wallace's Wittgenstein." *Review of Contemporary Fiction* 12 (1993): 199–225.

Orphir, Ella Zohar. "Toward a Pitiless Fiction: Abstraction, Comedy, and Modernist Anti-Humanism." *Modern Fiction Studies* 52 (2006): 92–120.

Ostas, Magdalena. "Kant with Michael Fried: Feeling, Absorption, and Interiority in the *Critique of Judgment.*" *symploke* 18 (2010): 15–30.

Park, Robert E., and Ernest W. Burgess, *Introduction to the Science of Sociology.* Chicago: University of Chicago Press, 1921.

Parrish, Tim. "Invisible Ellison: The Fight to Be a Negro Leader." In *Cambridge Companion to Ralph Ellison,* edited by Ross Posnock, 137–56. Cambridge: Cambridge University Press, 2005.

Parsons, Charles. "Quine's Nominalism." *American Philosophical Quarterly* 48.3 (July 2011): 213–28.

Passmore, John. *The Perfectibility of Man.* London: Duckworth, 1970.

Pater, Walter. "Conclusion" to *The Renaissance*. In *The Norton Anthology of Theory and Criticism,* edited by Vincent B. Leitch et al., 389–41. New York: Norton, 2001.

Pease, Donald E. "Ralph Ellison and Kenneth Burke: The Nonsymbolizable (Trans)Action." *boundary 2* (2003): 65–96.

Percy, Walker. *Love in the Ruins.* New York: Farrar Straus, 1971.

———. *Lost in the Cosmos.* New York: Picador, 1983.

———. *The Message in the Bottle: How Queer Man Is, How Queer Language Is, and What One Has to Do With the Other.* New York: Picador, 2000.

———. *The Moviegoer.* New York: Vintage, 1998.

———. *The Thanatos Syndrome.* New York: Farrar, Straus and Giroux, 1987.

———. *Signposts in a Strange Land.* Edited by Patrick Samway. New York: Picador, 1991.

Perkins, David, ed. *English Romantic Writers.* 2nd ed. New York: Harcourt Brace, 1995.

Pinkard, Terry. "Was Pragmatism the Successor to Idealism?" In *New Pragmatists,* edited by Cheryl Misak, 142–68. New York: Cambridge University Press, 2007.

Pinker, Steven. *The Better Angels of Our Nature: Why Violence Has Declined.* New York: Viking, 2011.

———. *The Blank Slate: The Modern Denial of Human Nature.* New York: Viking, 2002.

———. *The Language Instinct: How the Mind Creates Language.* New York: William Morrow, 1994.

Pippin, Robert. "Authenticity in Painting: Remarks on Michael Fried's Art History." *Critical Inquiry* 31 (2005): 575–98.

———. "Natural and Normative." *Daedalus* 138 (2009): 35–43.

———. Review of *Beyond Moral Judgment*, by Alice Crary. *Analytic Philosophy* 52 (2011): 49–60.

———. "What Was Abstract Art? (From the Point of View of Hegel)." In *The Persistence of Subjectivity: On the Kantian Aftermath.* Cambridge: Cambridge University Press, 2005.

Pitcher, George, ed. *Wittgenstein: The Philosophical Investigations—A Collection of Critical Essays.* Notre Dame, IN: University of Notre Dame Press, 1966.

Plato. *The Complete Works.* Edited by John M. Cooper. Indianapolis, IN: Hackett, 1997.

Pocock, J. G. A. *The Machiavellian Moment: Florentine Political Thought and the Atlantic Republican Tradition.* Princeton, NJ: Princeton University Press, 1975.

Podhoretz, Norman. "What Happened to Ralph Ellison?" *Commentary* 108.1 (July 1999): 46–58.

Poe, Edgar Allan. *Essays and Reviews.* Edited by G. R. Thompson. New York: Library of America, 1984.

Posnock, Ross. *Color and Culture: Black Writers and the Making of the Modern Intellectual.* Cambridge, MA: Harvard University Press, 1998.

———. "Fathers and Sons." *Raritan* 31 (2012): 104–18.

———. "Ralph Ellison, Hannah Arendt, and the Meaning of Politics." In *The Cambridge Companion to Ralph Ellison,* edited by Ross Posnock, 201–16. Cambridge: Cambridge University Press, 2005.

———. *Renunciation: Acts of Abandonment By Writers, Philosophers, and Artists.* Cambridge, MA: Harvard University Press, 2016.

Poteat, Patricia Lewis. *Walker Percy and the Old Modern Age: Reflections on Language, Argument, and Telling of Stories.* Baton Rouge: Louisiana State University Press, 1985.

Poteat, William H. "Reflections on Walker Percy's Theory of Language." In *The Art of Walker Percy: Stratagems of Being,* edited by Panthea Reid Boughton, 192–218. Baton Rouge: Louisiana State University Press, 1979.

Pound, Ezra. *The Literary Essays of Ezra Pound.* New York: New Directions, 1968.

Powers, Richard. *Galatea 2.2.* New York: Picador, 1995.

———. *The Gold Bug Variations.* New York: Harper Perennial, 1991.

Prinz, Jesse, and Andy Clark. "Putting Concepts to Work: Some Thoughts for the Twentyfirst Century." *Mind & Language* 19 (2004): 57–69.

Putnam, Hilary. "The Content and Appeal of Naturalism." In *Naturalism in Question,* edited by Mario De Caro and David Macarthur, 59–70. Cambridge, MA: Harvard University Press, 2004.

———. *Pragmatism: An Open Question.* Oxford: Wiley-Blackwell, 1995.

———. *Realism with a Human Face.* Edited by James Conant. Cambridge, MA: Harvard University Press, 1992.

———. *Renewing Philosophy.* Cambridge, MA: Harvard University Press, 1992.

Pynchon, Thomas. *V.* New York: Vintage, 2012.

Quigley, Megan M. *Modernist Fiction and Vagueness: Philosophy, Form, and Language.* Cambridge: Cambridge University Press, 2014.

Quine, W. V. O. *The Time of My Life.* Cambridge, MA: MIT Press, 1985.

———. "On What There Is." In *From a Logical Point of View: Nine Logico-Philosophical Essays*, 1–9. Cambridge, MA: Harvard University Press, 1953.

———. *Word and Object*. Cambridge, MA: MIT Press, 1960.

Rahv, Philip. "The Cult of Experience in American Writing." *Literature and the Sixth Sense*, 22–25. Boston: Houghton Mifflin, 1970.

Rampersad, Arnold. *The Art and Imagination of W. E. B. Du Bois*. Cambridge, MA: Harvard University Press, 1976.

Rankine, Patrice D. *Ulysses in Black: Ralph Ellison, Classicism, and African-American Literature*. Madison: University of Wisconsin Press, 2006.

Rawls, John. *A Theory of Justice*. Cambridge, MA: Harvard University Press, 1971.

Ravitch, Michael. "Just the Facts." Review of *Plowing the Dark*, by Richard Powers. *New Republic*. May 14, 2001. 45.

Reed, Adolph. *The Jesse Jackson Phenomenon: The Crisis of Purpose in Afro-American Politics*. New Haven, CT: Yale University Press, 1986.

Rieff, Philip. *The Triumph of the Therapeutic: The Uses of Faith After Freud*. Chicago: University of Chicago Press, 1966.

Robbe-Grillet, Alain. *For a New Novel*. Translated by Richard Howard. New York: Grove Press, 1965.

Robinson, Marilynne. *Absence of Mind: The Dispelling of Inwardness from the Modern Myth of the Self*. New Haven, CT: Yale University Press, 2010.

———. *The Death of Adam: Essays on Modern Thought*. New York: Picador, 1998.

———. *Gilead*. New York: Farrar, Straus and Giroux, 2004.

———. *Home*. London: Virago, 2008.

———. *Housekeeping*. New York: Farrar, Straus and Giroux, 1980.

———. "Hysterical Scientism: The Hysterical Realism of Richard Dawkins." *Harper's*. November 29, 2006. 83–88.

———. *Lila*. New York: Farrar, Straus and Giroux, 2014.

———. *When I Was a Child I Read Books*. New York: Farrar, Straus and Giroux, 2012.

———. "Writers and the Nostalgic Fallacy." *The New York Times Book Review*. October 13, 1985. http://www.nytimes.com/1985/10/13/books/writers-and-the-nostalgic-fallacy.html?pagewanted=all. Accessed January 20, 2016.

Roiland, Josh. "Getting Away From It All: The Literary Journalism of David Foster Wallace and Nietzsche's Concept of Oblivion." In *The Legacy of David Foster Wallace*, edited by Samuel Cohen and Lee Konstantinou, 25–52. Iowa City: University of Iowa Press, 2012.

Rorty, Richard. *Achieving Our Country: Leftist Thought in Twentieth-Century America*. Cambridge, MA: Harvard University Press, 1998.

———. *Consequences of Pragmatism*. Minneapolis: University of Minnesota Press, 1982.

———. "Derrida and the Philosophical Tradition." In *Truth and Progress: Philosophical Papers, Volume 3*, 327–50. Cambridge: Cambridge University Press, 1998.

———. "The Higher Nominalism in a Nutshell: A Reply to Henry Staten." *Critical Inquiry* 12 (1986): 463–64.

———. *Contingency, Irony, and Solidarity*. Cambridge: Cambridge University Press, 1989.

———. "Philosophy Envy." *Daedalus* 133 (Fall 2004): 18–24.

———. "The Priority of Democracy to Philosophy." In *Objectivity, Relativism, and Truth: Philosophical Papers 1*, 175–96. Cambridge: Cambridge University Press, 1991.

———. "Ten Years After." In *The Linguistic Turn: Essays in Philosophical Method*, edited by Richard Rorty, 361–70. Chicago: University of Chicago Press, 1992.

Rosenberg, Alexander. "Disenchanted Naturalism." In *Contemporary Philosophical Naturalism and Its Implications*, edited by Bana Bashour and Hans D. Muller. New York: Routledge, 2014.

———. "The Disenchanted Naturalist's Guide to Reality." http://nationalhumanitiescenter. org/on-the-human/2009/11/the-disenchanted-naturalists-guide-to-reality/. Accessed April 17, 2016.

Roughgarden, Joan. *The Genial Gene: Deconstructing Darwinian Selfishness.* Berkeley: University of California Press, 2009.

Ruckert, William, ed. *Critical Responses to Kenneth Burke.* Minneapolis: University of Minnesota Press, 1969.

Ryan, Judith. *The Novel After Theory.* New York: Columbia University Press, 2011.

Samway, Patrick H., S. J., ed. *A Thief of Peirce: The Letters of Kenneth Laine Ketner and Walker Percy.* Jackson: University Press of Mississippi, 1995.

Samway, Patrick H., S. J. *Walker Percy: A Life.* Chicago: Loyola, 1997.

Sand, George, and Gustave Flaubert. *George Sand- Gustave Flaubert Letters.* Translated by Aimee L. McKenzie. New York: Boni & Liveright, 1921.

Saunders, Laura. "Ellison and the Black Church: The Gospel According to Ralph." In *The Cambridge Companion to Ralph Ellison*, edited by Ross Posnock, 35–55. New York: Cambridge University Press, 2005.

de Saussure, Ferdinand. *Course in General Linguistics.* Translated by Roy Harris. La Salle, IL: Open Court, 1983.

Sawyer, R. Keith. "Improvisation and the Creative Process: Dewey, Collingwood, and the Aesthetics of Spontaneity." *The Journal of Aesthetics and Art Criticism* 58 (2000): 149–61.

Schaub, Thomas. Interview with Marilynne Robinson. *Contemporary Literature* 35.2 (1994): 231–51.

Schalkwyk, David. "Fiction as 'Grammatical' Investigation: A Wittgensteinian Account." *Journal of Aesthetics and Art Criticism* 53 (1995): 287–98.

Schlovsky, Viktor. "Art as Technique." in *Literary Theory: An Anthology*, edited by Julie Rivkin and Michael Ryan, 8–14. Oxford: Wiley-Blackwell, 2017.

Schryer, Steven. *Fantasies of the New Class: Ideologies of Professionalism in Post-World War II American Fiction.* New York: Columbia University Press, 2011.

Schwartz, Joseph. "Kenneth Burke, Aristotle, and the Future of Rhetoric." *College Composition and Communication* 17 (1966): 210–16.

Selisker, Scott. "Simply By Reacting? The Sociology of Race and *Invisible Man*'s Automata." *American Literature* 83 (2011): 571–96.

Sellars, Wilfrid. *Empiricism and the Philosophy of Mind.* Edited by Robert Brandom. Cambridge, MA: Harvard University Press, 1997.

———. "Philosophy and the Scientific Image of Man." In *Science, Perception, and Reality*, 1–40. New York: The Humanities Press, 1963.

Selzer, Jack. *Kenneth Burke in Greenwich Village: Conversing with the Moderns, 1915–1931.* Madison: University of Wisconsin Press, 1996.

Shapiro, Johanna, et al. "Teaching the Humanities to First Year Medical Students: Evaluation of an Elective Literature and Medicine Course." *Education for Health* 17.1 (March 2004): 73–84.

Shy, Todd. "Religion and Marilynne Robinson." *Salmagundi* 155/6 (Summer 2007): 251–64.

Simon, Herbert A. *The Shape of Automation for Men and Management.* New York: Farrar, 1965.

Simons, Herbert S., and Trevor Melia, ed. *The Legacy of Kenneth Burke*. Madison: University of Wisconsin Press, 1989.

Skinner, B. F. *Beyond Freedom and Dignity*. Indianapolis, IN: Hackett, 1971.

Skinner, Quentin. *The Foundations of Modern Political Thought: Volume 1: The Renaissance*. Cambridge: Cambridge University Press, 1978.

Smith, Sidonie. "Narrating Lives and Contemporary Imaginaries." *PMLA* 126 (2011): 564–74.

Smith, Stan. *W. B. Yeats: A Critical Introduction*. London: Rowman & Littlefield, 1990.

Snow, C. P. *The Two Cultures*. Cambridge: Cambridge University Press, 1998.

Snyder, Sharon. "The Gender of Genius: Scientific Experts and Literary Amateurs in the Fiction of Richard Powers." *Review of Contemporary Fiction* 18 (1998): 84–96.

Soames, Scott. "David Lewis's Place in Analytic Philosophy." In *David Lewis*, edited by Barry Loewer and Jonathan Schaffer, 80–98. Oxford: Wiley, 2015.

———. *Philosophical Analysis in the Twentieth-Century, Volume 2: the Age of Meaning*. Princeton, NJ: Princeton University Press, 2005.

Sontag, Susan. *Against Interpretation*. New York: Farrar, Straus and Giroux, 1966.

———. "Introduction to *The Best American Essays, 1992*." In *Essayists on the Essay: Montaigne to Our Time*, edited by Carl H. Klaus and Ned Stuckey-French, 149–52. Iowa City: University of Iowa Press, 2012.

Sophocles. *Antigone*. Translated by Richard Emil Braun. New York: Oxford University Press, 1973.

de Sousa, Ronald. Review of *Virtues and Vices*, by James D. Wallace. *Noûs* 16 (1982): 161–65.

Spiro, Howard, et al., ed. *Empathy and the Practice of Medicine: Beyond Pills and the Scalpel*. New Haven, CT: Yale University Press, 1993.

Stephens, Gregory. *On Racial Frontiers: The New Culture of Frederick Douglass, Ralph Ellison, and Bob Marley*. Cambridge: Cambridge University Press, 1999.

Stuckey-French, Ned. *The American Essay in the American Century*. Columbia: University of Missouri Press, 2011.

Sundquist, Eric. "Dry Bones." In *The Cambridge Companion to Ralph Ellison*, edited by Ross Posnock, 217–30. Cambridge: Cambridge University Press, 2005.

Taylor, Charles. *The Ethics of Authenticity*. Cambridge, MA: Harvard University Press, 1991.

———. *The Explanation of Behavior*. London: Routledge and Keegan Paul, 1964.

———. *Hegel*. Cambridge: Cambridge University Press, 1977.

———. *Human Agency and Language: Philosophical Papers, Volume 1*. Cambridge: Cambridge University Press, 1985.

———. *Modern Social Imaginaries*. Durham, NC: Duke University Press, 2003.

———. *Multiculturalism: Examining the Politics of Recognition*. Princeton, NJ: Princeton University Press, 1994.

———. *Philosophical Arguments*. Cambridge, MA: Harvard University Press, 1995.

———. *Sources of the Self: The Making of the Modern Identity*. Cambridge, MA: Harvard University Press, 1989.

———. "What's Wrong With Foundationalism? Knowledge, Agency, and the World." In *Heidegger, Coping, and Cognitive Science: Essays in Honor of Hubert L. Dreyfus, Volume 2*, edited by Mark Wrathall and Jeff Malpas, 115–34. Cambridge, MA: MIT Press, 2000.

Telotte, J. P. "Charles Peirce and Walker Percy: From Semiotic to Narrative." In *Walker Percy: Art and Ethics*, edited by Jac Tharpe, 65–79. Jackson: University Press of Mississippi, 1980.

"To Walker Percy, Man's Prognosis is Funny." *National Observer*. May 24, 1971. 17.

Tolson, Jay. *Pilgrim in the Ruins: A Life of Walker Percy.* New York: Simon and Schuster, 1992.

Tracy, Thomas. "The Formative Years: David Foster Wallace's Philosophical Influences and *The Broom of the System*." In *Gesturing Toward Reality: David Foster Wallace and Philosophy,* edited by Robert K. Bolger and Scott Korb, 157–75. London: Bloomsbury, 2014.

Trilling, Lionel. "On the Teaching of Modern Literature." In *The Moral Obligation to Be Intelligent: Selected Essays,* edited by Leon Wieseltier, 381–401. Evanston, IL: Northwestern University Press, 2000.

Turing, Alan. "Computing Machinery and Intelligence." In *Mind Design II,* edited by John Haugeland, 29–56. Cambridge, MA: MIT Press, 1997.

Tymoczko, Dmitri. "Dear Stanley." *Journal of Music Theory* 54 (2010): 5–23.

Vargish, Thomas, and Delo E. Mook. *Inside Modernism: Relativity Theory, Cubism, Narrative.* New Haven, CT: Yale University Press, 1999.

Wallace, David Foster. *Both Flesh and Not: Essays.* Boston: Little, Brown and Company, 2012.

———. *Consider the Lobster and Other Essays.* Boston: Little, Brown and Company, 2005.

———. *Everything and More: A Compact History of Infinity.* New York: Norton Books, 2003.

———. *Infinite Jest.* Boston: Little, Brown and Company, 1996.

———. *The Last Interview and Other Conversations.* New York: Melville House, 2012.

———. *Oblivion.* Boston: Little, Brown and Company, 2004.

———. *The Pale King.* Boston: Little, Brown and Company, 2011.

———. *A Supposedly Fun Thing I'll Never Do Again: Essays and Arguments.* Boston: Little, Brown and Company, 1997.

———. *Time, Fate, and Language: An Essay on Free Will.* Edited by Steven M. Cahn and Maureen Eckert. New York: Columbia University Press, 2010.

Wallace, James D. *Moral Relevance and Moral Conflict.* Ithaca, NY: Cornell University Press, 1988.

———. *Virtues and Vices.* Ithaca, NY: Cornell University Press, 1978.

Walton, Kendall. *Mimesis as Make-Believe: On the Foundations of the Representational Arts.* Cambridge, MA: Harvard University Press, 1990.

Wampole, Christy. "The Essayification of Everything." *The New York Times.* May 26, 2013. http://opinionator.blogs.nytimes.com/2013/05/26/the-essayification-of-everything/. Accessed April 1, 2016.

Warren, Kenneth. "Chaos Not Quite Controlled: Ellison's Uncompleted Transit to *Juneteenth*." In *The Cambridge Companion to Ralph Ellison,* edited by Ross Posnock, 188–200. Cambridge: Cambridge University Press, 2005.

———. *So Black and Blue: Ralph Ellison and the Occasion of Criticism.* Chicago: University of Chicago Press, 2003.

———. *What Was African-American Literature?* Cambridge, MA: Harvard University Press, 2011.

Watt, Ian. *The Rise of the Novel: Studies in Defoe, Richardson, and Fielding.* Berkeley: University of California Press, 2001.

Watts, Jerry Gafio. *Heroism and the Black Intellectual: Ralph Ellison, Politics, and Afro-American Intellectual Life.* Chapel Hill: University of North Carolina Press, 1994.

Weinstein, Philip. *Unknowing: The Work of Modernist Fiction.* Ithaca, NY: Cornell University Press, 2005.

Wendel, Saskia. "A Critique of Feminist Radical Constructivism." In *Belief, Bodies, and Being: Feminist Reflections on Embodiment,* edited by Deborah Orr, 185–96. London: Rowman & Littlefield, 2006.

West, Cornel, and Eddie S. Glaude, Jr., ed. *African-American Religious Thought: An Anthology*. Louisville, KY: Westminster John Knox Press, 2003.

Whitworth, Michael H. *Einstein's Wake: Relativity, Metaphor, and Modernist Literature*. New York: Oxford University Press, 2001.

———. "The Physical Sciences." In *A Companion to Modernist Literature and Culture*, edited by David Bradshaw and Kevin J. H. Detmar, 39–49. Oxford: Blackwell, 2006.

Will. Frederick. *Pragmatism and Realism*. Edited by Kenneth R. Westphal. Lanham: Rowman & Littlefield, 1996.

Will, George F. "Shallow Look at the Mind of an Assassin." *The Washington Post*. September 22, 1988. A25.

Williams, Bernard. *Ethics and the Limits of Philosophy*. Cambridge, MA: Harvard University Press, 1986.

———. *Shame and Necessity*. Berkeley: University of California Press, 1993.

Williams, Jeffrey. "The Last Generalist: An Interview with Richard Powers." *Minnesota Review: A Journal of Committed Writing* 52–54 (2002): 95–114.

Williams, Malcolm. *Science and Social Science: An Introduction*. London: Routledge, 2000.

Williams, William Carlos. *Selected Poems*. Edited by Charles Tomlinson. New York: New Directions, 1985.

Wills, Gary. "Superficial & Sublime?" *New York Review of Books*. April 7, 2011. http://www.nybooks.com/articles/archives/2011/apr/07/superficial-sublime/. Accessed September 3, 2015.

Wilson, E. O. *Sociobiology: The New Synthesis*. Cambridge, MA: Harvard University Press, 1975.

Wittgenstein, Ludwig. *The Blue and Brown Books: Preliminary Studies for the 'Philosophical Investigations'*. New York: Harper & Row, 1960.

———. *Philosophical Investigations*. Rev. 4th ed. Translated by G. E. M. Anscombe, P. M. S. Hacker, and Joachim Schulte. Oxford: Wiley-Blackwell, 2010.

———. *Tractatus Logico-Philosophicus*. Translated by. C. K. Ogden. London: Routledge, 1999.

Wood, James. "Human, All Too Inhuman." *The New Republic*. July 24, 2000. http://www.newrepublic.com/article/61361/human-all-too-inhuman; Accessed August 22, 2014.

———. *The Irresponsible Self: On Laughter and the Novel*. New York: Farrar, Straus and Giroux, 2004.

———. "The Homecoming." *The New Yorker*. September 8, 2008. http://www.newyorker.com/magazine/2008/09/08/the-homecoming. Accessed January 20, 2016.

———. "Acts of Devotion." *The New York Times*. November 28, 2004. http://query.nytimes.com/gst/fullpage.html?res=9E00E4DC103FF93BA15752C1A9629C8B63&pagewanted=all. Accessed January 20, 2016.

Woolf, Virginia. "Mr. Bennett and Mrs. Brown." In *Essentials of the Theory of Fiction*, 3rd ed., edited by Michael J. Hoffman and Patrick D. Murphy, 21–35. Durham, NC: Duke University Press, 2005.

———. "Modern Novels." http://xroads.virginia.edu/~class/workshop97/gribbin/modern.html. Accessed October 2, 2016.

———. "Philosophy in Fiction." In *Contemporary Writers*, 67–70. New York: Harcourt Brace Jovanovich, 1965.

Wright, John S. "Ellison's Experimental Attitude and the Technologies of Illumination." In *The Cambridge Companion to Ralph Ellison*, edited by Ross Posnock, 157–71. Cambridge: Cambridge University Press, 2005.

Wright, Robert. "2004 *Time* 100." *Time* (April 26, 2004). http://content.time.com/time/specials/packages/article/0,28804,1970858_1970909_1971671,00.html. Accessed March 27, 2016.

Yeats, W. B. *Per Amica Silentia Lunae.* New York: Macmillan, 1919.

Zerilli, Linda. "The Turn to Affect and the Problem of Judgment." *New Literary History* 46 (2015): 261–86.

Zhang, Dora. "Naming the Indescribable: Woolf, Russell, James, and the Limits of Description." *New Literary History* 45 (2014): 51–70.

Index